SOUNDING AUTHENTIC

AMS Studies in Music

JANN PASLER, *General Editor*

Editorial Board

Conceptualizing Music:
Cognitive Structure, Theory, and Analysis
Lawrence Zbikowski

Inventing the Business of Opera:
The Impresario and His World in Seventeenth-Century Venice
Beth L. Glixon and Jonathan Glixon

Lateness and Brahms:
Music and Culture in the Twilight of Viennese Liberalism
Margaret Notley

The Critical Nexus:
Tone-System, Mode, and Notation in Early Medieval Music
Charles M. Atkinson

Music, Criticism, and the Challenge of History:
Shaping Modern Musical Thought in Late Nineteenth-Century Vienna
Kevin C. Karnes

Jewish Music and Modernity
Philip V. Bohlman

Changing the Score:
Arias, Prima Donnas, and the Authority of Performance
Hilary Poriss

Rasa:
Affect and Intuition in Javanese Musical Aesthetics
Marc Benamou

Josquin's Rome:
Hearing and Composing in the Sistine Chapel
Jesse Rodin

Details of Consequence:
Ornament, Music, and Art in Paris
Gurminder Kaur Bhogal

Sounding Authentic:
The Rural Miniature and Musical Modernism
Joshua S. Walden

SOUNDING AUTHENTIC

The Rural Miniature and
Musical Modernism

Joshua S. Walden

OXFORD
UNIVERSITY PRESS

OXFORD
UNIVERSITY PRESS

Oxford University Press is a department of the University of Oxford.
It furthers the University's objective of excellence in research,
scholarship, and education by publishing worldwide.

Oxford   New York
Auckland   Cape Town   Dar es Salaam   Hong Kong   Karachi
Kuala Lumpur   Madrid   Melbourne   Mexico City   Nairobi
New Delhi   Shanghai   Taipei   Toronto

With offices in
Argentina   Austria   Brazil   Chile   Czech Republic   France   Greece
Guatemala   Hungary   Italy   Japan   Poland   Portugal   Singapore
South Korea   Switzerland   Thailand   Turkey   Ukraine   Vietnam

Oxford is a registered trade mark of Oxford University Press
in the UK and certain other countries.

Published in the United States of America by
Oxford University Press
198 Madison Avenue, New York, NY 10016

© Oxford University Press 2014

Library of Congress Cataloging-in-Publication Data
Walden, Joshua S.
Sounding authentic : the rural miniature and musical modernism / Joshua S. Walden.
pages   cm.—(AMS studies in music)
ISBN 978-0-19-933466-7 (hardback)—ISBN 978-0-19-933467-4 (electronic text)
1. Music—20th century—History and criticism. I. Title.
ML197.W38   2013
780.9′04—dc23   2013022443

1 3 5 7 9 8 6 4 2

Printed in the United States of America
on acid-free paper

For Zuzia and my mishpokhe

Men can do nothing without the make-believe of a beginning.
—George Eliot, *Daniel Deronda*

CONTENTS

ACKNOWLEDGMENTS

This project began in another form as a dissertation at Columbia University, and I am grateful to Walter Frisch for always providing insightful suggestions, sage advice, and supportive words from the early stages of that project to the final manuscript of this one. I also wish to thank Mark Anderson, Anna Maria Busse Berger, Karol Berger, Giorgio Biancorosso, Andrea F. Bohlman, Philip V. Bohlman, Christopher Doll, Judit Frigyesi, Boris Gasparov, Lila Ellen Gray, Karen Henson, Carol Hess, Mark Katz, James Loeffler, Christopher Reynolds, Elaine Sisman, Mark Slobin, and Richard Taruskin for their ideas and feedback. Many thanks also to my Hungarian language instructor Carol Rounds, without whose warm, patient teaching I could never have embarked on this research.

I continued working on this project at the University of Oxford and I owe thanks to the leadership and staff at Merton and Wolfson Colleges for creating such fruitful environments for research and collaboration. I enjoyed the opportunity to share meals and teach tutorials with Suzannah Clark and Daniel Grimley; and I am thankful to my friends and colleagues during my years in Oxford, especially Andy Byford and Nicolette Makovicky. I completed the book at Johns Hopkins University and Peabody Conservatory with the support of the Andrew W. Mellon Postdoctoral Fellowship, and deeply appreciate the advice of Gabrielle Spiegel, Andrew Talle, Elizabeth Tolbert, Susan F. Weiss, and my other Hopkins colleagues.

I conducted research for this book at a number of archives and I am thankful to the librarians and archivists at the Bartók Archívum in Budapest, the Bibliothèque nationale de France, the Bodleian Library, the British Library, the Music Division of the Library of Congress, the New York Public Library for the Performing Arts, and the YIVO Institute for Jewish Research. I am grateful to Paul Glasser, Lyudmila Sholokhova, László Somfai, Jonathan Summers, and László Vikárius for sharing their time and suggestions at these archives. I also wish to acknowledge the research funding of the Harold Powers World Travel Fund from the American Musicological Society, the Foreign Language and Area Studies Fellowship, and the Vladimir and Pearl Heifetz Memorial Fellowship from the YIVO Institute for Jewish Research.

Some of the material in Chapters 2, 5, and 6 of this book has appeared in other forms in "'The Hora Staccato in Swing!': Jascha Heifetz's Musical Eclecticism and the Adaptation of Violin Miniatures," *Journal of the Society for American Music* 6, no. 4 (November 2012): 405–31; "Music of the '*Folks-Neshome*': 'Hebrew Melody' and Changing Musical Representations of Jewish Culture in the Early Twentieth-Century Ashkenazi Diaspora," *Journal of Modern Jewish Studies* 8, no. 2 (July 2009): 151–72; and "'On the String in the Peasant Style': Performance Style in Early Recordings of Béla Bartók's *Romanian Folk Dances*," in *Performers' Voices across Centuries, Cultures, and Disciplines*, ed. Ann Marshman, 151–62 (London: Imperial College Press, 2011). I thank the publishers of these articles for granting permission to reprint these passages.

I am most grateful to Jann Pasler for her insightful feedback and editing and to Suzanne Ryan, Jessen O'Brien, Erica Woods Tucker, and Patterson Lamb at Oxford University Press for their invaluable work in creating this book. My interest in this topic emerged from my love of the violin repertoire, and I wish to thank my violin teachers Elizabeth Gibson, Anne Crowden, Gillian Findlay, Serban Rusu, and Anahid Ajemian for instilling that knowledge and passion in me; and my piano teacher Elizabeth Swarthout, who helped me write my first composition (it would incidentally turn out to be one of my last), which I named "Sara's Gypsy Dream" in honor of my grandmother. I now realize, upon looking back, that this was, in its own naïve way, a rural miniature. And I must thank my parents Judith Schelly and Michael Walden for providing me with these music lessons. Not only that, but they have always been my most critical, insightful, and steadfast editors and interlocutors on music, and I am indebted to them for the hours of immeasurably valuable conversation and ideas. My brother Danny has been a marvelous collaborator—and sometime duet partner—throughout the process of writing this book. And my wife Susanna Berger is a source of continual inspiration who has offered her support at every stage of the project. It is for this reason that I dedicate this book to my parents, my brother, and Susanna.

SOUNDING AUTHENTIC

INTRODUCTION

In 1918, the renowned Russian Jewish violinist Toscha Seidel published a work for violin and piano titled "Eïli, Eïli." The phrase "Traditional Yiddish Melody" appeared under the title, indicating that the work was based on a preexisting folk song, and rather than listing the violinist as the composer, the score stated that the music was "Transcribed by Toscha Seidel." The solo part, in a slow and lilting triple meter, featured a plaintive hummable melody with prominent augmented seconds and alternating duple and triple rhythms that evoked Eastern European Jewish song. When Seidel performed the work at Carnegie Hall that same year, the critic for the *New York Times* identified the piece as Seidel's "own arrangement of the Hebrew prayer 'Eïli Eïli.'"[1] The violinist Mischa Elman, also a Russian Jewish immigrant and formerly a student in the same St. Petersburg studio where Seidel had studied with Leopold Auer, published a new adaptation of the same source melody in 1922, in a score that described the music as "A Traditional Jewish Melody."

During the 1910s and 1920s, "Eïli, Eïli" was performed and recorded repeatedly by violinists as well as vocalists, who sang the melody's original Hebrew text, an adaptation of Psalm 22, verse 2, which begins, "My God, my God, why hast Thou forsaken me?"[2] This text and melody were also the subject of ethnographic collection, included in 1910 and again in 1917 in anthologies of transcribed Jewish religious and folk songs published by the Society for Jewish Folk Music, an organization founded in 1908 at the St. Petersburg Conservatory that was devoted to the study of the traditional music of Jewish communities and the development of a "Jewish" national style of composition.[3]

In live performances and on records produced by major labels, Jewish cantors including Yossele Roseblatt and Shloimele Rothstein intoned the melancholy song.[4] It was later reported: "When Yossele Rosenblatt chanted 'Eïli, Eïli,' angels in heaven seemed to sing along with him."[5] Opera singers also performed "Eïli, Eïli," beginning with Sophie Breslau's acclaimed 1917 rendition at the Metropolitan Opera. Rothstein's 1920 disc identified the music as a "Religious Prayer";

and among other singers' interpretations, vaudevillian Belle Baker's 1919 record stated that the text was "In Jewish" and opera singer Rosa Raisa's called it a "Traditional Hebrew Melody." The music made its way into other artistic genres, too—for example, it was performed hundreds of times by the orchestra that accompanied screenings of the 1920 silent film *The Golem*, based on a Jewish legend, during its run at the Criterion Theatre in New York.[6] Indeed, by 1920 the melody had become so popular and ubiquitous that it was the subject of a playful parody in Leo Wood and Archie Gottler's song "That Eili Eili Melody," whose chorus began, "That melody called 'Eili, Eili,'/ Is always haunting me."

How, then, did this cherished Jewish religious song find itself at the center of a heated copyright infringement case brought by the Yiddish operetta composer Jacob Koppel Sandler against the music publisher Joseph P. Katz, argued before the Honorable John C. Knox, in a New York City federal courtroom in 1925? Sandler claimed that "Eili, Eili" was not a traditional folk song or prayer but an original composition he had written in 1896 for a production of M. Horowitz's Yiddish operetta *The Hero and Brocha, or the Jewish King of Poland for a Night*, directed by the Yiddish theater impresario and actor Boris Thomashefsky at the Windsor Theatre in New York. He had composed the number for the actress Sophie Karp to sing as she hung from a crucifix, enacting a young woman's medieval martyrdom for refusing to repudiate her Jewish faith (Figure 0.1).[7] Sandler attempted to copyright "Eili, Eili" only in 1919, however, after learning that the song had become an international success, and he was suing Katz for violating his copyright by continuing to publish arrangements of the music.

Katz testified that he had no knowledge that the melody was by Sandler; to the contrary, his father, a Jewish immigrant from Eastern Europe, had hummed it to him decades earlier, and it was so common in Jewish traditional contexts that it was assumed to be a Jewish folk song imported from Eastern Europe. At trial, as the *Times* reported, Yiddish theater actors including Jennie Moskowitz and Mischa Nechamkus testified for the plaintiff, while Lazare Saminsky, a composer, author, and performer who had been a founding member of the Society for Jewish Folk Music and was now musical director of New York's Temple Emanu-El, recounted that he first heard the song in St. Petersburg with other Society members and they had "concluded that the composition was a folksong," following which it was published in Germany and Russia, and included in "a Russian encyclopedia."[8] Elman's accompanist Joseph Bonime, too, told the court that when he was young his father had often sung him the song, evidence that it was plausibly a folk song.[9] At the same time, however, it was also established that a number of musicians who had played in the orchestra during the production of *The Hero and Brocha* had returned to Russia in the intervening years; perhaps it was through them that the melody became known there.[10]

At the end of the trial, Judge Knox decided in favor of the defendant, the publisher Katz, on a technicality of copyright law: too much time had elapsed

FIGURE 0.1:   Jacob Koppel Sandler, "Eili, Eili," arranged by Louis Friedsell, 1908. Heskes Collection, Music Division, Library of Congress, C.D. Box 2, Folder 247.

between the alleged composition of the tune and the filing of the lawsuit. "Of course it is to be regretted that Sandler, if he in fact wrote 'Eili, Eili,' cannot enjoy the fruits of his labor," Judge Knox told the court, "but it is difficult to find that he did not, for many years, acquiesce in the wide-spread publication of the song. No sufficient reason for the delay is revealed by the evidence."[11] Judge Knox reviewed the equivocal evidence, noting that although it appeared that "Eili, Eili" may be a genuine folk song, the piece, "as it now exists, was not generally known in Russia before 1908. And it was in 1896 that Sandler claims to have written the song. It is, therefore, not impossible that 'Eili, Eili' originated in America, and was carried abroad."[12] In response to the verdict, Sandler reportedly lamented, "What I feel is—is like a father that's told he can't have his own child."[13] Judge Knox later wrote in his autobiography that in reaching his verdict he had felt sorry for Sandler: "It is probable, nevertheless—or so it seems to me—that Sandler, the poor New York Jew, really wrote it, but I did not have to decide the matter. The injunction was asked for on the basis of Sandler's copyright."[14] By the time Sandler filed his application for copyright, the music had "entered the public domain. . . . His copyright, therefore, could not avail him."[15]

Was "Eili, Eili," then, an authentic Russian Jewish folk song—as assumed by many scholars and immigrants and as implied or stated in published sheet music, in concert reviews, and on record labels—or was it, to the contrary, a number composed by Sandler for the fin-de-siècle New York Yiddish operetta? Although the latter appears to be the true story of the music's origins, the widespread impression of the former is instructive for the historian of early twentieth-century music, as exemplary of the values and priorities of so many musicians, publishers, composers, and listeners during this era. In many of Europe's urban centers as well as among New York's immigrant communities, folk music was frequently cast as a symbol of nationality, ethnicity, and race, a notion that led composers and performers to search for inventive ways to incorporate folklore into their works for the purpose of depicting modern identities. In cases like that of "Eili, Eili," this pursuit led to the construction of a discourse of authenticity around some newly composed melodies too, in a process of folklorization involving music that was anything but "traditional."

This book examines a genre of arrangements of folk music and original "folk-like" works for solo or small ensemble that I call the "rural miniature." Works in the genre, such as Elman's and Seidel's versions of "Eili, Eili," Manuel de Falla's *Siete canciones populares españolas*, Joseph Achron's "Hebrew Melody," and Béla Bartók's *Romanian Folk Dances*, were played frequently in recitals in the early twentieth century, and many have persisted to this day as canonic "encore" pieces and pedagogical exercises for students of violin, cello, piano, and other instruments. They can be difficult to master, incorporating flashy techniques that allow the musician to display virtuosity. The composition of rural miniatures in the early twentieth century emerged from the synthesis of recent changes in the methodology of folk music collecting, developing ideologies of political nationalism, and the rapid burgeoning of sound recording technologies. Although the music on which rural miniatures were based was not always rural—in the case of many works in the genre by Jewish composers, the source melodies came from Jewish music of urban areas—they were generally associated nevertheless with the entrenched ideo-logical distinction between urban "society" and rural "community." The genre was founded upon the belief that musical structures, notation, and perfor-mance could be employed to represent the musical traditions of rural and minority European cultures in a realistic manner. The rural miniature thus provides the basis for a broad case study examining the search for authenticity that preoccupied so many musicians during the modernist period, in their exploration of folk music and incorporation of new ethnographic findings into the composition and performance of art music.

Authenticity is a discursive construct rather than a property inherent in music, and it is always subjective and mutable.[16] In the period under discussion, authenticity was a central concept in many nationalist ideologies, in which it was used to define the collective members of a nation as united and separate from other nations. At the same time, authenticity was an important trope in anthropological and ethnographic scholarship, where it frequently underpinned descriptions of folklore, crafts, music, and other subjects of study as intrinsic features of the social and cultural groups to which they belonged.[17] The notion of authenticity has thus been a central component in the construction and expression of shared identities across social groups.[18] Studying historical ideas of authenticity allows us to contemplate why many musicians have defined what they believe to be true and inherent to their identities through the ar-rangement of folk melodies as works of art music, and how changes in cultural identities over time have led to variations in the ways such works were per-formed and discussed long after their composition.

This book explores the pursuit of authenticity in art music by examining musical realism, an aesthetic mode according to which musicians depicted folk music traditions in a manner that was interpreted by many listeners, critics, and other musicians as accurate and objective. Musical realism was predicated on the notion that instrumental music could evoke a perceived reality; working in this mode, musicians developed a set of techniques aimed at persuading listeners that their compositions offered an authentic image of rural life. It emerged in part under the influence of the new sound recording technologies and their early reputation for providing objective representations of musical performances. The concept of musical realism is helpful in characterizing the process of representation involved in folk music transcription and arrange-ment, as well as the inevitable gap between source melodies and the ethno-graphic transcriptions and art music compositions and performances based on them. Indeed, any effort to notate sound involves a transformation in the medium of musical transmission, as a unique and ephemeral performance becomes fixed on the printed page. The composition of a work based on a collected melody also requires significant changes associated with the con-trasting conventions of folk and art music, and the interpretation of such a piece is typically undertaken by a performer who has had a different form of training than the original musician and plays for audiences with different expectations. These changes along the path between the initial rendition of a folk melody encountered during fieldwork and the performance of the rural miniature, however, do not preclude an aesthetic mode of realism in transcription and arrangement. The ethnographer and composer may still aim to be as accurate as possible, or to create the impression of accuracy, in spite of the alterations they make, and their audiences may be persuaded to some degree by the truthfulness or verisimilitude of what is revealed by the finished product. The study of musical realism thus helps to explain why and how composers and performers attempted to depict folk music accurately in their works, while it also allows for a richer understanding of the nature of the gap between the musical representation and that which it represents.

In the first decades of the twentieth century, musical realism was deeply entwined with the conceptions of authenticity associated with folk music. When rural miniatures were reinterpreted and adapted in changing contexts and for different audiences as the century progressed, other stylistic traits were frequently adopted to purvey authenticity in new ways. Achron's 1911 "Hebrew Melody," for example, was performed and recorded frequently over the first three and a half decades after its composition, and was adapted by performers, filmmakers, and lyricists as a short Zionist film, a concert aria, a popular song, and, finally, a recital piece for the theremin (see Chapter 5).[19] The persistent purpose of these artists was to achieve through their realizations the authenticity of expression they believed this work, reportedly based on a traditional melody, made available to them in their varied contexts.

Rural miniatures were also made to serve as signifiers of social and cultural identities for listeners far away from the works' stylistic origins. In America, for example, a number of European rural miniatures resurfaced in the influential guidebook for silent movie scoring, *Erno Rapée's Encyclopædia of Music for Pictures*, as tools ensemble leaders could use to heighten a film's portrayal of setting and character. Rapée wrote that in developing the accompanying score for a silent feature film, "Firstly—determine the geographic and national atmosphere of your picture,—Secondly—embody everyone of your important characters with a theme," using music that corresponds to the filmic depiction of places and identities.[20] Rural miniatures are listed under multiple headings throughout the encyclopedia, which is divided into sections by themes, regions, moods, and genres. Under "Hebrew Music," for example, Rapée suggests the ensemble play Achron's "Hebrew Melody" and several editions of "Eili, Eili"; under "Hungarian" he recommends programming Brahms's *Hungarian Dances* and Jenő Hubay's "Hejre Kati"; and under "Spanish" he lists rural miniatures by Isaac Albéniz, Enrique Granados, and Pablo de Sarasate. If rural miniatures in concert programs were a vehicle for offering urban listeners insight into rural and minority cultural artifacts and thereby depicting the sounds of the nation, here the same repertoire functioned as a tool of authenticity to enhance a silent film's photographic representations of place and to "embody" its characters by contributing a sense of realism to the two-dimensional image.

RACE AND HYBRIDITY

The genre of the rural miniature emerged out of urban European composers' encounters with folk and popular music, encounters that took place in some cases through active involvement in ethnographic fieldwork and analysis and in others through the study of writings by ethnographers. Bartók conducted fieldwork throughout East Central Europe and elsewhere, and Falla studied Spanish traditional music with musicologist and collector Felipe Pedrell and consulted ethnographic anthologies, while Achron worked with ethnographers as a member of the Society for Jewish Folk Music. Many of the musicians and critics who figure in this study believed race to be a principal determinant of identity, although definitions of race differed from place to place and person to person.

The scientific study of race gained footing and became systematic in the late nineteenth century as a field that was considered to provide empirical evidence of the inherent traits of differentiated groups of people.[21] This contributed to a racial turn in folk music collection and taxonomy, and the search for authentic examples of the music of different populations, including ethnographers' own nations and communities. This racial turn often evinced a preoccupation with the search for origins and the belief that pure and unmodified folk songs could provide insight into the history of a race.[22] Thus, for example, the French composer and folklorist Jean-Baptiste Weckerlin stated in 1886 that French folk songs, or *chansons populaires*, contain evidence of "the memory and the history of races that have sometimes been lost or disappeared"; he produced collections of folk song arrangements, presenting them as cultural artifacts of the French and other global racial groups.[23] Indeed, the search for national and racial origins provided an important impetus for the collection and arrangement of chansons populaires in France. Louis-Albert Bourgault-Ducoudray wrote that the songs allowed listeners as well as composers seeking new languages of musical innovation to look backward "to the origins of music";[24] and Julien Tiersot described chansons populaires in the 1880s as "the chronicles through which the people conserve their memory of past times."[25] In the first decades of the twentieth century, Bartók and Achron, seeking to represent Hungarian national and Jewish diasporic identities, respectively, also turned to the arrangement of folk music.

The emergence of racial ideology in the study of music furthermore manifested itself in pronouncements about the putative authenticity or inauthenticity of the music of diasporic groups, particularly Jews and Roms (sometimes referred to as Roma or Gypsies). Franz Liszt, for example, wrote in his *Des Bohémiens et de leur musique en Hongrie* (On the Gypsies and Their Music in Hungary), published in 1859 and later translated as *The Gipsy in Music*, that in their music Roms "repeat sentiments applying to all individuals of the same race—sentiments which go to form their interior type, the physiognomy of their soul, the expression of their entire sentient being."[26] Decades later the American critic Olin Downes implied a similarly idealized view of race as a source of musical authenticity in describing Ernest Bloch's "Schelomo" as "racial, ancestral, it is the voice of sages and prophets, which never dies, resounding in the souls of the peoples for unnumbered ages."[27]

This idea of race has by now been largely discredited in academic discourse, both as a result of new understandings of what science can and cannot reveal about human identities, and in recognition of the role of the concept in horrifying acts of war and genocide during the twentieth century and continuing into the twenty-first. Scholars today generally view race to be not a historical and biological given but an invented category that gradually became ingrained as ideology in the West, and ultimately had an important role in the rhetoric used to justify destruction and genocide during World War II.[28] Many academic authors prefer the concept of ethnicity, understood as a social tool used in identity construction, over that of race as a heritable social "essence" passed on by blood.[29] The study of the early twentieth century and its music nevertheless demands the interrogation of historical understandings of race and the ways the concept's meanings changed over the period and varied among different communities. *Sounding Authentic* considers the influence of racial theories on the use of folk music in composition and the ways in which notions of identity and authenticity were defined in relation to the musical boundaries people erected using the concept of race.

Much of the historical discourse around the rural miniature, in the writings of composers, performers, and critics of the early twentieth century, relied on the idea of a stable binary relationship between the urban and rural spheres. In spite of efforts in academic studies to move beyond this conceptual trope, it has left a lasting impression on the reception and study of Western music and its relation to non-Western and folk repertoires. It is crucial in examining the rural miniature, however, to recognize this urban/rural binary as another construction and to look instead at the remarkable intertextuality of composition and performance during the period, and at the fluidity between the perceived boundaries between self and other and among folk, popular, and art musics. This approach allows for a more nuanced understanding of the forms of appropriation and arrangement found in the genre.

In his pioneering 1978 book *Orientalism*, Edward Said described a paradigm that accounted for representations by Christian scholars in the West of Muslim subjects in the East in the academic discipline of orientalism.[30] Said's work left its enduring mark on scholarship, and in part as a result of his legacy orientalism has typically been viewed primarily as a category of colonial discourse, a language of the West's imperial assertion of domination over Islam and the East. The prominence of this West-East and Christian-Muslim paradigm has meant the general avoidance until more recently of the study of many other complex forms of orientalism that account for representational gazes in different geographical and cultural directions and that stem from motivations other than the assertion of hegemonic power.[31] European Jews, for instance, were long the subject of an orientalist perspective in Western writings that cast them as Europe's internal other. In spite of this, and in part in response to it, some Central European Jewish scholars also became active in the field of orientalism in the nineteenth century. The work of these scholars provides evidence that not all orientalist works involved the language of imperial domination; their writings on Jewish culture in Muslim Spain, for example, often exhibited more empathy toward their Muslim subjects than the orientalist research of Christian scholars.[32] Some scholars and artists within the West turned to orientalism in projects of self-definition as well; this was particularly prevalent among peripheral and non-state cultures and further complicates the West-East, imperialist paradigm of orientalism. The Jewish orientalists who engaged in the study of Muslim Spain, for example, did so partly in response to the history of European anti-Jewish orientalism, hoping to carve out a stronger, more respected position for modern Jewish culture within Europe.[33]

Exoticist and orientalist representation in music has also occurred in multiple directions, not only from West to East or imperialist to colonial subject: in non-Western and subaltern cultures, some musicians have shown an impulse to represent the West as exotic "other," while within Europe exoticism has also been used in typically urban art forms as a language for depicting neighboring rural cultures.[34] The rural miniature, in the variety of its forms and functions across diverse cultural contexts, demonstrates how complex the boundaries had become in the racial and geographic imagination of modern Europe of the early twentieth century, even within a framework dominated by the reductive conceptual binaries of West and East, rural and urban, and self and other. The study of this genre, therefore, benefits from a focus on the notion of hybridity, a crucial and common though often overlooked element of composition, performance, and listening in the modernist period.

In his essay on hybridity in literature "Discourse in the Novel," Mikhail Bakhtin writes that language

> becomes "one's own" only when the speaker populates it with his own intention, his own accent, when he appropriates the word, adapting it to his own semantic and expressive intention. Prior to this moment of appropriation, the word does not exist in a neutral and impersonal language . . . but rather it exists in other people's mouths, in other people's contexts, serving other people's intentions: it is from there that one must take the word, and make it one's own.[35]

It is helpful to conceive of composition and performance as based upon a diversity of musical gestures, tropes, and idioms, analogous to the multiplicity of speech types for which Bakhtin develops the term "heteroglossia." In creating music people appropriate and adapt elements from various musical styles and genres that are found in the prior work of other musicians.

As an amalgamation of what composers learned about rural musical traditions through collections, recordings, and transcriptions of folk music, and of what they absorbed of the elements of art music practice during their training, the rural miniature privileges musical heteroglossia. Rural miniatures constitute a hybrid genre that was frequently perceived and performed not simply as "classical" or "folk" music, but as a new form that exhibited elements listeners associated with both. Bakhtin discusses hybridity in the novel as a deliberate artistic device by which authors use language to "creat[e] the image of language": "Hybridization . . . is a mixture of two social languages within the limits of a single utterance, an encounter, within the area of an utterance, between two different linguistic consciousnesses, separated from one another by an epoch, by social differentiation or by some other factor."[36] He continues, "the novelistic hybrid is *an artistically organized system for bringing different languages in contact with one another,* a system having as its goal the illumination of one language by means of another."[37] The rural miniature is likewise the product of musical encounters, and a genre that self-consciously foregrounds its hybridity. Works such as Achron's "Hebrew Melody" and Bartók's *Romanian Folk Dances* were performed on both didactic lecture recitals about the history of regional folk musics and classical concert programs alongside works by Bach and Beethoven. Pablo de Sarasate's "Zigeunerweisen," a virtuosic showpiece for accompanied violin based on the music performed by Rom musicians, entered the repertoire of some Rom ensembles after becoming well known in concert halls and being distributed internationally on professional sound recordings. And "Hebrew Melody," "Zigeunerweisen," and Jascha Heifetz's "Hora Staccato," already arrangements of religious and folk music for classical violin and piano or orchestra, were adapted as popular songs in the style of Tin Pan Alley during the 1940s.

Because the study of folk music and the composition of rural miniatures were typically undertaken by scholars and musicians who believed that folk music exhibited a unique purity that arose from its development in rural communities that had remained untouched by outside influences, some of these ethnographers and composers—including Bartók, in his early essays, as shown in Chapter 6—conceived of hybridity negatively in relation to the ideal of musical purity and as a potential result of the erosion of the supposedly unspoiled cultural artifacts of rural populations.[38] But the description of folk music as pure and authentic was often ideologically motivated; the music of rural communities in Hungary, for example, was in many cases more directly influenced by traveling Rom ensembles than Bartók allowed in his earlier writings. Ethnographers, furthermore, often had as strong an impact on folk music performers at this time as the music had on their work.[39]

From our current standpoint, with the recognition that purity was an aesthetic ideal that could never in fact be located, the term "hybridity" can be of assistance in establishing how new musical styles and genres emerge from cross-cultural encounter. This understanding of hybridity does not impede the recognition of the ways such encounters might also lead to essentialization. Because of the nationalist ideologies that were frequently behind the composition of folk music arrangements, and the fact that the notational and technological media in which they were composed, printed, and recorded were developed in cosmopolitan Europe, rural miniatures often displayed homogenizing and generalizing assumptions about ethnic groups and their music. "Hybridity" allows us to recognize, however, that the will to adapt elements from folk music into new compositions also frequently grew out of musicians' positive intentions to define, clarify, and perform their national and diaspora identities through the study of rural and ethnic groups and the recognition of shared cultural characteristics.

THE RURAL MINIATURE AND THE "PERIPHERY"

The rural miniature predominated in communities often perceived as peripheral to those Central and Western European countries that had by the early twentieth century become widely associated with the central achievements in the field of classical music, principally Germany, Austria, Italy, and France. The notion of a musical center originated in the nineteenth century with the rising conception of German composers as the dominant, even universal upholders of the art form, in the quality, taste, and cultivation of their work. In response, musicians in countries peripheral to this growing "center" came increasingly to view themselves as musical "others," and if they sought to work in the "universal" musical style, their surest ticket to an international audience was, increasingly, the adaptation of regional folk music into art music.[40] A composer in the musical periphery, by representing local cultures through the use of folk themes in his work, could present his music for the consumption of those with "cultivated" taste in the mainstream style of German art music.[41] And through this process, out of the notion of national folk music, there emerged a new category of national art music, which typically involved the selection and adaptation of regional traditional music in new compositions.[42] The rural miniature developed from this social and cultural delineation between "center" and "periphery" and the perceived necessity for musical self-representation, as well as from the increasingly "scientific" aims of accuracy and objectivity in the field of folk music collection that followed the invention of technology for recording sound. The rural miniature thus arose in part from the effort to showcase musical artifacts from areas perceived as peripheral—and this meant both bringing rural musics to urban performers and presenting new compositions by artists in nations not generally viewed as centers of classical music to audiences both at home and abroad, as new contributions to the art music canon. In the context of the privileging of literacy and the "cultivation" of art music in Europe's cosmopolitan centers, the transformation of melodies from the oral tradition to the written through transcription and harmonization for piano, as found as early as the late eighteenth and early nineteenth centuries in England, Germany, and elsewhere (see Chapter 1), also served as a way of moving folk music from the periphery of modern life to the center.

In the late nineteenth and early twentieth centuries, folk song arrangements and rural miniatures were composed internationally, as musicians and folklorists turned to traditional music in order to present artistic achievements in composition that were at once mainstream and regionally marked, able to represent specific national and racial identities on the world stage. A selective survey of arrangements of folk songs and dances shows the broad scope of folk music settings in Europe and beyond. French scholars of chansons populaires in the nineteenth century considered the repertoire they collected, particularly from rural areas in France, to be useful tools in promoting unity behind a French national identity.[43] In this spirit Bourgault-Ducoudray wrote, "a people who ignores its *chansons populaires* does not know its own 'soul,' whose spontaneous melodic inspiration is like the imitation or the living reflection."[44] Weckerlin, Burgault-Ducoudray, Tiersot, Vincent d'Indy, and others arranged chansons populaires with piano accompaniment, often publishing these settings in collections that presented the songs as "pure" historical relics, shared cultural artifacts of a French national identity, and inspiration for progress in the field of composition. In his three-volume *Échos du temps passé*, which featured *chansons* by trouvères including Adam de la Halle, composers such as Machaut and Lully, French kings, and other historical figures in addition to religious songs and regional folk songs, Weckerlin introduced most of his arrangements with a few paragraphs about the original songs' historical context and performance style. His description of a *Chanson Normande* sung to him by a "simple farmer," for example, relates, "We have often heard the peasants of Normandy singing in the countryside; they produce their voices at the top of their lungs and sustain them on each note until their breath is extinguished. Their airs are almost always in minor, and resemble psalmody more than songs."[45] Weckerlin sets the bucolic outdoor scene for the song that follows in its arrangement for the bourgeois indoor ensemble of voice and piano, and his depiction of the performance evokes an unrefined but intense mode of expression made to seem more transcendent by the identification of the song with characteristics of church music, despite its folkloric origins.

In northern Europe, folk music arrangements of the early twentieth century grew out of an active and long-standing tradition of folk song collecting and arrangement. In the Preface of Edvard Grieg's *Slåtter*, Op. 72, a collection of piano arrangements of seventeen folk tunes published in 1903, Grieg writes that these "Norwegian peasant dances," originally played on the Hardanger fiddle and transcribed by Johan Halvorsen "in a manner reliable even for research-work," were collected from the playing of Knut Dahle, a performer from the southern Norwegian region of Telemark.[46] Grieg, who had himself experimented with the transcription of Hardanger fiddle music a few years before composing *Slåtter*,[47] claims that this musical tradition achieves its authenticity in part because it originated in isolation, uninfluenced by surrounding cultures: it is "handed down to us from an age when the culture of the Norwegian peasant was isolated in its solitary mountain-valleys from the outer world, to which fact it owes its whole originality." He describes the melodies in terms that would become standard in characterizations of folk music by composers and ethnographers during the modernist period, as combining earnest simplicity and barbaric violence: "Those who can appreciate such music, will be delighted at the originality, the blending of fine, soft gracefulness with sturdy almost uncouth power and untamed wildness." As Bartók would soon argue about his own early rural miniatures (see Chapter 6), Grieg states that his aim in *Slåtter* "was to raise these works of the people to an artistic level, by . . . bringing them under a system of harmony." A number of the arrangements are introduced with retellings of local legends, or provided with notes describing the tempo, instrumentation, or other attributes of their initial form.

In Britain, Cecil J. Sharp and others wrote rural miniatures based on folk music from various regions of the nation. His 1911 *Four Folk-Airs*, for example, featured settings of "Morris Dance Tunes Collected from Traditional Sources and arranged with pianoforte accompaniment." Other collections were historical in nature; for example, in *Six Country Dances of the 18th Century* (1921), Ernest Newton produced piano arrangements of British folk songs, following their titles with the years they were first published in anthologies.

Rural miniatures were also composed outside of Europe, with the arrangement of folk music for piano in nations and colonized regions from America to Australia. Justin Elie's piano adaptations of Haitian melodies transformed the island's traditional music into miniatures for performance in cosmopolitan concert venues. A review of his 1923 Carnegie Hall performance of a series of dance arrangements, in which a dancer called Hasoutra performed as he played the piano, stated that the dancer's "interpretation of these works is essentially original and absolutely authentic."[48] Reviews of Elie's three-part *The Ancient Mountain Legends* praised the composer for his authentic depiction of Haitian folklore; one critic write that the work, "built on genuine primitive themes," demonstrates Elie's skill at composing "a characteristic harmonization, however keeping the full value of the original mood of the songs."[49] Moreover, Elie's arrangements of the music of indigenous groups in Latin America were viewed as uniquely authentic due to his work as an ethnographer; thus Conrad

H. Ratner wrote in 1923 that Elie "has devoted ten years to concentrated in-vestigation among tribes, living among them, at times at the very risk of his life, leading the simple and picturesque existence of a people so capricious, carefree and degenerate."[50] Ratner overstates Elie's encounters with Native American musicians, carried away by his attempt to depict Elie's works as uniquely accu-rate in their representation of folk music, possessing an authenticity whose roots lie in Elie's involvement in the field of ethnography.

In Clarence Elkin's 1923 *Maori Melodies (with Words) Collected and Arranged for Pianoforte*, published in Australia, the Preface invokes ethnographic encoun-ter in a description of the work's composition: "The Compiler of these Maori Melodies was charmed whilst touring New Zealand, on several occasions, with the beauty of their Folk-Songs and Poi Dances." The Preface acknowl-edges his ethnographic sources by name, thanking them "for assistance in col-lecting these sweet little melodies," and follows with a brief retelling of a Māori legend, "The Story of Hinemoa and Tutanekai."[51] Song titles, written in Māori, are followed didactically by the English name of the original genre.

Arthur Farwell's *American Indian Melodies*, first published by the Wa-Wan Press in 1901, featured ten miniatures, most of which are based on melodies written down by the ethnographer Alice C. Fletcher or transcribed directly from the wax cylinders she compiled during fieldwork; each is introduced by a short excerpt of Fletcher's interpretation of the song's original text.[52] In the Introduction, Farwell describes the songs he has chosen as providing evidence of the transcen-dence and authenticity of music in Native American religious practice: "Song, an invisible agent, is to the Indian the direct means of communicating with his in-visible god."[53] The Introduction proceeds to relate Fletcher's fieldwork experi-ence and methodologies. Farwell offers suggestions to enable the performer to imbue each song with its corresponding ethos. His explanation refers to German art music in order to distinguish his arrangement from these "cultivated" and "universal" genres, but at the same time also to compare Native American folk songs favorably with the works of "the masters":

> "Inketunga's Thunder Song" would sound ridiculous interpreted after the style of a nocturne, moment musical, impromptu, or any purely musical form with which we are familiar, but gains an exalted and beautiful significance the moment we bring to its interpretation the knowledge that it stands for the direct communication of a human soul with its god, and a deeply-felt assurance, to its fellow man, of that communication. Thus it will be seen that a seriousness no less than that which we accord the works of the masters, must be brought to the interpretation of these songs, the spontaneous utterance of a people whose every word, action or tone invariably bears a deeply vital significance.[54]

The simple, cross-cultural understanding of religious conviction, therefore, is all that is needed to perform these ancient melodies with the authentic spon-taneity and seriousness they demand. In works such as Elkin's, Elie's, and

Farwell's, the music of native populations of Polynesia, the Caribbean islands, and the Americas, having been transformed from the oral tradition to the literate through ethnographic transcription, were brought even further from the "periphery" toward the "center" of art music culture through the arrangement, publication, and performance of rural miniatures.

Rural miniatures appealed not only to members of the national and ethnic groups they represented through their adaptation of folk themes but also beyond their borders toward the modern musical "center," where the "periphery," as a place of cultural "otherness" assumed to lack the cultivation of Central Europe, came to evoke stereotypes of musical authenticity, purity, and simplicity that were linked with romantic notions of the pre-modernized rural and the pre-hybridized folk. But it is also for this reason that while many rural miniatures did enter the canons of piano or violin pedagogy and recital repertoire, they generally failed to be adopted into the more general canons of Western music still dominated by Austro-German composers. Indeed, as Richard Taruskin writes, "Without the native costume, a 'peripheral' composer would never achieve even secondary canonical rank, but with it he could never achieve more."[55] While the use of folk themes became a way for the composers of the "periphery" to make themselves heard by broad international audiences, it nevertheless often restricted them from gaining a respected place in the highest ranks of the musical canon.

The rural miniature thus played an important role in the efforts of many musicians and listeners to construct national identities and negotiate processes of adaptation and assimilation in the face of displacement across the diaspora. It was a tool in the construction of personal and group identities among composers, performers, and listeners, and the hybrid origins, uses, and recontextualizations of works in the genre are testimony to the nuance and variability of such social negotiations. A compelling by-product of this complex role of the genre was the frequent use of rural miniatures as training vehicles, through which the unrefined young student could be taught to play with cultural sophistication, and also as encore pieces, in which a prominent performer could demonstrate the technical virtuosity popularly associated with both "high culture" classical training and the supposedly authentic, expressive emotionality of rural music.

MUSIC AT THE BORDERS: TRANSCENDING "HIGH" AND "LOW"
IN THE PERIPHERY

This study of music and periphery brings to the fore questions of genre and the distinctions among "folk," "art," and "popular" music, and between "high" and "low" culture, by combining score-based readings with the study of music's manifestations in other media—such as sound recording and film soundtracks—as well as the of discursive values that developed around music. In examining music's roles in peripheral cultures it becomes critical to consider musical functions, adaptations, and performances to understand the ways music reflects the processes of cultural encounter and exchange that occurred regularly in borderland regions and among diasporic groups.[56] In such communities, music often thrived at the borders between folk, popular, and artistic genres. The study of music among these groups can thus reveal the overlaps between the categories of "high" and "low" music, the prolific instances of cross-cultural musical adaptation and appropriation, and the freedom with which music was adapted between genres and styles in the early twentieth century, a period marked by rapid developments in nationalism and technology, and the increasing rate of migration from rural to urban spaces and across national borders.[57]

Even the simplest rural miniature—as an adaptation of a folk melody into a work of art music, an original composition based on preexisting material, and a transposition of the oral tradition into the written—demonstrates that musical styles during this era can be more accurately characterized as points along a fluid continuum than as distinct and easily differentiated cultural forms. But as so many of the rural miniatures explored in this book demonstrate, the genre was rarely this straightforward. In the case of "Eili, Eili," as Judge Knox concluded, the rural miniature Seidel published as a simple folk tune arrangement was more likely a composition for the popular genre of operetta that had become folklorized and then assimilated into the canon of violin recital music at the same time that it became a standard religious song in the repertoire of celebrated cantors. But that was not the end of the story. Later still, the piece was performed by artists known for their work in far different styles, from the crooner Johnny Mathis to the *klezmer* clarinetist Dave Tarras to the big band trumpeter Harry James. This book's discussions of "Hora Staccato," "Zigeunerweisen," "Hebrew Melody," and other rural miniatures further demonstrate how common it was that works in the genre reached fluidly across a continuum of musical styles typically conceived of as popular, folk, and art, and moved between national and ethnic idioms as diverse as rural folk music, urban Rom numbers, European classical repertoire, and American swing.

The rural miniature complicated the constructed distinctions between "folk," "art," and "popular" music, not only in its composition but also in its reception and performance. Like many of the violinists of his and the preceding generation, Heifetz recorded and performed adaptations for violin of songs and dances associated with folk and popular traditions while always remaining devoted to the standard works of the violin repertoire and the new compositions of his peers.[58] In a 1946 article in the *New York Times*, he boasts of his broad-minded musical taste for the folk and popular song of his adopted country:

I have never hesitated to play Stephen Foster's "Jeanie With the Light Brown
Hair." . . . It's a fine song, American to the core. Why should I go hunting for its
Viennese or Parisian equivalent and try to palm that off as art because it has a
foreign name? Foster's tune is art in its class. So are the songs of Kern, Gershwin
and Berlin. I think Irving Berlin's "White Christmas" is a grand tune, and it pleases
me to play it in concert or on the radio.[59]

As is shown throughout this book, similar statements arise in the writings of
Bartók, Falla, and members of the St. Petersburg Society for Jewish Folk
Music when they argue that their representations of musical identities raise
folk song and dance, through arrangement and adaptation, to the level of art
music.

By employing the genre of the rural miniature in part to "elevate" folk and
popular melodies to the prestige of art music, musicians displayed their reliance
on these entrenched stylistic categories while at the same time they under-
mined this taxonomy, highlighting the fractures in the supposed barriers
between musical genres. The rural miniature thus carved out its space at the
perceived borders between musical genres and styles. It acts as a lens through
which to view the fluidity of the music of the early twentieth century along a
stylistic continuum, and it allows us to consider the dynamic effects of cultural
encounter and appropriation in communities at the peripheries of art music
culture during this period.

THE RURAL MINIATURE FOR VIOLIN IN SPAIN, THE JEWISH DIASPORA, AND HUNGARY

Rural miniatures were written for numerous instrumentations; most were
arranged for solo piano—an instrument that because of its omnipresence in
bourgeois culture and its ability to incorporate both melody and harmony was
an obvious candidate for "elevating" folk music to the level of cosmopolitan
high art while recontextualizing it with Western harmonies or experimenting
with the modes and scales of traditional musics. Many others were arranged
for accompanied string instrument, and some were for clarinet, chamber ensemble, or chamber orchestra. This book focuses in particular on rural miniatures for violin with piano or orchestral accompaniment. In works in the
genre for string instruments, composers and performers often sought to
achieve a quality of musical realism, taking advantage of the violin's common
association with international folk musics, which provided the sense of a direct
correlation between rural miniatures and the traditions on which they were
based. With its durable frame and portable size, the violin was a typical member of folk and popular music ensembles throughout Europe, as well as one of
the most ubiquitous instruments in the art music canon; thus Jean-Jacques
Rousseau wrote of the violin in his *Dictionnaire de musique* in 1768, "There is

no instrument from which one obtains a more varied and universal expression."[60] For this reason, in the rural miniature the violin could act as a perfect medium for bringing together the musical "periphery" and "center," for staging an encounter between rural and urban spheres and traditional and classical repertoires. It also became a common symbol of national, religious, and cultural identities for a number of Europe's rural and minority groups. Its timbre was often described as imitative or evocative of the voice, and therefore as able to communicate human sentiments without the requirement of language, a universalizing quality that allowed people to perform and listen to the folk music of the world's ethnic and national groups without the necessity of understanding the languages in which they communicated. The rural miniature's popularity was propelled in large part by prominent violinists including Heifetz, Szigeti, Elman, and Zoltán Székely, who edited violin arrangements of works in the genre for solo piano and frequently performed them. Rural miniatures based on Spanish, Jewish, and Eastern and East Central European melodies dominated the recital and recording repertoires of these violinists, becoming most widely known among international audiences. For this reason, this book focuses primarily on rural miniatures originating in these settings.

Sounding Authentic is divided into two parts. The first is devoted to the aesthetic and theoretical aspects of the composition and performance of folk music arrangements for accompanied violin. Part II opens with a consideration of the precursor to the rural miniature in the *style hongrois* and continues with several case studies in the genre of the rural miniature, viewing realism's development in the contexts in which it was most widespread: the composition and performance of works based on traditional music from Spain, the Jewish diaspora, and Hungary.

Chapter 1 explains the identification and labeling of the genre and explores the concept of realism in music. It examines the types of melodic, harmonic, formal, and rhythmic elements that produce the effect of realism, referring to excerpts from a range of works in the genre in order to compare how composers from different regions and cultures represented rural traditions in their works. The chapter also investigates the ways composers developed the aesthetic mode of realism to achieve what they considered to be authenticity in music. It provides a stylistic analogy and context by viewing nineteenth-century examples of realist representation in painting, literature, and photography, and discusses musical realism in relation to early twentieth-century methods of folk song collection and transcription, and beliefs about and uses of recording technology.

Chapter 2 considers the performance and recording of rural miniatures during the first half of the twentieth century. The chapter first addresses the contexts in which violinists played rural miniatures in recital programs, radio broadcasts, and performances for commercial recording studios, and it explores the ways performers actively took part in the composition of rural miniatures, focusing in particular on a historical and analytical case study of Heifetz and Grigoraş Dinicu's "Hora Staccato." The chapter addresses the performance style that many prominent violinists developed in playing rural miniatures, characterized by the combination of a variety of aural tropes to evoke the sounds urban listeners typically associated with folk and ethnic performance traditions. The rural musician, as an ideological construction in the urban imagination, was not professionally trained, and played an instrument weathered from outdoor use in an emotionally authentic manner that evoked the ethnic soul of the community. Common gestures that violinists used to project this sonic character were rough timbres, heavy downbeats, slides, accented bowings, and ornaments including trills and grace notes.

Part II opens in Chapter 3 with a consideration of the nineteenth-century virtuosic repertoire for violin in the style hongrois, which provided an important precedent to the rural miniature and the realist representational mode, both as a model and as a genre that later musicians reacted against. The chapter addresses the history of the style and its roots in mythologies of Rom culture throughout Europe. Roms were victims of racism and abusive government policies and were often depicted in anthropological and fictional writing as well as in the visual arts, with some variation, as wild, pre-literate denizens of bucolic areas, and as natural musicians who played with expressive passion and authenticity and danced sensuously. Stereotypes about Rom music were first disseminated in the eighteenth century in the writings of Heinrich Grellman, and were further propagated in Franz Liszt's *The Gipsy in Music.* The chapter investigates Sarasate's "Zigeunerweisen," analyzing the score as well as recorded performances by Sarasate and Heifetz, to suggest how the work acted as a predecessor to the rural miniature.

Chapter 4 explores rural miniatures based on the traditional music of Spain and Hispanic cultures by composers and violinists from Spain and Paris. It deals especially with Manuel de Falla's works for piano and their arrangements for accompanied violin. Falla showed great interest during an early period of his career in the study of Spanish folk music, and his personal library contained numerous anthologies in which he made extensive marginal notations. The chapter considers Falla's relationship with the Spanish musicologist and nationalist Felipe Pedrell, and examines the rhetoric about Spanish traditional music that can be found in the collections in Falla's library and in his own writing on flamenco *cante jondo* (deep song). The chapter turns to a discussion of Paweł Kochański's arrangement for violin and piano of "Jota," from Falla's *Siete canciones populares españolas*, and analyzes recordings of this movement by Manuel Quiroga and Jacques Thibaud.

Chapter 5 reviews the role of the rural miniature in the work of members of the St. Petersburg Society for Jewish Folk Music, who shared a belief that the genre offered a crucial method of representing Jewish musical traditions for broad audiences. It investigates theories about the music of Eastern European Jewish communities propagated in contemporary texts about Jewish traditional and art music and discusses the metaphorical association, invoked commonly in the writings of members of the Society and in literary and artistic depictions of Eastern European Jewish culture, between the timbres of the violin and the popular nationalist concept of a "Jewish voice" expressed in music. The chapter focuses on Achron's "Hebrew Melody," viewing the history of its composition, performance, reception, and adaptation.

Chapter 6 focuses on the role of musical realism in Bartók's ethnomusicology and composition. It begins with a review of his essays and letters discussing recording technology and nationalism, which demonstrate Bartók's understanding that one can determine the inherent traits of particular ethnic groups by studying their folk music. The chapter offers an extended analysis of *Romanian Folk Dances*, which Bartók wrote in 1915, after a three-year hiatus from composition during which he dedicated himself exclusively to ethnomusicological research. It examines the wax cylinder recordings of the original source melodies, Bartók's transcriptions and anthologies, manuscript sketches of *Romanian Folk Dances*, and recordings of Székely's arrangement for violin and piano. In his attempt to produce a work that would be perceived as simple and objective, Bartók considerably altered the embellishments and rhythmic complexities of the original melodies he collected.

Viewing the rural miniature in Spain, the Jewish diaspora, and Hungary enables a comparison of the genre's composition and performance in different political settings, and a study of the ways the rural miniature developed in relation to state and diaspora nationalism. It also permits us to view how, despite such differences and the dependence of the genre on new technologies and politics, the rural miniature in these three contexts remained deeply rooted in the style hongrois and nineteenth-century mythologies of Rom music. Analyses of early sound recordings of rural miniatures further reveal the impacts on the genre of increasing globalization in the fields of music performance and sound recording during the first half of the twentieth century. *Sounding Authentic* explores representations of ethnic and national identities in the rural miniature in contexts across Europe as a product of the intersecting influences of political movements, aesthetic modernism, and technological innovation.

PART I

AESTHETIC AND THEORETICAL APPROACHES TO THE RURAL MINIATURE

CHAPTER ONE

MUSICAL REALISM RECONSIDERED

The Rural Miniature and Representation

To renew the old world—that is the collector's deepest desire
when he is driven to acquire new things.
—Walter Benjamin, *Illuminations*, trans.
Harry Zohn (New York: Schocken,
1968), 61.

A folk song in a book is like a photograph of a bird in flight.
—Attributed to Charles Seeger. Evan
Eisenberg, *The Recording Angel: Music,
Records and Culture from Aristotle to
Zappa* (New Haven: Yale University
Press, 2005), 102.

NAMING THE GENRE OF THE RURAL MINIATURE

The genre of the rural miniature emerged during the early years of the twentieth century in the midst of rapid developments in the field of musical ethnography. Composers of rural miniatures found material for their works among the
fruits of ethnographers' research, the newly recorded, transcribed, and catego-
rized melodies they collected. The activities of many of these composers and
ethnographers were motivated by prevailing fears that rural communities were
vanishing in the face of modernization and urbanization, and as a consequence
of war and poverty.[1] Salvage ethnography was founded on the understanding
that by preserving folklore, scholars could begin to counteract the disappearance of the past. In creating rural miniatures, musicians attempted to preserve
musical traditions that they feared were vanishing, by representing them in new

compositions; and one important intended function of many works in the genre was to bring the urban listening public into contact with folk songs and dances.

The rise of the rural miniature followed the development of sound recording technologies around the turn of the century, as new portable devices initiated changes in the ways ethnographers engaged in fieldwork and listeners interacted with performances of contemporary art music. The genre's decline came with the devastating effects of the World War II, around forty years later. The war changed the course of ethnographic research in Central and Eastern Europe, with the destruction of many rural and diaspora communities, whose populations were dispersed and fragmented by genocide and emigration. Béla Bartók, Joseph Achron, and a number of the other composers of rural miniatures left their homes for the United States and other regions as new immigrants and refugees, far from the villages and towns in which the source music for their compositions had been collected.

The "rural miniature" has not previously been given a lasting designation. This is largely because generic names most commonly arise in the field of art music when groups of musical works share title words based on their forms or functions, such as the string quartet or the sonata. One of the typical characteristics of the rural miniature, however, is the avoidance of shared title words. Rural miniatures are named after a broad variety of traditional song and dance types. This variety of technical names is integral to the works' aesthetic style and performance and reception histories but has obscured the common genre they inhabit.

The prior failure to name this genre has also been a result of the common assumption that during the modernist age, genre became outmoded in the composition of art music, surpassed by an increasing tendency to value the autonomy of the individual musical work.[2] Theodor W. Adorno described the trend toward nominalism, or the tendency of modernist composers to write new pieces in what he viewed to be unique forms not shared by other works, as resulting in a "decline of aesthetic genres as such."[3] Carl Dahlhaus also wrote of the "disintegration of genres, the final consequences of which are the individualizing yet abstract titles of the last decade and a half."[4] But Fredric Jameson explains such an understanding of genre as a "strategic feature of what must be called the *ideology of modernism*."[5] Adorno's and Dahlhaus's descriptions of the waning of musical genre in the twentieth century conform to modernist aesthetic values, as they demonstrate the authors' tendency to favor individuality and innovation, characteristics that may seem to preclude a composer's conformance to genre.

In practice, the concept of genre can be a crucial tool in the study of twentieth-century music, precisely because it helps listeners to consider individual pieces of music in relation to other works that are similar in their composition, performance, or reception. Northrop Frye explains in *Anatomy of Criticism* that the study of genre is more than taxonomy; it clarifies "traditions and affinities, thereby bringing out a large number of literary relationships that would not be noticed as long as there were no context established for them."[6] It is common to conceive of genre in literature as a form of social contract among members of an art world that directs audiences' expectations about a particular work and dictates to artists the constraints within which they are expected to create new works.[7] According to this metaphor, the composer, by writing in a specific genre, makes an implicit commitment to abide by a number of the rules of that genre, and other members of the art world tacitly agree to perform, publish, and listen to the work according to the standards preordained by past experiences with the genre. Contrary to the claims of Adorno and Dahlhaus, genre continued to be a salient force in twentieth-century music, and the interpretation of meaning in music from this period has been based to a large extent on sets of shared assumptions that guide the composition, performance, publication, and reception of musical works.

For the modernist composers who incorporated elements of folk music into their work, genre was an important topic because it had been integral to folk music studies since the previous century. Although the rural miniature itself was not named at the time, it was heavily defined by genre, both in the way that it looked back toward the precedent set by earlier forms of folk music adaptation and in the naming of rural miniatures after the songs and dances on which they were based. Genre formed the basis of musical taxonomies in Bartók's research and in the anthologies of Spanish and Jewish musics studied by rural miniature composers, as it did in the very distinctions between folk and art music as they were conceived at the time.[8] Almost any project of collecting music in the oral tradition and appropriating it into the written tradition through transcription and composition involved the idea of genre as an organizing principle that allowed scholars to identify individual songs and dances in relation to one another in terms of form, function, and culture.[9] Genre also permitted ethnographers to conduct comparative studies of folk music within and between cultural groups, in efforts to find similarities and distinctions between traditions and to form conclusions regarding the effects on music of such matters as geographical movement, cross-cultural influence, and stylistic origins.

In many cases these turn-of-the-century genre-based explorations of folk repertoires were inspired by nationalist ideologies.[10] The process by which rural miniature composers selected folk songs and dances for arrangement often reflected the same concerns, as composers sought to draw comparisons through the juxtaposition of melodies, support claims of the cultural purity of folk songs, and define social and national boundaries on the basis of their musical choices. The approach to the genre of the rural miniature in this book adopts the concept of genre as it has been theorized in the field of ethnomusicology, to reflect the understanding that genres develop and change in relation to other genres within greater musical systems.[11] This study aims to balance aesthetic

matters regarding the rural miniature's form with questions of its social function.[12] Overall, the book employs the notion of genre to provide the infrastruc-
ture for a transnational study of the similarities, differences, and mutual
influences between approaches to folk music in the work of composers across
several regions and cultures, as well as of the ways "folk" and "classical" performers interacted with and inspired these composers in their work.

In naming this genre of arrangements the "rural miniature," I employ the
word "miniature" to indicate the common formal characteristics of this body of
works, describing both their brevity and instrumentation. A variety of genres
through centuries of the history of Western music have been identified by the
term "miniature." François Couperin's and Carl Philipp Emanuel Bach's character pieces and musical portraits are often called miniatures, as are many of the
short, programmatic piano works of the nineteenth and early twentieth centuries by composers including Robert Schumann, Felix Mendelssohn, and
Claude Debussy. When used to describe such pieces, the term implies a concise,
often simply constructed work that portrays one recognizable intellectual concept or theme. C.P.E. Bach represents human characteristics in miniatures such
as "La Capricieuse"; Schumann depicts human subjects in "Chiarina" and other
movements of *Carnaval*; and Debussy evokes visual tableaux in "Voiles" and
elsewhere. Rural miniatures continue this musical tradition, as short pieces that
evoke themes related to rural life and minority cultures.

The designation "miniature" is additionally intended to allude to the function of miniaturization as a tool of memory, nostalgia, and appropriation.[13] As
representations of ethnic cultures, rural miniatures recall travel souvenirs and
postcards, portable depictions of foreign locales that serve as aids for recollection and often as proof of a voyage abroad. Affordable and easily mass produced,
postcards were a popular and ubiquitous form of travel photography in early
twentieth-century Europe, available in shops, at fairs, and in arcades in urban
centers. Rural miniatures fulfill an analogous aesthetic purpose. They are col-
lectible items—in the forms of recordings and scores and as numbers on recital
programs—that provide an inventory of representations of rural musical traditions. It was common for violinists to combine rural miniatures representing
different cultures' folk music in concerts and on recordings. Such programs, as
well as multi-movement rural miniatures such as Bartók's *Romanian Folk
Dances*, constructed of arrangements of multiple songs or dances, resemble catalogues of folklore, rather like the "topographical" collections of postcards that
became popular during the period between 1907 and 1920.[14] In Ernest Bloch's
1923 *Baal Shem: Three Pictures of Chassidic Life*, this visual analogy is made explicit: the title implies that the movements depict tableaux of life in the Jewish
towns of Eastern Europe. Like travel photography, rural miniatures serve a documentary purpose as portrayals of folk music traditions for urban audiences.
Additionally, as in the case of *Romanian Folk Dances*, rural miniatures often

serve as certificates of proof of the composer's firsthand knowledge of genres and regions that are often unknown or inaccessible to urban listeners.

Susan Stewart has explained of the souvenir miniature, "On the one hand, the object must be marked as exterior and foreign, on the other it must be marked as arising directly out of an immediate experience of its possessor."[15] Like souvenir miniatures, rural miniatures provide evidence of the difference and distance between the urban centers where they become popular and the rural regions they represent, while simultaneously functioning as proximate appropriations of these regions' traditions. They produce an impression of authenticity, while in fact they offer representations of folk music traditions that have been modified for consumption by cosmopolitan listeners. Works in the genre also invoke narratives of travel, by implying that the composer and perhaps also the performer have been to the source of the ethnic song and dance traditions depicted in the music. At the same time, rural miniatures appeal to popular nostalgia, representing a world that is distant spatially and perhaps also temporally, one threatened with disappearance due to the destructive forces of urbanization and modernity.

The term "rural" in the genre designation "rural miniature" refers to the conception, common during the nineteenth and early twentieth centuries, of folk music as belonging to the rural realm, which was defined in opposition to the urban. During the period in which rural miniatures became popular, many inhabitants of European cities defined the rural against the urban. Believing themselves to be literate and sophisticated, they considered inhabitants of rural areas to be the opposite, that is, uneducated, primitive, and virtuous, and as such the nation's source of folklore. The notion of the folk was thus closely allied with the notion of the rural, as an artifact of this conceptual binary.[16] This geographic distinction helped to fuel the emergence of the concepts of "folk music" and "art music" at the end of the eighteenth century.[17] Folk music was believed to have originated in the past among "primitive" members of a racial or national group and to be kept alive in the present day by the rural or diasporic "folk." By the early twentieth century, the conceptual distinction between urban society and rural community was at the core of definitions of folk music. Not all rural miniatures were in fact based on the music of rural areas; those that borrowed from Jewish traditional musics in particular often referred to sources collected in the small towns and the areas of larger cities in which many Jews lived in Europe and Russia. Nevertheless, such rural miniatures still reflected the conceptual distinction between the urban sphere as cosmopolitan and modern and the rural as homogeneous and more deeply rooted in tradition, with the resulting notion that in order to locate their roots and study their cultural artifacts, urban citizens must look outward to the rural (or to Jewish communities in circumscribed areas of cities and in small towns).

The dichotomy between urban and rural was described in the social theories laid out by Ferdinand Tönnies in his book *Gemeinschaft und Gesellschaft*, first published in German in 1887. Tönnies's subject is a pair of social bodies in dialectical opposition. *Gemeinschaft*, often translated as "community," is based on "real and organic" relationships, and associated with kinship and folk customs. *Gesellschaft*, often translated as "society," is based on "imaginary and mechanical" structures of relationships, and associated with the rationality of law and the organized state.[18] Mapping this dichotomy regionally, Tönnies writes that "all praise of rural life has pointed out that *Gemeinschaft* among people is stronger there and more alive; it is the lasting and genuine form of living together." *Gesellschaft*, more common in urban areas, is, by contrast, "transitory and superficial."[19] Describing folk traditions, Tönnies explains,

> Custom and mores are . . . the animal will of human *Gemeinschaft*. They presuppose an often-repeated common activity which, whatever its original meaning, has become easy and natural through practice and tradition and is therefore considered necessary under given conditions.[20]

Along such lines, rural musical performance style was often assumed, during this period, to be rooted in the organic relations between the peasant and the natural world: music was popularly considered one of the principal forms of community expression in rural areas and a typical component of traditional rituals that were thought to exhibit expressive spontaneity and improvisation.

In the following decade, the British composer and musicologist C. Hubert H. Parry saw "civilization" as posing a threat to the survival of folk music, which was gradually being overtaken by the popular music genres developed and enjoyed by the "leisured classes":

> The features which give [folk music] its chief artistic and historical importance (apart from its genuine delightfulness) are those which manifest the working of the perfectly unconscious instinct for design, and those in which the emotional and intellectual basis of the art is illustrated by the qualities of the tunes which correspond with the known characters of the nations and peoples who invent them. Folk-tunes are the first essays made by man in distributing his notes so as to express his feelings in terms of design.[21]

For Parry, folk music was the basis of art music, "an epitome of the principles upon which musical art is founded"; but at the same time its existence was endangered by the widening of access to art and popular music.[22]

By the first half of the twentieth century, the perception of rural life as defined by traditional kinship relations, organic human nature, and folklore, and of urban society as characterized by mechanical and unnatural forms of relations, was an influential element of urban modernist intellectual thought. Thus, over half a century after Tönnies first published his text, articles such as "The Folk Society," written by Robert Redfield in the *American Journal of Sociology* in 1947, offered a definition of "folk" still based on the assumption that "primitive, or folk, societies" were those "least like our own," that is, they were the opposite of the modern and urban.[23] Like Tönnies, Redfield describes rural folk society as "small, isolated, nonliterate and homogeneous, with a strong sense of group solidarity."[24]

Bartók's definitions of folk music also relied on the distinction between rural and urban musical traditions. This binary is implicit in the title of his 1931 essay "The Influence of Peasant Music on Modern Music," in which he contrasts the Romantic musical tradition, which he argues is characterized by unbearable excess, with "peasant music," which "is simple, sometimes primitive, but never silly."[25] Describing the methodology by which he encountered and collected folk music, Bartók continues, "Hungarian composers went into the country and made their collections there. . . . The effects of peasant music cannot be deep and permanent unless this music is studied in the country as part of a life shared with the peasants."[26] Bartók's description of rural folk music, in this and other essays from the time, as a cohesive idiom created by the rural Hungarian peasantry and rooted in a historic past contradicted the official Hungarian nationalism that postulated the gentry as the national folk, and Rom music as the true expression of the Hungarian soul.[27] In a conservative critique of the Hungarian musical avant-garde, Emil Haraszti in 1929 articulated the value of Rom music in Hungarian society: "Hungarian sighs are carried to the four corners of the world by the Gypsy violin, and Hungarian hearts are heard beating in the music."[28] Bartók's claims were thus radical and even threatening, an explicit rejection of the notion that the national character of Hungary was defined by the urban gentry.[29] Many members of the middle class who rejected his modernist music and ideas about rural folklore did so from the perspective of a conservative view of Hungarian society that continued to consider the gentry as its folk.[30]

According to Bartók and Zoltán Kodály, the most effective way to redirect the path of modern music, and to tear it from the grips of Romantic tradition, was to travel to rural areas and study their regional music traditions. These avant-garde composers and their progressive audiences conceived of themselves in a complex relationship with the rural realm. They viewed its landscapes and social structures as the opposite of theirs, yet considered it to hold at its core the foundational material of the nation's soul and the vestiges of the originary, organic relationship between its people. The genre of the rural miniature grew out of these ethnographic and nationalist impulses.

MUSICAL MATERIAL

The parameters of a specific genre are never entirely fixed, nor will any instance of a genre display all of the genre's identified characteristics. Rather, genres are mutable, changing over time and operating differently in varied cultural contexts, and works need confirm only as many elements of the genre as are necessary to be identified as examples of that type.[31] Rural miniatures changed with political and social developments around Europe, and works that were written in different places emphasize varying characteristics of the genre. In most cases, however, rural miniatures were composed with the stated or implied goal of accurately representing folk songs and dances in works of art music. This realist style can be interpreted as a break from the parody or self-conscious mimicry that is inherent in so many exoticist works in the style hongrois and the Turkish style, compositional idioms developed in the previous century and a half for the evocation of "exotic" musical cultures, particularly the traditions of Rom ensembles and Turkish Janissary bands. The perceived authenticity of rural miniatures also, however, provided cover for the significant modification of the music of rural areas that occurred in setting melodies for classical instruments and urban audiences. The incorporation—and in some cases invention—of folk songs and dances in art music allowed composers to work with novel scales, sonorities, and timbres; but as they experimented on the basis of the new expressive freedoms folk music afforded, composers also significantly transformed rural melodies and musical practices through processes of notation, harmonization, and arrangement for classically trained performers and instruments. Thus, despite apparent differences between the style of rural miniatures and trends in musical exoticism, the chasm was in some ways not so vast: composers of rural miniatures borrowed numerous techniques from the Romantic idioms of musical exoticism, and in their reception, works in the genre were often favored for their exotic quality, while at the same time praised for their accuracy and realism.

Songs and dances taken along the journey from rural folk song to urban art genre underwent a process of homogenization. In the transformation of these melodies for urban audiences, a host of locally specific modal, formal, and performance customs were represented by a limited handful of tropes, which operate in a manner analogous to those literary details that produce what Roland Barthes called "l'effet de réel" or the "reality effect."[32] Barthes explained that in fiction, the mimetic portrayal of external reality is a product of the addition into a narrative of "interstitial" details that, although they might have no bearing on plot, produce a sense of verisimilitude.[33] He suggested by example a description of a room in Gustave Flaubert's "A Simple Heart," from *Three Tales*, in which Flaubert writes, "an old piano supported, under a barometer, a pyramidal heap of boxes and cartons."[34] This description offers information that appears irrelevant to the narrative: although the piano might indicate the bourgeois social class of its owner and the heap of boxes the disorganization in his home, "no purpose seems to justify reference to the barometer, an object neither incongruous nor significant."[35]

Although Flaubert's barometer and other similar details in literature do not carry out any function with regard to the progression of the story, they suggest proof of the accuracy of the story's setting and characters, indicating that they are

EXAMPLE I.IA: Joseph Achron, "Hebrew Melody," measures 73–4

true to life. These details announce, "*we are the real*; it is the category of 'the real' (and not its contingent contents) which is then signified; . . . the *reality effect* is produced, the basis of that unavowed verisimilitude which forms the aesthetic of all the standard works of modernity."[36] In rural miniatures, such reality effects are produced by compositional details and facts printed in the published score about the origins and functions of the individual songs and dances, thereby impressing on listeners the notion that the rural melodies are accurately and authentically reproduced.

Rural miniatures vary in construction from one-movement works such as Achron's "Hebrew Melody" and "Scher" (opus 42), Joel Engel's "'Chabad'er Melodie" (opus 20, number 1) and "Freilachs" (opus 20, number 2), and Enrique Granados's "Spanish Dance" (transcribed for violin and piano by Fritz Kreisler), to multi-movement collections of rural songs and dances, such as Bartók's *Hungarian Folk Tunes* and *Romanian Folk Dances*, Bloch's *Baal Shem*, Achron's *Stempenyu Suite*, and Paweł Kochański's *Suite populaire espagnole*, based on Falla's *Siete canciones populares españolas*. Individual movements tend to be formally simple, generally containing only one or two principal melodic themes, often followed by a coda; and from time to time the structure is interrupted at

EXAMPLE 1.1B: Joseph Achron, "Märchen," measures 41–2

its climactic point by a solo bravura passage for the primary instrument. In some cases, as in "Hebrew Melody," this is marked as a cadenza (Example 1.1a); in others, as in Achron's "Märchen" (opus 46), a group of measures function in this manner though without being explicitly marked as such (Example 1.1b). The coda is typically built loosely on the earlier themes and often contains a series of runs, double stops, or held trills, marking the zenith of the passion that has increased with the restatements of the themes.

The composers of rural miniatures tend to evoke the melodic scales found in folk music traditions by mixing major and minor, writing in "medieval" modes, or inflecting diatonic scales with additional accidentals. Many rural miniatures are composed in the minor with phrase endings in the major tonic. This occurs throughout the repertoire, notably in the first movements of *Romanian Folk Dances* ("Joc Cu Bâtă"), in A minor with A major phrase endings (Example 6.2); *Baal Shem* ("Vidui"), in E minor, ending in an E major triad; and *Stempenyu Suite* ("Stempenyu Plays"), which begins in D minor, with D major phrase endings, and concludes in A minor, with a final A major triad. Granados's "Spanish

EXAMPLE 1.2:   Enrique Granados, "Spanish Dance in E minor," arranged by Fritz Kreisler, measures 89–96

EXAMPLE 1.3:   *Ahavah rabbah* mode

Dance," in Kreisler's transcription, also begins and ends with a key signature of E minor, but with prominent phrase endings in E major (Example 1.2).

Rural miniatures based on Jewish traditional music were often written in the melodic modes of Eastern European Ashkenazi folk and liturgical music. These modes are theoretical constructs, composite scales created by the alignment of motifs that typically occur together in religious chants, in opening, intermediate, and closing phrases.[37] One of the most common of these is referred to in the context of Ashkenazi synagogue music as the *Ahavah rabbah* (With great love) mode, and in other contexts, including Yiddish and Hasidic song, as the *freygish* mode, a Yiddish term that characterizes it as an altered Phrygian.[38] The *Ahavah rabbah* resembles the minor scale with an augmented second produced by lowering the second scale degree and raising the third (Example 1.3). This scale was common in both Jewish and non-Jewish musics of Southeast Europe, and is equivalent to the Arabic *maqām hijaz*.[39] Each mode is said to carry its own character or ethos; the *Ahavah rabbah* was often considered symbolic of lament.[40] Around the turn of the twentieth century the mode, and the augmented second on its own and in other modal contexts, were adopted into Yiddish popular song and Yiddish theater, and into art music by composers who wished to represent Jewish culture

EXAMPLE 1.4:   Béla Bartók, *Romanian Folk Dances*, arranged by Zoltán Székely, movement 3, "Pe Loc," measures 1–8

and tradition.[41] It appears in Engel's rural miniature "Freilachs" and Achron's "Hebrew Lullaby" (opus 35, number 2), in which it is produced by setting the tonic pitch as A in a key signature of one flat, with the raised third scale degree creating an augmented second between B-flat and C-sharp and a major triad at some phrase endings.

The second movement of *Romanian Folk Dances*, "Brâul," is in the Dorian mode, which Bartók creates by raising the sixth scale degree from D-natural to D-sharp in the key signature of F-sharp minor. Among the most typical scale inflections is the raised fourth scale degree in the minor, producing an augmented second against the third scale degree, as in Bartók's "Pe Loc," the third movement of *Romanian Folk Dances*, in which the G-natural is repeatedly raised to G-sharp in the key of D minor (Example 1.4); and Achron's "Hebrew Melody," in which the D-natural is raised to D-sharp in A minor (see the transcription on which the work is based, Example 5.1). In the context of Achron's work, this scale evokes the *Mi sheberakh* (May the one who blessed) mode, also referred to as the "Ukrainian Dorian."[42]

Rural miniatures often draw from a number of stock rhythmic tropes. These include hemiolas and juxtapositions of triple and duple rhythms, both "horizontally" in individual voices, for example, in a melodic line in which duple and triple groupings immediately follow one another, and "vertically," for instance, between violin and piano, or between the two hands of the piano. This contributes a sense of rhythmic groove, which is compounded by the creation of syncopated patterns with ties over the beat and across the bar line. Ornamental gestures are a typical reality effect in rural miniatures; trills, turns, and grace notes add color to musical themes. In some rural miniatures, avoidance of double stops and chords and adherence to a narrow tessitura evoke the range and tone of the human voice. Similarly, some performance instructions prescribed timbres expressive or imitative of traditional instruments. A common example is the instruction to play phrases with the left hand in higher positions on lower strings than those on which they would otherwise naturally be played (often notated with Roman numerals I through IV, indicating the E through G strings). Playing a melody in high positions produces a warm, throaty timbre, lending itself to a

EXAMPLE 1.5:   Joseph Achron, "Sher," measures 1–11

EXAMPLE 1.6:   Igor Stravinsky, *Histoire du soldat*, violin part, measures 37–42

rich, resonant, and plaintive style of performance (as in Achron's "Scher," Example 1.5). Other idiomatic effects written into violin parts include left-hand pizzicato (often marked by a "+" sign over the pitch to be plucked, as in Sarasate's "Zigeunerweisen" and Kochański's arrangement of Falla's "El paño moruno," from *Suite populaire espagnole*, Example 4.3), and whispering, flute-like harmonics, as found in "Pe Loc" (Example 1.4).

Another typical reality effect that evokes folk violin performance involves the use of simultaneous open strings. In Stravinsky's *Histoire du soldat*, the violinist plays in a manner that resembles the sounds of tuning and out-of-tune strings (Example 1.6). The passage resembles the performance of a damaged instrument: as the soldier, who recently bought a violin in the narrative of the work, says of his purchase, "It didn't cost much, the tone's not rich,/ You have to keep screwing it up to pitch."[43] This technique is also found in "Iber di hoyfn" (Over the Fields), movement two of *Five Songs from the Yiddish* (c. 1913–21), a song cycle for tenor, baritone, and string quartet by Leo Zeitlin, a member of the Society for Jewish Folk Music. The text of this song is an amalgam of lyrics from Yiddish songs about Jewish musicians, opening with the refrain of "Tsen brider" (Ten Brothers).[44] In this song about Jewish brothers living in Russia,

EXAMPLE 1.7:   Béla Bartók, *Contrasts*, movement 3, "Sebes," measures 1–12

each verse recounts the death of another brother, and the refrain is a call to the local *klezmorim* (musicians) to perform their violin and bass for the funeral: "Yidl mitn fidl,/ Khaykl mitn bas,/ Zingt zhe mir a lidl/ Oyfn mitn gas" (Yidl with the fiddle,/ Khaykl with the bass,/ Sing me a little song/ In the middle of the street).[45] Inspired by this invocation of stringed instruments, Zeitlin instructs all four instruments to play only open strings for the first seventeen measures. At the start of the piece, the cello and viola play upward from the C to A strings, and the violins play downward from E to G, sounding the full range of open string sonorities and pitches across the ensemble, and recalling the timbres of tuning, as the instrumentalists check their strings.

Bartók too evokes the sonorities of violin tuning and open strings in the third movement, "Sebes," of his 1938 trio *Contrasts* for violin, clarinet, and piano (Example 1.7). At the opening of this movement, which is based on a Bulgarian dance type, the violinist plays the role of a rural performer, gradually and haphazardly tuning his instrument before joining the other musicians, who have already begun to play more complicated melodic lines. The violinist plays with scordatura strings: the E string is lowered to E-flat, and the G string is raised to G-sharp, producing tritones in the two outer intervals and a fifth between the middle strings. The first seventeen bars of the violin part consist of open strings played simultaneously; this is followed by thirteen bars in which the violinist repeatedly plays double stops with the first finger on the A and E strings and second on the G and D strings, to evoke an alternate tuning, perhaps a botched attempt on the part of the violinist to retune the open strings. Between measures 30 and 35, Bartók allows the violinist time to put down this violin and replace it with another that is tuned traditionally in fifths, to play the dance melody of rapid sixteenth and eighth notes that have already been introduced in the clarinet. In the first recording of the work, produced in 1940 with Bartók, Szigeti, and Benny Goodman, Szigeti mocks the sound of the out-of-tune "sawing" of a stereotyped rural violinist by playing loudly with unfelicitous accents at the starts of notes and a rough, unrefined timbre that brings out the dissonances produced by the tuning of the strings.

Finally, it was common for composers and publishers of rural miniatures to include ethnographic details about a work's source music in the score's paratext, the space outside of its main text—the musical notation—that typically includes the title, preface, instructions, and illustrations. The role of the paratext is to present the text, and to control and manipulate its reception.[46] The title is perhaps the foremost paratextual element to play a role in the realism of the rural miniature, because it is likely to be read on a score, in a concert program, or on a record casing before one hears any music. By giving a rural miniature a title derived from ethnographic research on rural cultures, the composer guarantees that the performer or listener will know of the work's basis in a cultural or national group's music, or even a specific traditional genre or melody. Titles such as Bartók's *Romanian Folk Dances* and *Hungarian Folk Tunes*, Achron's "Hebrew Melody" and "Hebrew Lullaby," Alexander Krein's *Esquisses Hebraïques* and "Caprice Hebraïque," Lazare Saminsky's "Hebrew Rhapsody," and Kochański and Falla's *Suite populaire espagnole* identify the regional and cultural roots of the repertory.[47]

Explanatory subtitles are common in paratexts of rural miniatures and reflect the methods of the taxonomic study of folk music found in anthologies. For example, parenthetical generic subtitles appear in the score of Engel's "Freilachs (Tanz)," Achron's "Sher (Hebräischer Tanz)," and the three movements of Ernest Bloch's *Baal Shem: Three Pictures of Chassidic Life*, "Vidui (Contrition)," "Nigun (Improvisation)," and "Simchas Torah (Rejoicing)." In some cases, the rural miniature's paratext was seen as a space for explicit didacticism: scores of Achron's "Hebrew Melody" and "Hebrew Dance," as well as Bartók's *Romanian Christmas Carols*, as published by Universal Edition in 1918, included melodic transcriptions of its source melodies.[48] Underlying each transcription in Bartók's collection is a fragment of the song texts in Romanian, and above each staff appears the city and county in which Bartók collected the song. Additionally, Bartók marks the refrain of each song with a bracket, in order to provide the performer with a fuller understanding of the formal structure of the original artifact.[49]

MUSICAL REALISM

The concept of realism depends on the understanding that an artistic, musical, or literary work can represent something that exists externally to its structure.[50] In 1921, the literary critic Roman Jakobson defined realism as "an artistic trend which aims at conveying reality as closely as possible and strives for maximum verisimilitude."[51] Common to the genre of the rural miniature is the attempt at documenting ethnic cultures by representing their musical artifacts in a realist manner. The genre is thus founded on a set of assumptions: that its structures constitute a close, or in some cases direct, transcription of musical artifacts, and its performance can be similarly imitative of the performance tradition associated with the source melodies; that these musical artifacts, often selected from ethnographic and folkloric research or from personal knowledge of ethnic traditions, are able to signify the ethnic groups from which they derive; and that the study of ethnic communities, in turn, reveals fundamental lessons about modern society and nationhood.

Of course, music can never objectively reproduce phenomena from life any more than other artistic media, and the transcription and arrangement of folk music are to be understood as realist modes of representation, processes that necessitate the mediation of members of the art world, including artists, performers, listeners, and patrons.[52] To consider the rural miniature's relationship with its source music as one of representation allows the listener to acknowledge the distance between the two that is telescoped by the realist mode. In the transcription and arrangement of folk music, a process involving the adaptation of a melody from the oral to the written tradition, the musical artifact undergoes considerable change, and the context and performance style associated with the printed score can never match those of the unique performance of the ethnic melody on which the work is based. Far from directly mirroring reality, the rural miniature is several steps removed from the tradition it represents.

The imprecise nature of the realist representation has been recognized since the early history of critical writing on the aesthetic mode. The nineteenth-century writer Champfleury, a promoter of the painter Gustave Courbet who initiated the use of the term "realism" as a positive description of the work of Courbet's circle, recognized that realism in the visual arts did not reproduce nature without mediation. He wrote, "The reproduction of nature by man will never be a *reproduction* nor an *imitation*, it will always be an *interpretation*."[53] The musical realism of the folk music setting was not a direct reproduction of the rural performance but rather an interpretation of a folk music performance heard firsthand or "read" in the form of an ethnographic transcription—or even, in some cases, an original composition created to accord with a set of characteristics associated with a particular traditional genre or style.

The aim of rural miniatures was often stated to be the evocation of the metaphysical entity of the "soul" of the ethnic communities being represented, and the "ethos" and "expression" of their musical traditions. Similar to paintings associated with nineteenth-century realist movements in the visual arts, arrangements of folk melodies were thought to represent truths about society, nature, and the act of listening, and in that way to represent folk cultures with a greater degree of accuracy than ever achieved before in composition. Musical realism was an aesthetic mode that musicians called upon to convey, in a seemingly accurate style, their conceptions of folk music and, more generally, the representational capacities of music.[54]

In late nineteenth-century writings on music, "realism" was occasionally invoked in reference to examples of tone painting. It was a technique that was often considered tolerable in limited quantities but unhelpful to the true aim of music, the evocation of interior emotions. Thus at the end of the nineteenth century, C. Hubert H. Parry wrote, "though realism is admissible as a source of suggestion, the object of the expressive power of music is not to represent the outward semblance of anything, but to express the moods which it produces, and the workings of the mind that are associated with them."[55] The more recent scholarly literature on realism in art music is scant, dominated by Carl Dahlhaus's historical and aesthetic study *Realism in Nineteenth–Century Music*.[56] Dahlhaus sees musical realism as an anti-Romantic musical style, employed by composers who sought to represent the outside world in a quasi-objective manner that avoided Romantic composers' emotionalism and quest for aesthetic autonomy.[57] Dahlhaus warns that any attempt to define the mode should avoid, among other pitfalls, the narrow consideration of only *Tonmalerei*, and should assume that the frequency with which the term appeared and the meanings it implied within the discourse around music during the period under examination may ultimately be unhelpful or misleading, as its use has been complex and inconsistent across its history.[58] The notion of realism in the arts developed in the nineteenth century alongside increasing doubt about the nature of reality that developed with the growth of epistemology. Realism was approached as artists aimed toward objectivity, casting off subjectivity as much as possible, even while understanding that subjectivity could never be entirely bypassed, making any sort of pure objectivity unattainable.[59]

For Dahlhaus, realism involved "(1) an—as far as possible—objective representation of (2) social reality, set in either (3) the present time or (4) a concrete past, a reality which (5) also extends to areas which were previously excluded from art as 'unsuitable,' and the depiction of which (6) frequently breaks the traditional rules of stylization."[60] Dahlhaus also associates realism with nationalism, as manifested in the use of speech rhythms—for example, in the music of Janáček—and in what he dubs the "folklike tone," as he finds in the compositions of Mahler.[61] Otherwise Dahlhaus focuses his attention primarily on works of nineteenth-century opera. In these discussions the reader might infer a restricted understanding of the term "music" as referring to the printed score, without accounting for the meanings that might emerge through interpretation in performance; furthermore, the correlation between music and modern technologies is overlooked. But musical realism in the early twentieth century, especially in the rural miniature, was propelled by new capabilities of sound recording devices and the way such technology helped to reframe common understandings of rural and minority groups' lifestyles and performances. An understanding of "music" to include all components of the score's text and paratext, as well as its actual and potential realization in performance, thus permits a reframing of realism in music that accounts for its role in the composition and performance of early twentieth-century instrumental music, particularly works based on folk song and dance, as exemplified by the rural miniature.

REALISM AND THE TRANSCRIPTION OF FOLK MUSIC

Roland Barthes writes that the movement of literary realism coincided with the rise of what he calls "objective history," and the growth of such practices and institutions as photography, tourism, collection, and archaeological exhibition.[62] These same developments, along with the invention of the phonograph decades later, also played important roles in the emergence of musical realism.[63] Research in folk music was inspired in large part by the association between folk song performance and nationhood, which dates back at least to the writings of Johann Gottfried Herder, who argued in his *Essay on the Origin of Language* (1772) that language is socially learned, not innate, and is shared by all members of a community. Because poetry and music were considered to be the "highest" forms of language, folk music, the pairing of poetry and music found in rural communities, was seen as the most important bond among members of the nation.[64] It was at the start of the nineteenth century that intellectuals such as the brothers Jacob and Wilhelm Grimm, collectors and authors of folk tales, would argue that the folk were socially organized and that they actively created folklore in response to their contexts and environments.[65]

Because these intellectuals considered folk music to be an original and authentic mode of expression, the collection of folklore thus became a crucial activity in the definition and construction of national identities. Musicians collected data on ethnic melodies, dances, and performance styles, transporting their discoveries back to cities, where they incorporated what they had learned into composition and performance practices. In many cases, this form of collecting was carried out by interested citizens; in others it was commissioned by state governments. The invention of technologies of mechanical reproduction—first photography, then sound recording and cinema—provided the means to document rural and suburban musical practices and bring the sights and sounds to cosmopolitan centers for display to city dwellers, contributing to the increase in folk music collecting and the publication of anthologies.

The growing interest in the history and folklore of rural populations at the turn of the twentieth century was propelled by the fear of what many writers and artists considered the perilous downside of modernity, the loss of tradition. Folklorists and ethnographers in the nineteenth century drew and photographed iconography, transcribed stories and music, and notated dance and religious rituals, with the belief that by transferring these fleeting images, sounds, and events onto paper and organizing them in archives, they would salvage them from disappearance and prepare them for study. The phonograph instantly became an invaluable tool for folklorists and ethnographers, providing a chance to capture ephemeral sounds on a lasting medium. Charles Cros, the French inventor who devised a machine much like the phonograph around the same time as Thomas Edison, but failed to turn his concept into a prototype, wrote a poem about his inspiration for his new invention: "Like the faces in cameos/ I wanted beloved voices/ To be a fortune which one keeps forever,/ And which can repeat the musical/ Dream of the too short hour;/ Time would flee, I subdue it."[66] Many ethnographers saw in the portable phonograph an opportunity to subdue time, to maintain forever the fleeting voices of their subjects.

Ethnographers began using wax cylinder recording technology as early as 1889 in the United States, and between 1890 and 1935 the phonograph was a widespread tool for European and American researchers in the field.[67] Enthusiasm for the phonograph's portability and apparent utility as an objective research tool initiated an intensified interest during the early years of the century in capturing and categorizing ethnic music genres throughout Europe. One of the first ethnographers to use the phonograph in his fieldwork was Jesse Fewkes, who wrote in 1890, "The phonograph imparts to the study of folklore, as far as the aborigines are concerned, a scientific basis which it had not previously had, and makes approximately accurate."[68] Franz Boas's insistence on the importance of the phonograph to ethnographers was described by Theodora Kroeber as "evangelical"; he promoted its use particularly for recording "virgin languages" that had not yet been studied.[69] Although it is generally recognized today that objectivity is an unattainable goal in ethnomusicology even with the use of recording technologies, the importance of the phonograph to the field's development was profound.[70]

In the ethnographic study of music at the start of the twentieth century, researchers devised a technique that has been called "realist ethnography," involving the creation of transcriptions that represent distilled and idealized paradigmatic versions of melodies, rather than depicting the details of particular performances.[71] This form of transcription, like the rural miniature itself, demonstrated that the authenticity associated with realism did not preclude the existence of a notable gap between the original performance and its representation; fieldwork recordings formed the basis for transcriptions that were sometimes quite different from what one hears when listening to the wax cylinders but that nevertheless were considered to offer accurate depictions of the melodies and genres of folk music. Bartók and Kodály transcribed their findings in this mode in collections including Bartók's *A magyar népdal* (The Hungarian Folksong, 1924) and Kodály's *A magyar népzene* (Folk Music of Hungary, 1952).[72] Jewish folk song collectors of the early twentieth century produced similar transcriptions in such books as Fritz Mordechai Kaufmann's *Die schönsten Lieder der Ostjuden* (The Most Beautiful Songs of the Eastern Jews, 1920), Yehuda Leyb Cahan's *Yidishe folkslider mit melodyes* (Jewish Folksongs with Melodies, 1912), and Moshe Beregovski's *Jewish Folk Music* (1934).[73] The development of realist methods of musical ethnography and the persistence of associations between musical folklore and national identity supplied composers with musical material on which to base new works and provided a primary influence for the realist mode of musical representation.

FOLK SONG TRANSCRIPTION IN RELATION TO OTHER REALIST
MOVEMENTS

Despite differences in chronology and artistic medium, proponents of early twentieth-century musical realism and the French movement of realist painting (approximately 1840 to the late nineteenth century) held similar goals of creating objective and truthful depictions of reality, categorizing and collecting worldly phenomena and incorporating into artistic representation the influence of new scientific technologies for recording imagery and sound.[74] Many French visual realists also shared with the realist composers of folk music arrangements a fascination with the representation of elements of society often considered marginal and peripheral. The working class had rarely before been portrayed with such earnest attention as in Courbet's *Burial at Ornans*, his iconic painting that depicted character types from society's marginal and dispossessed, engaged in the mundane ritual of burial, on a canvas the size of Jacques-Louis David's history paintings. In 1858, G. H. Lewes gave voice to the realist cause in language that demonstrated a sense of urgency to represent the margins of society that was shared by many of the ethnographers and composers occupied with the collection and representation of traditional music in the early twentieth century: "Either give us true peasants, or leave them untouched; either paint no drapery at all, or paint it with the utmost fidelity; either keep your people silent, or make them speak the idiom of their class."[75]

French literary realists also engaged in the depiction of the lower classes of society. Early in the nineteenth century, Honoré de Balzac took on the project of representing and cataloguing the social types that he believed inhabited French society and provincial life. He wrote in 1842 in *Comédie humaine*, "Does not Society make of man, according to the milieux in which his activity takes place, as many different men as there are varieties in zoology?"[76] The focus on marginal strata of society in French realist literature and painting was similarly a characteristic of realist representations of folk music in the rural miniature; for example, works such as *Romanian Folk Dances* and "Hebrew Melody" exhibited the attempt to raise to the level of high art the traditional music of the people of the Eastern European countryside.

French realists and the later musical realists shared an appreciation for scientific progress and the ideal of objectivity in the study of empirical phenomena that was associated with new methods of research and collection.[77] The stated aim of many artists in both visual and musical modes of realism was to represent what they perceived, visually and aurally, as phenomenal reality; although they were not necessarily scientific in the means by which they created their work, they valued scientific discovery and its provision of subjects and motifs for new artistic production. For many of the French realist painters, the new technology of photography was influential as a stylistic model in the attempt to produce visual verisimilitude and provided inspiration as a mode of objective scientific observation. At the end of the century the phonograph became important for composers of rural miniatures, who chose source melodies that in many cases became known only when captured on wax cylinders and emulated the sounds and expressive modes they heard in the recorded performances and found in folk music anthologies.

Realism in the nineteenth-century visual and literary arts was sometimes brought into contact with musical evocations of lower-class and marginal groups, as in the 1879 printed score of Jenő Hubay's *18 Eredeti magyar dal* (18 Original Hungarian Songs), a set of songs in the style of *magyar nóta* to texts by the Hungarian poet Sándor Petőfi and illustrated by Hungarian realist painters.[78] A virtuoso violinist who had been a pupil of Joseph Joachim in Berlin, Hubay later served as director at the Budapest Music Academy and taught Joseph Szigeti, Zoltán Székely, Stefi Geyer, and other successful violinists. For the texts of his eighteen songs, Hubay turned to the works of Petőfi, a poet who had been involved in the Hungarian *népies*, or populist, movement, which was inspired by French literary realism.[79] *Népies* writers adhered to nineteenth-century interpretations of Herder's writings on the value of folk culture, turning for subject matter to the Hungarian peasant classes.[80] The artists affiliated with the project were all Hungarian, and many were associated with the realist movement of Hungarian art, which sought to represent what many viewed as the authentic Magyar spirit uniting what was in fact an ethnically diverse nation, using a representational style inspired by French realism and Munich naturalism.[81] Most of the illustrations in this score, which appear above the opening measures of each song, show idealized pastoral scenes of work, battle, leisure, and romance among peasants or urban visitors to the countryside (Figure 1.1).

Fifteen years after the publication of Hubay's collection of songs, the composer wrote an article titled "Petőfi befolyása a magyar zenére" (Petőfi's Influence on Hungarian Music) in a pamphlet produced by the Petőfi Museum.[82] In a typical Romantic-era echo of the writings of Herder, Hubay explains that nations are distinguished principally by differences in language, and that "the most primitive phase of song music is in turn the folksong."[83] For this reason, the occupation of Hungary's present and future composers will be to study folk music and mold it into familiar art music forms, producing a uniquely Hungarian music; this is a critical task, he argues, as Hungary has almost no musical literature of its own that can stand up to the quality of musical works from other European nations. The elements of Petőfi's poetry that Hubay identifies as most influential to composers of folk and art song are "simplicity, immediacy, intensely developed rhythm, and brevity of form."[84] Many decades later Bartók would use similar adjectives to describe a different body of music, the folk songs and dances of rural Hungarian regions, which he praised for their "brevity of form and simplicity of means."[85] Hubay's illustrated score demonstrates some of the ways realism, as developed by French painters and writers,

FIGURE I.I: Jenő Hubay, "Kis furulyám szomorúfűz ága," from *18 eredeti magyar dal* (Budapest: Táborszky és Parsch, c.1881), 35, illustration by Mihály Munkácsy, text by Sándor Petőfi. © The British Library Board. Music Collections, H.1403.s.

could be seen to influence artists and composers beyond French borders in the representation of folk and Rom communities in the late nineteenth century.

Precedents to the development of nineteenth-century realism in the arts included such popular forms of visual media as the panorama, the diorama, and, most important for this study, the mass-produced book of prints.[86] The Industrial

Age brought developments in technologies for reproducing detailed prints, which could be marketed cheaply and thus purchased by members of both the working and upper classes. A genre of illustrated books documenting in detail the natural world or aspects of urban and rural everyday life became especially popular at this time. Exemplary were Thomas Bewick's *History of British Birds*, published around the turn of the nineteenth century, with detailed wood engravings depicting various regional species of bird, and W. H. Pyne's 1806 "*Microcosm*; or, a Picturesque Delineation of the Arts, Agriculture, and Manufactures of Great Britain in a series of above a Thousand Groups of Small Figures for the Embellishment of Landscape," which contained etchings detailing the labor of the British working classes and boasted images "accurately drawn from nature."[87]

Books such as these presaged the realist movement in the degree of detail of their illustrations and the role they played in artists' and scientists' burgeoning sense of duty to record the world, a task that had been made increasingly easier with the advent of improved printing presses and later by the daguerreotype and photography. The perceived divide between the urban and rural and the ideological dichotomy of society and community took on an important relevance as artists working in different media engaged in the creation of visual taxonomies of natural phenomena and human inventions. Books and novelty magazines that contained collections of images relating to human society or the natural world continued to be published throughout the nineteenth century and into the twentieth. Around the turn of the century, with improvements in printing technology, collection books began often to include photographs in the place of etchings, as their creators increasingly strived for greater degrees of representational objectivity. Books of this nature allowed the urban middle class to study and explore the wonders of the world from home: for instance, *Camera Mosaics*, a collection of travel photographs published in 1894, offered its readers "all the treasures of art in Rome and Florence and Paris and Dresden, and the feast is spread by the sitting-room window or under the fireside lamp."[88]

Around the same time, anthologies of folk songs were printed with increasing frequency in Europe, most prevalently in Germany. In much the same way that compendia of illustrations such as *History of British Birds* were forebears of realism in painting, the folk song anthology preceded the realism of the rural miniature. Anthologies of folk song adaptations appeared in the late eighteenth and early nineteenth centuries; William Hamilton Bird, for example, published *The Oriental Miscellany*, a collection of "the Most Favourite Airs of Hindoostan," in Calcutta in 1789, and at the beginning of the following century Edward Smith Biggs published selections from this compendium in *Twelve Hindoo Airs with English Words Adapted to them by Mrs. Opie and Harmonized for One, Two and Three Voices*, as well as collections of arrangements of Sicilian and Welsh songs.[89] In Germany, where Ludwig Achim von Arnim and Clemens Brentano's anthology of folk song texts *Des Knaben Wunderhorn* was published in 1806, the anthology became most popular rather later than collections of taxonomic sketches and etchings, due to the difficulties of fieldwork and the association between the compilation of folk songs and the rise of nationalism in Germany as the century progressed.[90]

The anthology *Deutsche Lieder für Jung und Alt*, from 1818, is one of the earliest books of German-language folk song texts to include melodic transcriptions presented in a manner that aimed at the appearance of objectivity: the songs are catalogued with no harmonization or at most bare accompaniment and were not arranged for performance.[91] Not unlike *History of British Birds*, *Deutsche Lieder für Jung und Alt* offers visual, two-dimensional representations of phenomena that occur differently in nature, birds as three-dimensional life forms and songs as ephemeral sound events. Both demonstrate the goal to record and categorize objects—species of birds, genres of songs—that occur in a large number of variations, and to elicit the observation of comparisons and contrasts between similar objects. Both limit their subjects nationally, the former defining its national boundaries geographically and the latter linguistically. The content of both books is also similar in their aesthetic character: the etching of the ringtailed eagle in *History of British Birds* and the transcription of "Es war ein König in Tule" in *Deutsche Lieder für Jung und Alt* offer ideal, paradigmatic forms of representation (Figures 1.2 and 1.3).[92] The images in these books of collections, furthermore, provided models from which later artists and musicians could adapt their own representations.

The style of folk music transcription found in *Deusche Lieder für Jung und Alt* continued to be developed into the following century by researchers who incorporated the phonograph into their work and created realist ethnographic transcriptions that aimed to categorize folk music in a thorough and accurate manner. Thus in his collection *The Hungarian Folksong*, Bartók states his ambitions "to constitute as rich a collection as possible of peasant tunes, scientifically classified," and "to determine, by careful comparison, every one of the musical styles recognizable in the above materials."[93] In an essay included in his posthumously published compendium *Rumanian Folk Music*, Bartók described his aim to "collect as much material as possible" and "with the greatest humanly-attainable precision, approaching in this regard the features and qualities of a so-called 'Urtext' edition."[94] The development of the phonograph, transcription methods, and realist ethnographic practices had a notable impact on the rise of the rural miniature and its associated styles of composition and performance.

THE PHONOGRAPH AND THE QUEST FOR ACCURACY IN COMPOSITION

Many of the composers who engaged in the arrangement of folk songs and dances for art music ensembles viewed the composition and performance of rural miniatures as useful methods of presenting listeners with the findings of

FIGURE 1.2:   "The Ringtailed Eagle," in Thomas Bewick, *History of British Birds* (Newcastle, 1816), 1:49. Library of Congress.

contemporary ethnographers. The wax cylinder recordings made on fieldwork expeditions were inaccessible to general audiences because they were housed in archives and private libraries, or, in many cases, discarded or lost. Transcription anthologies were limited in their utility to laymen without backgrounds in music and ethnography because of the technical nature of their taxonomic systems and

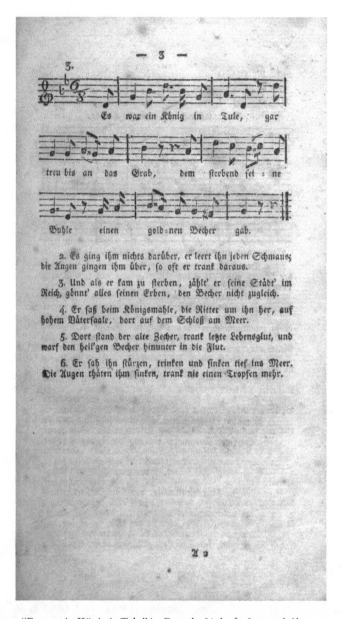

FIGURE 1.3:   "Es war ein König in Tule," in *Deutsche Lieder für Jung und Alt*, 3.

generalized treatment of melodies. On the other hand, through arrangements of
the melodies that were already documented on wax cylinders and in anthologies,
composers could present their findings to the public, in sales of scores and at live
performances; the widest audience would be reached through the marketing of
recordings of professional performers interpreting these works. The phonograph

thus had a significant impact on all stages of the artistic journey from the sonic event of the rural performance to the private act of playing a recording of a musician interpreting a rural miniature on the parlor phonograph.

From the time of the phonograph's invention, it immediately came to be associated with the idealist urge to produce a precise representation of sonic reality. Much as photography was viewed as a medium capable of depicting the world as it appears to the eyes, the phonograph was popularly believed to represent the world's sounds with objective accuracy. In both cases, the medium was perceived to recede into the background, leaving only the visual or aural evidence it provided. Historian Miles Orvell makes the case that the increasing ubiquity of machines capable of recording the phenomenal world in seemingly objective fashion around the turn of the century led to an aesthetic "culture of authenticity" that constituted, in the spirit of realism, "an effort to get ... beyond the manufacturing of illusions, to the creation of more 'authentic' works that were themselves real things."[95] This culture exhibited both a dependency on and an ambivalence toward new technology. Using techniques inspired by photography, artists sought to produce works that confronted their audiences with an expression of the authentic—"the real thing"—during an age in which many felt increasingly alienated by the industrialized modern world. New sound recording machinery had a similar impact on multiple facets of musical practice, including the composition and performance of the rural miniature.

Thomas Edison's project in inventing and perfecting the phonograph in the late nineteenth century was to produce a machine capable of recording sound with utmost fidelity to reality.[96] In his announcement of his new invention in the 1888 article "The Perfected Phonograph," Edison explained,

> The most skillful observers, listeners and realistic novelists, or even stenographers, cannot reproduce a conversation exactly as it occurred. The account they give is more or less generalized. But the phonograph receives, and then transmits to our ears again, every least thing that was said—exactly *as* it was said—with the faultless fidelity of an instantaneous photograph. We shall now for the first time know what a conversation really is; just as we have learned, only within a few years, through the instantaneous photograph, what attitudes are taken by the horse in motion.[97]

The phonograph was viewed not only as a product of mass entertainment but also as a tool of scientific study. Photography's capacity for objective and unmediated reproduction had similarly been claimed proudly in 1838 by Louis Daguerre in a description of his daguerreotype: "The daguerreotype is not merely an instrument which serves to draw nature. . . . [It] gives her the power to reproduce herself."[98]

Early advertisements for phonographs and records touted the medium's capability of producing a sort of aural mirror of the sonic world.[99] Victor's logo famously depicted a dog with its face to the phonograph's horn, looking for the source of the sound identified by the caption, "His Master's Voice." In one early poster, the Edison Company advertised its product as "The Acme of Realism," over a drawing of a boy poised to break his machine open with an axe, as though "Looking for the Band."[100] Around 1915, the Edison company initiated a series of live concerts around the United States in which a professional singer would stand next to a phonograph on the stage of a recital hall and perform with a recording of his or her voice, in the hope of convincing the audience of the machine's fidelity to reality.[101] And in 1918, an advertisement printed on the back of a number of concert programs juxtaposed images of Jascha Heifetz and a record of his music, over the words "The Victor Record of Heifetz is just as truly Heifetz as Heifetz himself. When you hear this wonderful young violinist on the Victrola it is as though you were hearing him in real life on the concert stage—and on the Victrola Heifetz is always ready to entertain you just as though he was always in your home."[102] This advertisement listed seven available discs of Heifetz playing a variety of miniatures, from "Ave Maria" to Achron's "Hebrew Melody."

Edison presaged the technology's utility for performers and composers when he wrote, "Instrumental and vocal music . . . can be recorded on the perfected phonograph with startling completeness and precision. How interesting it will be to future generations to learn from the phonograph exactly how Rubinstein played a composition on the piano."[103] He continued, "Musical composers, in improvising compositions, will be able to have them recorded instantaneously on the phonograph."[104] Novel conceptions of sound fidelity introduced in the early age of the phonograph contributed to a growing sense at the turn of the century that composition too could be a representational medium with the potential for producing fidelity to sonic events. The score could be seen as providing an authentic description of folk songs and dances, and also as a script for a future rendition that would accurately represent the performances of folk musicians.

The realism of the early twentieth-century folk music arrangement owes its development in large part to the popular understanding of the phonograph as an impartial conduit between a past performance and the ears of the listener. A 1915 publication released by the Edison Company for phonograph dealers put it as follows: "Mr. Edison has experimented for years to produce a sound re-creating instrument that has no tone—of its own. . . . There is no distortion of the true tone of the original music."[105] The phonograph depended for success on the perception of the disappearance of the medium, the collapsing of space between a past sound event and the listener's ears. The denial of mediation facilitated an ontological leap on the part of the rural miniature's listeners, who might consider a recording of a folk song arrangement to be authentic and accurate in its evocation of the sounds of rural folk music performance, much as, in the words of the Victor advertisement, the recording of Heifetz is "just as truly Heifetz as Heifetz himself."

A 1928 print advertisement for the Orthophonic Victrola, designed to play new electric-process discs, invoked both the technological realism associated with the phonograph and the musical realism of the rural miniature (Figure 1.4). Under the image of a dashing Rom violinist performing vigorously before an outdoor fire, surrounded by his community as they dance and clap along, a caption describes the sound of his playing as a nocturnal, disembodied vocal utterance: "A cry . . . half-human in its quality . . . floats out of the dark." The advertising copy continues:

> Kreisler . . . Elman . . . Heifetz. A violin, quivering with a thousand varied emotions that transcend words. Swiftly your surroundings vanish. You see a black Hungarian forest. Brooding pines look down on a gypsy fire, whose jagged flames silhouette the wild grace of a Romany dance. Showers of notes—furious as sparks—whirl into the night. You are at the concert—*in your own home!* So realistic, so lifelike, is reproduction through the Orthophonic Victrola, the artist seems to stand there before you. Whatever the season, this versatile instrument brings you and your friends the best of the world's music—with all the encores you wish. Only when you've heard it, can you appreciate its performance. Arrange now for a demonstration *in your home.*[106]

This advertisement describes the capacity of a recorded performance of a work based on Rom music to transport the listener to another space, as the music summons a distant landscape and the professional violinist becomes the Rom fiddler he evokes in his performance. "So realistic, so lifelike" is the Victrola's reproduction of the sounds of Heifetz's playing that it conjures—"*in your home*"—not simply "Heifetz himself," as other advertisements promised, but those very rural violinists Heifetz evoked in performing rural miniatures and works in the style hongrois. Two "versatile instrument[s]," the violin and the Orthophonic Victrola, bring their own forms of realism to persuade the home record collector that he hears a Rom dance as though it were performed before him, not in the event of a firsthand encounter, and not even in hearing an ethnographic recording of a Rom performer, but in listening to a studio disc of a favorite conservatory-trained violinist. Both media—the Orthophonic Victrola and the violinist himself—retreat to the background, as though bringing the listener into direct content with the mythic rural fiddler in his bucolic surroundings.

TRANSCRIPTION AND ACCOMPANIMENT

One of the less "realistic" attributes of arrangements of folk songs and dances for solo voice or instrument is the creation of harmonic accompaniment for melodies that were traditionally unaccompanied, or supported by a different harmonic idiom; but in fact the composition of Western-style harmonic accompaniment had already become common in many anthologies of folk songs

FIGURE 1.4: Advertisement for The New Orthophonic Victrola, in *Vanity Fair*, October 1928, 101. University of California, San Diego Library.

since the nineteenth century. The benefit of adding accompaniment to transcribed melodies was the subject of intense debate among ethnographers from an early date. Many engaged in the practice of writing accompaniments to the music they collected. In 1888, Julien Tiersot described arranging piano accompaniment for French chansons populaires as "dressing them with the clothes of harmony" to introduce them to audiences who "would not accept them in their bare simplicity."[107] James C. Filmore, who collaborated with Alice C. Fletcher during her fieldwork in the United States, believed that composing accompaniments brought to light latent similarities between all folk and Western musical languages. Others condemned this procedure; Erich M. von Hornbostel and Carl Stumpf wished to preserve what they viewed as the significant difference between the musical cultures.[108]

In many arrangements of folk music artifacts, accompaniment was composed in an attempt not to mimic a foreign musical tradition but rather to demonstrate the believed universality of musical expression. This apparent statement of universal brotherhood carried at the same time the imperialist implication that all cultures share musical roots that also contributed to the formation of Western art music. Alexander Rehding recounts that in 1902, Hugo Riemann, composing the violin and piano arrangement "Festive March on the Emperor's Entry into the Temple," which he published in the set "Six Authentic Chinese and Japanese Melodies Arranged for Violin and Piano," altered the original transcription of the melody as it appeared in J. A. van Aalst's 1884 anthology *Chinese Music*, changing rhythms to suit his metric theories and harmonizing it according to Western traditions. Riemann's procedure was to operate as an experiment intended to prove that Western harmony was in fact a latent universal practice, and the perception that the original transcription was accurate functioned to authenticate his experiment.[109]

Even in the work of twentieth-century ethnographers such as Bartók and Kodály, who were outspoken about the value of highlighting differences among the world's musical cultures, the practice of arranging folk music by representing traditional melodies within metric and harmonic structures idiomatic to European art music tradition might be read as the setting of rural musical expression into a stipulated universal musical language. Bartók described his project of writing folk music arrangements as an attempt "to collect from the Hungarian folksongs the most beautiful ones and, providing them with the best piano accompaniment possible, to elevate them, as it were, to the level of art song."[110] He thus claimed to undertake the scientific study of collecting folk songs with his phonograph and notating them in anthologies, while at the same judging them by urban standards of beauty and representing them in Western harmonic "clothing," a formulation that recalls Tiersot's earlier description of arrangement.[111]

This seemingly paradoxical interweaving of the empirical and the imperialist was commonly at the heart of the realist project of composing rural miniatures during the first half of the twentieth century. The ideals of scientific accuracy and objectivity undergirded the field of ethnographic research that inspired the rural miniature, and the resulting perception that ethnographers were engaged in compiling facts about rural communities and their music cultures allowed them to participate in bids to define national borders. The Jewish composer and ethnographer Abraham Zvi Idelsohn laid the foundations of his Zionist support for the foundation of a Jewish state in Palestine in the collection of music that he transcribed from other sources or recorded on wax cylinders in Jewish communities of Yemen, Iraq, Morocco, and other Central Asian, African, and Middle Eastern lands, his *Hebräisch-orientalischer Melodienschatz* (Thesaurus of Hebrew-Oriental Melodies), published in multiple volumes between 1904 and 1932. He compiled and juxtaposed folk musics to create the impression that far-flung Jewish communities formed a greater, coherent diasporic community that could come together in a new Jewish state.[112]

The decades-long project to create the German anthology *Landschaftliche Volkslieder* began between the world wars. Started by the German Folk-Song Archive, this project brought together folk songs in a compendium that redrew the borders of the German nation based on music. With the rise of the National Socialist party in Germany, these volumes began to incorporate music from outside the nation's official borders, using the "objective" claims of the existence of German folk music within neighboring areas in Central and Eastern Europe to support the cause of expansion.[113] Such efforts as Idelsohn's *Thesaurus* and the *Landschaftliche Volkslieder* project were not only inward-looking in their nationalist and imperialist goals of building diasporic communities and defining geographical borders for listeners that shared the cultures represented; they also aided in the outwardly oriented performance of identity for groups seeking national, ethnic, and political legitimacy.

Chapter 4 discusses the ways some Spanish folk song anthologies employed the language of scientific folk music research to argue for a unified Spanish nation in a period of intense regionalism and diverse musical traditions. And as Chapter 6 shows, Bartók's collections of folk songs in contested regions such as Transylvania were invoked by some musicians and political figures to make the case for a Hungarian nation that transcended its post–World War I borders. The rural miniature played a role in these processes too—for example, in lecture recitals held by the St. Petersburg Society for Jewish Folk Music and Budapest's New Hungarian Music Society that aimed to present the ethnic makeup and geographical borders of Jewish and Hungarian music cultures— and in multi-movement rural miniature collections such as Manuel de Falla's *Siete canciones populares españolas*, which brought together melodies from disparate regions.[114] The rural miniature also became popular because it helped to satisfy the nineteenth- and twentieth-century internationalist impulse, the increasing fascination with world travel, encounter, and discovery that was manifested in such globalizing phenomena as the rise of the academic field of orientalism and the staging of world expositions. As the gramophone became widespread in middle-class homes in the early decades of the twentieth century, the sound recording industry positioned itself at the center of this trend, releasing discs of European and American cantors, Yiddish operetta singers,

Rom instrumental bands, flamenco ensembles, and other musical genres. The recorded rural miniature became a commodity that helped to fulfill this global market imperative, as an object that could bring folk melodies—adapted and perhaps "elevated" to the idiom of art music—across the world, carrying their sounds as interpreted by such renowned recording artists as Pablo de Sarasate, Mischa Elman, and Heifetz, who themselves possessed exotic appeal and prestige as musicians known to come from the same European musical and cultural "peripheries." Thus, the seemingly objective basis of the rural miniature's realist aesthetic mode, an attribute that grew out of the genre's dependence on ethnographic research and therefore also its indirect reliance on sound recording technology, was crucial to its composition, performance, and programming at home and abroad.

CHAPTER TWO

THE RURAL MINIATURE IN PERFORMANCE
AND SOUND RECORDING

Temp'ramental Oriental Gentlemen are we:
Mischa, Jascha, Toscha, Sascha—
Fiddle-lee, diddle-lee, dee.
High-brow He-brow may play low-brow
In his privacy.
But when concert halls are packed,
Watch us stiffen up and act
Like Mischa, Jascha, Toscha, Sascha—
Fiddle-lee, diddle-lee, dee.

—"Mischa, Yascha, Toscha, Sascha."
By George Gershwin and Ira
Gershwin. Copyright © 1930
(Renewed) WB Music Corp.
(ASCAP). All Rights Reserved.
Used by Permission.

PERFORMING RURAL MINIATURES

In his 1921 memoir and textbook *Violin Playing as I Teach It*, Leopold Auer, professor of violin at the St. Petersburg Conservatory and the teacher of Jascha Heifetz, Mischa Elman, Toscha Seidel, and other world-renowned virtuoso violinists, writes that the role of the performer is to imbue the composer's work with a living soul:

> In each reincarnation of . . . a work, on each occasion that its inspiration charms the auditory sense and moves the heart, it is the part of the player—the sorcerer, whose bow is his magic wand—to give it a soul. And this soul is interpretation—interpretation which is *nuance* in its final and perfected annealing of component factors in the matrix of individuality.[1]

Auer describes a composition as a body that is imbued with a soul as it is given life in each unique interpretation by the performer. In the rural miniature, Auer's students and many of their contemporary violinists saw a compelling opportunity for interpretation as a form of embodiment, because the performance of works in the genre allowed for the metaphorical incarnation not only of individual pieces but also of the ethnic and religious cultures from which the source melodies were appropriated.

During the early decades of the twentieth century, the style in which many performers played rural miniatures in concert and in studio recordings involved a unique mode of sonic representation. Béla Bartók, Joseph Szigeti, Zoltán Székely, Heifetz, and other musicians interpreted the repertoire with the aim of evoking the playing style of rural musicians and depicting what they conceived of as the collective soul of the groups among which the music originated. Some performers had access to ethnographic research, having conducted it themselves or reviewed the work of their contemporaries. Bartók, for example, after undertaking considerable fieldwork and transcription, sometimes recorded his own works in the genre, both privately on wax cylinders and professionally in recording studios, and Szigeti and Székely reportedly discussed Bartók's findings with him, once even listening to his fieldwork cylinders, before recording his works (Chapter 6 describes Szigeti and Székely's relationship with Bartók and the impact of his research on their performances). Other performers based their representations on widespread urban assumptions about rural playing, which was often described as rough in articulation, intensely emotive, and suggestive of a collective folk "soul." These musicians constructed a system of sonic tropes for evoking authenticity through the depiction of traditional folk performance styles: their performances and recordings of rural miniatures were frequently described in reviews and articles as providing listeners with an experience akin to being in the audience at a folk fiddler's concert.[2]

A number of violinists took part in the composition and arrangement of rural miniatures as well. Szigeti and Székely, for example, arranged Bartók's rural miniatures for solo piano as duets for violin and piano. Szigeti's *Hungarian Folk Tunes* and Székely's *Romanian Folk Dances* received Bartók's approval, and both musicians performed their versions with Bartók at the piano. Rural miniatures based on Spanish folk music appeared in arrangements for violin and piano transcribed by violinists including Szigeti, Jacques Thibaud, Paweł Kochański, and Fritz Kreisler. Kreisler also wrote his own original works, including "La Gitana (Arabo-Spanish Gypsy Song from the Eighteenth Century)." Similarly, Heifetz, in addition to publishing numerous editions of works in the genre by Achron and others, composed the virtuosic rural miniature "Hora Staccato," based on a performance he heard during an encounter with a Rom musician in Bucharest, and Elman, who edited other composers' rural miniatures, composed his own "Tango" and "Eili, Eili."

Reviews of rural miniature performances in European periodicals often remarked upon the musicians' ability to suggest folk performance styles in their playing. In a 1929 review of Szigeti's interpretation of Bartók's first Rhapsody in Budapest, for instance, the influential Hungarian critic and musicologist Aladár Tóth marveled, "How Szigeti found this unprecedented ancient style of interpretation in this concert is a miracle of intuition."[3] The evocation of folk musicianship in classical violin playing involved not the mimetic reproduction of the sounds of wax cylinder recordings, however, but the representation of assumptions about rural playing based on an imagined notion of folk musicianship.

In the 1910s and 1920s, rural miniatures were often performed at concerts programmed by societies dedicated to the study of musical folklore and at arts organizations concerned with developing the profile of composition and performance in a particular culture or nation—for example, the St. Petersburg Society for Jewish Folk Music and the New Hungarian Music Society, an association founded in Budapest in 1911 by Bartók and Zoltán Kodály. The purpose of such programming was to educate audiences in both the ethnography of rural musical traditions and developments in contemporary nationalist composition. The Society for Jewish Folk Music and its offshoots in Central and Eastern Europe organized numerous concerts dedicated almost exclusively to the performance of rural miniatures based on Jewish traditional music. The Warsaw branch of the organization, for example, presented a concert in 1928 of sixteen rural miniatures by ten composers, including Achron, Ernest Bloch, Mikhail Gnesin, Moses Milner, and Solomon Rosowsky.[4]

Concert organizers often incorporated rural miniatures side-by-side with contemporary and older pieces in other genres, in an attempt to associate them with the prestige of canonic works of art music. Bartók and Kodály expressed such a goal in the preface of their 1906 pamphlet *Hungarian Folksongs for Voice with Piano*: "Hungarian folksongs in the concert halls! Sounds rather preposterous today. To be ranked with the master pieces of song literature on a world scale and also with the folksongs of foreign nations!"[5] In a concert of the New Hungarian Music Society on November 27, 1912, Bartók played a program that included miniature piano works by Rameau, François Couperin, and Domenico Scarlatti, a set of variations by Beethoven, and Bartók's rural miniature arrangements of *Three Hungarian Folksongs from Csík*.[6] A later concert combined the violin and keyboard Sonata in E major by J. S. Bach, additional miniatures by Scarlatti, and three groups of works identified by national boundaries: Ravel's *Cinq mélodies populaires grecques*, a set of "Old English and Italian Piano Pieces," and an arrangement of music by Mily Balakirev under the title "Old Russian Folksongs," probably selections from his folk song anthology.[7] Bartók's duo concert recitals with Székely and Szigeti continued to follow this pattern through the early 1940s: in April 1940, for instance, Bartók and Szigeti played Bartók's first Rhapsody alongside Ernest Bloch's *Baal Shem: Three Pictures of Chassidic Life*, concertos in D minor by J. S. Bach and Giuseppe Tartini, and Stravinsky's "Chanson Russe."[8]

Rural miniatures also appeared frequently on the recital programs and recording lists of many prominent European violinists of the first half of the twentieth century. Auer's pupils in St. Petersburg were exposed to rural miniatures during their training: Auer considered these works an important component of the violin repertoire and assigned Achron's "Hebrew Melody" and "Hebrew Lullaby" to students who had reached the stage at which they were able to play the violin concertos of Beethoven, Mendelssohn, Brahms, and Tchaikovsky, and the solo sonatas of Bach.[9]

In his 1925 *Violin Master Works and Their Interpretation*, Auer describes a series of compositional "types" in the violin training and performance repertoire, the second of which refers to the rural miniature:

> The second type of composition, one which is a feature of practically all contemporary recital programmes, is one which represents the development of characteristic folk-tune melodies in brilliant and idiomatic recital numbers. The folk airs and dance tunes of practically every nation have been drawn upon to supply pieces of this description and in some instances—as in Fritz Kreisler's developments of distinctively Viennese airs—they even reflect the musical folk-wise character of a particular city.[10]

Auer values rural miniatures for their realism, as well as for their brevity and technical virtuosity, which he considers appropriate for recital programs.

One important reason for the predominance of miniatures in the violin repertoire in the early sound recording era is that until the long-playing record was introduced in 1948, an individual side of a disc could hold up to a maximum of about four and a half minutes of continuous music, making miniatures particularly well suited to the technology and popular among recording artists and producers. Recordings of rural miniatures representing different cultures were sometimes released as A- and B-sides on the same disc. For example, in 1924 Victrola sold a 78-rpm recording with Heifetz's renditions of Sarasate's "Habanera" on one side and Achron's "Hebrew Dance" on the other.[11] In other instances rural miniatures were paired with excerpts and arrangements of the canonic repertoire, as in Columbia's disc of Toscha Seidel playing "Hebrew Melody," with an adaptation of Schubert's "Ave Maria" on side B.[12] The brevity of works in the genre also made them appropriate for radio broadcasts. For example, Heifetz performed works in the genre by Achron, Kodály, and others on the *Bell Telephone Hour* radio program throughout the 1940s and 1950s.

For several decades, beginning at least as early as his American debut on October 27, 1917, Heifetz favored a consistent programming structure: his recitals were divided into four sections, designated in the printed program by Roman numerals (Figure 2.1).[13] The first two included movements from concertos, sonatas, and other canonic genres of solo and accompanied violin music.

JASCHA HEIFETZ
NEW RUSSIAN VIOLINIST

AMERICAN DEBUT

CARNEGIE HALL

57th Street & 7th Ave., N. Y. City

Saturday Afternoon
OCTOBER 27th
At 2:30 P. M.

...Programme...

I.

Chaconne . . . . Tomaso Vitali (1650)
Arrangements de Leopold Charlier
(With Organ Accompaniment)

II.

Concerto in D Minor . . . . Wieniawsky
Allegro moderato
Romanze: Andante non troppo
Finale: A la Zingara

III.

a. Ave Maria . . . . Schubert
b. Menuetto . . . . Mozart
c. Nocturne in D major . . . . Chopin-Wilhelmj
d. Chorus of derviches (Etude) . . . . } Beethoven-Auer
e. March orientale (Scherzo) . . . . (From the Ruins of Athens) . . . }

IV.

a. Melodie . . . . Tschaikowsky
b. Capriccio No. 24 . . . . Paganini-Auer

MR. ANDRE BENOIST at the Piano.   MR. FRANK L. SEALY at the Organ.

Tickets: 75c., $1.00, $1.50, $2.00   Boxes: $15.00 & $18.00
On Sale at Box Office.

Management: - - WOLFSOHN MUSICAL BUREAU

STEINWAY PIANO USED

FIGURE 2.1:   Playbill of Jascha Heifetz's American debut recital at Carnegie Hall, October 27, 1917. Jascha Heifetz Collection, Music Division, Library of Congress, Box 218, Folder 1.

The third section typically consisted of a selection of three or four miniatures—including rural miniatures and arrangements of brief nineteenth-century pieces originally for keyboard—and the fourth and final section included one or two slightly longer virtuosic, show-stopping works, often compositions based on Spanish and Rom music by Sarasate. The recital programs of Elman and Szigeti followed a similar structure during this period.

Table 2.1 shows recital programs of Heifetz, Elman, Szigeti, and Thibaud. This method of organizing violin recitals meant that these performers included rural miniatures frequently in their programs. The tendency to play a selection of miniatures in the later parts of the program also created an opportunity for the juxtaposition of two or more rural miniatures representing musical traditions of different regions of the world. Thus in the fourth concert program in Table 2.1, Heifetz plays two of Achron's works representing Eastern European Jewish traditional music, along with Sarasate's representations of Hispanic dances.

In these programs, the sets of rural miniatures served by analogy to a travelogue or set of postcards, bringing audiences on a brief imaginary trip around the world to listen in on the traditional customs of various communities. By playing multiple rural miniatures in a single program, these violinists invited listeners to participate as amateur comparative ethnographers of music, reaching their own conclusions about the similarities and differences among traditional musics of different regions. Publishers of the handbills distributed at Heifetz's concerts often provided notes describing these rural miniatures in language that signified the practice of musical ethnography, in simple terms, and provided listeners with additional information about each stop on the musical "journey." The information presented was not always accurate, but it was aimed at conveying the impression of a scientific method behind the composition of these works and at evoking exotic foreign locales. The handbill to Heifetz's November 28, 1920, performance in the Royal Albert Hall included the following blurb describing Sarasate's "Zigeunerweisen":

> Gipsy Music is essentially the same, whether it is found in Hungary or Spain. The melodies and their rhythms are akin in every case. Their origin is, of course, uncertain, but their characteristics unmistakable, the sudden alterations of *tempi*, of mood, and of rhythmic structure. The tunes collected by Sarasate, on which he has written such a beautiful fantasia, are mostly from Southern Spain, his native province. On account of the piquant melodies and its technical brilliance, the piece has long been a favorite with virtuosi of the violin.[14]

This account is largely fictitious: in fact, "Zigeunerweisen" features a melodic quotation of a composition by Hungarian composer Elemér Szentirmay and is based on the genre of the *verbunkos*, a style of military recruiting dance that was widely disseminated during the nineteenth century, when government recruiting tours brought Rom ensembles along to Hungarian villages to provide entertainment as they attempted to persuade young men to join the army.

Jascha Heifetz:
October 27, 1917, New York City, Carnegie Hall[i]

I: Tomaso Vitali, "Chaconne" (arranged by Leopold Charlier)
II: Henryk Wieniawski, Concerto in D minor
    Allegro moderato
    Romanze: Andante non troppo
    Finale: À la zingara
III: a. Schubert, "Ave Maria"
            b. Mozart, "Menuetto"
            c. Chopin, arr. August Wilhelmj, Nocturne in D major
            d. Beethoven, arr. Auer, "Chorus of the Dervishes (Étude)"
            e. Beethoven, arr. Auer, "Marche orientale" (Scherzo), From
               the *Ruins of Athens*
IV: a. Tchaikovsky, "Mélodie"
            b. Paganini, arr. Auer, Capriccio No. 24

April 28, 1918, Metropolitan Opera House, New York[ii]
"For the benefit of the dependent families of the Jewish soldiers and sailors."

I: Bruch, Concerto in G minor
    Allegro moderato
    Adagio
    Finale
II: Saint-Saëns, Rondo Capriccioso
III: a. Chopin, Nocturne in E-flat major
            b. Brahms, arr. Joseph Joachim, Hungarian Dance No. 1
            c. Achron, "Hebrew Melody"
            d. Achron, "Hebrew Dance"
IV: a. Handel, arr. Hubay, "Larghetto"
            b. Sarasate, "Zigeunerweisen"

November 1918, Boston[iii]

I: Julius Conus, Concerto in E minor
II: J.S. Bach, Prelude, Menuetto, Loure, and Gavotte from Solo Violin Sonata No. 6
III: a. Chopin, arr. Auer, "Lithuanian Song"
            b. Schumann, arr. Auer, "Bird of Prophet"
            c. Leopold Godowsky, "Danse Macabre"
            d. Wieniawski, "Caprice in A minor"
IV: Sarasate, "Zigeunerweisen"

January 18, 1920, Chicago, Orchestra Hall[iv]

[I:] Vitali, "Chaconne"
[II:] Heinrich Wilhelm Ernst, Concerto in F-sharp minor, Op. 23
    Allegro moderato
[III:]   [a.] Bedřich Smetana, "Aus der Heimat"
            [b.] Achron, "Hebrew Melody"
            [c.] Achron, "Hebrew Dance"

[IV:]   [a.] Sarasate, "Habanera"
          [b.] Sarasate, "Malagueña"

Mischa Elman:[v]
January 19, 1909, The Philharmonic Society of New Orleans

I: Lalo, "Symphonie Espagnole," movement 3
II: Handel, Sonata in E Major, movement 4
III: a. Beethoven, "Minuet"
          b. Carl Ditters von Dittersdorf, "Deutscher Tanz"
          c. François-Joseph Gossec, "Gavotte"
IV: a. Schubert, arr. Wilhelmj, "Ave Maria"
          b. Sarasate, "Caprice Basque"

March 14, 1918, Private Residence Benefit for the Red Cross

I: Vivaldi, Violin Concerto in G minor
II: a. Elman, "Deep River Paraphrase"
          b. Albéniz, arr. Elman, "Tango"
          c. Chopin, arr. Sarasate, "Nocturne"
          d. Brahms, arr. Joachim, "Hungarian Dance"
III: a. Scarlatti, arr. Harrison, "Pastoral Caprice"
          b. Schubert, arr. Wilhelmj, "Ave Maria"
          c. Beethoven, arr. Auer, "Turkish March"
IV: Sarasate, "Zigeunerweisen"

Joseph Szigeti:
June 8, 1909, Draper's Hall, London[vi]

I: Mendelssohn, Violin Concerto, movement 1
II: a. Sarasate, "Malaguena"
          b. Sarasate, "Zapateado"
III: a. Anton Rubinstein, "Romanze"
          b. Hubay, "Hullámzó Balaton"

Late 1930s, New York[vii]

I: J.S. Bach, Violin Concerto in D minor (with orchestra)
II: Giuseppe Tartini, Violin Concerto in D minor (with orchestra)
III: Brahms, Violin Sonata in G Major (with Andor Farkas)
IV: Bartók, Rhapsody No. 1 (with Bartók)
V: Stravinsky, "Chanson Russe"
VI: Bloch, "Baal Shem Suite"

Jacques Thibaud:
March 11, 1920, Trinity Auditorium, Los Angeles[viii]

1. Lalo, Symphonie Espagnole
     Allegro
     Andante
     Rondo final

(*continued*)

TABLE 2.1: *(continued)*

---

2. Ernest Chausson, "Poème"
3.   a. Desplanes, arr. Nachez, "Intrada"
      b. Pierre Rode, arr. Thibaud, "Caprice"
      c. François Couperin, arr. Salmon, "Les Chérubins"
      d. J.S. Bach, Prelude in E Major
4.   a. Saint-Saëns, "Rondo Capriccioso"
      b. Wieniawski, "Polonaise"

---

[i] Jascha Heifetz Collection, Music Division, Library of Congress, Box 218, Folder 1.
[ii] Ibid., Box 218, Folder 3.
[iii] Ibid., Box 218, Folder 2.
[iv] Ibid., Box 218, Folder 6.
[v] Mischa Elman Collection, Howard Gotlieb Archival Research Center at Boston University, Box 12.
[vi] Joseph Szigeti Collection, Howard Gotlieb Archival Research Center at Boston University, Box 12.
[vii] Ibid., Box 11.
[viii] Jascha Heifetz Collection, Box 218, Folder 6.

When Heifetz performed Achron's "Stimmung" in a series of concerts in the United Kingdom in 1925, the handbill described the work in similarly fanciful terms:

> Joseph Achron is chiefly known in musical circles by his devotion to, and arrangement of traditional Oriental music, and understanding of "Stimmung" will be helped by letting the thoughts wander to distant climes and far-off times where life is expressed in vivid colours and when human emotions fought fiercely with iron laws.[15]

The same handbills also described Kreisler's arrangement of Dvořak's Slavonic Dance in E minor in terms that depicted the work as both authentic and exotic:

> The fascination of these Dances lies in their strongly national character. The themes, founded on traditional Bohemian folk-tunes, [reflect] the temperamental peculiarities of this people, and the treatment intensifies their significance. The Dances are too simple in form and too direct in expression to need description or analysis, but it should be pointed out that they more forcibly reflect the spirit of the composer than any other of his works. . . . They also show Dvorák's [*sic*] predilection for themes of five and seven bars so common to Bohemian folk-songs, and his naïve spontaneity in the form and harmonization. Above all, these measures are essentially out-of-door music of a land where the sky is blue and the sun is fierce, and life is fraught with keen sensations and emotional impulses.[16]

These characterizations of Sarasate's, Achron's, and Dvořak's compositions combine references to geography with national and ethnic stereotypes. The authors of these paragraphs emphasize that the works are based on folk music that originates far from the concert hall, though their facts are distorted or vague: "Zigeunerweisen" is reportedly constructed of southern Spanish "tunes collected by Sarasate," "Stimmung" is an "arrangement of traditional Oriental music," and the "Slavonic Dance" is "founded on traditional Bohemian folk-tunes," but appears also to emerge directly from Dvořak's own spirit, as it was shaped by his native folk song. These descriptions also characterize the works in language that refers to senses other than the aural, with the "piquancy" of Sarasate's music evoking the spiciness of Spanish cuisine, the "vibrant colors" of Achron's calling to mind exotic fabrics and architecture (despite the traditional black and white of Jewish religious costume and the run-down buildings of the small towns from which Achron's melodies derived), and the "fierce" Bohemian sun invoking hallucinatory heat. These sensory extremes become associated with emotional intensity and a spontaneous and naïve form of musical virtuosity.

By stating that they incorporated "collected" and "traditional" melodies into their compositions, these program notes depict Sarasate, Achron, and Dvořak as ethnographers of a sort, bringing melodies from remote areas to urban audiences in their compositions. Heifetz's performance, in turn, is expected to bring listeners back in the opposite direction, provoking them to "wander to distant times and far-off climes." The urban listener was presented with an opportunity to participate in an imaginary ethnographic field trip, with the timbres of Heifetz's playing standing in for those of the musicians who performed the original musical artifacts in rural areas, as well as serving as a medium to evoke the sounds, sights, and smells of distant landscapes and cultures.

Heifetz himself was sometimes depicted in his recital programs as an exotic relic of the distant East, as in a handbill for a 1919 performance in Michigan that cast him as a quasi-Messianic presence providing a direct connection to a different era and place,

> when America threw her defiant glove in the face of imperialism; when the people, in ever increasing numbers heard the call, and felt the mounting pulse of war in their homes and hearts; when the public, in the first stages of a growing excitement which bordered on hysteria, was ready for any sensation which could relieve the tension of the conflicting situations,—there came out of the turbulent east at the psychological moment in 1917, a veritable deliverer; that remarkable genius of the violin, perhaps the only real successor of the myth-enshrined Paganini,—Jascha Heifetz.[17]

The author of this "Biographical Sketch" proceeds to enshrine Heifetz in myth, painting him as a magician who reveals, in every composition, "new beauties, hitherto hidden, . . . in fresh and glowing tints, tonal nuances as fine and as delicate as the merging lines of the rainbow."[18] A psychological conjurer, Heifetz "lays bare the innermost thoughts of the composer. . . . Under the magic bow of Heifetz all music is made to speak a tongue that touches the heart, fires the mind, and brings endless joy to the music-starved soul."[19] In this description, repeated or paraphrased in numerous programs around this time, Heifetz is a magical figure from the East whose playing offers the listener access to music's inherent meanings and the composer's private thoughts, and by extension, through the performance of rural miniatures, to the essence of national and ethnic identities.

In combining diverse rural miniatures and juxtaposing works in the genre with more canonic compositions, violinists such as Heifetz, Szigeti, and Elman also brought the modern musical "periphery" in touch with the "center." They accomplished this in two ways. First, and perhaps most immediately, they were able to transform such compositions as Achron's "Hebrew Melody" and Sarasate's "Malagueña" into canonic works in their own right, through repeated performance around the world and by playing them side-by-side with standard repertoire, indicating an equivalence of musical value. Second, these violinists effected an encounter between periphery and center in a metaphorical sense by juxtaposing music by composers from Europe's musical "margins" and its "center," creating a meeting of national cultures that could occur on the recital stage as it might at a world's fair, with standard works programmed alongside arrangements of the traditional music of Russian Jews, Spanish and Hungarian Roms, and other ethnic minority and national groups. In this way these performers played a crucial role in helping to realize the more political goals of many composers of rural miniatures, by showcasing their compositions based on national and ethnic folk themes together with works exemplifying the German "cultivated" tradition of art music. Furthermore, by performing the Jewish-themed rural miniatures of Achron and other Russian Jewish composers in their international recital programs, Russian Jewish violinists placed themselves and their compatriots closer to the European social mainstream. In a time of growing anti-Semitism, with pogroms, restrictive legislation, and political movements increasingly marginalizing the Jews of Europe, these concert programs painted an alternate vision of the relationship between Jews and other European ethnic and national groups, trumpeting Jews' accomplishments as composers and performers of cultivated music, while depicting them as possessors of a unique folklore of a depth and quality to match that of so many other European groups in this period of rising nationalism.

PERFORMANCE, INTERPRETATION, AND CRITICAL RECEPTION OF RURAL MINIATURES

The musical score offers a set of instructions that cannot govern all aspects of performance; even when composers and editors provide exhaustive instructional notation, the performer must make interpretive decisions in realizing a piece of music. These include such elements of performance as the consistency and width of vibrato, the execution of accents and other timbral gestures that might be called for in the score but whose tone quality cannot be dictated by symbols, momentary inflections of tempo and dynamics, and the clarification of phrase and larger formal structures. Such elements might be planned in the practice room, but the performer must make decisions spontaneously in performance as well, in reaction to such matters as the location of phonograph trumpets or digital microphones, the acoustics of the performance space, and the sounds and reactions of the audience. Some interpretational details arise in response to other extenuating factors including the nervousness, health, and attitude of the musician at any given performance. All such attributes of any given performance have the potential to alter the public reception of a work.

In an interview, Yehudi Menuhin discussed the role of personal interpretation in performance: "During the first few months of playing the violin, when I was just five, I wondered, when will I be able to vibrate, 'cause that was my first desire, to vibrate. Looking back, I can see the logic of it, that for me it was a voice, it was something that had to mean something, convey a feeling, and I couldn't do that without lovely sound."[20] For Menuhin, the performer's role is to act as an interpreter who conveys musical meaning by embodying a composition, giving it voice. The violinist Ivry Gitlis has also described the importance of individuality in performance, arguing, "When someone says . . . 'That's how it should be played,' it is an insult to the music. It means that the music is very poor if there is only one way to play it."[21]

In writing about their early folk song arrangements, Bartók and Kodály recognized the performer's freedom to alter a work in interpretation and provided general suggestions to performers that they hoped would help them to bring life to the music frozen on the printed page. In particular, they indicate in their preface to *Hungarian Folk Songs for Voice and Piano* that firsthand knowledge of rural performance styles is helpful to the interpreter of their folk song arrangements: "Those who know the way common people sing in the villages will not err in performing the songs."[22] Furthermore, they assert that familiarity with the Hungarian language is important to the performance of their arrangements because it provides an understanding of the musical rhythms, which follow speech patterns: "Common folk never sing in a way to hurt one's sense of linguistic rhythm." Bartók and Kodály then advise against "exaggerated rubatos, as played by Gypsies," because these are not authentic to the performance tradition of rural peasants, but they suggest that performers should still experiment with different tempi: "One should not come to believe that each song has its own standard and regular tempo: folk singers very often sing the same song with greatly varying tempi. It is up to the performer to hit upon the right tempo by which a particular song is at its best." Finally, because folk singers, according to Bartók and Kodály, rarely alter their dynamics in performance, urban musicians playing these arrangements should imitate this convention by applying dynamic variation only "very sparsely."

Bartók and Kodály thus recommended that an authentic rendition of these works would be informed by the songs' language and cultural origins and would evoke the performance of an imagined rural musician. It is common for musicians and listeners to perceive performance gestures, including timbral effects, musical phrasing, and other elements of interpretation, as combining to create the impression of a musical character or personality. When newspaper music critics describe a performance by a violinist as "sweet," "charming," "violent," or "angry," for instance, these adjectives are generally employed to describe not the character of the musician but the persona he or she conveys through gestures produced in sound by motions of the hands on the instrument. In this way, the performance of instrumental music resembles dramatic acting: an actor in the role of Hamlet, for example, need not feel ambivalent himself in order to convey the ambivalence of his character. The performer projects a musical character by means of aural signs that convey expressive effects.[23] Violinists playing rural miniatures during the early twentieth century often projected the character of a stereotyped folk musician, by employing semiotic gestures that signified rural musical performance style as many urban audiences conceived of it. The style that these violinists adopted for their renditions of rural miniatures involved the use of tropes including particular kinds of ornamentation, articulation, and phrasing that, taken together in the performance of works based on folk music, were often interpreted to signify the sounds, and in turn the authenticity and expressive immediacy, that urban listeners commonly assumed to be typical of rural music making.

A survey of the early twentieth-century critical reception of recorded and live performances of rural miniatures and other works based on folk music reveals the tendency to hear rural miniatures as sonic representations of folk musicianship. Published reviews from the United States and United Kingdom often referred to the strangeness and intensity of violinists' renditions of rural miniatures, evoking such stereotypes as the primitive passion and entranced spirituality that were commonly associated with rural playing. Thus Rupert Croft-Cooke writes in an essay in *The Gramophone* that a Parlophone record of the violinist Edith Lorand and her orchestra performing a "Hungarian Dance" by František Drdla evokes "that peculiar abandonment which brings to one who has seen the gypsies play visions of their flushed and impassioned faces as they throw themselves into the spirit of their native music."[24]

Critical descriptions of performances of rural miniatures often incorporated sensual or even overtly sexual metaphors. A critic writing in 1935 in *Rimington's Review*, another magazine that like *The Gramophone* published brief reviews of the latest records to hit the market, referred in an article on Yehudi Menuhin's recording of Brahms's sixth "Hungarian Dance" and Sarasate's "Romanza Andaluza" to Eduard Reményi, the Hungarian violinist with whom Brahms performed in the 1850s and who influenced Brahms in writing his *Hungarian Dances*:

> With all our respects to the accounts we have of Remenyi's [sic] abundant temperament, it is difficult to believe that he could have filled this dance with such an abundance of Tsigane passion. He may have played it with more fire, more devil, but it is impossible to imagine phrasing more heavily perfumed, more languorously exciting than Menuhin's. If Brahms really conceived the piece to be played in this manner, it is a miracle that he did not commit bigamy.[25]

In a 1928 review in *The Gramophone* of Szigeti's recording of a work identified as "Saudades do Brasil"—most likely a reference to his disc containing Darius Milhaud's *Saudades do Brasil* no. 7, "Corcovado"—a critic writes, "Szigeti has a most attractive piece called Saudades do Brasil, a South American dance of the tango type. There is a lot of music in it, and it is played with a dark and mysterious rhythm that makes one long for distant shores where dark men dance with dangerous women all night."[26] Such references to violin performances as evoking thoughts of lascivious sensuality conflate titillating exotic fantasy with nineteenth-century mythologies of the demonic nature of Niccolò Paganini, as well as with stereotypical characterizations of Rom and klezmer violinists as devilish seducers.[27]

In other reviews, the qualities of passion and power are identified as the natural result of the synergy that emerges when performers interpret rural miniatures based on the traditional repertoire of their own ethnic and national cultures. In an article in the November 1925 issue of *The Gramophone*, the author, referring to Heifetz's famously still posture and inscrutable, stoic demeanor as a performer, writes that Heifetz's playing is generally "cold, calm, [and] dispassionate," and asks, "do we not feel slightly chilled, anxious perhaps for less mastery and more humanity[?]"[28] He continues,

> Heifetz does once give us a glimpse of his real self in the Hebrew Melody by Achron.... In the writer's opinion this is easily the most beautiful of his records, both from the interpretive and recording points of view. The tune, supported by an orchestral accompaniment is surely an old Hebrew one; appealing, therefore, to immemorial racial instincts and traditions in the Jew. It does seem to have penetrated beneath the outer shell of this curious personality.[29]

According to this critic, the barrier Heifetz had constructed against emotional expression in his performances is broken down by Achron's work, and Heifetz, confronted directly with an artifact of his own tradition, cannot help but be moved and convey his sentiment in his playing.

The review attributes the qualities of passion and authenticity in performance to the unique resonance between the repertoire and the violinist's ethnic identity. The critic's interpretation of this recording of course relies on a number of unverified assumptions about both the work and its performer. He asserts that Achron's composition is "surely an old Hebrew one," though it is in fact a contemporary setting of an unidentified melody that Achron claimed to recall from a childhood visit to a Warsaw synagogue. And on the basis of Heifetz's geographical origins and his family's Jewish ethnicity, the critic assumes that Heifetz must respond in a different and more personal way to a work based on Jewish music traditions than he does to any other piece in his repertoire.[30]

The performing partnership of Székely and Bartók was often celebrated in the Hungarian press in nationalistic terms. Thus a critic in the *Szegedi Napló* wrote, "Székely is a real pearl in the history of the violin to the glory of

Hungarian art and the pleasure of two continents."[31] In a similar spirit, Aladár Tóth wrote in the pages of the *Pesti Napló* that the two musicians were "both the pride of Hungary, one of Hungarian composition, the other of Hungarian violin playing."[32] Tóth credited Bartók and Székely with performances characterized by purity and authenticity, analogous to "shining . . . elementary colors," and lacking "any restraint or artificial coloring," but expressing the music "in the straightest way and in its naked truth."[33] This nationalist description of performance style echoes the language in Bartók's essays on the performance style of the rural musicians he visited and studied. Tóth associates the sounds Bartók and Székely produced with the authentic expression of "Hungarianness," exhibiting clarity and purity and lacking in any frivolity.

In the same review, Tóth portrayed the duo's interpretations of Bartók's rural miniatures in the following terms: "In its shaking, volcanic outbursts, in its pagan, mystic shiverings, in its ancient melancholy, painful melodies, and finally blood-boiling, wild outbursts, this miraculous vision of the world has never been painted more distinctly than by these artists."[34] Their performance of *Romanian Folk Dances* in particular is successful because of Székely's clear understanding of the idiom: "Székely presented us this very complicated musical structure so clearly that it was as if he had been playing a Schubert rondo, and the most demanding technical problems were solved magically."[35] Tóth implies in these writings that a musician's performance style can represent the authentic nature of rural life and ethnic identity. His interest in purity was echoed by critics outside of Hungary as well. One Dutch journalist, describing the 1925 performance of *Romanian Folk Dances* in Arnhem, writes that the work was "unlike that of the composers of the romantic school who went too far making things nice which were meant to be naked and honest."[36] The *Utrechtsch Nieuwsblad* similarly recalls, "A very unusual alternation of directness and restraint gave a very lively character to their playing in the *Rumanian Folk Dances*."[37] These critics located in Székely and Bartók's performances the ideals of authenticity, simplicity, and precision that Bartók valued in folk music and sought to replicate in composing rural miniatures. But their words also resemble the language that had been invoked since the nineteenth century to describe the music of Rom, klezmer, and other minority and rural musicians and performing ensembles. In the reviews quoted here, the critics hear primitivism, sensuality, ethnicity, nationality, and personal identity, and contextualize their discussions of these performances in relation to the social and historical backgrounds of the performers and the folk music traditions represented in the rural miniatures they played.

HEIFETZ'S EDITIONS OF ACHRON'S RURAL MINIATURES

The performance style described in the reviews quoted earlier was evident not only in performances and sound recordings but also in the printed scores these violinists produced as arrangers, editors, and composers. Heifetz's involvement in the publication and recording of rural miniatures provides a particularly rich example of the roles performers played in generating works in the genre and devising the evocative style in which they were performed. Throughout his career, Heifetz arranged numerous rural miniatures for violin and piano duet, including Isaac Albéniz's "Sevilla, sevillanas," Mario Castelnuovo-Tedesco's "Ritmo di Tango," Kodály's "Danube-Tisza," and Sarasate's "Zapaeado" and "Malagueña." Among Achron's works, Heifetz produced editions of "Hebrew Melody," "Hebrew Lullaby," and "Hebrew Dance." His editions of Achron's music followed others by Auer and Efrem Zimbalist. He called such miniatures "itsy-bitsies," and characterized them as both challenging and rewarding because they afforded the violinist only three or four minutes in which to evoke the wide range of expressive modes and technical virtuosity that are more dispersed in genres such as the sonata and concerto.[38]

As he worked on his editions, Heifetz wrote his annotations by hand directly onto copies of the original scores published by the St. Petersburg Society for Jewish Folk Music.[39] In addition to contributing fingerings, bowings, and other markings, Heifetz replaced the Yiddish and German titles, dedications, and performance instructions with English. His editions of Achron's rural miniatures differed from those of other violinists in the emphasis he placed on the works' basis in folk music in the paratext of the scores as well as in his introduction of numerous performance instructions.

Where Achron's original version of "Hebrew Lullaby," published by the Society for Jewish Folk Music, opened at the top of the score with a transcription of his source melody in small print, Auer's edition, published in 1919, omits the introductory transcription. Auer's editorial markings are restricted to dynamics and fingering indications. He adds frequent "hairpin" swells that contribute a lilting oscillation of generally quiet dynamics, ranging from *pianissimo* to *mezzo forte*. His fingering instructions suggest useful shifts and explain how one might play some of the challenging double stops in the second half of the piece. Auer indicates twice that passages that could be attempted in first position should be played in higher positions on lower strings: in measure 13 he writes a Roman numeral III, instructing that the passage should be played on the D string (it in fact reaches the higher regions of the D string already in the previous measure because of his fingering indications), and in measure 27, he similarly indicates that the performer should play high on the A string a phrase that naturally falls on the E string. The muted, dulcet timbre that can be created by playing in high positions is appropriate to the performance of a quiet lullaby.

In his new edition of the work from 1936, Heifetz reintroduces the origins of "Hebrew Lullaby" in folk music by including the opening transcription in small print, and labeling it in an English translation of Achron's German caption, "Original version of the melody, as recorded by S. Kisselgof."[40] Heifetz adds a number of slides and increases Achron's initial tempo marking (Auer had omitted any tempo indication) from 78–84 to the eighth note, to 92–108.

He suggests a more prolonged and pronounced expression of the husky timbre of high positions on lower strings by marking the opening of the violin part *pianissimo* rather than the original *piano*, and instructing the violinist to play the opening phrases (measures 7–20) entirely on the D string, whereas Auer indicated a return to the A string at measure 11. Heifetz also instructs the violinist to experiment with rubato tempo fluctuations: he writes "*rit.*" in measure 33, returning *a tempo* in the next measure; he adds "*meno*" during the cadenza-like runs in measure 49, again followed by *a tempo* in the next measure; and finally he concludes *morendo* in the last two measures.

For the first time in the publishing history of "Hebrew Lullaby," Heifetz adds instructions to play portamentos between notes, indicated by upward and downward slanted straight lines between consecutive pitches.[41] Heifetz's fingering instructions are also devised to produce frequent portamentos even in the absence of diagonal lines between pitches. The violinist's choice of whether to shift along the fingerboard or to remain in the same position in performing a phrase establishes whether or not there will be a clean articulation or a slide between successive pitches.[42] When one finger is used to stop the string on two or more successive notes, the sound of that finger's motion along the string is often audible, creating a glissando. Heifetz's markings suggest that the player's left hand glide over the strings in narrow motions, often using a single finger rather than neighboring fingers to play adjacent notes. In measures 10–12 (Example 2.1), rather than marking the phrase in first position (with a fingering 2-3-4-3-2-1-0/4) or in fifth position shifting down at the end to third (2-3-4-3-2 [shift] 3-2), or other simpler alternatives, Heifetz requires the violinist to play half-step intervals twice without changing fingers, an option that is likely to produce additional slides (on the D string: 2-3-4-3-3-2-2).

Heifetz's editorial markings in "Hebrew Melody" are similar to those in "Hebrew Lullaby." He increases the tempo that appeared in the original 1911 version, from 60–3 to 72–80 to the eighth note. He also adds instructions to play multiple phrases high on lower strings and to fluctuate the tempo with isolated rubatos. In his version, Heifetz inserts articulations that did not appear in the original version—for instance, tenuto marks at the violin's first entrance and on the frequent pattern of alternating sixteenth-note fourths that first appears in measure 11, and accent marks on the second and third beats of measure 15.

EXAMPLE 2.1: Joseph Achron, "Hebrew Lullaby," edited by Jascha Heifetz, violin part, measures 10–12

Heifetz notates slides with diagonal lines between pitches continuously throughout the work, and his fingering instructions again indicate additional portamentos.

Heifetz's editions of Achron's rural miniatures contributed to the development of a distinctive mode of performing these works. The abundance of slides, heavy articulations, rubato, and narrowly shifting fingerings implies an expressive, melancholy performance style, as the violinist drags the fingers poignantly from note to note and applies pressure with the bow on the beats. Heifetz's fingerings are not aimed at suggesting easy alternatives for the benefit of the performer, as are Zimbalist's and Auer's; to the contrary, they frequently complicate the performance, making the violinist's work more difficult and highlighting the sounds produced by shifting fingers. Whereas violinists' editions of the repertoire often provide fingering suggestions that seek to produce a fluid, intuitive performance with the left hand, Heifetz wishes the audience to hear the motions of the fingers along the strings, to be made aware of the mechanics of performance and the technology of the instrument. This suggests the performance style that evoked the sounds of an imagined rural violinist for many listeners and critics of the early twentieth century. The Hasidic male vocalists recorded by Kiselgof and other Russian Jewish ethnographers whose collections inspired Achron's works often also sang portamentos from pitch to pitch, singing in a heavy tone. One performer recorded in 1913 in the Kiev region, Moishe Bilotserkovsky, for example, slides profusely in the Hasidic music he performed for ethnographers, emphasizing important pitches in the phrase with increased volume, upward glissandos, and vibrato, and peppering the melodies with expressive, energetic grace notes.[43] Heifetz's editions of Achron's rural miniatures and his recorded performances of these works evoke such a style of *nigun* performance—the *nigun* is a typically wordless vocal genre of Hasidic worship—through the use of portamento, grace notes, vibrato, and other timbral, structural, and ornamental techniques. But this was not a pure imitation; it was a reinterpretation of the traditional performance styles of Jewish vocalists and klezmer musicians that was based on, and fed into, urban, cosmopolitan impressions of a music that was being collected at the time by ethnographers but rarely encountered directly by the listeners who made up Heifetz's audiences.

"HORA STACCATO" AND HEIFETZ'S AMATEUR ETHNOGRAPHY

Heifetz's role in the history of the rural miniature extended beyond arrangement, editorship, and performance to the composition of new works as well. His "itsy-bitsy" show-stopper "Hora Staccato" provides a rich example of both the eclectic hybridity of Heifetz's composition and performance repertoire, and the surprising impact of the field of ethnography on his method of devising the work, his publisher's marketing approach, and the piece's reception over several decades. During his studies with Auer from the age of nine at the St. Petersburg Conservatory, Heifetz was a friend and collaborator of a number of members of the Society for Jewish Folk Music, which had been founded two years prior, and he came into contact with the ethnographic work being done under the organization's auspices. It was here that he became particularly close to Achron, whose pianist brother Isidor was to serve as his long-term accompanist. In 1927, Achron dedicated his Violin Concerto No. 1, Op. 60, to Heifetz. On Heifetz's personal copy, Achron dated and signed the front cover and wrote a short melody over two staves set to the repeated syllables of diminutive versions of Heifetz's first and last names, written in Russian (Figure 2.2).[44] The tune, the main theme on which he based the concerto's second movement, "Improvisations sur deux thèmes yemeniques," is in a dance-like 2/4 time, set in the A Dorian mode, and divided into two simple four-measure phrases and one six-measure phrase. Achron alternates snapping rhythms of dotted eighth and sixteenth notes, alongside syncopated measures, and adds a triplet turning ornamentation in the third-to-last measure. This personalization of the Yemeni melody to Heifetz's name demonstrates the affectionate relationship between the two musicians and their mutual interest in folk music.

Heifetz seems likely to have been aware of the goals and accomplishments of the Society for Jewish Folk Music. He owned a copy of *Lieder-Sammelbuch für die jüdische Schule und Familie* (in Yiddish, the *Lider-zamelbukh far der yidishe shul un familie*, Collection of Songs for the Jewish School and Family), an anthology of Jewish traditional melodies compiled by the Society's ethnographer Susman Kiselgof, edited by Alexander Zhitomirsky and Pesach Lvov, and published in 1912 in St. Petersburg by the Society's printing house, and in Berlin by Leo Winz.[45] Kiselgof signed the front page of Heifetz's copy, dating his autograph January 1914 and personalizing it with the words, "My modest work, to the master and commander of the violin, my dear pupil Jascha, for his thirteenth birthday" (Figure 2.3).[46] Although it is not certain whether Kiselgof implies that Heifetz studied with him or was merely a pupil at the Conservatory when he worked there, Kiselgof apparently served in some way as a mentor to Heifetz during the early 1910s. Under his greeting and signature, Kiselgof writes, "The people's song is the people's soul. The unhappy soul of the Jewish people is reflected in this sad and melancholy song." This statement summarizes Society members' common characterization of beliefs about traditional song, which was often held to express the collective soul of the Jewish diaspora and to evoke the history of Jewish suffering.

In 1929, Heifetz engaged in his own amateur ethnographic expedition during a visit to a Bucharest café, where he heard a performance by the Rom violinist Grigoraș Dinicu, a student of the prominent violin pedagogue Carl Flesch and graduate of the Bucharest Conservatory. The piece Heifetz heard Dinicu play was "Hora Staccato," which Dinicu had arranged in 1906, based on

FIGURE 2.2: Cover of Jascha Heifetz's personal copy of Joseph Achron's Violin Concerto No. 1, Op. 60, with handwritten message by Achron. By permission of Jay Heifetz. Jascha Heifetz Collection, Music Division, Library of Congress, Box 15, Folder 3.

the melody of a Romanian hora, a genre of circle dance. Heifetz saw the potential to adapt, publish, and perform a new version of this showpiece and signed an agreement with Dinicu to buy publication rights to the music for 16,000 Romanian lei, on the agreement that their names would appear together as co-authors.[47]

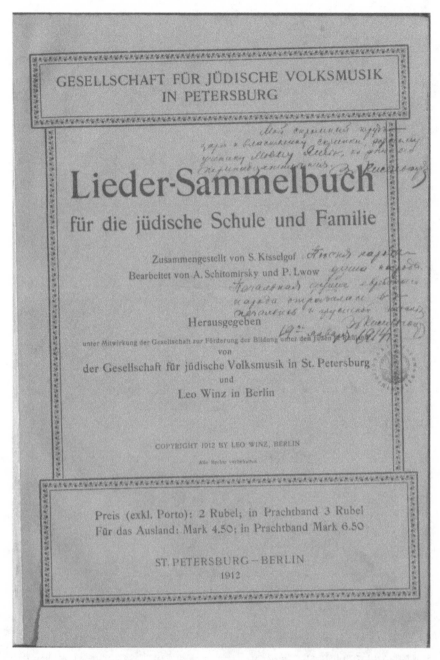

FIGURE 2.3:   Cover of Jascha Heifetz's personal copy of Susman Kiselgof's *Lieder-Sammelbuch für die jüdische Schule und Familie*. By permission of Jay Heifetz. Jascha Heifetz Collection, Music Division, Library of Congress, Box 206.

Published versions of Heifetz's work were usually attributed to "Dinicu-Heifetz" or "Heifetz-Dinicu." In an early handwritten manuscript copy dated March 29, 1930, Heifetz settled for the first time on the final title: his piece was to be called "Hora Staccato," followed by the parenthetical geographic and ethnic attribution "(Roumanian)."[48] This title—adhered to for a number of years in reprints of the score, sheet music catalogues, concert programs, and sound recording contents lists—functions to identify a folk genre and its regional location of origin, in the manner of the titles and other accompanying information provided in the paratexts of so many rural miniatures.

Heifetz's arrangement of "Hora Staccato" is in a 2/4 time signature, with a generally consistent repeating "oom-pah" pattern of eighth notes exchanged between the left and right hands in the piano part, alluding to the traditional *esztam* pattern, characterized by pairs of pitches of equal duration often played by bass and upper string or cimbalom in Rom ensembles.[49] The main focus of the solo part, and the feature that gives the work the other half of its name, are the recurring passages of slurred staccato sixteenth notes written to be performed at a fast pace with long down-bows and up-bows. This is difficult to play crisply and precisely, especially on the down-bow, but Heifetz could execute this virtuosic technique masterfully, and no doubt chose to arrange Dinicu's melody in part to provide himself the opportunity to show off his skill. The work is characteristically simple and repetitive, in a structure of A–A'–B–B'–A". There are frequent passages of pedal tones, and for most of its duration the piece is in E-flat major, with only one brief modulation to the IV key of A-flat major, beginning in measure 99, where the tonic chord with added flat 7th scale degree takes on the role of the dominant V^7 of A-flat major, resolving in measure 101. The tonality begins to shift back to the original tonic in measure 111.

Harmonic irregularities and the evocation of foreign modality are produced by the use of an octatonic scale. Heifetz and Dinicu repeatedly juxtapose E-flat major tonic chords with an oscillating scale that conforms to the octatonic profile on E-flat, but without the F-flat: E-flat–F-sharp–G–A-natural–B-flat–C–D-flat; this scale appears in the piano in measures 1–2 and in the violin throughout sections B and B' (Examples 2.2a and 2.2b). The scale clashes dissonantly with its context, and because of the omission of F-flat, it incorporates an augmented second between the first and second scale degrees. Additional non-chord tones create unexpected dissonances elsewhere, especially in the piano on every second beat in measures 77–87 (Example 2.3). Other gestures that resemble common tropes in the rural miniature are trills, grace notes, heavily accented downbeats, chromatic scales (e.g., measure 44), slides (measures 65, 87–8, and 101), and triplets that jauntily contrast with the otherwise consistent duple rhythms (measures 59, 67, 71, 83, 87, 113, and 129).

EXAMPLE 2.2A: Jascha Heifetz and Grigoraş Dinicu, "Hora Staccato," measures 1–3

EXAMPLE 2.2B: Jascha Heifetz and Grigoraş Dinicu, "Hora Staccato," measures 45–8

The hybrid nature of Heifetz's version of "Hora Staccato," based on the music of Rom bands but written for classically trained performers, contributed to its substantial popularity and inspired its arrangement in a variety of instrumentations and musical idioms. New editions appeared for cello, viola, B-flat clarinet or tenor saxophone, E-flat alto saxophone, accordion solo and duet, piano solo and duet, and other combinations of instruments. In 1938, Carl Fischer published arrangements for orchestras increasing in size from small to "full" and "symphonic," by Adolf Schmid, an orchestrator who worked at the National Broadcasting Company. Schmid's editions featured an explanatory blurb that told the story of Heifetz's initial composition of the piece:

> This brilliant work has the most romantic origin that may be imagined. Its discovery illustrates Mr. Heifetz's acute sensitivity to outstanding materials which, when transcribed will enrich violin literature. One evening, while in a café in Bucharest, Roumania, Mr. Heifetz was suddenly aware of a strangely exciting melody played by a young gipsy violinist. He was intrigued by the unusual character and rhythm of the piece, and upon inquiry, learned that it was the player's own composition. The performer's name was Dinicu, who, astonished at the great virtuoso's interest in his work, seized a napkin and quickly produced on the linen, a rough sketch of his composition. This was presented to Mr. Heifetz, and out of this source was developed the transcription known as "Hora Staccato," a virtuoso number of bewildering effects and surprises, demanding technical left-hand ability of the highest order and unusual skill in staccato bowing.[50]

This tale casts Heifetz's rural miniature as emerging from a quasi-ethnographic discovery he made during a trip abroad. Dinicu's training and identity are

EXAMPLE 2.3: Jascha Heifetz and Grigoraş Dinicu, "Hora Staccato," measures 77–87

reduced to the descriptive phrase "young gipsy violinist," apparently aimed to conjure for American audiences the stereotype of an untrained Rom fiddler devoted solely to playing popular music in public settings. Dinicu wrote a rough, spontaneous transcription of the music on a napkin, which, this account implies, Heifetz transported on the journey back to the West, to arrange the melody for his edition.

"Hora Staccato" quickly met with tremendous success. In 1939, Heifetz performed it in the Samuel Goldwyn film *They Shall Have Music,* in which he starred as himself, helping to protect a music school that offers free lessons to disadvantaged children in New York City. Led by Frankie (Gene Reynolds), a young violinist saved from living on the streets by the school's director, the students meet Heifetz in front of Carnegie Hall, where they are busking to raise money for the indebted school, and Heifetz agrees to send the students a film reel of his performances. Heifetz is seen in this reel playing the opening of

FIGURE 2.4:   Film still from *They Shall Have Music*. Directed by Archie Mayo. Samuel Goldwyn Company, 1939. New York: HBO Video, 1992.

"Hora Staccato" in a shot of the projector's lens, and his performance continues in a new shot of the screen in the front of the room where the student body and their teachers look on enthralled (Figure 2.4). In images of the school audience, Frankie's eyes are glued to the screen in admiration, his mouth agape, and even his rough, streetwise sidekick Limey, smacking his chewing gum, begins to smile. Young violinists imitate Heifetz's fingering on the necks of their instruments as they listen. In his performance, Heifetz, with his back straight and sporting a stiff tuxedo, barely moves, apart from some minimal rocking back and forth. His face remains still and stoic throughout, and his technique is precise and clean. The students onscreen are no doubt amazed, along with much of the film's audience, by his technical ability, and particularly his fast and flawless performance of the slurred staccato passages. Indeed in the context of the speed and virtuosity required by the composition, Heifetz's demeanor makes his technique appear all the more effortless and impressive.

At the time *They Shall Have Music* was released, the published editions of "Hora Staccato" still credited Heifetz and Dinicu and mentioned Romania as the work's original geographic location of reference, but as time progressed, the piece gradually shed its associations with Eastern European Rom culture, appearing with increasing frequency in the context of American jazz and swing. It was scored for trumpet and piano in 1944; in a dance arrangement for piano, strings, brass, and percussion by Paul Weirick in 1945; and for xylophone and piano in 1947. In some of these editions, the reference to the music's geographical origins was reduced by the elimination of the word "Roumanian" for the first time since the piece's initial publication.

FIGURE 2.5:   Film still from *Bathing Beauty*. Directed by Sidney George. Metro-Goldwyn-Mayer, 1944. Burbank, CA: Warner Home Video, 2007.

In the 1944 film *Bathing Beauty*, trumpeter Harry James performs "Hora Staccato" on a dancehall stage with his band after the emcee makes an introduction that refers back to the work's Romanian origins:

> Ladies and gentlemen, next we present a musical phenomenon: some years ago, in a little café in Romania, Jascha Heifetz, the famous violinist, heard a Gypsy fiddler play a selection that made such an indelible impression on his mind that later, he wrote a brilliant adaptation of it. Tonight, for the first time, we present these—uh—violin fireworks as transcribed for the trumpet by Harry James. Ladies and Gentlemen, "Hora Staccato."

The performance that follows opens with a brief introduction in the brass section, after which the strings play a descending lick. The lighting highlights the violins and violas while mostly hiding the performer's bodies in shadow (Figure 2.5). Although this is an arrangement for the trumpet, the origin of the work in violin performance is thus implied at the start by the row of glowing violins, manipulated by disembodied hands. Harry James's performance of the solo, which alternates with recurring phrases in the strings, generally follows Heifetz's violin part, as James plays at a rapid pace, vibrating on longer notes and adding glissandi up to some of the higher pitches. At the conclusion of the performance the lights go up as James plays a long ascending slide to the dominant followed by the tonic in a high tessitura, below which members of the brass section hold a blue note on the lowered seventh scale degree.

The emcee's introduction suggests that Heifetz's composition is particularly valuable because Heifetz discovered the authentic "Gypsy" melody at its distant source, in a "little café in Romania." At the same time, however, the performance's immediate success had the effect of severing the piece from its exotic source. The 1944 trumpet arrangement was published without reference to Heifetz's discovery, instead simply identifying the music with the advertisement, "As Featured by Harry James in the Metro-Goldwyn-Mayer Picture 'Bathing Beauty.'"[51]

In 1947, another band arrangement composed by David Bennett replaced the typical blurb with new notes:

> "Hora Staccato" achieved instant success in its original form as an arrangement for violin and piano. While it is not, in its entirety, a "tune for humming," the unusual treatment of the scale as a subject and the exotic style of the motifs in the second part make it "catchy" and hence easily remembered. It has appeared in many versions, including accordion solo, trumpet (featured by Harry James), viola, cello, saxophone, clarinet (featured by Benny Goodman), piano solo, and two pianos, and has now been issued as a popular song under the title "Hora Swing-cato."[52]

The piece's origins in Bucharest and the earlier implications of authenticity derived from the description of Heifetz's foreign musical encounter are here reduced to the words "exotic style of the motifs." This introduction omits any details of the work's history, focusing instead on recent adaptations in the performances of Harry James and Benny Goodman, and the song "Hora Swing-cato."

"Hora Swing-cato" had been published in 1946 by Carl Fischer. Its title is a hybrid of the original genre "hora" and the new genre "swing," though the original manuscript score of the new version shows that an initial experimental title was "The Horrible Staccato," a name Heifetz was known to call "Hora Staccato" because of its difficulty and ubiquity.[53] This joking title is mimicked by the illustration on the polka-dotted cover of the sheet music, which shows two dancing couples, one in embroidered, ruffled representations of Romanian traditional costume, and the other in 1940s swing dancing garb (Figure 2.6).[54] The song is attributed to Jim Hoyl and lyricist Marjorie Goetschius, who together had published two other songs in the same year, "So Much in Love," and "When You Make Love to Me (Don't Make Believe)," which was recorded by Bing Crosby and also in a solo piano version by Heifetz himself. The daughter of music theorist and composer Percy Goetschius, Marjorie Goetschius was a known lyricist; Hoyl's identity, however, remained a mystery until October 1946, when Heifetz revealed in Hollywood that he was the songs' composer, using the name "Jim Hoyl" as a pseudonym, or, as one critic put it, a "nom de swing."[55] Heifetz had written these songs, according to an article in *Time* magazine, "to prove how easy it was."[56]

The modal mixture and evocative dissonances of the rural miniature are replaced in this arrangement for piano and voice by jazz chords and blue notes, and the perpetual motion of the violin part is condensed to a swinging, syncopated melody with the following lyrics:

FIGURE 2.6: "Hora Swing-cato." Lyrics by Marjorie Goetschius, arr. Jim Hoyl. Adapted from "Hora Staccato" by Grigoraş Dinicu and Jascha Heifetz. Copyright © 1945 Carl Fischer, Inc. All rights assigned to Carl Fischer LLC. International copyright secured. All rights reserved. Used with permission. Cover image from The Lester S. Levy Collection of Sheet Music, Johns Hopkins University.

It goes like this:
"Diga, diga, diga, diga, da, doo-da, doo-da"—
It's making history, that melody,
The Hora Swing-cato.

You couldn't miss
"Diga, diga, diga, diga, da, doo-da, doo-da"
From Maine to Oregon it's catching on,
The Hora Swing-cato.

Why, even Tommy plays it and
Sammy sways it and
Jascha plays it up in Carnegie Hall.
It's the mania way back in Roumania
Where they cry for curtain calls!

And when you hear
"Diga, diga, diga, diga, da, doo-da, doo-da"
You're hep to ev'rything if you can sing
The "Hora Staccato" in swing![57]

The violin part in Heifetz's score is imitated in "Hora Swing-cato"
in a simpler scalar melody sung to scat-like syllables (Examples 2.4 and
2.5).

The initial selling point of "Hora Staccato" as a work derived from quasi-
ethnographic research has been reduced here to the mere mention of Romania. In the bridge of the song, Jascha Heifetz lists people who have performed
the melody, omitting Dinicu completely and giving himself third billing, after
Tommy and Sammy (presumably references to bandleaders Tommy Dorsey and
Sammy Kaye). On the words "Where they cry for curtain calls," the composer
introduces a brief *ossia* staff above the right hand of the piano that interacts
rhythmically and harmonically with piano and voice to represent the exotic
and emotional implications of the text (measures 26–8, Example 2.6). In this
interpolated voice, the dotted rhythms in measures 26 and 27 create syncopated
cross-rhythms with the other voices, perhaps inspired by the rhythms of Rom
music. Dissonances created between the piano and *ossia* lines in measure 27 by
the juxtaposition of F, E, and E-flat appear to imitate both the blue notes of
swing music and the modality of Rom numbers. The descending contour of
the melody in measures 27–8 acts as tone painting to imitate crying, though
rather than the sort of cries indicated in the text (the screams for a curtain call),
this is a musical pun that depicts tearful crying, of the sort associated with melancholy, an emotional characteristic often linked in popular culture and the arts
with Rom and other Eastern European ethnic musical idioms. The melody in
these extra few measures of material is repeated in canon two beats later by the
left hand of the piano. In the text, the role of Romania is reduced from the

EXAMPLE 2.4:   Violin theme in Jascha Heifetz and Grigoraş Dinicu, "Hora Staccato,"
measures 9–12

EXAMPLE 2.5:   Adaptation of violin theme in Jim Hoyl (Jascha Heifetz) and Marjorie
Goetschius, "Hora Swing-cato," measures 7–8

"Dig - a, dig - a, dig - a, dig - a,   Da   doo - da, - doo - da" -

EXAMPLE 2.6:   Jim Hoyl (Jascha Heifetz) and Marjorie Goetschius, "Hora Swing-cato,"
measures 25–9

source of the melody to another setting, "way back" far away, where the swing
versions of "Hora Staccato" are popular.

Heifetz's most famous foray into composition was thus recast over time, as
the work became known in many circles as a swing melody and was gradually
divorced in numerous new editions and performances from the initially popular

story of its origins as a representation of an ethnographic discovery abroad. At first, "Hora Staccato" was interpreted as offering an accurate evocation of traditional Eastern European music, in performance through the display of virtuosity associated with Romany music making and in print through its tale of origins as a composition born of a personal cross-cultural encounter between musicians trained in Western classical and Romany popular idioms. As swing became popular and Heifetz and many of his listeners grew progressively deracinated from European cultural origins in the United States, Heifetz's adoptive home, the adaptation of "Hora Staccato" to swing instruments and tropes perhaps seemed a logical course of development.[58] The successive versions of "Hora Staccato" show the evidence of increasingly hybridizing, fractured musical perspectives, as these renditions of the work gesture less toward ethnography than nostalgia and exoticism through the combination of techniques of classical and popular genres from Europe and America. In the 1922 song "Mischa, Jascha, Toscha, Sascha," quoted in the epigraph of this chapter, George and Ira Gershwin affectionately tease the four prominent Jewish immigrant violinists from Russia—Elman, Heifetz, Toscha Seidel, and Sascha Jacobsen—asserting that beneath the high-brow façades they maintain, these musicians privately nurture swinging souls. The variations in published and recorded versions of "Hora Staccato" from the 1920s through the 1940s provide insight into the important role of violinists in the development of the rural miniature, and the ways that changes to musicians' conceptions of their own identities, brought about by immigration and encounters with new forms of popular music, prompted the gradual reinterpretation of many rural miniatures to foreground new ideas of what was authentic in music.

PART II

HISTORICAL CASE STUDIES

CHAPTER THREE

THE RURAL MINIATURE'S PRECEDENTS

Representations of Rom Performance in Nineteenth-Century Violin Repertoire

Ven ikh derher tsigayner melodi
A lid fun libe dringt in harts arayn.
—"Tzigeiner Veisen,"
Miriam Kressyn

This chapter explores a principal nineteenth-century precedent to the rural miniature, the repertoire of virtuosic compositions for accompanied violin based on the music of Rom ensembles. The compositional style of these works, the style hongrois, emerged in the eighteenth century as a trope signifying the music of Hungarian Roms in works by Haydn, Mozart, and their contemporaries, and was further developed by nineteenth-century composers including Franz Schubert, Franz Liszt, and Johannes Brahms.[1] The Rom ensemble's performance style was frequently romanticized in literature and the arts, and the style hongrois was developed largely to create space in art music performance for the characteristics of virtuosity, passion, and expressive authenticity commonly invoked in descriptions of Rom playing. Rom groups were admired for their public performances of repertoire that typically comprised waltzes, polkas, and opera and operetta numbers, as well as popular pieces in dance and song types developed by Hungarian composers, particularly the *verbunkos* and *csárdás* dance forms, and the song genre of the *nóta*.[2]

Among the most successful compositions based on the music of Rom ensembles were Brahms's twenty-one *Hungarian Dances* for piano four hands (published 1869 and 1880) and Liszt's nineteen *Hungarian Rhapsodies* (1846–85). Joseph Joachim's arrangements of the *Hungarian Dances* assumed a canonic place in violin recitals during the first half of the twentieth century. Numerous discs of these works were made by violinists of the first recording generation, Joachim,

Arnold Rosé, Leopold Auer, and Fritz Kreisler, as well as by younger violinists including Jascha Heifetz, Celia Hansen, Toscha Seidel, Joseph Szigeti, and Mischa Elman. Pablo de Sarasate's "Zigeunerweisen" (1878) was also recorded repeatedly, performed on numerous recital programs, and incorporated by instructors into violin pedagogy, in which context it still plays an important role today. Because of the clear compositional overlaps between the popular Rom *verbunkos* and art music in the style hongrois, examples of the latter, such as passages of operetta, Brahms's *Hungarian Dances*, and Sarasate's "Zigeunerweisen," would enter the performance repertoire of some Rom bands. In this way, musical influence flowed in a circular manner between these ensembles and performers of art music. Compositions like Sarasate's "Zigeunerweisen" thus demonstrated the hybrid influences of both Rom and art music and introduced new expectations about what constitutes expressive authenticity in violin performance.

The popular conception of Rom performance as passionate and emotionally authentic would exert a profound influence on composers of the early twentieth century as they developed the rural miniature as a medium for representing disparate European cultures. As the following chapters show, Manuel de Falla embraced Spanish flamenco as the key to developing a national language of art music. A number of Jewish composers of the St. Petersburg Society for Jewish Folk Music, in creating a "Jewish" art music to represent themselves as a united subculture within Russia, incorporated techniques from the style hongrois, the style in which nineteenth-century composers had represented Roms as a different minority "internal other" residing in their own nations. Bartók's early compositions reflect his initial enthusiasm for Rom repertoire and performance technique; but with his later rural miniatures he aimed to represent Hungarian and Romanian rural cultures in an authentic and "pure" manner by rejecting the Rom music that was so popular in Budapest. The style hongrois, developed as a way of depicting Rom music and the ideals of spontaneity and authenticity that formed part of the stereotype commonly associated with Rom culture, was therefore an important precedent that was to be adopted, borrowed from, or explicitly rejected by composers of rural miniatures in the first decades of the twentieth century.

HISTORICAL APPROACHES TO ROM PERFORMANCE

The style hongrois was founded on notions of Rom culture that had origins in anthropology and literature. Many of the tropes that became common in discussions of the subject were first disseminated widely in print with the publication of Jakob Thomasius's *Gründliche historische Nachricht von denen Zigeunern*, based on his 1652 doctoral *Dissertation de Cingaris*.[3] Although written in a scholarly tone, this text incorporated both slander and mythology and concluded that the solution to the problems Roms bring to society was banishment.[4]

Thomasius's theories, however poisonous, became standardized in subsequent writings.

It was in Heinrich Grellmann's *Historischer Versuch über die Zigeuner*, which appeared in 1783 and was soon republished in English, French, and Dutch translations, that the stereotypes associating Roms with the ideal of a natural virtuosity in music and dance became a fixed part of the mythology.[5] Grellmann writes that Roms specialize in musical performance, showing "great proficiency in the art; besides some wind instrument, they have generally a violin: many have attained to so great a perfection on that instrument, as to be employed in the chapels of the nobility, and admired as great masters."[6] He cites the renowned Rom violinist Barna Mihály as an "Orpheus of this kind," in reference to his popular label as the "Hungarian Orpheus," and although he describes some untrained Rom violinists as "scrapers," he reassures his readers that others are so talented that they are invited to play at high society events great distances from their homes.[7] He continues, "Music is the only science in which the Gipsies participate, in any considerable degree; they compose likewise, but it is after the manner of the Eastern people, extempore."[8] Grellmann writes that Rom girls are taught to dance from a young age in a lascivious and indecent manner, "to divert any person who is willing to give them a small gratuity."[9]

Grellmann's depiction of Rom culture became a model for Rom characters throughout Romantic literature.[10] Clemens Brentano and Achim von Arnim, creators of the folk song anthology *Des Knaben Wunderhorn*, were also prolific authors of tales about Roms. Brentano's 1817 *Die mehreren Wehmüller und ungarischen Nationalgesichter*, a text in the genre of the *Zigeunerromantik*, incorporates the stereotype of the passion and virtuosity of Rom music. Brentano's Wehmüller, a painter of mass-produced commercial portraiture, meets the Rom violinist Michaly—a literary version of Barna Mihály—whose art is characterized, in contrast to Wehmüller's, as always unique and authentic. Michaly's beautiful sister Mitidika, who sings and dances, resolves the main conflict of the story, finally compelling Wehmüller to ally with his professional nemesis. The art of the Rom characters serves as the chief motivator of peace between enemies and across political borders.[11]

Elements of the mythology surrounding Roms in Spain appeared in literature as early as 1499 in Fernando de Rojas's *La Celestina*, but it was Miguel de Cervantes Saavedra who, with "La gitanilla" (The Gypsy Girl) from *Novelas ejemplares* (Exemplary Novels, 1610–13), provided the most influential of early depictions of Spanish Rom characters.[12] The racial ideology in Cervantes's text strongly conveyed negative beliefs about Roms but was made ambivalent by the character of the protagonist, the beautiful and good Preciosa who, it is discovered, is in fact not Rom but Spanish, having been kidnapped as a child. "La gitanilla" helped to create the cultural conception of the exotic and alluring

Rom woman, a character type that became a standard subject in literature, drama, and opera.

In the late eighteenth century and through the nineteenth, French authors perpetuated and augmented this Rom mythology. Travel writers offered gripping descriptions of Rom dance as overtly sexual. Pierre Beaumarchais, in a letter of 1764, characterized the fandango as an "obscene dance" whose "charms consist in certain lascivious steps and gestures."[13] Jean-Marie-Jérôme Fleuriot de Langle stated in his travelogue *Voyage de Figaro en Espagne* that the fandango dancer Julia Formalaguez was so seductive she could make a hermit lose his head, swoon with desire, and relinquish his habit and sandals to the devil.[14] French literature of the following century propagated the notion of the combined allure and evil of Rom culture, with Victor Hugo's *Han d'Islande* (1823) and *Notre Dame de Paris* (1831), in which the good-hearted Esmeralda is, like Preciosa, a Spanish woman who had been kidnapped by Roms as a baby.[15] With Prosper Mérimée's *Carmen* (1846), the recurring Preciosa character type was born a Rom, rather than a kidnapped outsider in Rom society, and thus was capable of embodying both the enticement and the transgressions associated with her people.[16] This change in the typical narrative helped to bolster the already prevalent tendency in French culture to conflate Roms and Spaniards in representations of Spain.[17]

The most influential nineteenth-century text on Rom music was Franz Liszt's *Des Bohémiens et de leur musique en Hongrie*, completed with the assistance of his companion Princess Caroline Sayn-Wittgenstein, who acted as ghostwriter for various passages. This document, intended as an introduction to the *Hungarian Rhapsodies* but published separately as a book in 1859 (and later in an English edition, *The Gipsy in Music*), shows the influence of Grellmann's writings. Liszt's book strongly influenced conceptions of Rom music and marked a new direction in the approach to its subject, as it aimed at improving the reputation of Roms by recasting as dignified those characteristics previously depicted as evidence of debasement.[18]

In order to effect this rehabilitation, Liszt employed Hegel's characterization of art—grouped with religion and philosophy—as the most elevated outward evocation of a people's spirit (*Geist*), and his description of the epic as the earliest literary genre and an expression of national character.[19] Opening his treatment of Rom music, Liszt writes, "In the infancy of nations, at a time when they have not yet entirely lost the remembrance of their pastoral habits . . ., their imagination readily feeds . . . on poems; which awaken their taste of heroic emotions."[20] These poems, authentic and spontaneous, "rank among their first necessities and most precious enjoyments; and afford them the satisfaction of creating an ideal representing the grandest of that which they deem to be exceedingly beautiful."[21] Over time, the poems develop organically, until one emerges "from popular instinctive choice" as the subject of a national epic, "which, in point of inspiration, was most identical, and in respect of form, most in agreement with the genius of the nation."[22]

Liszt weaves an account that represents Roms as different from other social groups that develop as a nation and spin national epics out of their native poetry. Roms embody the wildness and freedom of nature and are unattached to any specific geographical location. They are a people "so strange as to resemble no other in anything whatever," who sought on arrival in Europe neither to subjugate the people nor to possess the lands they encountered, nor would they accept subjugation themselves.[23] They "lead what is practically an animal existence," and are united not by law or religion, but "only by gross superstition, vague custom, constant misery and profound abasement."[24] Yet, of utmost importance, Liszt argues, is the fact that Roms are a people who "retain somewhere within its heart a trace of noble quality."[25] Although Rom poems, unlike the epic-forming poetry of other people, "refer to no event, ... what they really do is to repeat sentiments applying to all individuals of the same race—sentiments which go to form their interior type, the physiognomy of their soul, the expression of their entire sentient being."[26] Furthermore, instrumental music, not written or spoken poetry, is their primary source of artistic expression because it is unburdened by the specific meanings of language and provokes the passions "to flow directly from the heart."[27] Liszt proposes, therefore, that because Roms are unlettered and lack the common memory to produce a poetic epic, any Rom epic would properly take the form of instrumental music.[28] He finds himself in the position of undertaking the creation of this musical "Bohemian Epic" in his set of *Hungarian Rhapsodies*.[29]

Liszt depicts Roms as a people who experience extremes of pain and pride, and who express these emotions in instrumental music. He writes that an approximate representation of Rom music by non-Rom musicians requires, first, the imitation of its virtuosity, followed by "the marvels of its colouring, the unexpected keys, the luxuriant ornamentation and the exotic intervals which stupefy our senses."[30] Liszt defines virtuosity as a creative act comparable to composition: "The virtuoso is ... just as much a creator as the writer; for he must virtually possess, in all their brilliancy and flagrant phosphorescence, the written passions to which he has undertaken to give life."[31] Rom virtuosos emphasize their music's rhythmic character and ornament the melodies, "seeming to throw upon each ... the prism of a rainbow or the scintillation of a multi-colored sash."[32] But any accurate reproduction of Rom music is impossible outside of their milieu because their skills, training, and sentiment differ from those of other European musicians and listeners. He writes that the music's "expression of Bohemian sentiment is too manifest and its adaptation of Bohemian type too close for it to be anything else than a pure Bohemian art."[33] Among those characteristics that Liszt argues are most integral to Rom performance are its freedom and lack of rules, being bound only to the musician's immediate feeling;[34] sudden key changes and non-diatonic intervals;[35] a unique scale;[36] rhythmic language;[37] and pervasive ornamentation and appoggiatura.[38] The characteristic that Liszt identifies most strongly with Rom performance is its unmediated and passionate expression of the Rom soul.

Liszt buttresses his arguments about the value of Rom music by contrasting it with the music of another diaspora: he casts Jewish music and musicians in a negative light, presenting them as a foil to elevate Rom music. But while this derogatory approach to the music of European Jews was common, it was not exclusive in contemporary literature. George Eliot, an acquaintance of Liszt who was deeply knowledgeable about music, depicted Jews in her 1876 novel *Daniel Deronda* as an inherently musical people.[39] The Jewish protagonists—principally Mirah Lapidoth, a "poor Jewess" from London's marginal Jewish working-class community who sings Hebrew songs and European repertoire from the past, and Herr Klesmer, an assimilated, cosmopolitan Jewish immigrant pianist who composes and performs a progressive music of the future—far outshine most of their gentile peers and patrons with their organic musical talent.[40] The music these characters perform is depicted as authentic and pure, an unmediated form of expression: Eliot describes Mirah's voice as possessing "that wonderful, searching quality of subdued song in which the melody seems simply an effect of the emotion."[41] Deronda himself, who has been raised as a gentleman but discovers toward the end of the novel that he was born to Jewish parents (in a reversal of the plot twist in early novels about Rom young women such as Preciosa who learn that they were in fact of Spanish birth), also possesses a natural musicality, though he is only an amateur performer. After the revelation of his Jewish identity, he describes himself by analogy to "a cunningly-wrought instrument, never played on, but quivering throughout in uneasy mysterious meanings of its intricate structure that, under the right touch, gives music."[42] In the manner of literary portrayals of Rom musicians, *Daniel Deronda* depicts a diasporic population as possessing an inborn capacity for musical virtuosity and portrays music as the authentic mode of expression for this often misunderstood community.

SARASATE'S "ZIGEUNERWEISEN" AND THE MYTHOLOGIES OF ROM PERFORMANCE

When Liszt addresses the typical structural elements of Rom music, he writes as if he is describing their ethnic folk music. It was not in fact their repertoire, however, as much as the style in which Rom ensembles played that seemed to have been of particular interest to Liszt, Grellmann, and many other writers on Rom culture. European Roms received ambivalent treatment in fiction, anthropology, and musicology throughout the nineteenth century, but their history of musical performance in European cities and the notion of the inherent virtuosity and passionate spontaneity of their playing inspired the development of a body of compositions for the salon and the concert hall, as well as the domestic piano.

Sarasate's "Zigeunerweisen," one of most frequently recorded examples of late nineteenth-century repertoire for accompanied violin in the style hongrois, incorporated numerous characteristics associated with the mythology of Rom culture and music. Sarasate was born in Pamplona, the capital of the region of Navarre, in northern Spain, and while he spent most of his career in Paris from his youthful conservatory studies onward, he retained strong ties to his home city, where he was celebrated as a local hero.[43] A renowned violin virtuoso, Sarasate also composed his own scores, mostly for accompanied violin, publishing numerous works including opera fantasies, arrangements of miniatures by other composers, and pieces based on Spanish folk music. Although many of his compositions, inspired by traditional genres, incorporate fully invented melodies, others use preexisting tunes. His "Caprice Basque," for example, employed phrases from a pair of Basque dances in the genre of the *zortzico*; his violin duet "Navarra" was founded partly on melodies associated with Pamplona's annual *Fiesta de San Fermín*;[44] and "Jota aragonesa" opened with an adaptation of a dance found in the anthology *Repertorio de Jotas*, by Santiago Lapuente.[45]

For the violinists of Sarasate's and the subsequent generation of violinists, Sarasate was widely considered most influential for having achieved an unprecedented degree of virtuosity. The performer and teacher Carl Flesch wrote, "For all who played the violin during the last quarter of the nineteenth century, Pablo de Sarasate . . . was a magic name, and even more: he stood for aesthetic moderation, euphony, and technical perfection."[46] According to Flesch, Sarasate served as a model to other violinists in this regard: "From him, in fact, dates the modern striving after technical precision and reliability, whereas before him a somewhat facile fluency and brilliance were considered the most important thing."[47] Similarly Eugène Ysaÿe is reported to have said, "It is he who taught us to play correctly."[48] Leopold Auer remembered, "I was impressed by the beauty and crystalline purity of his tone."[49] As a technical virtuoso he was credited with promoting the composition of new concertos and with popularizing important contemporary works by composers including Camille Saint-Saëns and Édouard Lalo.[50] Most commentators concurred that Sarasate's legacy was to set new milestones for technical proficiency, provoking other violinists to pursue unprecedented goals by dint of his reputation as well as the physical demands of his compositions, in particular "Zigeunerweisen."

Violinists highly praised Sarasate's compositions for their value in pedagogy and recital programming as well as their apparent authenticity as arrangements of traditional music. Flesch described Sarasate's *Spanish Dances* as simple and correctly written paraphrases of Spanish folk songs and dances of intense melodic charm. There is no "development"; invariably, we only find the bare themes, at times garnished with virtuoso runs, but with no other compositorial additions. . . . Sarasate's simple folk music, infinitely charming in its lack of make-up, bears the same relation to our contemporary arrangements as a fresh, rosy-cheeked peasant girl to a made-up city lady.[51]

Auer, too, perceived Sarasate's dances as accurate representations of Spanish traditional music and, more broadly, of the character of its culture, "warmly colored with the fire and romance of his native land."[52]

Flesch called "Zigeunerweisen" "probably the most popular and most grateful virtuoso piece of all time."[53] Auer was particularly moved by "Zigeuner-weisen," and, arguing that he was well situated to make such a judgment, having composed his own *Hungarian Rhapsody*, he stated that the work is an authentic and accurate depiction of Rom music: "Zigeunerweisen deserves to be called the most brilliant piece of *Hungarian* airs every written. . . . [It] is written abso-lutely in the style and character of the original type of music which one may hear played at its best in the large *cafés* and restaurants of Budapest, the Hungar-ian capital."[54] The charm of Rom music, for Auer, resides in the improvisational quality of the lead violinist's performance, and Sarasate was considered uniquely able to evoke this character in his work:

> Sarasate, in his "Gipsy Airs" adheres absolutely to the style of the *tzigane* originals as he had heard them played; no son of the Hungarian soil could have improved upon him. In the Introduction the melancholy mood dominates; the melody is presented by the violin together with the well nigh uninterrupted cadenzas which imitate those of the zimbalon, thus reflecting the distinctly racial character of the music.[55]

What Flesch and Auer admired in Sarasate's work was what they perceive to be the authenticity of its depiction of Rom performance techniques and its poten-tial to allow classically trained violinists to evoke this style of playing.

Sarasate raised the notion of cultural role-play through musical performance in a letter to the composer Alexander Mackenzie in 1894. Describing Macken-zie's *Pibroch Suite*, written for the violinist on the basis of Scottish traditional music, Sarasate wrote, "I will endeavor on this occasion to show myself as a pure-blooded Scot—minus the costume—and to prove that the national music of your country is one of the most beautiful and poetic that exists in the world: you know that I am fanatic about it."[56] According to Sarasate, the violinist in performance could masquerade as a member of another national or ethnic group. In this spirit, nineteenth-century editions of "Zigeunerweisen" were published with a blurb that directed the performer to approximate the tech-nique and style of the Rom violinist: "It is impossible to express in words the manner of performing this Composition. The interpretation is to be free and the Character of the Zingara (Gipsy) Music improvised as much as the ability of the performer will admit."[57] The violinist is recommended to perform the work with the spontaneity and ineffable expressiveness associated with Rom playing since the writings of Grellmann.

Although the musical material in "Zigeunerweisen" is predominantly original, the piece's most lyrical passage is an invention on a nineteenth-century song by Elemér Szentirmay called "Csak egy szép lány van a világon" (There Is Only One Fair Girl in the World).[58] Born János Németh, Szentirmay composed instrumental music and songs, and during the latter part of his career he primarily wrote operettas for the Hungarian folk theater (*népszínház*). Sarasate published "Zigeunerweisen" without mentioning Szentirmay's authorship of the tune. Upon learning of the work, Szentirmay wrote a letter to Sarasate asking for due credit; Sarasate replied in December 1883 that he had not known of the melody's origins, having learned it from a Rom ensemble. Sarasate praised Szentirmay and promised to remedy the problem, but Szentirmay was disappointed to find that his name continued to be omitted in subsequent reprints and concert programs.[59]

In addition to entering the repertoire of Hungarian Rom bands, many of Szentirmay's songs were available in arrangements for voice and piano accompaniment, published with ornate, calligraphic cover pages. Adaptations of his melodies have been identified in works by Brahms, who appears to have quoted Szentirmay in two of the *Hungarian Dances*,[60] and by Bartók, who included "Utca, utca" (Street, Street) in the first volume of his 1906 collection of Hungarian folk songs, co-authored by Zoltán Kodály.[61]

"Csak egy szép lány" was printed in several arrangements and editions after its initial publication. In 1891, for example, it was included in a multi-volume collection of "Hungarian Melodies" translated into English and provided with accompaniment and introductory and concluding phrases by the composer Francis Korbay. In his introduction to the first volume, Korbay describes these melodies with nationalist fervor as products of the "Hungarian spirit."[62] Most Hungarian folk songs, he writes, "grow like wild flowers, in the country, among the peasantry." These songs, and those by professional composers including Szentirmay, become so widely familiar from repeated performance in Budapest that they often "lose some of their fine petals," despite the "inherent worth" that is proven by the interest shown by listeners outside of Hungary and the composers Liszt, Brahms, and Joachim.

Korbay's extended botanical metaphor reflects a tendency during the late nineteenth century to depict Roms as representative of an idealized free, natural, and unconstrained rural life, despite the fact that by this point many Roms lived in cities and were no longer nomadic.[63] Charles G. Leland, a British philologist, gave voice to the growing conception of Roms as providing a human bond between modern European society and wild, primitive rural nature when he wrote in 1882 that they "are human, but in their lives they are between man as he lives in houses and the bee and bird and fox, and I cannot help believing that those who have no sympathy with them have none for the forest and road and cannot be rightly familiar with the witchery of wood and wold."[64] Artists frequently portrayed bucolic scenes inhabited by Roms, standing for the antithesis of urban bourgeois society, a distinction that, although perhaps seemingly positive in intent, was also at the root of many of the official policies and racist acts against this group always considered to be outside the social mainstream. The covers of many published scores of "Zigeunerweisen" reflected this trend in the visual arts. An 1898 edition of "Zigeunerweisen" published by N. Simrock, for example, features a cover illustration of a violin and tambourine resting on a branch below a floral canopy. This imagery even extended to Sarasate's manuscript copy of the violin part, the first page of which features a hand-drawn border of vines surrounding four systems of the score, the large leaves overlapping the title and first two clef marks.[65]

"Zigeunerweisen" is built of four sections with different tempo markings, *Moderato—Lento—Un poco più lento—Allegro molto vivace*, dividing the work into slow and fast sections that correspond to the *lassú* and *friss* components of the *verbunkos*. The slow portion is in C minor, and in sections 1 and 2, which are largely built of scalar and arpeggiated phrases, Sarasate frequently raises the fourth and seventh scale degrees, creating augmented-second intervals between the third and fourth and sixth and seventh degrees. These two sections are structured largely in the style of fantasias: brief melodic phrases are intercut by held notes under fermatas and fast runs and arpeggios notated as sixty-fourths in smaller type but not measured out to fit precisely into the meter, indicating that they should be played with rhythmic freedom (Example 3.1). Sarasate makes space for the violinist to play in an improvisational style, with frequent changes in dynamic and expressive markings such as *très passioné* (measure 13), *ritenuto espressivo* (measure 17) and *ad libitum* (measure 23), and by composing a simple and flexible accompaniment—much of it is built of half-note tremolos or chords on the beat. He also includes virtuosic techniques such as alternating natural and artificial harmonics and runs combining bowing and left-hand pizzicato (Example 3.2).

The setting of Szentirmay's "Csak egy szép lány" in the third section of the work is song-like and structured in parallel phrases, by contrast with what came before. The lyrics of the original rhapsodize the singer's young beloved, to whom the song is addressed: it begins, "There is only one beautiful girl in the world:/ My dear rose, my dove."[66] Sarasate's arrangement indicates that the violinist should produce a sweet tone using the mute, *avec beaucoup d'expression*, in a dynamic range from pianissimo dropping near the end of the passage to triple-piano under a fermata. Sarasate employs typical rhythmic tropes of the *nóta*, the genre of Szentirmay's song and a common component in the repertoire of Hungarian Rom bands, including the *esztam* accompaniment pattern. The short-long rhythms in the melody here (Example 3.3a) represent a change from

EXAMPLE 3.1: Pablo de Sarasate, "Zigeunerweisen," measures 10–20

EXAMPLE 3.2: Pablo de Sarasate, "Zigeunerweisen," measures 28–32

EXAMPLE 3.3A: Pablo de Sarasate, "Zigeunerweisen," measures 49–56

EXAMPLE 3.3B: Elemér Szentirmay, "Csak egy szép lány," measures 4–11

the first printed piano reduction of Szentirmay's version (Example 3.3b), but it is not necessarily a sign that Sarasate has purposefully altered Szentirmay's composition: if, as Sarasate claimed, he learned the melody from an encounter with Rom performers, those musicians might have diverged from the printed score. Sarasate's arrangement of the melody is followed by another rhythmically free, quasi-improvisational passage of slow trills and runs, rounding out the slow portion of the work on a half note under a fermata.

The fast half of the work follows with a sudden change of tempo and double-forte dynamic marking. This section comprises a succession of six- and eight-bar phrases that allow the violinist to demonstrate facility with a variety of challenging techniques in a brilliant style. These include passages of staccato sixteenth notes in perpetual motion, broad leaps across strings, moving double stops in parallel thirds, swift changes between bowed and left-hand pizzicato and between normal tones and harmonics, and fast runs requiring multiple changes of position up the highest string. The pervasive pattern of rising and falling staccatos in this section can be found in a number of Szentirmay's melodies as well, demonstrating similarity especially around cadences. Examples 3.4a and 3.4b show Sarasate's swirling sixteenth-note runs from the end of the work and a characteristic passage in one of Szentirmay's songs. In the closing measures of "Zigeunerweisen," the violinist is instructed to gain speed, *plus animez*, through the concluding bar, which comes to a crashing halt on two pizzicato chords, a vigorous end to a piece that runs the gamut between melancholy song-like vocality and virtuosic fireworks, in an influential representation of the stereotypical spontaneity and expressive variety of Rom music.

EXAMPLE 3.4A: Pablo de Sarasate, "Zigeunerweisen," measures 162–7

EXAMPLE 3.4B: Elemér Szentirmay, "A költő álma," end of *friss* 1. Kerényi, *Szentirmay Elemér és a magyar népzene*, 29.

RECORDINGS AND ADAPTATIONS OF "ZIGEUNERWEISEN"

During the first half of the twentieth century, "Zigeunerweisen" was recorded by many of the most prominent violinists, including Jascha Heifetz, Mischa Elman, Ruggiero Ricci, Ida Haendel, Miron Polyakin, and Toscha Seidel, in some cases multiple times. The first known recording of "Zigeunerweisen," from 1904, is by Sarasate himself. Sarasate's performance diverges from the printed score in a number of respects, offering a glimpse of the partly improvisatory approach he reportedly adopted in performing his works. In the opening two sections, Sarasate adds slides between pitches, varies the lengths of some notes, and makes other decisions regarding rhythm and pitch that are not prescribed by the sheet music. He plays rapidly in passages printed with small note heads, rushing sufficiently that at times the individual pitches are impossible to make out.

Example 3.6 shows the violin part in measures 10–20, repeated three times, first as printed in the score, and then with annotations describing the interpretations heard in the 1904 disc of Sarasate and a 1919 recording of the work by Heifetz.[67] A legend describing the performance symbols in this annotated score appears in Example 3.5.[68] Sarasate adds a small trill of one note on the final beat of measure 10. He does not hold the fermata in measure 11 particularly long, moving on to the arpeggios with small note heads, which speed up during the opening notes to a rapid tempo that is maintained until the highest pitch. At his entrance in the *lento* section in measure 13, Sarasate slides twice during shifts upward. He also modifies the rhythm here: instead of playing the B-natural

EXAMPLE 3.5:   Legend with analytical symbols

and D as two sixteenth notes on beat four, he displaces them earlier by one sixteenth and holds the D for an eighth note. The bravura run in measure 15 is so fast as to render its pitches nearly indiscernible, and the downbeat on measure 16 sounds arguably like a pick-up to the measure (this is not notated in Example 3.6 because of its ambiguity).

Sarasate slides up to the G at the start of measure 16, then again in the leaps at the start of measures 17 and 19. He slides twice upward to repetitions of pitches in measures 18 and 19. In these cases, as there is no alteration in pitch, there is no need for him to slide or move the left hand at all; the slide requires an unnecessary change in position, as the left hand reaches below the pitch and glides back up. Although it is difficult to hear, perhaps as a result of degradation of the original disc, Sarasate appears to omit the sixteenth-note C and B-natural in beats 2 and 3 of measure 17, playing trilled quarter notes in their place. In measure 19, he lengthens the D that he reaches after a slide on the second note of beat three but then does not follow his own *ritenuto* and *stringendo* markings, instead playing the runs at a relatively steady, rapid pace. Sarasate plays six or seven accented B-naturals under the slur in measure 20, rather than the four that are notated.

Other departures from the score follow along the same lines: Sarasate continues to add slides, change tempo, and sometimes diverge from the printed durations and pitches. The most significant alteration is the omission of section three, the passage based on Szentirmay's song. Before this section, Sarasate and his pianist stop playing briefly and a voice can be heard—it appears likely that this is Sarasate's voice, instructing the pianist to make the cut, but it is impossible to discern the words on the recording.[69] The pianist then plays the first four-and-a-half bars of section three, but when Sarasate fails to enter on the violin part, the pianist stops playing and skips ahead to the *friss* passage of the work, at a fast tempo. It seems likely that Sarasate and his pianist made this cut to guarantee that the opening and closing sections would fit within the duration of the disc.

Other violinists employ and elaborate on many of Sarasate's performance techniques in their renditions of "Zigeunerweisen." In his 1919 recording, Heifetz adheres more closely to Sarasate's printed pitches and expressive marks and follows the older violinist's lead in adding frequent slides. He is also freer with his variations of the rhythms and tempos, however, playing in a dramatic rubato and lengthening and shortening notes, counteracting what listeners are

EXAMPLE 3.6: Transcriptions of Pablo de Sarasate's and Jascha Heifetz's recordings of "Zigeunerweisen," measures 10–20

Original

Sarasate

Heifetz

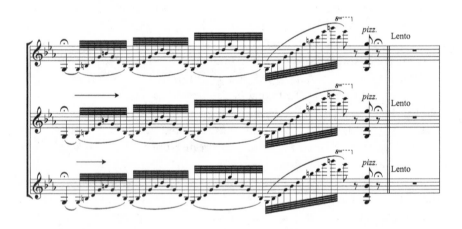

EXAMPLE 3.6: *(continued)*

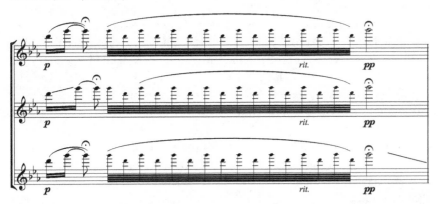

likely to anticipate in order to evoke the qualities of spontaneity and freedom. Heifetz holds the first notes of beats three and four in measure 10 and the downbeats of measures 11 and 14 so that the meter feels disjointed in unexpected moments, heightening the sense that the performance is improvisational, that the violinist is not a transparent conduit conveying the composer's intention but a co-creator, a quality that resonates with Liszt's characterization of the virtuoso. Like Sarasate, Heifetz plays the runs printed in small note heads at a fast tempo, but he employs rubato in many of these passages: he begins more slowly and speeds into the tempo in measure 11, and again speeds into the alternating notes in measure 16, then slowing down into the final note of the bar. Also in the manner of Sarasate's recording, Heifetz alters the rhythm of beat three in measure 13, but he holds the F on beat four longer, pausing briefly before continuing. He also follows Sarasate in playing more than the four prescribed B-naturals in measure 20, with what sound like eight slurred, accented notes.

The work's virtuosity and the opportunity it offers for staging the idealized notion of the authenticity and spontaneity of Rom performance have provoked the work's adoption on other instruments and infusion with other styles. For example, in mid-century the Mexican trumpetist Rafael Méndez played "Zigeunerweisen" in a short pedagogical film designed to demonstrate the trumpet's range of capabilities, with the accompaniment of a brass-heavy dance band off camera, playing an arrangement with jazz chords and blue notes. "Zigeunerweisen" has more recently been recorded and performed by both Zhou Yu and George Gao on the erhu; by the bluegrass trio of Béla Fleck, Edgar Meyer, and Mike Marshall; and by Korean rock electric guitarist Lee Hyun Suk. "Zigeunerweisen" is also performed by Rom bands; for example, the violinist György Lakatos plays "Zigeunerweisen" with an ensemble that highlights the sound of the hammered dulcimer on his 1988 album *Souvenir from Hortobágy*. The broad range of performers who have adopted "Zigeunerweisen" into their repertoire speaks to the appeal of the work's improvisatory style and the opportunity it provides musicians to invoke sonic tropes of expressive authenticity. This eclectic performance history has also meant that the piece, already a hybrid combination of elements from the Western art music tradition and Rom *verbunkos* and *nóta* genres, has undergone further hybridization, being incorporated into styles as diverse as rock, jazz, bluegrass, and traditional Chinese music, and even returning to the Rom tradition on which the original composition was based.

"Zigeunerweisen" and other contemporary works like it, as representations of Hungarian Rom music and performance style and of the authenticity associated with Rom playing in both popular stereotype and scholarly writing, left a lasting mark on the violin repertoire and inspired many subsequent novel interpretations. The rural miniature and the discourse surrounding it grew out of nineteenth-century works in the style hongrois and adopted many of the style's methods for conveying the ideal of direct, expressive authenticity. At the same time, the rural miniature is the product of the reaction against what was sometimes viewed as the superficiality of nineteenth-century depictions of folk music, in this case the music of Rom ensembles.

CHAPTER FOUR

THE RURAL MINIATURE BASED ON

SPANISH FOLK MUSIC

Ceci est donc absolument une collection d'Airs populaires
[d'Espagne]. En outre, ces airs appartiennent à la musique
nationale la moins européene peut-être de tout notre
continent. . . . La musique du zône Sud est fille d'un art
étranger, rêveuse, mélancolique et passionnée plutôt que
dansante.

—P. Lacombe, preface to P. Lacombe and
J. Puig y Absubide, *Echos d'Espagne:*
chansons et danses populaires
(Paris: Durand, Schoenewerk, 1872), iii.

In an article published in two parts in the *Musical Times* in 1919, Leigh Henry writes enthusiastically of the potential of the recent London performance of Manuel de Falla's ballet *The Three-Cornered Hat* to end a long drought in the British reception of the music of Spanish composers and performers. Finally with this work, he explains, "Spanish music attains the first adequate expression of that spirit of mingled fantasy, decorative grace, humour, and mental clarity which has been apparent in Spanish literature from the times of Cervantes and Calderon to the literary and dramatic writers . . . of Spain to-day."[1] This unique Spanish spirit, for Henry, is a product of "the racial elements which go to make up the Spanish nation," resulting from centuries of cultural encounters on the Iberian peninsula, and producing the hybrid mixture of traits locatable in Spanish art.[2] Among the most important of these traits, apparently borne into Spanish culture by the arrival of the Moors from North Africa, was "that liberty of expression so imperatively necessary to all creative development."[3]

In a manner that was rather typical among contemporary descriptions of Spanish folk music, Henry overlooks other cultural agents involved in the development of this repertoire, including most importantly the Gitanos, or Spanish Roms, when he attributes what he sees as its integral rhythmic, ornamental, harmonic, and improvisational characteristics to Moorish and Greek musical and mathematical precedent.[4] Because of Spain's multiple regions, diverse population, and history of complex relationships between its ethnic communities, its traditional music genres demonstrate a diversity of forms and origins. Musicians, critics, and ethnographers of the first half of the twentieth century varied widely in their acknowledgment of the roles of Roms, Jews, Moors, and other groups in the development of traditional music in Spain.

In the work of Spanish composers beginning in the nineteenth century, Henry finds parallels with Spanish folk music. For example, Enrique Granados, the Spanish pianist and composer who studied in Paris and was active in Spain in the late nineteenth and early twentieth centuries, conveys "that dramatic element which finds fluid expression in the melodic flow and poetic themes of the Malaguenas, and in the rhythmic nuances and movements of the popular Spanish dances."[5] For Henry, Spanish composers and performers are most successful when they convey their Spanish identity, or "spirit," in their music, and it is because of this spirit and its foundation in the unique Spanish racial admixture that their work deserves the attention of listeners elsewhere in Europe. The concept that the Spanish "spirit" was a quality inherent in the best contributions of Spanish musicians would adhere for decades. It appealed to many composers and performers as a source of both exotic and national inspiration and pride. At the same time, the notion of what techniques and references evoke Spanish culture was interpreted variably and debated by musicians and commentators inside and outside Spain.

Spanish music in a variety of forms was heard, read about, transcribed, and published across Europe well before Henry wrote his two-part essay. Among the multiple compendia of Spanish folk song transcriptions published outside Spain, *Echos d'Espagne: chansons et danses populaires receuilles et transcrites par P. Lacombe et J. Puig y Absubide*, originally published in France in 1871, assembled thirty-eight songs arranged for piano and voice with texts in French and Spanish and an introductory essay and guide to pronunciation.[6] Visitors to the 1889 Exposition Universelle encountered multiple performances of Spanish musics; Julien Tiersot described these performances in his *Musiques pittoresques: promenades musicales à l'Exposition de 1889*, published in Paris the same year.[7]

In the field of art music, Sarasate had a definitive impact on the development of the so-called Spanish style in his work as a performer at the end of the nineteenth century. He was supportive of many of the prominent composers of the day, collaborating with them by programming their works alongside established canonic repertoire and commissioning new pieces. A number of these composers, in admiration of his playing and in gratitude for the publicity he brought them, dedicated music to him. Inspired by Sarasate's seeming embodiment of popular myths of Spanish identity and culture, several wrote pieces representing Spanish traditional music. Examples include such canonic works as Camille Saint-Saëns's *Introduction and Rondo Capriccioso*, Édouard Lalo's *Symphonie Espagnole*, and Max Bruch's Violin Concerto No. 2.[8]

Sarasate particularly provoked an interest in Spanish traditional music in Saint-Saëns and brought the composer on a trip to Spain to tour the country and perform.[9] Saint-Saëns, who had adapted melodies that he transcribed during his travels in the 1904 *Caprice Andalous* for violin and orchestra, wrote in *Au courant de la vie* of the influence on his violin repertoire of Sarasate's advice and performances of his works around the world.[10] The two maintained a friendly epistolary correspondence, sharing news, praise, and compositions.[11] For his part, Bruch wrote in a letter of 1877 that he was inspired, in writing his Violin Concerto No. 2, by a trip with Sarasate through Germany, during which the violinist described to him the beauties of the Basque landscape and the devastation of Spanish battles, and sang Spanish songs. Bruch imagined mournful marching and funeral music, bells and trumpets, and from this blanket of sounds, he mused, his concerto was conceived.[12]

Around the turn of the century, composers including Granados, Isaac Albéniz, and Manuel de Falla wrote works based on Spanish dance genres, often rural miniatures for solo piano. The popularity of such piano repertoire, combined with the success of Sarasate's earlier showpieces based on Spanish and Rom music, inspired other violinists to arrange many of their works for violin. Performers including the prominent Viennese violinist Fritz Kreisler and the Odessan-born violinist Paweł Kochański adapted works by Albéniz, Granados, and Falla as rural miniatures for violin and piano. Some professional violinists also composed their own works based on Hispanic song and dance genres, such as Kreisler's "La Gitana," Elman's "Tango," and Heifetz's arrangement of Manuel Ponce's "Estrellita." In 1928, the Spanish violinist Manuel Quiroga recorded several rural miniatures of his own, "Danza Española," "Rondalla (Jota)" and "Segunda Guajira." Falla and many of his contemporaries embraced Spain's diversity and the heterogeity of its musical traditions. In his rural miniatures, Falla proudly demonstrated the influence of Rom culture and the flamenco genre of *cante jondo*, or deep song, as well as other Spanish regional music traditions, producing a repertoire that evoked the nation's ethnic and regional diversity in the music's hybridity.

FALLA AND SPANISH FOLK MUSIC RESEARCH

Born in Cádiz in 1876, Falla lived and worked in Paris from 1907 to 1914, during which period he met the premier French and expatriate composers of the time, including Debussy, who had a profound influence on him. Falla had wished to remain in Paris and send for his family to join him but found he had little choice but to return to Madrid with the start of the World War I. After his return, Falla continued to write music on Spanish themes, a technique he had developed during his Parisian years, and he periodically wrote about his visions for art music in Spain.

In his 1917 essay "Nuestra música" (Our Music), Falla described the importance of Spanish folk song as a model for contemporary composition but advised that composers should represent the Spanish musical "spirit" through the imitation of folk music's typical characteristics rather than the quotation of its particular melodies:

> Some consider that one of the means to "nationalize" our music is the strict use of popular material in a melodic way. In a general sense, I am afraid I do not agree, although in particular cases I think that procedure cannot be bettered. In popular song I think the *spirit* is more important than the *letter*. . . . Inspiration, therefore, is to be found directly in the people.[13]

Falla would repeat this admonishment in a later statement: "The essential elements of music, the sources of inspiration are nations and people. I am against music resting on authentic folklore documents; I believe, on the contrary, that one must start from the natural living fountainheads, and use the substance of sonority and rhythm, not their outward appearance."[14]

This disavowal of the quotation of preexisting folk music in favor of the creation of new melodies based on personal resonance with the "spirit" of rural musical cultures was not uncommon among the composers of rural miniatures; the Swiss Jewish composer Ernest Bloch, for example, offered similar descriptions of his method of creating his so-called Jewish works such as the *Baal Shem: Three Pictures of Chassidic Life* (1923). In 1917, the same year Falla published "Nuestra música," Bloch stated, "I believe that those pages of my own in which I am at my best are those in which I am most unmistakably racial, but the racial quality is not only in folk-themes: it is in myself!"; in another article that year, he explained, "I am not an archaeologist."[15] Falla and Bloch, in these statements, were eager to characterize themselves not as mere scientific researchers but as living practitioners of the music traditions they represented in their compositions, able to create new "folk" songs by tapping directly into the cultural spirit.

In spite of such claims, however, Falla in fact borrowed from folk music anthologies in a number of compositions—and in this his method again resembled that of Bloch, who also quoted preexisting tunes he found in books of ethnographic transcriptions more frequently than he acknowledged.[16] Falla owned numerous ethnographic studies and anthologies of Spanish folk music, and occasionally he turned to these to find melodies for his compositions.[17] Folk music research and the publication of anthologies of transcriptions in Spain had begun in earnest in the nineteenth century and often focused on regional traditions.[18] Studies in Falla's library, many of which display his marginal annotations and other signs of use, include texts on music from around the world, such as Louis-Albert Bourgault-Ducoudray's *Trente mélodies populaires de Grèce & d'Orient* (Thirty Popular Melodies of Greece and the Orient, 1897) and Judith Gautier's *Les musiques bizarres à l'Exposition de 1900* (Strange Musics at the Exposition of 1900, 1900–1), in which musicological essays are followed by piano-vocal settings by Louis Benedictus of music from Asia and Africa heard at the 1900 Exposition Universelle. Falla also owned collections of Spanish folk music, including José Hurtado's *100 cantos populares asturianos* (One Hundred Popular Asturian Songs, 1889), the composer José Inzenga's *Ecos de España* (Echos of Spain, 1874), and Felipe Pedrell's *Cancionero musical popular español* (Spanish Popular Music Songbook, 1918–22).[19] Pedrell was a Catalan composer and ethnographer of music whose professional activities corresponded to his nationalist project of creating a Spanish national school of music. In addition to collecting Spanish folk music, he became involved in the curation of Spanish early music, particularly as editor of the works of the sixteenth-century composer Tomás Luis de Victoria.

Although Falla's experience of folk song transcription was mostly limited to his study of anthologies, he also briefly experimented with ethnography himself, creating, around 1903–4, a collection of nine *villancicos* (Christmas carols) that he heard in Cádiz and possibly Madrid. He called this set *Cantares de Nochebuena* (Songs of Christmas Eve) and arranged the songs for voice and guitar, or in the first two cases, voice, *rabel* or *chicharra*, *zambomba*, and guitar.[20] Falla's focused interest in the use of folklore began during his training with Pedrell, who also for a time instructed Albéniz and Granados. Each of these composers maintained that their tutelage under Pedrell influenced their work in crucial ways. Albéniz wrote in a 1902 article in *Las noticias* that he was indebted to Pedrell, whose nationalist operatic trilogy *Los Pirineos* was "the cornerstone of the edifice of *our future lyric nationality*."[21] Granados invited Pedrell to speak twice during the early years of the Granados Academy; the first address, delivered in 1902, was titled "On National Music."[22]

Although Pedrell worked to develop Spanish national opera as a composer, it was his work as a writer and teacher that most significantly influenced the course of composition and musicology in Spain during the late nineteenth and early twentieth centuries. Pedrell promoted a pan-Spanish form of nationalism rather than Catalan regionalism, and his three most prominent students adopted a similar notion of overarching Spanish nationalism in their writings and compositions.[23] In "Nuestra música," Falla credits Pedrell with teaching Spanish composers "what the national way should be—a direct consequence of our popular music."[24]

In his private lessons, public lectures, and essays including "La música del porvenir" (The Music of the Future) and "Por nuestra música" (For Our Music), published in 1891 to accompany the score of *Los Pirineos*, Pedrell promoted both a Wagnerian style of operatic composition and a nationalist technique for creating a specifically Spanish musical idiom based on folk music.[25] Falla owned and annotated a copy of "Por nuestra música," which opens with a starkly nationalist quotation spuriously attributed to the eighteenth-century theorist Padre Antonio Eximeno: "each people should construct its musical system on the basis of its national folk song."[26]

Pedrell later produced edited anthologies of early music by Spanish composers, including the 1894 *Hispaniae Schola Musica Sacra* (Spanish School of Sacred Music) and a 1902 edition of Victoria's liturgical music, as well as collections of Spanish folk music in transcriptions with piano accompaniment—including the *Cancionero musical popular español*, which also includes early Spanish compositions. These influential publications disseminated Pedrell's project of a Spanish national style of composition based on the early music and folk song of Spain. In the 1923 article "Felipe Pedrell" in *La revue musicale*, Falla wrote that Pedrell "led Spanish musicians towards a profoundly national and noble art," by demonstrating that composition in Spain "must find its inspiration on the one hand in the strong and varied Spanish tradition, and on the other in the admirable treasure left to us by our composers of the sixteenth, seventeenth and eighteenth centuries."[27] He praised the *Cancionero* as "a fundamental work" that conveys "the manifold modal and harmonic values that emerge from the rhythmic-melodic substance" of Spanish music and "unfold[s] before our eyes the evolution of popular song, and its technico-musical treatment in our primitive and classical art, that is, between the thirteenth and the eighteenth centuries."[28]

Pedrell's notion of pan-Spanish national identity and Falla's interest in the varied musics of Spain's multiple regions and ethnic groups were consistent with common conceptions of race in late nineteenth- and early twentieth-century Spain. Although in the fifteenth century Spain defined its nation by blood purity laws, leading to the mass expulsions of the Inquisition that were orchestrated to create a "pure" Spanish identity and population, at the turn of the twentieth century the notion of race, or *la raza*, was not strictly exclusive or based on notions of biological identity as it was in many other European contexts. Rather, Spanish race was commonly conceived as a fusion, a product of Spain's ethnically diverse makeup. Many scholars who were engaged in the scientific study of race viewed this in a positive light and approached their field through the investigation of how the cultures of Spain's multiple ethnic groups combined in a unified identity.[29] The anthropological study of Spanish race as fusion also emerged from a desire to foster a sense of Spanish unity in the face of growing regional divisions, economic disparities, and differences in political ideologies that threatened to divide the nation.[30] In France, too, where Falla spent so many influential years early in his career, theorists of race in the nineteenth century had developed a complex understanding of the concept that accommodated multiple meanings. When invoked by French theorists, "*la race*" often signified the culture that served as a link among French citizens, even across a diverse set of cultural and religious identities.³¹ It seems likely that Falla absorbed some of his thinking from the Spanish and perhaps also French theorists of *la raza* and *la race* in developing his own understanding of Spanish culture and its music.

Falla's belief in the significance of adapting folk songs and dances in compositions during the 1910s and early 1920s was evidently heightened by the themes of nationalism and urgency that are found in many of the writings in the anthologies and *cancioneros* to which he likely had access during this time. In *Por nuestra música*, Pedrell invokes folk music's authenticity and describes its essential importance to the composition of new music:

> Folk song, this *voice of the people*, the genuine primitive inspiration of the great anonymous singer, passes through the alembic of contemporary art and turns out to be its quintessence: the modern composer nourishes himself with this quintessence, [and] assimilates it. . . . Folk song provides the accent, the foundation, and modern art provides a conventional symbolism, the wealth of forms that are its heritage. It is the perfect equation of a statement of elevated beauty emanating from the harmonious relation that exists between form and content.³²

In the *Cancionero*, Pedrell designates traditional music as "*música natural*," contrasting it with art music, which he calls "*música artificial*"; *música natural* is, for Pedrell, a product not of learning but of the "gut predisposition and the incentive of passion for singing." In turn, he writes, "the generating cell for this artificial music is the natural music."³³ In a 1921 article on Spanish music folklorists in *La revue musicale*, Pedrell further expounded upon his notion of folk and art music, which in French he called "musique *naturelle*" and "musique *artificielle*." The latter, he writes, is produced out of the former, which "did not demand from the individual, for singing, anything other than a soul in a state of grace or the stimulant of passion."³⁴ He argues that man was given an intuitive understanding of a musique *naturelle* that was "not enslaved to circumstances and rules," and that expresses, like language, human "sorrows, pains, sufferings, joys, with an emotion more or less vehement and in a manner vague or precise."³⁵ This music preserves "the memory of the souls and sentiments that are dissolved through the course of the ages into other sentiments and other souls, transmitting from century to century the pure word of the emotion of an individual who was, and who created the music that others feel as he did."³⁶

Other texts of the late nineteenth and early twentieth centuries—many in Falla's collection—similarly describe Spanish folk music as expressive of the Spanish soul and characterize its study as a matter of urgency. In his 1903 *Cancionero popular de Burgos* (Popular Songbook of Burgos), Federico Olmeda writes of the necessity of studying and collecting folk music, in regionalist and nationalist terms that were typical by this time.³⁷ In the introduction to *Cantos españoles: Colección de aires nacionales y populares* (Spanish Songs: Collection of

National and Popular Airs), Eduardo Ocón emphasizes the importance of accuracy in folk music transcription, trumpeting the realism of his own arrangements. He states that in arranging the songs contained in the anthology, all of which are from Andalusia, he has eschewed the common practice of harmonizing them to recreate the melodies as artistically pleasing and refined. Instead, he explains, he has endeavored to reproduce harmonies with the greatest possible "exactitude and truth," even if at times these harmonies are coarse and crude; and the melodies, he writes, are "always rare and extremely original," and the true expression of Andalusian musicians.[38]

In *100 cantos populares asturianos,* Hurtado writes, similarly, that Asturian popular music should be conserved in its purest form.[39] His description of folk song emphasizes themes of spontaneity and nature, recognizing the value of folk song as a source for artistic creation: "Popular music, a fount of natural beauty, divine emanation, and spontaneous expression, by means of sound, of the character, customs, and inclinations of the natives of a region, offers broad scope to the artist for his studies, and is an inexhaustible source of inspiration."[40] Asturian folk song's expressive modes, according to Hurtado, depict the sweetness of the Asturian character, the simplicity of the region's customs, and the strong will and integrity of its people.

Although Falla's library does not appear to have included a copy of Inzenga's 1888 *Cantos y bailes populares de España* (Popular Songs and Dances of Spain), his use of the author's earlier *Ecos de España* as a creative source for composition indicates the possibility that he was familiar with Inzenga's other writings. *Cantos y bailes populares de España* also characterizes folk music as the authentic expression of the people and warns that unless it is collected immediately, this repertoire will disappear. Inzenga argues that popular music of the lower classes, characterized by primitive simplicity and unique qualities of tonality and rhythm, can be found in all nations around the world.[41] Such music originates in the mundane and repetitive areas of life: "With song . . . the mother lulls to sleep the fruit of her love in the cradle, the farmer lightens his laborious tasks of the field, the prisoner bears his dejected spirit, the sailor finds distraction from his melancholy."[42] Inzenga provides a lengthy quotation of nineteenth-century folklorist Francisco Asenjo Barbieri to describe popular songs as "the most spontaneous and pure language of the sentiment represented by melody, which is the soul, the *sine qua non,* of the art of music."[43]

Inzenga writes that the collection of folk music requires fieldwork in the towns where the music is still performed. This is urgently needed in order "to preserve forever, in the medium of musical notation, these simple and spontaneous manifestations of the sentiment and joy of our people," because the music is in danger of disappearing in the progress of modernity.[44] This sense of urgency is echoed in the 1922 pamphlet that Falla wrote about the flamenco genre of cante jondo, titled *El cante jondo (canto primitivo andaluz):*

> That rare treasure, the pure Andalusian song, not only threatens to disintegrate, but is on the verge of disappearing permanently. . . . What we can usually hear of the Andalusian song is a sad, lamentable shadow of what it was, of what it should be. The dignified, hieratic song of yesterday has degenerated into the ridiculous *flamenquism* of today. In this latter, the essential elements of Andalusian song, those which are its glory, its ancient nobility titles, are adulterated and (horror!) modernized.[45]

Falla laments that cante jondo is imperiled by the encroaching force of urbanization and the increasing popularity of what he considers the inauthentic *café cantante* concerts in which flamenco was commonly performed.

Many ethnographers and musicians who studied Spanish traditional music were concerned with determining the origins of Spanish genres. There is much disagreement to be found among these writings. In his 1928 *La música de la jota aragonesa*, Julián Ribera y Tarragó offered a survey of recent hypotheses about the origins of the dance genre of the *jota*, which is typically associated with the region of Aragon, though variants are performed throughout Spain.[46] Inzenga argued that the *jota* has ancient Greek origins; Tomás Bretón considered it a modern descendant of the *fandango*; Pedrell said it grew by conglomeration of genres and influences, layered atop each other like geological strata; and still others saw it as an offshoot of Northern European airs.[47]

Such a diversity of arguments appears common in writings on Spanish song and dance genres from the period, but one element that is typically agreed upon is the influence on Spanish music of minority and immigrant groups in Spain, including Moors, Roms, Jews, and visitors from other European regions. This does not appear to have interfered in such writings with notions of folk music as the authentic and pure expression of Spain. Whereas contemporary ethnographers of Jewish and Hungarian traditional music often sought what they considered a pure folk song lacking in outside influence, as later chapters show, many Spanish ethnographers argued that the authenticity of Spanish folk music derived from its inherent hybridity. Inzenga, for example, stated that much Spanish music had ancient and foreign origins, because Spain, isolated on the Iberian Peninsula with its mild climate and rich soil, had tempted greedy conquerors throughout its history and absorbed their cultural influences.[48] Thus, he argued, Asturian dance is rooted in the Hebraic choirs of the Bible; the *muñeira gallega* derives from Pyrrhic dances, described in Homer's epics; the Andalusian *polo*, *jácara*, and *caña* originated in part from melancholy Arabic song; music of the Catalonian mountains exhibits vestiges of medieval Provençal music; and the *zortzico vascongado* is an imitation of sacred dances of the Pharaohs and Ptolemies.[49] Inzenga's theories evidently produced some controversy—Ribera wrote that they "can pass for imaginary hypotheses"—but they also provide a useful example of the tendency among turn-of-the-century Spanish writers to characterize the hybrid sources of their traditional music as originating in cultures outside the country's borders.[50]

Falla's writings indicate that he absorbed the influence of a wide range of studies of Spanish folk music. They appear to have inspired his conception of folk music's expressive capacity and creative value as a sign of national and regional character, a product of Spain's history of cultural diversity, and a model for compositional practice. The use of folk music as a resource in composition was, according to Falla at this time, a critical avenue that would aid in the development of a Spanish national musical language. He saw the composition of arrangements of songs and dances, moreover, as a way of salvaging and increasing knowledge of Spanish traditional music.

ANDALUCISMO AND FALLA'S 1922 PAMPHLET ON *CANTE JONDO*

Most of the rural miniatures for accompanied violin based on the traditional music of Spain and Hispanic cultures are arrangements of piano works by Granados, Albéniz, and Falla. Their dominant stylistic idiom, known as *andalucismo*, involves a set of common tropes imitative of Andalusian flamenco. These tropes include the use of Phrygian harmonies; grace notes, turns, runs, and other *fioritura* melodic gestures; percussive rhythms and hemiolas; and harmonic, gestural, and timbral representations of flamenco guitar accompaniments.[51] In spite of the common occurrence of *andalucismo* in rural miniatures, composers during Falla's time developed an ambivalent relationship with it, feeling at some times loyal and at other times hostile to the style. Although many critics in and out of Spain viewed Falla's *andalucismo* as an authentic representation of Spanish culture, others disagreed.[52]

Andalusian flamenco was historically performed in two principal contexts: the first and most common was among groups of men gathered to drink and sing, and the second was among women at carnivalesque fairs where flamenco song and dance provided an opportunity to break free of the behavioral restrictions of daily life.[53] In flamenco, singing is often melismatic, and texts emotionally expressive and accompanied by the guitar. Flamenco cante jondo emerged among Spain's diverse marginal underclasses, and while Roms were central to its development and performance, it was likely also influenced during its early formation by the musical practices of Moors; the rural castes of thieves and bandits; the incipient industrial classes of mine and port workers; and rural peasantry and day workers.[54] In the wake of the Napoleonic Wars, the growing middle classes in Andalusia appropriated flamenco as a nationalist symbol of authentic regional identity, supporting its performance and incorporating it into literature.[55] In the late nineteenth and early twentieth centuries, some scholars began to promote the argument that flamenco developed primarily from the influence of the Gitano population.[56] Antonio Machado y Álvarez (known as Demófilo) wrote essays about flamenco in the 1860s and 1870s, and co-founded societies devoted to folklore research.[57] With the publication of *Colección de cantes flamencos, recogidos y anotados por Demófilo* (Collection of Flamenco Songs, Compiled and Annotated by Demófilo) in 1881, flamenco was reimagined as an authentic musical symbol of the Spanish nation.[58] Demófilo viewed Andalusian Gitanos as unknowingly but potently able to give voice to Spanish national identity in their performances of flamenco because their poverty, suffering, and peripheral role in Spanish society as street musicians afforded them the capacity to express uniquely Spanish emotions.[59]

Members of the Spanish modernist movement at the turn of the century further elevated flamenco to the role of a national symbol: Pablo Picasso, Federico García Lorca, dancer Antonia Mercé (known as La Argentina), and Falla all created an aesthetic hybrid between high and low art forms by integrating flamenco tropes into the "cultivated" genres of painting, literature, dance, and music.[60] Falla expressed empathy toward the Spanish Rom population in his writings and compositions, and in his "Gypsy ballet" *El amor brujo* (Love, the Magician), he offered a view of Rom culture that posed a challenge to common negative conceptions. He invited the Rom singer Pastora Imperio to consult with him on the score and perform in the premiere and even wrote that in composing the work he "tried to live it" as a Rom to learn how to "express the soul of the race."[61] In 1922, Falla produced his pamphlet dedicated to the flamenco genre of cante jondo, which he argued was a product of Andalusia's Moorish and Rom populations.[62] He cited recent research indicating that the Gitanos, a term he used to signify a pure Rom identity, originated in India and arrived in Spain in the fifteenth century. As a result of this geographic trajectory, he argued, the "essential elements of the *cante jondo*" share traits with music of India and "other oriental countries."[63]

Falla's pamphlet on cante jondo was published to coincide with a two-day competition called the *Concurso del cante jondo* that he organized with Lorca in Granada. The competition, held at the Alhambra during Corpus Christi in June of 1922, was open only to non-professional musicians, in reaction against the growing commercialization of flamenco in the popular *café cantante* and *ópera flamenca*. Falla and Lorca viewed these professional contexts for flamenco as deleterious in their effects on the music, resulting in too great a level of polish and uniformity to the music, and in a decline in the authenticity and spontaneity of expression they considered to be inherent qualities of flamenco performance in its traditional contexts.[64]

After the event, Falla continued to promote the genre by working with the recording company Odeón to produce five 78-rpm discs, released in late 1922 and 1923, of cante jondo performances by the singers Manuel Torre and Diego Bermúdez (called *El Tenazas de Morón*), both of whom had been involved in the contest.[65] Falla's decision to focus in particular on cante jondo and his avoidance of the term "flamenco" were in part attempts both to sidestep recent public criticisms of flamenco as cheapening Spanish culture, by intellectuals and critics including Miguel de Unamuno and José Ortego y Gasset, and to draw greater attention to a sub-genre that was perceived to express extremes of passionate and emotional authenticity.[66] Falla and Lorca characterized cante jondo as a historic basis for contemporary flamenco and therefore as a powerful expression of Spanish identity.[67] In Lorca's words, the music was "the soul of our soul."[68]

For Falla, cante jondo was the most authentic of lyric forms of flamenco, an ideal medium for expressing deep-seated emotions. He explained that those tropes that contribute to the emotional ardor of cante jondo and have analogues in the music of "oriental countries" include quarter tones and vocal portamento; the rarity of melodic contours beyond the interval of the sixth; the "repeated, even obsessive, use of one note, frequently accompanied by an upper or by a lower appoggiatura"; the use of ornament "to express states of relaxation or of rapture"; and audience members' shouts of support to the performers.[69] The declamatory repetition of a single note that often disables the sense of meter in cante jondo is evidence to Falla that cante jondo is a pre-linguistic mode for expressing pure emotion.[70]

Falla appears to have developed his conception of cante jondo in reading studies of the history and culture of Andalusia, musicological texts including Pedrell's *Cancionero* and *Emporio científico é histórico de organografía musical antigua española* (Scientific and Historical Treatise on Old Spanish Musical Organography, 1901), and collections of transcriptions of North African and flamenco music.[71] A number of his ideas about Rom music and history derive in part from the anthropologist F. M. Pabanó's *Historia y costumbres de los gitanos* (History and Customs of the Gitanos, 1915), a book illustrated with photographs that presents a study of the origins, customs, language, and physical and moral characteristics of Spanish Roms. In his personal copy of this book, Falla made numerous marginal notes and jotted an index listing his own annotations.[72] Pabanó describes Andalusian songs in idealized and romantic terms: they are simply structured and passed on orally, they are "tender and sentimental," and in their poetry and guitar accompaniment, "every vibration is a passionate kiss, a tear, a sigh."[73] Acknowledging the hybrid cultural influences of the genre, Pabanó writes that cante jondo singers perform music that "recalls the poetic melancholy of the Arab peoples, absorbing those who listen to it in inexplicable ecstasy."[74]

In keeping with nineteenth-century conceptions of sensuality in Rom dance, Pabanó characterizes Gitano flamenco steps by analogy to the movements of the *bayadera*, or Indian temple dancer, and the *odalisca*, the odalisque of the Turkish harem, female professions associated with images of lascivious dancing in the exotic East.[75] Flamenco dances, writes Pabanó, are "not very original or varied, but they express the fire and the joy of life, provoke erotic fervor and burning insolence."[76] Flamenco practice was in fact often deeply enmeshed with the consumption of alcohol and the erotic portrayal of female sexuality in lyrics and dance; but Pabanó's charged language perpetuates an interpretation that is rooted in nineteenth-century exoticizing conceptions of Rom music and dance.[77] Falla provides a less romantic characterization than does Pabanó, and he does not focus on the element of sexuality, but his pamphlet follows Pabanó in arguing that Gitanos originated in India and that cante jondo also exhibits Moorish music elements, and he similarly describes cante jondo as a spontaneous and authentic mode of musical expression.

In his pamphlet on cante jondo, Falla invokes *L'acoustique nouvelle*, a book by Louis Lucas that promoted a compositional method based on supposedly natural consonances. Lucas wrote that the major triad has roots in nature because its pitches occur in the overtone series. He also argued, with reference to folk music traditions from around the world, that composers should progress beyond the tendency to use only major and minor modes and scales in which the semitone is the smallest interval. Drawing on Lucas's theory, Falla states that modality, semitones, and portamento in cante jondo singing are signs of the music's origins in nature, vocal expression, and the sounds made by birds, animals, and the "infinite rumblings of matter."[78] Many sources on Falla's life and works have claimed that the composer's chance encounter with Lucas's book influenced his development of new harmonic methods in his compositions, including the *Siete canciones populares españolas*. Falla's well-worn copy of *L'acoustique nouvelle* and other notated documents in his archive show that he gave much thought to Lucas's ideas.[79] While Falla found the text inspiring, however, his harmonic practice shows limited signs of its influence; the book's importance to Falla's development of harmonic techniques appears to be largely an exaggeration initiated by Falla's early biographers.[80] More influential to Falla's harmonic experiments was his study of anthologies and books about folk music from around the world and, in particular, his knowledge of Andalusian cante jondo.[81]

In order to persuade composers of the value of cante jondo as a source of inspiration, Falla, in his 1920 essay "Claude Debussy et l'Espagne," looked beyond the borders of Spain to Debussy, whom he had come to know during his seven-year residence in Paris and whose influence and importance he acknowledged as providing "the point of departure for the deepest revolution ever in music history."[82] It is Debussy's absorption of cante jondo, writes Falla, that allows him to break ground in the French tradition of musical representations of Spain. Whereas Bizet and his contemporaries composed "à l'espagnole," Debussy, employing cante jondo "in its most authentic form," was able to write "*in Spanish*, or rather, *in Andalusian*."[83] In Falla's characterization in this essay, cante jondo, with its pre-linguistic origins, is the basis of a uniquely Spanish musical language, no matter the national identity of the composer.

RURAL MINIATURES ON SPANISH THEMES
AND THEIR TECHNIQUES

The work of ethnographers of Spanish folk music and the notion that the country's traditional music should provide the basis for a "Spanish" style of art music inspired Spanish composers to write recital works based on Spanish songs and dances using both found and invented melodies. The most widely recorded rural miniature for violin based on a composition by Granados is the arrangement by Fritz Kreisler of "Andaluza," the fifth of Granados's *Twelve Spanish Dances*, also published in its original form as "Playera." Kreisler's edition was printed variably under the titles "Andaluza" and "Spanish Dance in E minor." Granados composed his set in the late 1880s and its components were first published individually and in small groups early in the next decade by Barcelona's Casa Dotesio. The first of Granados's works to become popular internationally, *Twelve Spanish Dances* received praise from composers including César Cui, Saint-Saëns, and Grieg, and prompted Jules Massenet to dub Granados "the Spanish Grieg."[84] Granados appears to have invented the melody of "Andaluza," rather than basing it on a preexisting dance.[85] With its *fioritura* melodic ornamentation and the repetition of grace notes in the accompaniment redolent of guitar tropes, the movement is a clear example of the *andalucismo* style. Kreisler recorded his adaptation around 1916, and in the following two decades it appeared on discs by Heifetz, Yehudi Menuhin, and Jacques Thibaud, who also made recordings of his own arrangement of the sixth dance, the "Jota" or "Rondalla aragonesa," published in 1920 by Carl Fischer as "Danse Espagnole," and of another of Granados's arrangements labeled "Andaluza playera."

Among Albéniz's works, the "Tango" was arranged multiple times, by the violinists Samuel Dushkin, Sam Franko, and Kreisler. This rural miniature derives from the second movement of the 1890 composition *España: Six feuilles d'album*.[86] Other popular versions of Albéniz's music were two miniatures arranged by Kreisler, both titled "Malagueña," one from the third dance in *España*, "Malagueña," and the other from "Rumores de la caleta (Malagueña)" (Murmurs of the Cove), the sixth movement of *Recuerdos de viaje* (Souvenirs of a Journey), composed in 1886–7. Heifetz's 1934 recording of "Sevilla, sevillanas" was based on the third part of Albéniz's 1886 *Suite española no. 1*, and Dushkin's 1928 recording of "Jota Aragonesa" was an adaptation of "Aragón (Fantasía)," part six of the suite, also printed in 1889 as movement one of *Deux morceaux caractéristiques*.

Kochański's collection *Suite populaire espagnole*, based on six of the seven movements of Falla's *Siete canciones populares españolas*, became the most frequently performed violin arrangement of Falla's rural miniatures. Kochański was a violin prodigy who studied during his teens at the Brussels Conservatory and would replace Auer at the St. Petersburg Conservatory in 1913. Kochański and Falla met a few years before this, in 1907, when Juan Carlos Gortázar, the secretary of the Bilbao Philharmonic, organized a performance for the two musicians in Bilbao. Kochański's agent helped to arrange Falla's journey to France later that year.[87] In addition to the *Suite populaire espagnole*, Kochański also arranged a set of three movements based on *El amor brujo*, "Danza del terror" (Dance of terror), "Pantomima" (Pantomime), and "Danza ritual del fuego" (Ritual Fire Dance).[88] Other rural miniatures for violin based on Falla's compositions are Fritz's Kreisler's "Danse espagnole," a setting of music from the first tableau from Act II of Falla's lyric drama *La vida breve* (Life Is Short), and Joseph Szigeti's "Miller's Dance," from Part II of the ballet *El sombrero de tres picos* (The Three-Cornered Hat).

In rural miniatures representing Spanish traditional music, the tropes associated with *andalucismo* appear alongside elements common to other rural miniatures, such as fast runs, ornamentation, melodic lines that resemble vocal writing in their range and contour, and challenging performance devices such as successions of double stops, artificial and natural harmonics, and the alternation between arco and pizzicato techniques (Example 4.1). The sonorities and performance practice of guitar playing were common points of reference for composers inside and outside of Spain creating works based on Spanish traditional music, and in this repertoire of violin arrangements, composers used pizzicato to imitate the two principal methods of playing guitar, *rasgueado* and *punteado*. *Rasgueado* involves strumming chords with downward or upward sweeping motions of the right hand across all or most of the strings; in this technique, chords are usually changed by altering only one pitch at a time, resulting in a pedal point.[89] *Punteado* entails plucking individual notes in succession.

At the opening of Szigeti's arrangement of the "Miller's Dance," the violinist is instructed to play a series of quadruple-stop chords, *molto ritmico e pesante*, with upward and downward arrows indicating the changing directions in which the right hand should strum rapid successions of sixteenth-note and eighth-note triplet chords. The downward arrow dictates a strum away from

EXAMPLE 4.1: Enrique Granados and Jacques Thibaud, "Danse Espagnole," measures 41–4

EXAMPLE 4.2A: Manuel de Falla and Joseph Szigeti, "Miller's Dance," violin part, measures 1–7

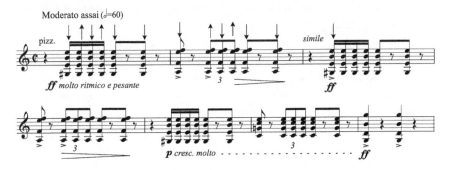

EXAMPLE 4.2B: Manuel de Falla and Paweł Kochański, "Jota," violin part, measures 25–32

EXAMPLE 4.3:   Manuel de Falla and Paweł Kochański, "El paño moruno," violin part, measures 65–74

the body, from the lowest to highest strings, and the upward arrow means a strum towards the body, from highest to lowest (Example 4.2a). Kochański's "Jota" from *Suite populaire espagnole* also imitates *rasgueado* strumming; here, the direction in which the hand strums across the quadruple-stop chords is indicated by the down-bow and up-bow symbols (Example 4.2b). The open E string in all the chords will ring out resonantly beyond the stopped pitches. In four-measure phrases, the chords change only in stepwise motion in one voice, imitating the stasis and pedal point of *rasgueado* guitar.

Rasgueado-style chords and *punteado*-style melodies combine in Thibaud's arrangement of the sixth of Granados's *Twelve Spanish Dances* and in Kochański's arrangement of "El paño moruno" in *Suite populaire espagnole* (Example 4.3). In both, the violinist is instructed to alternate plucking the strings with fingers of the left and right hands. Kochański indicates this with a + and the marking *m.g.*, for *main gauche* (left hand), while Thibaud uses only the + sign over the note to be plucked by the left hand. This method permits the violinist to play pizzicato runs at greater speed, and as a challenging technique to master, it provides the opportunity to show off one's skill.

KOCHAŃSKI'S *SUITE POPULAIRE ESPAGNOLE*

Falla composed *Siete canciones populares españolas* in 1914, on a contract with the publisher Max Eschig, at the end of his seven-year stay in Paris. He had become an important figure in the music of the French capital and an acquaintance of the city's prominent musical figures. He encountered many of these musicians, including Ravel, Stravinsky, and M. D. Calvocoressi, at the meetings of the artists' group *les Apaches*, to whom he was introduced by the Spanish pianist Ricardo Viñes.[90] Falla wrote that his time in Paris provided him the opportunity to flourish as a composer, stating, "without Paris, I would have remained buried in Madrid, submerged and forgotten."[91] Another result of his stay in Paris was his absorption of the French conception of Spain, and especially of Andalusia. Spain was often evoked in French literature as France's peripheral exotic neighbor and in music through the use of tropes of *andalucismo*, particularly after the Expositions Universelles of 1889 and 1900, during which critics widely celebrated what they perceived as the authenticity and accuracy of the representations of Spain and Andalusia.[92]

The composition of songs based on traditional music was not uncommon among French composers in Falla's circle. After the loss of the Franco-German War of 1870, French music publishers and government organizations had begun to sponsor the collection and transcription of French folk songs, or chansons populaires, in the interest of finding a new source of national pride. Performance societies incorporated transcriptions of chansons populaires on programs that also included works from the history of art music by French composers, and many composers turned to the anthologies of chansons populaires for the creation of what was hoped would be a uniquely French idiom of art music.[93] Falla's friend Ravel accepted commissions to transcribe chansons populaires of France and other nations, and he wrote *Cinq mélodies populaires grecques* in 1904–6 and *Chants populaires* in 1910.[94] He was busy composing *Deux mélodies hébraïques* during the same year that Falla began work on *Siete canciones*.[95] The idea to write *Siete canciones* came to Falla after an experiment at harmonizing a Greek folk song at the request of a Greek singing teacher.[96] He was intrigued by the exercise, and when asked by a Málagan singer who had performed in the Opéra Comique premiere of *La vida breve* to identify Spanish folk songs that she could perform in recital in Paris, he agreed to compose a set himself.[97] Falla played in the work's inaugural performance, with the singer Luisa Vela, at a concert honoring Falla and Joaquín Turina at the Madrid Ateneo in January 1915.[98]

The individual movements of *Siete canciones* represent the musical traditions of several Spanish regions, in keeping with Falla's celebration of a brand of nationalism based on Spain's cultural and regional hybridity.[99] Four movements of *Siete canciones*, "El paño moruno," "Seguidilla murciana," "Jota," and "Canción," are modeled after transcriptions in *Ecos de España*, a collection of songs with piano accompaniment; "Asturiana" is based on a song in *100 cantos populares asturianos*; and "Polo" adapts a number in Eduardo Ocón's 1876 *Cantos españoles*.[100] The movement "Nana" incorporates a preexisting lullaby found at the end of *Las flores*, a play by the brothers Serafín and Joaquín Álvarez Quintero.[101]

In *Suite populaire espagnole*, Kochański changed Falla's ordering of the movements and omitted the second, "Seguidilla murciana." Despite their conception as components of a suite, individual movements of Kochański's arrangement were often singled out by violinists for performance alone. "Jota," the fourth song in Falla's *Siete canciones* and the sixth in the version for violin and piano, is the movement heard most commonly on sound recordings; in the 1920s and 1930s it was recorded by Flesch, Quiroga, Thibaud, Kreisler, and Heifetz.

The *jota*, a dance that is usually in the major mode with a harmonic structure built of alternating tonic and dominant harmonies, is traditionally associated with the Spanish region of Aragon, although some ethnographers, including Olmeda in *Cancionero popular de Burgos*, have argued that the genre is in fact diffuse, found throughout the Iberian Peninsula.[102] Falla's movement is based on a category of *jota* most directly linked to Aragon and characterized by alternating fast refrains for solo guitar and slower verses for voice.[103] In spite of its regional point of reference, the movement and its violin arrangement incorporate multiple stylistic traits associated with *andalucismo*. Although scholars tended for decades to assume that Falla's "Jota" is fully invented, seemingly lacking an obvious melodic source, it appears to be based on "La jota arangonesa" on page 81 of Inzenga's *Ecos de España*.[104] Falla employs much of the text in Inzenga's version and retains the opening intervals and general melodic contour of the vocal part. In the words of a young man singing to his beloved, the text describes a true love that must be kept a secret; and though he knows that his beloved's mother does not approve of their affections, he says farewell until tomorrow.

Falla plays with the harmonic tradition of the *jota* by employing mostly tonic and dominant harmonies in the key of E major, but prolonging the first dominant with a B pedal point beginning in the first measure that does not resolve to the tonic key until as late as measure 37.[105] In Falla's song, three passages of solo piano in 3/8 time alternate with two verses and a brief coda for voice in 3/4. This is in keeping with the form of the traditional *jota*, which typically opens with an instrumental introduction and alternates sung passages with instrumental interludes.[106] The piano introduction and first interlude in Falla's work are each built of four eight-measure phrases in which the musical material remains largely the same but the texture changes, interspersing passagework imitative of *punteado* and *rasgueado* figuration (Examples 4.4a and 4.4b). The second interlude begins in the same manner but dies away prematurely with

EXAMPLE 4.4A: Manuel de Falla, "Jota," from *Siete canciones populares españolas*, measures 1–6

EXAMPLE 4.4B: Manuel de Falla, "Jota," from *Siete canciones populares españolas*, measures 17–22

the instructions *perdendosi* and *poco rit.*, and is then cut short by the entrance of the vocal coda, marked *tranquillo*.

The textural evocation of the guitar further demonstrates the inspiration of the source in Inzenga's collection, where the passage on which Falla's instrumental introduction and interludes are based is marked with rolled chords and the words "*imitando la bandurria*" (Example 4.5). Carol Hess has shown that the four-note motif that Falla borrows from Inzenga's transcription, first appearing in "Jota" on the notes E–D-sharp–E–C-sharp–B (measures 1–2), becomes a recurring motif throughout the movement. This gesture dominates the introduction and interludes, reenters in augmented rhythmic form in the bass during the verses (measures 51–4, 55–7, 109–11, and 113–5), and is played in canon between the left and right hands (measure 125–40).[107]

Following standard *jota* tradition, the verse of Falla's song is formed of a quatrain with lines of seven or eight syllables, which are extended in his setting over seven four-bar phrases of music. The melodic fragments and lines of text repeat irregularly and in different ways in both verses (Table 4.1). While most of the phrases stand alone, with the voice entering on beat two—a common trait in *jota* text setting—the fourth and fifth phrases, in both melody and text, combine to form a composite eight-bar phrase with a contour that rises toward the center and falls on the final notes. The final two bars of each verse elide with the opening of the piano interlude. The music's frequent but irregular repetitions create the impression of cyclicality thrown off-kilter. This quality, created on the larger formal level by the alternation of instrumental and vocal passages, and on a lower formal level by the irregular recurrences of musical and

EXAMPLE 4.5:   José Inzenga, "La jota aragonesa," measures 62–5, from *Ecos de España.*
Christoforidis, "Manuel de Falla's *Siete canciones populares españolas*," 224

imitando la bandurria

TABLE 4.1:   Structure of textual and musical phrases in verses of Falla's "Jota"

Verse 1:	
Music:	A-B-A-C-D-B-A
Text:	A-A-B-C-D-A-B
Verse 2:	
Music:	A-B-A-C-D-B-A
Text:	A-A-B-C-D-D-A

textual phrases in the verses, is emphasized at the gestural level by the frequency of hemiolas setting two against three in contrasting voices.

Kochański retains the form of Falla's movement, but in his arrangement the violin plays throughout, imitating both guitar and voice. During the opening and interludes, the violin plays a series of figurations, many of which imitate *punteado* and *rasgueado* guitar with varied pizzicato techniques. In the introduction, the violin first plays a melodic *punteado* line for eight bars, followed by eight bars of *rasgueado*-style chords, every other beat producing a hemiola (Examples 4.6a and 4.6b). This is pursued by eight bars of *arco* playing of the simple melodic line with a drone on the open E string, and finally eight bars of rapid strummed pizzicato (Example 4.2b). In the first interlude, by contrast, after remaining silent in the opening eight-measure phrase (other than the concluding note of the elided ending of the verse), the violinist plays varying arco figures, beginning with *ponticello* sixteenth notes, then the melody in accented octaves, followed by the return of the melody with the open E drone, before a repetition of the strummed pizzicato chords on sixteenth notes in the final phrase. During the second interlude, the piano plays alone much of the time; the violin enters only in the second phrase, with a single line of pizzicato in *punteado* style.

During the verses, the violin imitates the human voice. It performs only in a single-voiced texture, without any multiple stops, and although it plays in different registers in verses one and two, in each it retains a narrow, singable tessitura. Kochański inserts performance markings in the verses that heighten their vocal quality. He adds breath marks before triplet turns (measures 35, 43, 51, 93, 101, and 109), and his markings indicate a delicate, expressive tone: he

EXAMPLE 4.6A: Manuel de Falla and Paweł Kochański, "Jota," from *Suite populaire espagnole*, measures 1–6

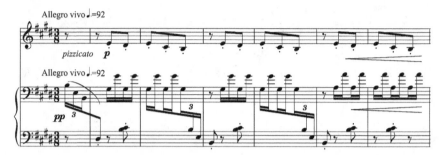

EXAMPLE 4.6B: Manuel de Falla and Paweł Kochański, "Jota," from *Suite populaire espagnole*, measures 9–14

writes *pochissimo più mosso* and *dolce* (measure 45) leading into the melodic climax in the first verse, and adds a fermata over the highest note in the corresponding measure in verse two (measure 106). This character is enhanced by the instructions to play the concluding phrases of each verse in fifth position on a lower string, rather than in the first position on a higher string, a technique creating a richer, throatier timbre (measures 57–60 and 115–20).

RECORDED PERFORMANCES OF "JOTA"

In their recordings of "Jota," Manuel Quiroga (from 1928–9) and Jacques Thibaud (from 1930) suggest the timbres of the guitar and voice in the alternating formal sections, as Kochański dictates in the score. They play briskly and relatively steadily in the introduction and interludes, and dramatically depart from the notation in the verses. But even when they convey metric regularity and retain the basic contours and textures of the score in the introduction and interludes, both violinists flaunt the freedom of their interpretations as they vary the figuration on the printed page, thereby evoking the spontaneity and expressive authenticity popularly associated with the performance of Spanish traditional music.

In Thibaud's rendition of the introduction, he rushes considerably in the bowed passage, during the third of the four eight-measure phrases, and he slightly delays and rushes the sixteenth-note triplets, as though they are fast ornamental turns (measures 17–24). It is unclear in the following eight-measure phrase if Thibaud strums as written in the score; it sounds as though he plays eighth notes rather than sixteenths, but the impaired quality of the recording might make the quieter upward plucking inaudible (measures 25–32). Quiroga maintains the notated patterns in the introduction, but like Thibaud he rushes the third eight-measure phrase, and he decreases speed dramatically at the end of the section. During the first interlude, Thibaud varies the rhythms in measure 72, playing octaves in two pairs of sixteenths and one eighth note, instead of the written pattern of three eighths with a triplet turn in the lower voice of the middle beat. In the fourth phrase of the interlude, he again seems to play strummed eighth notes rather than sixteenths following the first two beats, which sound like divided sixteenths as notated (measures 83–90). Quiroga also changes Kochański's figuration in the interlude: in the second eight-measure phrase, he performs the entire passage pizzicato, though it is marked as bowed, and in the second half of the phrase he omits the triplets, playing eighth notes in a descending pattern (measures 67–74).

Because both Thibaud and Quiroga interpret verse one similarly to verse two, this analysis focuses on verse one. Thibaud rarely plays portamentos in this passage, limiting himself to short, subtle slides between reiterations of the same pitch, C sharp, in measures 38 and 54. His interpretation of this passage departs most markedly from the printed score in its fluctuating tempos and altered rhythms. In particular, where the first bar of each phrase begins with a pair of quarter notes on beats two and three, he shortens the second beat and moves swiftly on to the downbeat of the following measure. He also rushes the sixteenth-note triplets (measures 35, 43, and 51) and thirty-second-note runs (measures 39 and 55), playing them—as he did in the introduction—as fast ornamental finger-work rather than measured notes. In the central eight-measure phrase, he rushes the first two measures, then drags as he approaches the climactic highest note on E, which he holds as though under a fermata, before continuing on in a sweet, poignant timbre as he pushes the tempo through the next two measures (measures 45–51). Finally, he drags the final two measures, as marked, though it sounds as though he does not play on the G string.

Example 4.7a offers a transcription of Quiroga's recording of the first verse for comparison with the violin melody as it is printed in the score, copied in Example 4.7b. The rhythms shown here are approximate; the transcription is merely a visual guide to the ways Quiroga's recording departs from the rhythmic and metric instructions in the score. Unlike Thibaud, Quiroga does play slides frequently during the first verse, between changing and repeated pitches. His rhythmic interpretation is stylized and takes considerable license. In the

EXAMPLE 4.7A: Transcription of Manuel Quiroga's recording, Manuel de Falla and Paweł Kochański, "Jota," from *Suite populaire espagnole* measures 33–58

EXAMPLE 4.7A: *(continued)*

EXAMPLE 4.7B: Manuel de Falla and Paweł Kochański, "Jota," from *Suite populaire espagnole* violin part, measures 33–58

first, third, and seventh phrases, he alters the downbeat rhythms of the second measure, playing what sounds more like dotted rhythms than even pairs of eighth notes (measures 34, 42, and 58). He similarly varies the rhythms as though playing dotted notes at the ends of measures 34 and 38, where he arrives early on the final note and lengthens it, and in the longer two-part phrase, in which the notated successions of quarter notes are played with jaunty syncopation (measures 47–50). He arrives early on the thirty-second run and sixteenth triplet in measures 39 and 51, as well as on the beginning of the sixth phrase (measure 53), and from measure 46, the tempo subtly fluctuates in a lilting rubato. Quiroga also holds the climactic pitch, though more briefly than Thibaud, as though under a fermata (measure 48).

In addition to their interpretive, individual approaches to the verse's rhythms, both violinists and their accompanists significantly alter the meter in the five-beat accompaniment pattern that links the end of one phrase to the start of the next, repeated three times between the first and fourth phrases: they double the tempo, playing quarter notes at the speed of eighth notes (measures 35–7, 39–41, and 43–5). Rather than sounding like a clear change in tempo, however, this technique distorts the sense of meter, disrupting the flow of the verse. It is unpredictable and makes understanding the source of the metric change immediately difficult; and thus this technique contributes to the perception of the spontaneity and capriciousness of the composition and its performances.

The Spanish "spirit" described by Leigh Henry in his article on Falla in the *Musical Times* receives its sonic enactment in these recordings, in which it is enacted by the violinists' departure from the instructions in the printed musical notation. By asserting their own creative authority in their performances, Quiroga and Thibaud signify the performance-centered practice of the oral tradition of folk music. The meter appears clear and familiar as a basic uninterrupted 3/4 time signature in the score, but the way they play with it makes it sound destabilized and even indiscernible where they alter it, embodying the spontaneous expression and sensual intoxication conceived as inherent to folk music performance in Spain, as depicted elsewhere in the popular, artistic, and ethnographic representations of Spanish culture of the late nineteenth and early twentieth centuries.

FIGURE 4.1:   Jacques Thibaud and Émile Vuillermoz, "Malagueña." In *The Art of Violin*. Directed by Bruno Monsaingeon. West Long Branch, NJ: Kultur, 2000.

A 1940 short musical film in which Thibaud performs an arrangement of Albéniz's "Malagueña" (from *España*, Op. 165) shows, through the juxtaposition of Thibaud's playing with an evocative visual track, the way that Thibaud's free rhythmic interpretation of Spanish rural miniatures—his sonic suggestion of this mythic Spanish "spirit"—reflects the genre's function as a sort of aural souvenir miniature of rural and foreign locales. The film was produced by the Compagnie des Grands Artistes Internationaux (CGAI), an organization founded by Thibaud to create short films of musical performances. This short piece and others produced by the CGAI were made under the supervision of Émile Vuillermoz, a French pianist and music critic who studied under Gabriel Fauré at the Conservatoire de Paris, worked as editor of *La révue musicale*, and wrote multiple books about French music of the early twentieth century. Vuillermoz had been a member of *les Apaches*, and he later became interested in film as a critic, curator, and producer. Also a composer, he amassed a small body of works that included a collection of arrangements of folk songs for piano and voice, the 1910 *Chansons populaires françaises et canadiennes* (Popular French and Canadian Songs).

As Thibaud performs the slow central passage of "Malagueña" in the film, he stands alone in concert dress, captured in a close camera shot. The scenario appears to depict Thibaud's internal thoughts, his personal, imaginative perspective as he performs the piece with his eyes closed. The work opens with violin alone, and when the piano enters periodically with brief upward rolled chords, an image of the pianist fades in and out briefly in front of Thibaud's face as though a figment of his thoughts. After several phrases, a montage shows the musical score and an abstract representation of expanding sound waves, followed by images of a southern European landscape, with a grove of palm trees and several shots of an aged white building complex, partially ruined, amid an arid terrain (Figure 4.1).

As the sound waves continue to pulse subtly over the visual track, the film implies that the music—as Thibaud transforms it from score into sound—conjures reveries of a warm, quiet, exotic Spanish vista. A small circle superimposed over the image of the sheet music shows Thibaud's face again as he plays the brief cadenza-like trills at the climax of the piece; as the circle expands, Thibaud's image overtakes the screen, to indicate that his daydream has come to an end. The film thus represents Albéniz's rural miniature as a souvenir that incites Thibaud's imagination to transport him to the distant climes where the folk music on which the work is based originated. With his fantastical film and his recordings, Thibaud realized in sight and sound the spontaneity, freedom, and authenticity so many associated with the Spanish national "spirit," often also considered a hybrid racial "soul," as it was represented in rural miniatures in the first half of the twentieth century.

CHAPTER FIVE

THE RURAL MINIATURE IN THE CULTURE
OF THE JEWISH DIASPORA

> Gleich anderen Völkern sollen wir sagen können: "Unser
> Volkslied vereint uns."
>
> —Susman Kiselgof, "Das jüdische
> Volkslied," in *Jüdische Musik in
> Sowjetrußland: Die 'Jüdische
> Nationale Schule' der zwanziger
> Jahre*, ed. Jascha Nemtsov
> and Ernst Kuhn (Berlin:
> Ernst Kuhn, 2002), 45.

The rural miniature based on Jewish traditional music was developed during the first decade of the twentieth century as a vehicle for the creation of a new style of Jewish national art music. Most of its proponents began their work in Russia and continued to compose rural miniatures in Central Europe, the United States, and Palestine, as they moved throughout the diaspora in the 1920s and 1930s. Many were affiliated with the Society for Jewish Folk Music, which was founded in 1908 at the St. Petersburg Conservatory by ethnographers concerned with developing collections and taxonomies of Jewish traditional music, in collaboration with composers occupied with the task of creating a Jewish art music tradition from the ground up. In a 1924 essay, the Russian musicologist Leonid Sabaneev coined the term "Jewish National School" to describe the original members of the Society.[1] For these artists, who considered themselves united to Jews around the world as members of the diaspora, the rural miniature was considered a principal stage in the creation of a new musical style built on representations of ethnographic research. They intended to begin their task of developing a folk-inspired musical idiom by composing simple arrangements first and later moving onto larger-scale compositions that used folk melodies and techniques in more abstract ways.

The activities of the Society brought into high relief a question that concerned composers involved in the invention of Jewish national art music internationally: how should one define "Jewish music"? This question became the
focus of numerous Jewish figures in the field of music across the diaspora, and
its answers consistently varied from place to place and over time. Abraham Zvi
Idelsohn shifted the focus of his definition of "Jewish" and "Hebrew" music
during different periods of his life and in different geographical and political
contexts. Idelsohn worked prolifically during the early decades of the twentieth
century as a composer, ethnomusicologist, and professor, and his numerous
scholarly works included the ten-volume collection *Hebräisch-orientalischer Melodienschatz* (Thesaurus of Hebrew-Oriental Melodies, 1914–32).[2] In the first
two decades of the twentieth century, Idelsohn became deeply involved in the
Zionist cause, and he had a foundational influence on the music of the Yishuv,
the Jewish settlement in British Mandate Palestine. He lived in Jerusalem from
1907 to 1921, where he composed, taught music, and compiled folk music anthologies and songbooks. Engaged in the ideological project of creating a
"Hebrew music" that would uniquely give expression to the Jewish community of Palestine, he voiced disdain for Eastern European Yiddish song in favor
of music that was "Oriental" and "ancient," rooted in the Middle Eastern landscape and its history and apparently uncorrupted by foreign influence and assimilation.[3] He was the composer of "Hava Nagila," which became one of the
best-known Hebrew "folk songs," but which reveals the hybridity that was in
fact at the heart of the "Hebrew music" project, as it was based on the melody
of a Hasidic *nigun* from Bukovina, Ukraine.[4] When he moved to America later
in life, his position on the definition of Jewish music gradually changed as he
shifted from advocating a Zionist "Hebrew music" to promoting a broader
diasporic program that would accommodate what he perceived as the cultural
and musical needs of American Reform Jews.[5]

In his 1929 text *Jewish Music in Its Historical Development*, a book that demonstrates the diaspora-oriented focus of his American period, Idelsohn contrasts
two compositions based on preexisting traditional Jewish melodies in order to
arrive at an understanding of the term "Jewish music."[6] First, he describes Max
Bruch's *Kol Nidrei* for cello and orchestra, Op. 47, which incorporated a melody
associated with the recitation that opens the Yom Kippur holiday, Kol Nidre,
taught to Bruch by the cantor Jacob Lichtenstein in the early 1860s.[7] Turning
away from his earlier rejection of Eastern European song, Idelsohn offers as a
contrast to Bruch's work the Russian Jewish composer Joel Engel's *Fuftsig
kinder lider far kinderheymen, shuln un familie* (Fifty Children's Songs for the
Child's Home, School, and Family), based on secular Yiddish songs and set for
voice with piano accompaniment.[8]

Idelsohn rejects Bruch's *Kol Nidrei* as an inauthentic adaptation of the
original prayer and affirms Engel's song cycle as an authentic and persuasive

representation of its source music. Bruch's work, in Idelsohn's judgment, is "not a Jewish *Kol-nidré*": by setting the melody at a fast tempo, and incorporating it into a polyphonic texture, the composer "did not express as a background of the tune the *milieu* out of which it sprang, the religious emotions which it voices." But in Idelsohn's explanation, Engel's work, which contained arrangements of folk songs adapted from various children's anthologies and the folk song collection published by the Society for Jewish Folk Music, exemplifies the compositional ideals of the Jewish National School. The composers of this school are "saturated with Jewish sentiments [and] feel the emotions which gave birth to these tunes with the intense and profound sense of artists; and they try to pour these sentiments into artistic moulds." They had studied the history of Jewish traditional music and the social contexts in which it originated. In "Jewish music," Idelsohn concludes, "the vibrations of the Jewish pulse will be reechoed."[9] Elsewhere he writes, "Jewish song achieves its unique qualities through the sentiments and the life of the Jewish people. Its distinguishing characteristics are the result of the spiritual life and struggle of that people."[10] According to Idelsohn, Jewish identity in music was based on more than simply the evocation of Jewish religious ritual; it required the composer to be in touch with a set of emotions shared by dispersed members of the Jewish nation.

Thus Idelsohn locates authenticity in "Jewish music" as emerging from the precise mixture of the objective and the subjective. The objective element consists of composers' use of melodies compiled during ethnographic scholarship as the principal themes of their compositions. The subjective component involves evoking the sentiment of what many authors describe as the Jewish "soul." In his remarks at the Fifth Zionist Congress in Munich in 1901, the philosopher Martin Buber also invoked both the objective element of ethnographic science and the subjective soul when, describing Jews as "a singing and music-loving people," he promoted the aims of ethnographers who collected Jewish liturgical and folk music, and composers who incorporated their findings into new works.[11] Jewish traditional music, he argued, provided "documentation of our soul's history with which [artists] can begin and on which they can build."[12] Sometimes referred to in Yiddish writing as the *folks-neshome* (folk-soul), the Jewish "soul" described in intellectual writings on Jewish culture and music was conceived as both personal and collective, uniting Jewish composers from across the diaspora. The categories of objective and subjective representation were invoked as characteristics of Jewish music in the writings of authors of both Jewish and non-Jewish descent and philo- and anti-Semitic sympathies during the first four decades of the twentieth century.

The melodies that Society members incorporated into their anthologies and their rural miniatures derived from a range of musical genres and practices from

Jewish tradition. These include Torah cantillation; prayer chant, called *nusach*,[13] and para-liturgical song; Hasidic *nigun*; instrumental wedding dances performed by klezmer ensembles; secular children's songs and folk songs of daily life; and songs composed for the Yiddish theater.[14] As they arranged traditional music in a way that would appear accurate both to the source music heard during eth-nographic fieldwork and to the expressive qualities of the mythologized Jewish soul, composers modified the chants, songs, and dances they worked with, sometimes inventing entirely new melodies. They added harmonic accompani-ment and virtuosic passages for the violin, expanded musical forms, and made other significant alterations in adapting music that originated in the synagogue and the home for the classical concert hall. The rural miniatures that emerged from this movement embodied a pair of dichotomous functions: like souvenir miniatures, they attempted to bring cosmopolitan listeners into contact with the traditions of Jewish communities in segregated urban areas and rural small towns, while at the same time they emphasized the difference and distance of these traditions.

JEWISH ETHNOGRAPHY AND THE SOCIETY FOR JEWISH FOLK MUSIC

At the start of the twentieth century in Russia, the concept of race operated as a central tenet in the construction of Jewish difference. Under the late imperial government, race (*rasa*), a construction that had gained currency later in Russia than in Central and Western Europe, came to be understood in two senses that sometimes intersected: it could signify the divisions of population groups on the basis of a systematic notion of skin color, or it could be considered in rela-tion to stereotypes of other physical traits and ethnicity.[15] Russians saw the empire as defined by its diversity and viewed this diversity as manifest in the distinct racial attributes of different population groups. Thus anthropologist Aleksei Arsen'evich Ivanovskii wrote in 1902, "The ethnic composition of Russia's population is distinguished by an incredible physical as well as cultural diversity, which we do not find in any Western European country. . . . All the ethnic groups and all the tribes develop their own particular racial characteris-tics."[16] It was according to the second of the two components of the Russian conception of race that Jews were generally viewed as different from other groups, distinct in their physical characteristics, language, religion, and cultural traditions, and thus "outsiders" within Russia.[17]

Anthropologists generally remarked on the difficulty of defining iron-clad divisions between Russia's populations, but many considered Jews the excep-tion to this rule, with enough unique characteristics to be considered members of a fully differentiated race;[18] Ivanovskii wrote that Jews were "a complete and an entirely isolated anthropological group that is not adjoined to any other group."[19] Among Russians working in fields such as anthropology and medicine in which race was typically studied as a science in Western Europe, most scholars remained skeptical of the notion of race as biologically determined, but race was nonetheless invoked increasingly during this time in scientific and political publications.[20] Also by the early twentieth century, anti-Semitic racism and stereotype had become widespread, especially with the rise of right-wing publications and political groups after the Revolution of 1905.[21]

It was partly as a result of these developments in racial consciousness in turn-of-the-century Russia that many Jews also came to view themselves as a distinct nation within the larger Russian nation. In the Jewish communities of Russia, a number of Jewish nationalist movements were formed during the late nineteenth and early twentieth centuries, at the same time as the development of nationalist movements in many European countries. Despite the ideological differences among the various Jewish nationalist groups in Europe during this era, they typically conformed to Anthony D. Smith's definition of nationalism as "an ideological movement for attaining and maintaining autonomy, unity, and identity for a population which some of its members deem to constitute an actual or potential 'nation.'"[22] Whether or not they supported the foundation of a Jewish state, these movements shared the aims of achieving Jewish cultural and sometimes political autonomy from the mainstream, often anti-Semitic, societies in which they lived; of creating unity among the Jews based on shared cultural, linguistic, religious, and political pursuits; and of promoting a collective sense of Jewish identity across a geographical area that transcends political and linguistic borders, based on common roots and traditions.[23] Members of the Society for Jewish Folk Music viewed music as a fundamental tool in the attempt both to help unify Jews within Russia and to create a sense of brotherhood with Jews elsewhere.

The Revolution served as a turning point in the history of Jewish culture in Russia. Until then, the tsarist regime had imposed severe limitations on Jewish life, meaning that Jewish cultural societies, literary works, and periodicals were relatively few and subject to strict oversight and censorship. With revolution, however, came Tsar Nicholas II's October 17 Manifesto, offering freedom of speech and assembly and introducing an elected parliament, the Duma.[24] The tsar's concessions allowed Jews to establish a multitude of new journals, professional and cultural societies, and political parties. One organization established after the Revolution was the Jewish Historic-Ethnographic Society, founded in 1908 and based on the Historic-Ethnographic Commission, which had been formed in 1892 as a part of the only certified Russian Jewish cultural institution of the time, the Society for the Dissemination of Enlightenment. With the creation of the Jewish Historic-Ethnographic Society, the movement of Jewish ethnography reached full throttle. Its aims, as described by its co-founder, the writer and activist Simon Dubnow, were to collect and assemble historical and ethnographic documents, to found a central archive and museum of Jewish history and ethnography, and to disseminate findings through lectures, essays, and publications.[25]

Ethnographers had already begun to compile and publish collections of Jewish folk songs at the end of the nineteenth century. The Protestant theologian Gustaf Hermann Dalman published one of the earliest anthologies of Yiddish folk music, with texts in German translation, in his 1888 *Jüdischdeutsche Volkslieder aus Galizien und Russland* (Jewish-German Folksongs from Galicia and Russia).[26] Engel kept a detailed notebook of folklore and music during the 1890s, and Saul M. Ginzburg and Pesach S. Marek collected songs in Yiddish during the century's final years, publishing their texts in the 1901 anthology *Yiddish Folksongs in Russia*. Along with Engel at the forefront of the new post-Revolution Jewish ethnographic movement were Shlomo An-sky and Susman Kiselgof, who were pioneering field researchers: An-sky traveled on numerous expeditions to collect folklore of various kinds, while Kiselgof specialized in the collection of ethnic musical artifacts, visiting communities including the Habad Hasidim in Lubavichi, in the Mogilev province, in 1907.[27]

In a 1909 letter to Chaim Zhitlovsky, the prominent Yiddishist and diaspora nationalist, An-sky described his research plans as critical to the survival of Jewish culture:

> If we manage to make our culture live, we will live, but if we do not manage it, we will be tormented to death. No surgeon will be able to sew onto us an alien head and an alien heart. . . . Now I have a project . . . that the Jewish Historic-Ethnographic Society send me . . . to collect Jewish folksongs, proverbs, folk tales, sayings, in short, folk art. If it works out, I would gladly occupy the rest of my life with it.[28]

As his comment demonstrates, during this early period of renewed freedom for Russian Jews, An-sky felt strongly that by collecting and studying Jewish folklore and music before what he feared to be the culture's imminent disappearance, he would be able to rehabilitate endangered traditions, to invigorate Russian Jewish culture with renewed strength, and to resuscitate the Jewish "head," or intellect, and "heart," the emotional and spiritual center of being—the *neshome*.

In 1912 the Jewish Historic-Ethnographic Society provided funding for An-sky, Kiselgof, Engel, and the photographer Solomon Yudovin to collect folklore including Hasidic melodies and Yiddish songs and dances from small towns in the provinces of Kiev and Volyn.[29] During this trip, the "Jewish Ethnographic Expedition in the Name of Baron Horace Guenzburg," An-sky transcribed Hasidic stories, Engel and Kiselgof used a wax cylinder phonograph to produce sound recordings of Jewish folk music genres, and Yudovin documented visual ornamentations and designs he found in the towns they visited.[30] An-sky enlisted the help of composer-ethnographers Lazare Saminsky and Hirsch Kopït to transcribe melodies from the more than 500 wax cylinder phonograph recordings compiled by his team between 1912 and 1914. An-sky's ambitious goal, which would remain unrealized, was to complete what he called his "Jewish Ethnographic Program" with the publication of these transcriptions as part of a forty-volume anthology of data compiled during the expedition.[31]

These ethnographers believed that Jewish folklore and folk music were crucial artifacts of Jewish cultural and social history because they expressed the collective Jewish soul, which was described in a 1912 editorial in the periodical *Di yidishe velt* (The Jewish World) as "the folk-soul, the deepest and purest source of culture."[32] In the introduction to *Yiddish Folksongs in Russia*, Ginzburg and Marek acknowledge a debt to Johann Gottfried Herder's writings on folk music as inspiring their work. They adopt Herder's explanation that, in their paraphrase, folk music reveals "the psyche of a people, . . . the opinions, memories, hopes of this folk or another, the everyday needs, and the attitude to surrounding phenomena."[33] Ethnographer Yehuda Leyb Cahan, in his essay "The Yiddish Folksong," describes the value of folk music in similar terms:

> A genuine folksong . . . is created from the folk body, and therefore it also expresses its general character in a natural, not artificial form, and it reflects the most hidden corners of the collective folk-soul [*folks-neshome*]. A genuine folksong cannot be read, recited or declaimed; it must only be sung, because it has coalesced with the melody, like a body and soul, each one of which cannot exist without the other.[34]

Kiselgof emphasized the importance of folk music in Jewish culture, writing in the introduction to his *Lider-zamelbukh far der yidishe shul un familie* (Collection of Songs for the Jewish School and Family) that because Jewish folk song reflects a variety of moments in the life of the Jewish people, it is a crucial tool in educating Jewish children about their cultural legacy. He explains, "All this plants a love for the folk in a child's heart."[35]

It was in parallel with the founding of the Historic-Ethnographic Society, that the group of composers and ethnographers established the Society for Jewish Folk Music at the St. Petersburg Conservatory, an institution that had been formed by Anton Rubinstein in 1862 and was rare among higher educational institutions in its admission of Jewish students.[36] On April 3, 1908, composer Solomon Rosowsky, pianist Leonid Nisvitsky, and singer Joseph Tomars visited their local official, General Drachevski, hoping to register the Society for Jewish Music. The general could not be convinced that such a genre as Jewish music existed; recalling, however, that he once heard a Jewish folk song played at a wedding he had attended in Odessa years earlier, he allowed the musicians to found instead a Society for Jewish Folk Music.[37] The Society was founded on an ideology formulated by Engel and dubbed by Rosowsky the "Engel Doctrine" that held that the survival and renewal of Jewish culture depended on the invention of a new style of Jewish art music based on the ethnography of folk songs and dances.[38] Inspired by the doctrine, the founders of the Society envisioned this new Jewish art music as combining contemporary compositional techniques with the formal, harmonic, and melodic characteristics of Jewish traditional music. Saminsky, who became an early member of the Society, would describe his belief in the importance of this compositional style in an article published St. Petersburg in 1914, as follows: "Only through a return to its pure old font can Hebrew composition add to universal art something of indisputable worth. Only thus, a newly directed craft, a bearer of yet unknown melodic vein and harmony may emerge."[39]

The Society for Jewish Folk Music counted among its membership Joseph Achron, Mikhail Gnesin, Kopït, Kiselgof, Alexander Krein, Pesach Lvov, Moses Milner, Saminsky, Ephraim Shklyar, Leo Zeitlen, and Alexander Zhitomirsky. An-sky was elected a member of the executive board of the Society in 1912.[40] In composing settings of folk music, these musicians often appropriated melodies that they had found in the collections assembled by Kopït, Kiselgof, and other ethnographers, or that they recalled from personal experience or had taken as dictations during their own fieldwork. By the middle of the 1910s, the Society had hundreds of members and had established branches in other Russian cities. It promoted compositions on Jewish themes following the "Engel Doctrine" by sponsoring concerts that featured rural miniatures, publishing scores, and organizing public lectures on Jewish traditional music, such as An-sky's 1911 educational lecture at the St. Petersburg Conservatory about the spirituality and emotional authenticity of folk music.[41] In his article "Notits vegn yidisher muzik" (Essay on Jewish Music), Achron celebrated the accomplishments of the Society, beginning with a nod to the importance of Engel's research. He boasted of the commitment of the Society members, the breadth of their composition in various genres, and their influence on Jewish musicians around the world, including Ernest Bloch, Darius Milhaud, and Mario Castelnuovo-Tedesco. Achron also explained the influence on contemporary Jewish composers' craft of both ancient religious tropes—the melodies employed in the chanting of the Torah—and the more modern Yiddish folk songs and Hasidic works.[42]

The rural miniature became a crucial vehicle for composers and performers who aimed to carry out the "Engel Doctrine," because it merged the representation of musical artifacts often collected in ethnographic research with the invocation of an idealized collective Jewish soul. The genre's capacity to convey nationalist ideology was based on the assumption that it represented a homogeneous Jewish folk music tradition, and thus the genre attained authority as a symbol of the ideal of a timeless coherence of dispersed Jewish populations. A one-page flyer published by the Society in 1909 to advertise the publication of their first edition of folk music transcriptions demonstrates the role of diaspora nationalism in motivating members of the Society to carry out the "Engel Doctrine" by combining the fields of ethnography and art music composition:

> From the Administrators of the Society for Jewish Folk Music:
>
> During the time when, amongst the Jewish people, a national consciousness is awakening that expresses itself in a great interest in all that is done in the domain of Jewish culture, Jewish art and, above all, Jewish music cannot, of course, remain unnoticed. The Jewish folksong, which sharply mirrors in itself the voices and experiences, the sorrows and joys of the Jewish folk, must be studied in the most serious manner.
>
> The Society for Jewish Folk Music, which takes as its goal contributing to the development of Jewish folk music, has from the beginning of its activity undertaken the collection of folk themes, and the work of arranging them artistically.
>
> Now the organization has published the first series of folk songs.
>
> Persuaded that they thus satisfied an essential life requirement, the Society did not stop for any difficulties and disturbances.
>
> The administrators of the Society for Jewish Folk Music call on everyone to whom the interest of Jewry is dear, to participate with all possible effort—to disseminate the songs that the Society has published. At Jewish musical evenings, in Jewish schools, in the family—Jewish folk songs should be heard everywhere, and everywhere take their appropriate place.
>
> The success of the ongoing activity of the Society in the same direction now turns only on the favorable response that the first edition receives.[43]

The Society for Jewish Folk Music adhered to the goals stated in this advertisement and thrived for just more than a decade.

Ethnographic research into Jewish folk music continued throughout Eastern and Central Europe during this era, resulting in the publication of Cahan's *Yidishe folkslider mit melodyes* (Jewish Folksongs with Melodies, 1912), Alexander Eliasberg's *Ostjüdische Volkslieder* (Eastern Jewish Folksongs, 1918),[44] Fritz Mordechai Kaufmann's *Die schönsten Lieder der Ostjuden: Siebenundvierzig ausgewählte Volkslieder* (The Most Beautiful Songs of the Eastern Jews: Forty-seven Selected Folksongs, 1920), and Moshe Beregovski's *Jewish Folk Music* (1934). The artistic influence of Jewish ethnography was to extend into many areas of the arts. For example, when An-sky wrote his play *The Dybbuk*, he described it in a letter to Zhitlovsky as "a *realistic* drama," innovative in combining ethnography and narrative storytelling.[45] He collaborated with Engel, who composed incidental music for the play in time for its Hebrew performance in 1922 by the Habima Theater.[46] An-sky claimed to be inspired in writing his play by the Hasidic song "Mipney ma?" that was popular in the Vitebsk region in which An-sky was born; this melody also infused Engel's score and the subsequent orchestral suite.[47] When *The Dybbuk* was published in New York in 1926, the script's preface featured a transcription of "Mipney ma?" and an explanation of Hasidism by Zhitlowsky.[48]

Revolution returned to Russia in 1917 with the overthrow of Nicholas II and the rise of the Bolsheviks, creating an unstable political situation that brought difficulty for the Jews in St. Petersburg, and by 1922, poverty, hunger, and illness hindered artists from continuing to participate in the Society. As a result, the Society and many of its subsidiary organizations could no longer afford to continue operating.[49] A new Society for Jewish Music was active in Moscow from 1923 to 1931, while others were founded in Poland and Vienna. Many of the members of the St. Petersburg Society emigrated from Russia during this time. Achron, Gnesin, and Engel moved to Berlin, a common destination to which Russian Jewish artists went temporarily before traveling on to Western Europe, Palestine, and the United States.[50] In Berlin, these composers ran publishing houses devoted to the dissemination of the works of former members of the Society and other Jewish composers. The first to be established, Jibneh, was directed by Achron and Gnesin, while the second, Juwal, was headed by Engel. Unfortunately, these companies did not work well together. They scheduled concerts that competed for a limited audience, and Engel spent the majority of his house's funds on reprinting the early works of Society members—and in particular his own pieces—rather than fostering new talent and instigating fresh compositional activity. Both houses were forced to fold within a few short years in the face of financial crisis.[51] Despite their troubled, brief histories, however, these publishing houses, in addition to the Society's earlier printing department, were crucial in the dissemination of rural miniatures during the first decades of the twentieth century.

The former members of the Society for Jewish Folk Music continued to move away from Central and Eastern Europe, emigrating widely throughout the diaspora. Achron went to Palestine briefly in 1924 before continuing on to the United States. Engel, who also settled in Palestine that year, remained there until his death in 1927. In the United States, Society members including Achron, Rosowsky, and Saminsky kept alive the hopes of the Society in essays, compositions, and concert programs. The three joined with other immigrants in New York in 1931 to found the American-Palestine Institute of Musical Sciences, known by its Hebrew acronym MAILAMM, to continue to promote research and composition in the United States and Palestine, and to provide support to Jewish musicians in search of refuge in New York (when Achron later moved to Los Angeles, he founded a new West Coast arm of the organization).[52] MAILAMM, which was to remain active until 1939, also established ties with a short-lived group in Palestine called the World Centre for Jewish Music in Palestine, which itself maintained a connection with the Jüdische Kulturbund in Berlin.[53] But despite these efforts, the cohesion and idealism of many of these musicians faded with time and distance, as the ethnography of Eastern European Jewish music became increasingly difficult. The dispersal of the Jewish National School around the globe meant that their once unified effort to save and promote Russian Jewish culture by bringing the study of ethnography to bear on Jewish art music style in urban St. Petersburg became increasingly attenuated.

SONGS WITHOUT WORDS: THE ICONOGRAPHY
OF THE VIOLIN IN JEWISH CULTURE

Jewish folk music was often associated in the writings of composers, performers, critics, and the members of the Society for Jewish Folk Music with metaphors of the "voice," "lips," and "singing." In describing traditional music as an authentic voice emanating from the collective soul of the Jewish nation, commentators relied on a traditional metaphysical understanding of the voice as a conduit conveying interior sentiments to the outside world. Thus Idelsohn stated, "Jewish music is the song of Judaism through the lips of the Jew,"[54] and Kiselgof described Hasidic instrumental music as "vocal music without words," in order to express the mystical spirituality he heard in this music as transcending language, while grounded in the human voice.[55] The metaphor of a song of Judaism made its way during the first half of the twentieth century into the discourse surrounding art music. Saminsky asserted in his 1934 *Music of the Ghetto and the Bible*, "The emotional tonus of the Jewish composer is marked by his tragic position, one best defined as *singing the song of Zion in exile*."[56] For Saminsky, the wordless timbres of instrumental music could express, in the manner of a voice, the thoughts of the collective Jewish soul. It became commonplace to describe the message conveyed by this voice as tragic and melancholy, as a result of the Jewish conditions of exile and subjugation.

The association in rural miniatures of the Jewish "voice" with the sounds produced by stringed instruments no doubt derived in part from the common invocation of singing as a metaphor for soaring violin virtuosity in European culture from at least the late eighteenth century. A number of treatises about violin performance from around 1800 recommend that the violinist use his instrument to imitate singing. In his *Nouvelle méthode théorique et pratique pour le violon*, for example, Giuseppe Maria Cambini wrote, "The bow is the soul, the thought, the spirit of the violin ... only the bow makes it speak and sing, therefore it is more difficult to control than the voice itself. All its inflections come from the hand that handles it; and as good as the violin may be, this hand can extract as it pleases the tones of Orpheus or the voice of a coachman."[57] François-Joseph Fétis described Paganini metaphorically as "a skillful singer"; and Paganini characterized Louis Spohr as "the premier and most outstanding singer on the violin."[58]

The violin was also prevalent in klezmer, the tradition of professional instrumental ensembles that played at weddings, funerals, and other Jewish celebrations and life cycle events. The itinerant klezmer fiddler was a common fixture in Eastern European Jewish communities, where many musicians made their living by working as itinerant wedding performers. The field of klezmer was generally male and hereditary, and *klezmorim* (the plural form of klezmer, a word that refers to both the music and the musician who plays it), were often distrusted, considered outside the social mainstream and capable of stealing people's belongings and seducing their daughters.[59] Klezmorim even developed their own argot, *klezmer-loshn*, which shared linguistic traits with the *ganovim-loshn*, the argot of thieves.[60] In his autobiographical story *Funem yarid* (From the Fair), Sholem Aleichem explains that in the 1870s, "playing violin was one of the necessary skills... .Thus, almost all the most respectable young men in town learned to play."[61] The long-established metaphor of the vocality of the stringed instrument, coupled with the violin's prevalence in traditional Jewish ensembles, contributed to the proliferation starting in the late nineteenth century of the violin as an icon in literature, visual arts, and music representing Eastern European Jewish life.

The violin and its performer were the subject of works of Yiddish theater and operetta in Europe and New York including I. L. Peretz's *Vos in fidele shtekt* (Involving the Violin) and *Yosl der fidler* (Yosl the Fiddler), Joseph Lateiner and Sigmund Mogulescu's *Dos fidele* (The Violin) and *Dovids fidele* (David's Violin), and Boris Thomashefsky and Joseph Rumshinsky's *Tzebrokhene fidl* (Broken Violin), as well as in a number of Yiddish short stories, such as Sholem Aleichem's "Afn fidl" (On the Violin) and Peretz's "A Musician's Death."[62] The central character in Sholem Aleichem's novel *Stempenyu* was a klezmer violinist; the story inspired Achron's *Stempenyu Suite* for accompanied violin based on his incidental music to a theatrical version of the tale. The poignant vocalic timbres produced by Jewish violinists were also described in the memoirs of Yekhezkel Kotik and Moissaye Olgin, who were brought up in the *shtetl*, the predominantly Jewish Eastern-European small town.[63]

The violin also featured in Yiddish-language film musicals of the 1930s: in *Yidl mitn fidl* (Yidl with a Fiddle, 1936), the eponymous character Yidl, played by Molly Picon, is a violinist in a Polish Jewish small town who becomes successful in America;[64] and in *Mamele* (Little Mother, 1938), Picon's character falls in love with a concert violinist. The lyrics to a great number of Yiddish popular songs begin with an invitation to an unnamed fiddler to perform: in Abraham Ellstein's "Shpil Klezmer Shpil," for example, the singer requests, "Play with strength, so that smoke comes from your fiddle./ Play and give my soul a caress, *oy/ vey iz mir, klezmer*, when your fiddle speaks."[65] Ellstein's "Der Nayer Sher" opens with the entreaty, "Hey you, klezmer, pick up your fiddle,/ Play your new song,/ And we'll dance to the new *sher*."[66] Another Yiddish song begins, "Play for me, fiddle, play me a *doyna*" and later continues, "In its playing are our feelings,/ Like a little song on a fiddle."[67] In an example from children's literature, the Russian-Jewish poet Leib Kvitko's 1928 pamphlet *Dos fidl* tells a story in Yiddish verse, illustrated with color woodcuts, about a young boy who makes a fiddle from a tree and plays so beautifully that his music summons all of the animals from the rural family farm and the adjacent woods to be still and listen.[68] In visual culture, the klezmer violinist was a recurrent symbol in the paintings of Marc Chagall, as well as in Eastern and Central European postcards representing Jewish life.[69]

Depictions of this iconic klezmer fiddler throughout the arts incorporated both the nostalgic idealization of life in the shtetl and the acknowledgment of its hardships and sadness. The shtetl, as it appeared in artistic representation and even in some ethnographic writing, was almost entirely fictional; it was, to borrow from Benedict Anderson, an "imagined community," characterized by a robust sense of fraternity and unity between people who would never all encounter one another.[70] It constituted a homogenized version of distinct Eastern European Jewish populations, a small town inhabited by stock folkloric characters—the rabbi, the bride, the dairyman, the fiddler, and so on.[71] The ideological evolution of the shtetl reached a pinnacle after World War II, when a number of authors wrote about the shtetl with the intent to resuscitate what had been destroyed before their eyes. In the 1952 ethnography *Life Is with People*, Mark Zborowski and Elizabeth Herzog expand the shtetl mythology, declaring: "The small-town Jewish community of Eastern Europe—the shtetl—traces its line of march directly back to Creation. The Exodus from Egypt, the giving of the Law on Mount Sinai, are seen as steps along the way, historical events no less real than the Spanish Inquisition or the Russian Revolution."[72]

In the 1919 Yiddish one-act musical drama *Moyshe der fidler* (Moyshe the Fiddler), written by Joseph Cherniavsky, the protagonist exemplifies the iconographic character type of the Jewish fiddler of the Russian shtetl.[73] Moyshe makes his living by performing at weddings; he plays so beautifully that, in the words of his friend Shmerl, a listener will forget the name of his own mother at the sound of his violin. But Moyshe is devastated by the loss of his young son Velvl, who, playing on Moyshe's instrument, produced so sublime a sound that he provoked the interest of an urban visitor, on an ethnographic visit to the shtetl to study Jewish wedding rituals, who took him to St. Petersburg to study at the conservatory. Velvl's patron intercepts Moyshe's letters to his son, and Moyshe never hears from the boy. Years later he learns that Velvl, who has changed his name to the gentile Russian Vladimir and emigrated to the United States, has become a celebrated American violinist. As Moyshe goes mad in a monologue that ends the play, he holds and kisses his fiddle, explaining that it is his only friend in the world, and his only way to express his unbridled sorrow.

In *Moyshe der fidler*, the violin plays two divergent roles, incorporating a dialectical symbolism that is common in a number of literary and art works from the Jewish Diaspora in the late nineteenth and early twentieth centuries. In depictions of the shtetl that feature the violin, the instrument generally acts both as a medium for the personal expression of those Yiddish-speaking Jews bound by poverty and tradition to life in Eastern Europe, and as an agent responsible for the inevitable dispersal of this population through emigration. This typical plot trajectory, which reflects literary trends regarding the representation of the shtetl as a mythic place of origin and a dying locale, offered artists a useful pre-mise on which to create works exploring the ambivalent exchanges between tradition and modernism that were so central to Jewish life in the first half of the twentieth century.[74] It was also based on some degree of truth: there were nu-merous Jewish violinists including Heifetz and Elman—whose grandfather was a klezmer fiddler—who had been raised in Eastern European Jewish commu-nities and achieved international acclaim.[75] Isaac Babel's semi-autobiographical short story "The Awakening," from 1931, pokes fun at the dream of many Rus-sian Jewish parents who brought their young children anxiously to violin lessons in hopes of discovering the "next Heifetz." The model provided by Auer's suc-cessful Jewish students gave the parents in Babel's story hope that a prodigiously talented child could rescue them from poverty.

The ambivalent symbolism of the violin influenced the genre of the rural miniature, which conjured an image of Jewish musical tradition in a manner both apparently accurate and, increasingly over time, nostalgic and melancholy, and which, while bringing rural traditions to the attention of urban listeners, also served to highlight the distance and difference of rural life. Indeed, the characterizations of the Jewish fiddler and folk music throughout the arts had long embodied a melancholy tone; in Sholem Aleichem's 1889 novel *Yosele Solevey*, the narrator asks, "What is it in Jewish singing and Jewish music that evokes only sorrowful thoughts?"[76] In visual representations from the 1920s and onward, the violinist often appeared to play music that tragically heralded the end of a way of life. This figure thus bears resemblance to Orpheus, the musi-cian from Greek legend whose lyre playing swayed the powers of nature and the will of the gods, but who was unable to save his own life or that of his beloved Eurydice. Orpheus uses music to persuade Hades to return Eurydice from the underworld, on the condition that Orpheus not look at her until they arrive on land. But he glances back, and she descends again. Orpheus is dis-membered by a band of enraged women, and his head floats downstream on his lyre, as both continue to murmur their melancholy music.[77]

The Orpheus legend, about the mystical and transcendent power of music over man and nature, was repeatedly invoked in the nineteenth and early twen-tieth centuries in discussions of virtuosos, including the Rom violinist Barna Mihály (see Chapter 3). Describing the "perfect virtuoso," Carl Czerny wrote, "in his own person, he appears to render probable and worthy of belief the celebrated fables of *Orpheus* and *Amphion*."[78] The Orpheus legend inspired Marc Chagall, who depicted the mythological Orpheus as well as his Jewish incarnation, the shtetl violinist, sometimes combining features of both in a single image.

When the impresario Aleksey Granovsky opened the Moscow Yiddish Chamber Theater, he commissioned Chagall to paint frescoes on its walls in time for the theater's opening performance on January 1, 1921, of a set of three short plays by Sholem Aleichem. These frescoes abound with images of fiddles and fiddlers. One of the paintings, the twenty-six-foot *Introduction to the Jewish Theatre*, teams with character types from the Yiddish cultural imagination, including three violinists (Figure 5.1). In the middle of the panel is a pair of consecutive rings like a bull's eye, at the center of which stands a violinist, in traditional garb to signify his Jewishness, and surrounded by members of his *kapelye*, or band. In an echo of the conclusion of the Orpheus legend, this musician's head, removed from his body, hovers above, as his open mouth appears to sing along with the fiddle's tune.

Across the theater from this painting, visitors to the Chamber Theater saw four frescoes depicting the "Jewish muses," *Music, Drama, Dance*, and *Literature*—or, in Chagall's description, "*klezmers*, a wedding jester, women dancers, a Torah scribe."[79] *Music* is a tall panel in which a violinist in traditional religious costume, his face green, stands larger than life on the top of the roofs of his shtetl and bows his instrument.[80] Townspeople and animals hover around Chagall's fiddler, enchanted by his music, and as the heavens roil, the houses seem to sway to the sound. This musician, like Orpheus, magically transfigures the landscape around him. The melancholy look on the fiddler's face and the barrenness of the shtetl recall the tragic consequences that befell Orpheus when he looked back at Eurydice.

Chagall's Moscow paintings embody the ambivalence of the symbolic Jewish violinist: the artist, looking back nostalgically toward his childhood in the Russian Jewish town of Vitebsk, evoked both the mystical allure of the Jewish musician and the sense of loss and dismemberment that was the penalty of looking backward. And yet the fiddler's music continues, just as Orpheus's head sang on as it floated down the river. As the following study of "Hebrew Melody" demonstrates, this complex symbolism and mythology played a significant role in the composition of rural miniatures based on Jewish traditional music, as well as in the way their reception changed throughout the twentieth century.

FIGURE 5.1:   *Introduction to the Jewish Theatre*, 1920 (tempera, gouache, and opaque white on canvas), Chagall, Marc (1887–1985). Tretyakov Gallery, Moscow, Russia / The Bridgeman Art Library. © 2013 Artists Rights Society (ARS), New York / ADAGP, Paris.

JOSEPH ACHRON'S "HEBREW MELODY"

The rural miniature was among the genres most frequently composed by members of the St. Petersburg Society for Jewish Folk Music and its later off-shoots. The publication histories of the Society and Jibneh demonstrate that after vocal and choral arrangements, the duo of violin or cello with piano was the most common ensemble for which these composers arranged folk songs.[81] Rural miniatures based on Jewish traditional music are typically constructed in short and repetitive melodic phrases and frequently incorporate augmented seconds, often in the context of the *Ahavah rabbah* mode, which was studied by Russian Jewish ethnographers and identified by Kiselgof as a link between dispersed Eastern European Jewish musical traditions.[82] These and other such techniques appeared earlier as orientalizing gestures in the music of Russian composers including Nikolai Rimsky-Korsakov to represent Jews and other ethnic minorities, as well as peoples living to the East of Russia.[83] The St. Petersburg *moguchaya kuchka*, or "Mighty little bunch," the group of composers nicknamed by Vladimir Stasov in 1867 and comprised of Rimsky-Korsakov, Mily Balakirev, César Cui, Modest Musorgsky, and Alexander Borodin, was strongly influential for the composers of the Society for Jewish Folk Music, and Rimsky-Korsakov was famously supportive of the study of Jewish folk music and development of a Jewish national style of composition.[84] The use of orientalizing gestures in musical depictions of Jewish culture relates in part to the powerful role of the symbolism of the east in Jewish culture. Synagogues are constructed to allow congregants to face east toward Jerusalem when they pray, and the word "east" appears in Sabbath prayers (in the Hebrew, *mizrakh*).[85] Yiddish songs and literature often address confrontations and negotiations between East and West (*mizrekh* and *meyrev*).[86] Additionally, the association between Jewish folk song and the Orient was a common subject among Jewish ethnomusicologists; Idelsohn, for example, having conducted research with a phonograph in the region around Jerusalem in 1911 in search of the most ancient and authentic forms of Jewish traditional music, devoted considerable space in his book to the study of the similarities between Jewish song and "the song of the other ancient Oriental peoples," that is, "Israel's ancient neighbors."[87] By conducting research to prove the "oriental" origins of Jewish folk song and evoking the Orient in their compositions, members of the Society depicted their own heritage as displaced within Russian borders, with ancient Eastern roots.[88]

Achron joined the Society for Jewish Folk Music in 1911 when, after performing a violin recital of works by Niccolò Paganini at the St. Petersburg Conservatory, he was confronted by Rosowsky, who spoke with him for several hours about Jewish music.[89] Achron became a devoted member of the Society, and Saminsky later described his loyalty to his Jewish heritage and its impact on his music, calling

Achron "a Jewish composer who does not wish to pose as a Pole or a Frenchman or a Dane, who insists on representing his own race and blood."[90] Shortly after joining the Society, Achron composed "Hebrew Melody," the first of many rural miniatures he would produce.

Critics and colleagues deemed "Hebrew Melody" to embody a convincing realism that combined apparent accuracy with essentially "Jewish" sentimentality. Idelsohn, for instance, characterized "Hebrew Melody" as a successful work of Jewish music:

> This composition is based upon a folk-tune in minor, with the Ukrainian augmentation on the 4 and 6 toward the end. [Achron] developed the melody in the violin and the piano part according to Jewish ways: by the sudden transferring of the tune to the upper third, giving vent to the outburst of suppressed pain and emotion, and then, toward the end, falling back exhausted to the first state of depression.[91]

As in his description of Engel's set of fifty songs, Idelsohn locates the authentic representation of Jewishness in the combination of the objective reference to ethnography and the subjective depiction of the Jewish soul.

"Hebrew Melody" appeared in at least four editions between its composition and 1933. It was first released in 1914 by the Society's printing press, followed by new editions by the violinist Efrem Zimbalist (G. Schirmer, 1918), Leopold Auer (Carl Fischer, 1921), and Jascha Heifetz (Carl Fischer, 1933). Achron and his publishers included in the score a transcription of the printed source melody, notated above the composition in the style of ethnographic transcription. This transcription, in small print without accompaniment, refers the piece directly to the cataloguing impulse of ethnographic exploration that appeared in folk music anthologies at the turn of the century. Although the language and precise wording of the expressive markings and performance instructions throughout the score varied from edition to edition, the short musical passage was always introduced with a caption identifying it as a traditional tune on which the larger piece was based, transcribed directly from the oral tradition by Achron (Figure 5.2). Nevertheless, musicologists have not yet found a religious or secular melody from the Jewish tradition that corresponds to Achron's transcription. It is possible that Achron misremembered the melody in writing it down years later, or that it has simply been forgotten and was never transcribed elsewhere. But it is also conceivable that Achron created the melody himself, adding the caption about transcription and printing it in bare ethnographic notation to add an aura of realism, persuading audiences of its authenticity.

The prefatory "ethnographic" transcription was a common feature of Achron's scores: "Scher" was published by Juwal in 1923 with a melody given the caption, "Das Thema im Original, (Volksmelodie) aufgenommen von S. Kisselgoff." The score of "Hebrew Lullaby," composed in 1912, also opens with a melody attributed to Kiselgof's ethnographic research.[92] Achron's 1914 "Hebrew Dance"

FIGURE 5.2:   First page of Joseph Achron, "Hebrew Melody," 1911. Published by Gesellschaft für jüdische Volksmusik, 1914.

opens with a tune in small print marked with the caption, "The original version of the melody, as recorded by H. Kopit."

   To make the notation in his opening excerpt appear as an objective account of a traditional melody, Achron offers no prescriptive performance instructions over his "original version," simply a descriptive tempo marking and the "ideal" pitches and durations. He depicts the tune in a generic form, as a transcription

of a melodic stereotype derived from listening to a particular performance, in
the style of transcription referred to as "realist ethnography." In his composition, Achron does not limit himself to following narrowly the formal structure
of the transcription, but instead he expands its dimensions. The work is structured in a basic three-part form, A–B–A; more closely, it breaks down as A
(measures 1–23)–A' (24–40)–B (41–57)–B' (58–73)–Cadenza (74)–A (75–87)–
Coda (88–108). The piece is in A minor and modulates to C minor in the B'
section, after which the cadenza begins on a diminished seventh chord on the
new leading tone B-natural and ends on a G major chord. In a short transitional
passage (75–9), the harmony returns to A minor for the final section and coda.

The transcription of the original melody, by contrast, is in binary form, a
(1–16)–b (17–32) (Example 5.1). The a section is in two parts, consisting of a
melody ending on E, the fifth scale degree (8), answered by an ornamented
repetition of the same material, ending on the tonic A (16). The b section is also
a two-part repeated melody, again ending on E in the first half (24) and finally
on A (32). The concluding three measures of the melodic line of each half of
the b section (22–4 and 30–2) echo the last three bars of each half of the a section in the transcription (6–8 and 14–16), except for one difference: in the b
section, the fourth scale degree D is raised to D-sharp, producing an augmented
second between the third and fourth scale degrees, and conforming to the
"Ukrainian Dorian" or *Mi sheberakh* mode.

Each larger section of Achron's work incorporates the equivalent half of the
transcription, so that section A in "Hebrew Melody" represents section a of the
transcription, repeated with alteration in A', and sections B and B' are based on
section b of the transcription. The final A section of "Hebrew Melody" does
not repeat the entire phrase again but elides into an extended coda of dream-
like trills and turns that rise upward in pitch and become ever quieter. The
work ends low on the G string, with an unaccompanied restatement of the
melody's closing bars. In the first half of "Hebrew Melody," A' and B' repeat A
and B with variation: A' is at a higher pitch than A, and B' adds runs and turns

EXAMPLE 5.1:   Transcription at opening of Joseph Achron, "Hebrew Melody" to the material in B, in both cases producing more expressive, impassioned re-statements of the thematic materials.

If the small-print source melody in the sheet music of "Hebrew Melody" represents a folkloric artifact in its ideal form, the score that follows, notated prescriptively with ornaments and performance instructions, constitutes a highly varied and elaborated interpretation based on similar musical materials. Whereas the original melody is printed without any performance instructions other than a tempo mark, the first iteration of the opening phrase of the same melody in Heifetz's edition of the violin-piano duo (measures 7–23), which follows a six-measure introductory solo for the piano, is copiously annotated with dynamic marks, hairpin crescendos and decrescendos, and detailed in-structions for the violinist's left hand, including fingerings, slides, and the sug-gestion to play in a high position on the G string. Heifetz also incorporates the expressive directions "with full lamenting tone" (7) and "with expression" (15), as well as indications for the violinist's right hand, including tenuto and accent markings and slurred bowings (Example 5.2).

In a surprising deviation between the transcription and its arrangement, whereas the melodic artifact is labeled "Moderate" with an indication that the eighth note matches 92 beats per minute on the metronome, the duet is marked "Tranquil and mournfully," the eighth note equaling 72–80. In editions by Efrem Zimbalist and Leopold Auer, it is even slower, at 60–3 to the eighth note. "Hebrew Melody" thus comes across as a languorous and wistful setting of the traditional melody, a mournful reflection on a recollection from Achron's past. Of course, when the source melody was performed—if it was in fact the melody of a preexisting *nigun* or other vocal genre as the score states—its singers doubtlessly at times adopted slower tempos, and even tranquil and mournful tones; the tempo indication that Achron ascribes to his paratextual transcription serves less as a reliable indication of ritual musical traditions than as a scientific control, contrasting to the tragic, lilting tempo indication that opens his setting of it as a chamber work.

The melodic transcription thus functions as a foil to Achron's composi-tion. Unadorned and concise in small typeface, it is a universal, generic anno-tation of a traditional artifact; by contrast, the composition that follows, embellished and lamenting, represents a particular rendition or appropriation of the same artifact. The inclusion in the score of a melodic transcription rendered in ethnographic notation contributes to the realism of "Hebrew Melody" by indicating that the work represents an actual traditional musical artifact that exists externally to the score. Achron and his editors attempted to indicate that "Hebrew Melody" represented authentic Jewish traditions by referring to ethnography, a field that, with the recent invention of the por-table phonograph, was increasingly considered scientifically objective in its methodologies.

EXAMPLE 5.2:   Joseph Achron, "Hebrew Melody," edited by Jascha Heifetz, measures 1–23

JASCHA HEIFETZ AND "HEBREW MELODY"

Heifetz recorded "Hebrew Melody" three times during his career: in December 1917, in an arrangement for violin and orchestra, with the conductor Josef Pasternack; in December 1926, to Isidor Achron's piano accompaniment; and in October 1946, with pianist Emmanuel Bay.[93] In considering Heifetz's three recordings together, one can hear that his interpretation of the work changed significantly since his earliest disc, and the variations in his approach over the course of three decades provide insight into the ways listeners' perceptions of "Hebrew Melody" changed with the rise of the Nazi Party, increases in immigration across the diaspora, and the destruction of Eastern European Jewish culture. Annotated analyses of Heifetz's recordings of the first forty measures of the violin part to "Hebrew Melody" appear in Example 5.3. Markings in the example identify bowings, slides, mid-phrase tempo alterations, and dynamics that are not regulated by the unedited first published version of the score. This passage, the A section of "Hebrew Melody," features a seventeen-measure phrase (following six measures of introduction in the accompaniment), which is repeated an octave higher in the following seventeen measures. In each of his recordings, Heifetz approaches the first half of this section with a stronger, richer timbre, by applying more pressure with the right hand on the bow and performing in high positions on the G string. He then plays the repetition in the second half at a quieter dynamic level, with a sweeter timbre on the A string. In each recording, he experiments with increasing dynamic variation, and by 1946 his interpretation involves both abrupt and gradual changes in volume, with swelling "hairpin" dynamics, as in measures 37–8 and 39–40, and the slow drop to *niente* at the ends of each half of the passage. As a result of the increasing frequency of changing dynamic gestures, each recording appears to be more broadly expressive than the one that came before, signifying more suddenly changing emotional states.

In these performances, Heifetz's tempo fluctuates frequently, but a pattern is evident: with every subsequent recording of "Hebrew Melody," Heifetz adopts a detectably slower overall tempo. The first editions of the work dictated a tempo of 60–3 to the eighth note, and, as remarked earlier, Heifetz's version of 1936 prescribes a faster tempo of 72–80. In his first recording of the work, Heifetz played the opening phrases in the violin at approximately 72 to the eighth note, in a performance that lasted approximately four minutes and twenty-six seconds; he thus took the piece faster than contemporary versions of the score indicated, and nearly at the tempo he would ultimately indicate in his edition. By 1926, Heifetz modified his conception of the piece, playing with a slower starting tempo of about 66 to the eighth note, in line with the instructions in the score, and this recording was almost half a minute longer, around four minutes and fifty seconds. Two decades later, having in the intervening years published his edition, Heifetz again recorded the work with the initial tempo of around 66 to the eighth note, but his tempo fluctuations and expressive playing resulted in a longer, more deliberate performance of around five minutes and four seconds.

The tempo variations between Heifetz's recordings of "Hebrew Melody" appear to reflect a change over time in the sentiment that musicians who were dedicated to the composition and performance of music based on Jewish

EXAMPLE 5.3: Transcriptions of Jascha Heifetz's 1917, 1926, and 1946 recordings of "Hebrew Melody," measures 1–40

tradition felt toward their goals. In 1917, "Hebrew Melody" was only six years old, and Heifetz was sixteen; the Society for Jewish Folk Music, under whose auspices Achron composed the work, was still actively pursuing the study of Jewish folklore and the manufacture of Jewish nationalist art music. In the context of the Society's ongoing attempts to perpetuate Jewish rural and urban musical culture, Heifetz's energetic rendition of the work seems to represent the Society members' interest in what they viewed as the straightforward, "pure" expression of folk music.

By 1926, many members of the Society had been forced to leave St. Petersburg, and with their departure, the hope of maintaining rural Jewish communities in Russia through music began to wane, as ethnographic research in the region—one of the tools many of these musicians believed would salvage an imperiled culture—became impossible. Slower tempos are often heard as musical analogues to the somatic effects of sadness, and Heifetz's tempo in the 1926 recording might therefore indicate a more dispirited approach to Jewish folkloric materials. It was indeed later that Heifetz published his faster-tempo edition, but the tragic events of the World War II intervened between then and his 1946 recording. At this point his interpretation of "Hebrew Melody," whose A minor key, repetitive phrases, and wild cadenza were already prone to interpretation as indexical signs of melancholy and passion, takes on the most downcast, yearning sound, becoming, perhaps, an elegy for the victims of the Holocaust.

Whereas the tempos and durations change in Heifetz's three recordings, the frequency and location of slides between adjacent pitches remain more or less the same. Each of the performances contains approximately sixteen or seventeen noticeable slides within the first forty measures. Slides often occur in repetitions of short musical phrases: for instance, in measure 10, which is a direct repetition of measure 8, Heifetz slides between the E and D, in each of his three recordings; and in the 1926 and 1946 recordings, he also slides in the subsequent two repetitions of this melodic unit, in measures 17 and 19. Similarly, in each of the recordings, Heifetz performs measure 26 without any slides, but does slide between E and D in the repetitions of this gesture in measures 28, 34, and 36. Heifetz's portamentos seem in most cases not to be employed out of any necessity based on the difficulty of individual shifts; in fact, in several instances, he slides between reiterations of the same pitch, where the fingering need not change at all. An example of this is his slide in each recording between the repeated E's in measures 14 and 15, and in the 1926 recording in the middle of measure 26. It seems that little changed in these four decades in Heifetz's use of portamento in his performances of Achron's work, as signifiers of sentimentality, as well as of klezmer performance technique.

With the increasingly slower tempos in Heifetz's interpretations of "Hebrew Melody" one also hears a growing propensity to apply rubato, with fluctuating tempos within measures and between phrases. In his 1917 recording, the orchestra keeps time with a strong, steady pulsation on the eighth-note beat in the bass. Heifetz rushes slightly in measure 21, entering early with the third beat and creating the impression of a syncopated rhythm, as he speeds through to the end of the phrase; and again, he follows the orchestra's increasing tempo through measures 39–40, and enters in the following section at a new and considerably faster tempo.

In the recording of 1926, the listener can detect more instances of rubato. Heifetz lingers briefly on the first beats of measures 15 and 17, and drags the tempo through the following beats of these measures, drawing out the dotted rhythms. He pulls back the tempo in the middle of measure 19, and then makes up for the lost time in the third beat of the bar; and, where he followed the orchestra's increasing tempo at the end of this section in his previous recording, here he appears to take greater initiative in directing the acceleration in measure 38 into the held final note of the phrase. In his 1946 recording, Heifetz takes the most liberated approach to tempo. He emphatically draws out the first pitches of measures 11, 19, and 36, and expands the held note in measure 31, as though it were written under a brief fermata. He seems to rush impatiently through the repeated descending sixteenth-note pattern that occurs first in measures 8 and 10, but drags back languorously at the ends of measures featuring repeated pairs of sixteenths, such as in measures 19, 21, 29, 36, and 38. These speed fluctuations, perceived along with the dramatic dynamic shifts, liberal use of slides, and slow tempo of the 1946 recording of "Hebrew Melody," combine to signify melancholy, nostalgia, and expressive passion. They convey the sense that Heifetz now looks back mournfully and fitfully at a work, a social movement, and a religious musical tradition that have been the victims of genocide.

THE AFTERLIFE OF "HEBREW MELODY":
A RURAL MINIATURE IN EXILE

As a result of emigration and the disappointed realization of many composers that it would be impossible to revive and refresh rural Eastern European Jewish life through musical practice as they had hoped, by the 1930s much of the intellectual fervor of the original members of the Society for Jewish Folk Music was replaced by a growing sense of loss as they created increasingly fictionalized depictions of musical traditions in later rural miniatures. The ethnographic component of the rural miniature became clearly less vital, so that by 1932, Achron fabricated dance melodies for his *Stempenyu Suite* and other works. This trend away from realism is evident not only in the composition of new rural miniatures but in new methods of transmission of the early ones as well. The history of the reception and adaptations of "Hebrew Melody" provides evidence of the gradual move away from the emphasis on ethnographic sources as providing scholarly access to living musical traditions and toward nostalgia as a more personal approach to the past in the genre of the rural miniature.

In the first years after its composition, "Hebrew Melody" was frequently performed during lecture recitals arranged by the Society for Jewish Folk Music and its offshoots. In a late example, a 1922 concert program of the Moscow Society opened with a lecture on Jewish music by Engel, and included performances of art songs and rural miniatures by Krein, Engel, Milner, and Gnesin, as well as "Hebrew Melody."[94] Professional violinists including Heifetz and Elman soon brought the work to international audiences. In one of the work's first American performances, Heifetz played it along with Achron's "Hebrew Dance" at the Metropolitan Opera in 1918, in a benefit concert earning $15,000 for Jewish soldiers and their families. The *New York Times* reported on the audience's emotional reaction to hearing these rural miniatures: "The celebrated violinist won an ovation from the house when he played on muted strings a Jewish melody and dance of Joseph Achron."[95] In the 1920s, the work appeared on Heifetz's programs throughout the world, including concerts in Tokyo and Osaka in 1923; Riga in 1926; Paris, elsewhere in Western Europe, and Sydney in 1927; and Carnegie Hall in 1929.[96] "Hebrew Melody" was included on recordings by Heifetz, Elman, Ida Haendel, Joseph Hassid, and other prominent musicians.

During the 1930s, a number of musicians and artists created new and innovative adaptations of "Hebrew Melody," recognizing the work's familiarity and capitalizing on the popular conception that it had begun to serve an unofficial anthem representing Eastern European Jewish culture. In the 1935 film *Hebrew Melody* (also advertised in the transliterated Hebrew translation of the title, *Shir Ivri*), a performance of Achron's rural miniature accompanied a montage of images of Jerusalem. The film combined the composition's musical realism with the visual techniques of cinematic realism to convey a Zionist message to German Jewish audiences. *Hebrew Melody* was created by a Berlin-based production company; its director, Helmar Lersky, and cinematographer, Walter Kristeller, were both German Zionists who had settled in Palestine around 1933.[97] The film's star was the Jewish violinist Andreas Weißgerber, a former child prodigy born in 1900 in a small Jewish town near Chernowitz, Ukraine. At the age of nine, Weißgerber studied for a time with Jenő Hubay in Budapest and later moved to Berlin to continue his performance career, finally relocating to Palestine shortly before the start of World War II.[98] The filmmakers worked under the auspices of *the Jüdischer Kulturbund*, which had been initiated in 1933 by the recently elected National Socialist party. Jews were now forbidden to participate in cultural practices such as attending art schools and playing in orchestras, and the Kulturbund was formed as an institution under which Jews could form a ghettoized cultural life, with their own orchestras, publishing presses, theater, and other cultural organizations.[99]

Hebrew Melody was filmed in Jerusalem's Old City and the surrounding hillside in the winter of 1934–5. Its soundtrack, recorded by the orchestra of the Jüdischer Kulturbund, opened with a prelude by the Jewish composer Arno Nadel, followed by Achron's "Hebrew Melody," as reorchestrated by Shabtai Petruschka.[100] In the spirit of travel documentary and ethnography, the producers filmed *Hebrew Melody* with the aim of bringing images of distant Palestine home to curious viewers in Germany. Creating a montage of images of the people, animals, architecture, and topography in the urban Jerusalem market and the countryside surrounding the city, the director uses techniques from the idioms of travel photography and ethnographic filmmaking to construct a Palestine that appears to be home to a society that is less technologically developed than Berlin's but possesses a more "authentic" humanity. In this context, "Hebrew Melody," Achron's slow and elegiac rendering of a traditional religious song that he reported to have heard long before in Warsaw, becomes anchored in the legendary Jewish Holy Land. Weißgerber performs the work as a spontaneous act of spiritual inspiration; the music seems to emanate from the landscape. *Hebrew Melody* is meant advertise a nostalgic and idyllic location, a remnant of the origins of Jewish culture that offers the potential for its renewal.

The film opens with credits superimposed over an image of men in robes leading trains of camels across a beach, backlit by the sun reflecting off the water. The music of Nadel's prelude enters, with soft, dissonant pulsing notes in the high winds, alternating with short, song-like fragments in a minor key. Shots of Old Jerusalem show a multi-ethnic population involved in the day's commerce. A black car pulls up, conspicuously more modern than the surroundings, and Weißgerber steps out holding his violin. In his suit and tie, he enters the market populated by figures wearing robes and headdresses; as a surrogate of the viewer, Weißgerber represents a curious explorer from the outside.

Weißgerber returns to his car, followed by an eager young boy in tattered clothing. The car drives off with the boy running behind; as they wind along the steep roads past city walls, the documentary shots of the landscape are paired with the orchestra's wind section playing a plaintive and folksy melody in a complex meter. The music is presented as a natural counterpart to the landscape. The car stops, and Weißgerber disembarks in a set of ruins at a hillside vista by Absalom's Pillar. Weißgerber, peering at the view, sees evidence of rural daily life, in the form of a pair of women carrying urns on their heads. The boy opens Weißgerber's violin case and playfully plucks the strings, whose sounds break through the orchestra, emphatically producing the first onscreen sounds in the film.

Weißgerber begins to perform "Hebrew Melody" at a slow tempo with dramatic rubato, finally settling on an unstable tempo of around 58 to the eighth note, approximately the speed dictated by Zimbalist and Auer in their editions, and considerably slower than the 72–80 indication that would appear one year later in Heifetz's. As the camera captures Weißgerber's performance in several shots from different angles, he plays the A section entirely on the G string to create a warm timbre. His fingerings produce frequent slides; for instance, in the first two bars of the melody, he plays the E with the third finger, but instead of remaining in position to play the D on the second finger, he shifts down with his third, to create an expressive slide. Similarly, he leaps from first position to play the D on the second finger in measure 12, so that he can slide more easily to the next pitch, C.

When Weißgerber begins to play section B, his eyes are closed but he is facing toward the expansive landscape beyond, and he plays with even more vibrato and slides between pitches and dramatically slows down the tempo at the climax of the phrase in measure 53. A new shot again begins at section B', showing only Weißgerber's face as he plays turns and runs of sixteenth-note triplets and thirty-second notes, with syncopations and tenuto emphases creating friction with the meter. As the music swirls ever faster into reverie, Weißgerber moves wildly as he plays, his eyes closed, brow wrinkled, and lips parted.

Just before the cadenza, the screen turns black, and a shot fades in showing only Weißgerber's fingers on the neck of the violin, as though to indicate that in the heat of his passionate playing, Weißgerber has lost consciousness; disembodied from his rational mind, his fingers flail wildly through the cadenza. As the cadenza winds down and the orchestral transition intercedes with a slow arpeggio in the harp, the screen turns black again, followed by a montage as though showing the viewer the stream of his thoughts. The image of an old Hanukkiah, the traditional candelabrum used during the holiday Hanukkah, is followed by a knotted tree, its branches curved in a similar shape. Next there appears a shot of grazing goats and sheep on a steep hillside, and finally Weißgerber reappears in a dramatic mid-length shot from below.

The sun's rays peek out from behind Weißgerber's face, as though God has divinely inspired his playing. Artifacts and images of Jewish ritual, the landscape and rural life of Palestine, and the religious implication of God's power are teamed with the music of Achron's rural miniature to convey the Zionist message of the film. After the high trills of the coda, captured mostly in another close shot of Weißgerber's fingers on the neck of his violin, a view from a greater distance captures his performance of the final solo bars (from measure 102), with the landscape behind him showing the city walls and the receding hills (Figure 5.3). In the film's closing image, Weißgerber performs the final three bars of the piece, and bows his head solemnly as he plays a diminuendo on the final note.

The expressive style the spectator hears from Weißgerber was a common feature of his performances and even provoked a critic to describe his playing as "almost realistic." He wrote that Weißgerber's performance of a solo movement

FIGURE 5.3:   Film still from *Hebrew Melody*. Directed by Helmar Lersky. Tobis-Klangfilm, 1935. In Bergmeier, et al., *Vorbei*, Hambergen: Bear Family Records, 2001.

by Bach conveyed a realist sound because "the diverse dynamics and rhythms were contrasted with each other under the strongest imaginable light, the chords were almost thrust into the strings, the runs and more agitated developmental passages presented with an apparently improvised freedom and relaxation."[101] For the critic, realism in performance was evoked by the heartfelt passion and spontaneity that Weißgerber seemed to exude in his violin playing. In this work of Zionist cinema, the spontaneity and passion evoked in Weißgerber's playing technique are depicted as an expression of his spiritual connection to his milieu through the medium of the rural miniature. The realism of the cinematic style, the rural miniature, and Weißgerber's playing combine to promote a message of nationalist propaganda. Thus "Hebrew Melody," originally published with an ethnographic transcription of its source music as an authentic representation of a melody appropriated from Polish Hasidic liturgical music, had been integrated two decades later into a Zionist film, in which it evokes the feelings of a European Jewish immigrant upon visiting Jerusalem and its rural outskirts.

"Hebrew Melody" was also transformed by performers in America, where it was set twice to text. One version, written by Achron's wife Marie Rap-hoph for the Russian singer Nina Koshetz, was published in 1929 with lyrics in English, Yiddish, Russian, and German. Each verse of this song repeats the line "Olden melodies return,/ Floating softly over hearts that burn." In sentimental and nostalgic language, these "olden melodies" are associated with "wails of the lowly,/ sayings most holy," "Israel's pain," and a "folk's long-buried pride." In the B section of the work, the Zionist message becomes apparent, as the lyrics explain that these traditional melodies incite the yearning for a Jewish Holy Land: "The nobility in every soul/ And the love for Zion's sacred goal/ Within me rise/ Till the tears come blinding to my eyes./ And the flooding tears, the ancient groan,/ Welling upward reach to Heaven's throne,/ Where the Lord of earth and sky/ Harks to that exceeding bitter cry."

In the place of Achron's increasingly wild violin part, Rap-hoph instructs the singer to perform the melody on extended, ornamented vocalizations of the syllable "Ah," as the piano accompanies with undulating notes. The cadenza here becomes a realization of the "exceeding bitter cry" that evokes the singer's yearning as, according to the lyrics, she weeps and calls out toward God. At the conclusion of the aria, Rap-hoph gives the singer, now unaccompanied on the final iteration of the opening theme, the instruction to hum the melody ad libitum. This arrangement thus maintains the sense of the cadenza as an improvised evocation of overwhelming spiritual feelings, as the vocalization represents the expression of emotions so powerful that they cannot be put into words.

"Hebrew Melody" was later set to text again, this time not as a concert aria but as a popular song adapted in Yiddish for the singer and Yiddish radio and film performer Seymour Rechtzeit, and recorded on a 78-rpm disc.[102] The Yiddish radio, which first emerged in New York in 1926 and remained active into the 1950s, was a quintessential product of the Jewish diaspora in the United States, representing in its intermixture of Yiddish- and English-language broadcasting and in the subject matter of its programming the foreign roots and new American identities of its multi-lingual and multi-generational Jewish audiences.[103] On Yiddish radio, one of the most popular of these hybrid musical forms was known by the phrase "Yiddish Melodies in Swing," a genre that typically involved the arrangement of Yiddish folk, theater, and religious songs as upbeat works in the style of American swing.[104] This resembled the common exercise among bands of the 1930s and 1940s of recreating classical works as swing hits, or "swinging the classics," as well-known compositions by prominent composers entered the repertoire of bandleaders including Tommy Dorsey and Benny Goodman.[105] Rechtzeit's "Hebrew Melody" reconfigured the composition—itself an arrangement of an Eastern European Jewish religious melody—into a stylistic hybrid exhibiting the characteristics of Tin Pan Alley.

The lyrics of this new arrangement were written by Rechtzeit's wife, Miriam Kressyn, another radio and film personality, and the accompaniment was by Abraham Ellstein, a composer who worked in New York Yiddish film and theater. The song offers a diaspora anthem about an exile's longing nostalgia for what the lyrics refer to as the "far-off East" (*vayten mizrekh*), the Holy Land in Palestine. Rechtzeit's adaptation of "Hebrew Melody" features melodramatic lyrics expressing a call to return to Israel: "Sounds are heard,/ From far-off East, there,/ Sounds enveloped in yearning/ With love from a heart that yearns./ An echo is heard,/ Come back from that time,/ When the ancestors from once-upon-a-time/ Gave us their treasures./ . . . Parting from you/ Was very difficult,/ Being with you/ Was my goal, my desire./. . . I won't leave you,/ Lovely bride of Israel."[106] The Hebrew melody of the title emanates from this distant space and embodies the artistic theme of Jewish yearning for a distant homeland, referred to as the bride the singer left behind when he was displaced in exile. The song's accompaniment features piano, strings, winds, and percussion playing gestures imported from Achron's composition as well as original material featuring instruments commonly heard in jazz and swing, such as the muted trumpet and glockenspiel, which alternately follow and diverge from the vocal line, punctuating transitions with diminished chords and arpeggios.

The muted trumpet intones the melodic line at the opening of the recording and returns to perform in unison with the singer in several passages. The violinist plays a solo line above the orchestra later in the recording, with a solo riff on a descending diminished chord that resembles both figuration heard in recordings of sentimental American songs and the augmented seconds common in klezmer's traditional modes. At the end of this phrase, Rechtzeit enters again as the violin plays along with his singing, with both newly composed gestures and references to the solo part of Achron's original. Rechtzeit's coda, sung wistfully to the repeated syllable "Ah" followed by a final reiteration of the refrain "beautiful bride of Israel," is accompanied by sparkling arpeggios on the glockenspiel. Achron's work, based on a melody he claimed to recall from a turn-of-the-century Polish synagogue, is adapted here for a Yiddish crooner with dance band accompaniment and becomes assimilated to its new musical context, with the incorporation of elements—instruments, melodic and harmonic gestures, and performance styles—associated with popular music of the United States. Rechtzeit's song is a nostalgic emblem of the idealized Jewish past that is made also to embody the change, social assimilation, and cultural appropriation that were experienced by many Jews throughout the processes of emigration, displacement, and resettlement in the diaspora.

The B-side of this recording contained a Yiddish song adaptation of Pablo de Sarasate's "Zigeunerweisen," which becomes a number about the singer's love for a *tsigayner meydl*, or Gypsy girl. Rom characters, particularly musicians, were frequently the subject of Yiddish theater and operetta—for example, in the show *Dos tsigayner meydl* (The Gypsy Maid), performed on stage and adapted for radio as a vehicle for Molly Picon. Kressyn's lyrics open with the words, "When I overhear a Gypsy melody,/ A song of love presses into my heart," reflecting and perpetuating longtime associations of Rom performance with passionate emotion.[107] Rechtzeit sings that when he plays his love song to his beloved, from whom he has been separated, the strings of the violin cry from his heart, and he asks her, "Give me love, if for one minute/ Because with you it is so sincerely good."[108] In the fast section, the singer describes his impassioned dance with the Rom girl, reflecting the age-old stereotype of the sensual dancing of Rom women:"Dance for me, my girl,/ wildly let's dance . . . / Two hearts, they pound without stopping/ Turn, girl, turn faster./ . . . Sing, Gypsy, jump, Gypsy,/ Dance to my song."[109]

In the orchestra, a violinist plays virtuosic runs from Sarasate's composition. Ellstein's band imitates the Rom ensemble, as filtered through Sarasate's nineteenth-century orchestration, but with instruments and harmonies of Tin Pan Alley. In the final strains, a vibraphone plays a blue note in the form of the sixth scale degree. In releasing Yiddish songs based on both "Hebrew Melody" and "Zigeunerweisen" on a single disc, Rechtzeit reveals the lasting influence of popular conceptions of Rom culture on Jewish self-representations, and of Sarasate's composition on rural miniatures based on Jewish themes, even as these artists assimilated to new musical idioms in New York City, far from the European communities in which Jews and Roms had been cast as "internal others."

Finally, in perhaps the strangest turn, "Hebrew Melody" appeared in an adaptation seemingly even more alien to its origins than the Palestinian landscape or Rechtzeit's jazzy rendition. It became part of the concert and recording repertoire of Clara Rockmore, a one-time child prodigy on violin and student of Leopold Auer, on the instrument on which she built her career during and after the 1920s, the theremin. Leon Theremin, born in St. Petersburg, was a scientist and inventor who created the eponymous musical innovation, an electronic device performed with subtle motions made by the hands as they hover over electrified metal rods. At Theremin's American debut of his instrument, the poster advertised "Music from the ether . . . produced by free movement of hands in the air."[110] From its inception the theremin was associated with the ether, ghosts, and the subconscious, due to its wailing, eerie timbres. It is most frequently heard in scores of science fiction and horror films—for instance, Miklós Rózsa's score to Alfred Hitchcock's *Spellbound*, in which the instrument's vibrating timbres accompany the beginning of Gregory Peck's character's subconscious dream, staged by the surrealist Salvador Dalí.

Rockmore performed "Hebrew Melody" for a recording produced by Robert Moog in 1977. As she plays it on the theremin, "Hebrew Melody" sounds otherworldly. In Rockmore's hands, the piece, originally a realist work closely associated with the scientific practice of musical ethnography, is transformed into a distant, ethereal voice, conjured by a novel electronic instrument. In an extant video recording, Rockmore appears to be in a trance as she plays "Hebrew Melody," as though presiding over a séance. She wears her hair up in a metallic headband, and her eyes are half-open. In the context of the associations between the theremin and the "music of the ether," the timbres of her performance evoke a sound emanating from a mystical and distant time and place.

Rockmore no doubt became familiar with "Hebrew Melody" while studying violin with Auer, but her revival of the work shows a common nostalgic impulse among Jewish immigrants in the wake of World War II. For many Jews in the diaspora who considered assimilating to the dominant culture of their new homes, reports of the destruction to Jewish communities in Eastern Europe created feelings of loyalty toward the places they and their families had left. Ethnographer Barbara Kirshenblatt-Gimblett writes, "It was one thing to reject East European Jewish culture while it was still flourishing on the other side of the ocean. But once the living communities that sustained that way of life were exterminated, ambivalence towards the world they had created became a desecration of their memory."[111] As a result, many authors and artists created works that memorialized Eastern European culture and even, as Rockmore seems to simulate in her performance, attempted metaphorically to conjure the spirits of the dead. Maurice Samuel, for instance, described his 1943 book *The World of Sholom Aleichem*, about Eastern European Yiddish literature, as "an exercise in necromancy, or calling up the dead."[112]

In a strange twist, Achron's attempt to evoke the soul of the Jewish people has been literalized in the decades after World War II: Rockmore appears to commune directly with the spirits of the dead. In this way, performers and adaptors of "Hebrew Melody" during the decades after its composition came to suppress the work's associations with ethnographic research. As Russian Jewish composers and performers were forced into exile and moved throughout the diaspora, the realist component of the enterprise of creating "Jewish" art music aimed at revitalizing the *folks-neshome* transformed into a metaphoric act of summoning ghostly impressions of a disappearing culture.

CHAPTER SIX

BÉLA BARTÓK'S RURAL MINIATURES AND
THE CASE OF *ROMANIAN FOLK DANCES*

The pure folk music can be considered as a natural phenomenon
influencing higher art music, as bodily properties perceptible
with the eye are for the fine arts, or the phenomena of life are
for the poet.

> —Béla Bartók, "The Influence of Folk
> Music on the Art Music of Today,"
> 1920, in *Béla Bartók Essays*, ed. Benjamin Suchoff
> (London: Faber and Faber, 1976), 318.

SETTING A PRECIOUS STONE

In 1912 Béla Bartók traveled to Igriş, Romania, where he asked a local musician who played the *furulya* (transverse flute) to perform dance music into the
bell of a wax cylinder phonograph. Bartók arranged one of the flautist's melodies for piano solo in 1915, naming it "Brâul" after the genre of the original
dance, and selected it to be the second movement of his piano solo *Romanian
Folk Dances (Román népi táncok,* BB 68).[1] In composing this movement, he
adapted the melody to the piano, added harmonic accompaniment, and altered
the original in other ways befitting its new cultural context, with the aims of
appealing to his audience's taste and also expanding their horizons by introducing them to folk music repertoire that was new to them. He would later
notate the same melody again in a more meticulous transcription in the ethnographic style, listening to the wax cylinder multiple times as he did so; this he
included as number 110 in the first volume of his compendium *Rumanian Folk
Music.*[2] Bartók adapted *Romanian Folk Dances* for string orchestra and approved
an arrangement for violin and piano by a frequent collaborator, the violinist
Zoltán Székely. Bartók performed and recorded the work on piano, participated in the preparation of a piano roll that reproduced his rendition, and

recorded the duet version with Joseph Szigeti.[3] Thus a dance melody played in a fleeting performance in a rural town made the long journey to an urban listener's phonograph collection.

This chapter examines *Romanian Folk Dances*, a work whose history shows Bartók's involvement in every stage of this musical journey, from cosmopolitan Budapest, where he joined a coterie of modernist intellectuals and developed an interest in folk music, to the Transylvanian landscape where he encountered local musical cultures of the villages and small towns he visited, and back to Budapest where he studied the music he had collected, composed *Romanian Folk Dances*, and performed and recorded the new work for a listenership predominantly made up of urban concertgoers and record owners. Throughout this process, Bartók significantly altered the forms and functions of folk songs and dances between his initial experience of hearing them performed during his fieldwork, his transcription of them in ethnographic notation, and his subsequent arrangement of them as works of art music. Bartók sought during the 1910s to develop a compositional method for representing folk music in a style that would locate emotional and cultural authenticity in rural musical expression and demonstrate to his performers and listeners both the affinity and the distance between Hungary's urban and rural cultures. This pursuit led him to write rural miniatures based on his folk music research.

In his essay "The Influence of Peasant Music on Modern Music," Bartók describes several methods of incorporating folk music into works of art music.[4] One of these methods involves the appropriation of a traditional melody to serve "as a 'motto' while that which is built around it is of real importance."[5] By contrast the composer can allude to folk music without direct quotation, inventing an original melody in imitation of known melodies; and at some later stage in his career he might even be able to "absorb" the folk music he studies as his "mother tongue," thus writing naturally in the style.[6]

Most relevant to the study of Bartók's process of composing his rural miniature *Romanian Folk Dances*, however, is the first method he lists in this essay: "Accompaniment, introductory and concluding phrases are of secondary importance, and they only serve as an ornament setting for the precious stone: the peasant melody."[7] Bartók developed this compositional method in *Romanian Folk Dances* and other works similarly constructed of series of brief arrangements of folk music including *Romanian Christmas Carols* (*Román kolinda-dallamok*, BB 67) and *Forty-Four Violin Duos* (*Negyvennégy duó két hegedűre*, BB 104). He would choose a selection of folk songs and dances, many of which he collected during his ethnographic fieldwork, and represent them as "precious stones" in seemingly straightforward, unadorned melodic arrangements, to which he would add harmonic accompaniments and titles derived from the genre names or lyrics of the source music. By this means, Bartók claimed to bring out the inherent beauty of his source melodies, in the manner of a jeweler who burnishes and sets a precious stone.

In *Romanian Folk Dances* and other rural miniatures, Bartók incorporated a set of musical tropes including spare but emphatic melodic ornaments, heavy chords and articulation marks on downbeats, and steady, repetitive rhythms in the left hand resembling *verbunkos* accompaniment patterns commonly played by Rom ensembles. These are the *dűvő*—in which pairs of pitches of equal duration are played by a stringed instrument with a portato stroke of the bow— and the *esztam*—a derivation of the *dűvő* in which each note in the two-beat units is played at alternately low and high pitches by different instruments, often bass and a higher string instrument or cimbalom.[8] The use of such tropes in *Romanian Folk Dances* helped convey Bartók's taste for the simplicity, purity, and authenticity that he attributed to "peasant music." Indeed, Bartók argued in his essays that music constituted the purest mode of expression of folk peoples, who represented the vestiges of an authentic community that had been lost in modern Budapest.[9]

Bartók obscures much of the invention involved in composing arrangements of folk music in his rural miniatures, producing the effect of apparent accuracy through a process of musical adaptation that is typical of the style of musical realism. Composing rural miniatures, for Bartók, required the careful removal of embellishment as though to reveal—but, more accurately, to create the impression of—a typical, skeletal melody underneath. Examining the conceptions of race and methodologies of comparative musicology that Bartók developed early in his career reveals the ideological context in which Bartók created rural miniatures, as well as the friction between claims about the authenticity of his rural miniatures and the works' actual deviation from their original sources. The compositional process he developed in writing rural miniatures, and the impact of his research on the performance practice associated with these works, become evident in the analysis of *Romanian Folk Dances*, viewed alongside Bartók's ethnomusicological field notations, his manuscript sketches, and recordings of the work by Bartók, Joseph Szigeti, and Zoltán Székely.

BARTÓK'S COMPARATIVE MUSICOLOGY AND HIS
CONCEPT OF RACE

Although the collection of rural traditional music in Hungary began after Herder published his seminal essay on folk music, the field of ethnography only became prominent in Budapest toward the end of the nineteenth century, and it often focused on the study of Hungary's multi-ethnic makeup.[10] In 1887 the Austro-Hungarian Monarchy sponsored the publication of the twenty-one-volume *Az Osztrák-Magyar Monarchia írásban és képben* (The Austro-Hungarian Monarchy in

Word and Pictures), produced, according to Archduke Rudolf's introduction, with the hope that because the book would show that "The national character of each nationality has been duly and respectfully recognized by the Monarchy's scientific observers," national groups would be able to "find their spiritual center of gravity inside the Austro-Hungarian Monarchy."[11] The Hungarian Ethnographic Society was founded in 1889, with departments set up to study the cultures of Hungarian, Romanian, Serbian, Slovak, and other ethnic groups within Hungary:[12] the Ethnographic Museum was created in 1892; and in 1896, the millenial of the Hungarian conquest was commemorated with the construction of an "ethnographic village" at the Hungarian Millenial Exposition.[13]

By contrast with the traditional correlation elsewhere in Europe of the concept of the nation's "folk" with the rural peasant classes, most Hungarians during the nineteenth and early twentieth centuries labeled the urban gentry and lower nobility as the Hungarian folk. For this reason, Hungarians generally viewed their folk music to be compositions of members of these social classes.[14] Because musical performance for financial gain was reserved for lower social ranks, the task of performing this genre of music fell most often to Rom musicians. Bartók had loved Rom music during his youth and incorporated *verbunkos* and *nóta* forms and melodies into patriotic compositions such as the 1903 symphonic poem *Kossuth* written in commemoration of Lajos Kossuth, the nationalist leader of the 1848–9 War of Independence. Bartók's later discovery of a different manner of folk music, performed not by urban Roms but by inhabitants of rural villages, has been traced to his youthful encounter with a servant named Lidi Dósa, whom he heard singing a Székely folk song she recollected from her childhood in Transylvania.[15] This event proved a turning point in Bartók's life, initiating a career collecting and writing about rural music traditions, and appropriating folk music into his compositions.

Another event that inspired Bartók's interest in ethnography was his first meeting with Zoltán Kodály on March 18, 1905. Kodály, who had already undertaken fieldwork and was completing a doctorate in Hungarian folk music, helped Bartók get his start in folk music research and appears to have introduced him to Béla Vikár, a scholar of Hungarian folk song and the first European to employ the phonograph in fieldwork.[16] Bartók's own fieldwork began in 1906 when he traveled to the north of the country to collect Slovak folk music. Over the next seven years, before his research was effectively put on hold by the events of World War I, he traveled around Hungary and beyond its borders, collecting Magyar, Slovak, Romanian, Ruthenian, Serbian, Bulgarian, and Arabic music.[17] According to Kodály, he and his colleagues hoped to use ethnography to revolutionize music and effect social change; he stated that upon "seeing the village folk, the wasted talents and the fresh vitality, the idea of an educated Hungary, reborn from the folk, dawned upon us. We devoted our life to its realization."[18] It was critical to Bartók and Kodály that they communicate the scientific character of their project in order to achieve their artistic and political goals. Bartók thus employed a wax cylinder phonograph to record performances he encountered because, he would write, the machine provided the only medium with which an ethnographer could accomplish his "ideal aim," the "elimination of the subjective element."[19]

Bartók's essays and letters suggest that race remained central to his ethnographic methodology and to his attempt to develop a "Hungarian" compositional language, even as his understanding of race varied significantly throughout his career as his political contexts changed.[20] Bartók argued that Hungary possessed two opposing musical styles, which he characterized as the authentic, pure music of illiterate rural peasants who had no contact with urban musicians, and the contaminated, hybrid music of the Hungarian gentry and Rom performers.[21] Some of the earliest demonstrations of this conceptual opposition between purity and hybridity appear in his private letters. In a September 8, 1903, letter to his mother, Bartók asserts his nationalistic fervor with the following vow: "For my part, all my life, in every sphere, always and in every way, I shall have one objective: the good of Hungary and the Hungarian nation."[22] He laments that most Hungarian citizens "incessantly commit wrongs against the Hungarian nation" by studying German and other European languages when they "ought to do all they can to foster the use of their mother tongue."[23] He chides his mother and sister for speaking in German at home and with friends, and asks them to "spread and propagate the Hungarian language, with word and deed, and with *speech*! Speak Hungarian between yourselves!!! . . . As for you addressing me in German—well, not even as a joke do I want this. You know how I am in the shops, and when anybody in the street asks me the way in a foreign language."[24]

On August 15 of the following year, Bartók wrote a letter to Irmy Jurkovics that further pursued this argument and its implications for the field of music:

> From what I know of the folk-music of other nations, ours is vastly superior to theirs as regards force of expression and variety. . . . Our intelligentsia comes, almost exclusively, from foreign stock (as shown by the excessively large number of Hungarians with foreign names); and it is only amongst intellectuals that we find people capable of dealing with art in the higher sense. And now our gentry lack the capacity; there may be the occasional exceptions, but such people are not in the least susceptible to our national art. A real Hungarian music can originate only if there is a real *Hungarian* gentry. This is why the Budapest public is so absolutely hopeless. The place has attracted a haphazardly heterogeneous, rootless group of Germans and Jews; they make up the majority of Budapest's population. It's a waste of time trying to educate them in a national spirit. Much better to educate the (Hungarian) provinces.[25]

Bartók shows contempt in these letters for the cosmopolitanism of Budapest and introduces an ideal alternative: the utopian, authentic, racially pure communities of the rural peasant classes.

Bartók's developing theory of folk music and the impact of his ideas on other Budapest intellectuals in the first two decades of the twentieth century can be viewed in the pages of the influential journal *Nyugat*, whose name means "West," referring to the area of Europe to which these innovators often looked for aesthetic inspiration and validation. The sense of being a nation alone on the periphery between East and West had been a dominant aspect of the Hungarian self-image since the early nineteenth century, and this geographical dichotomy became a characteristic symbol by which many Hungarian intellectuals considered a variety of aspects of their culture and landscape.[26] Founded in 1908, *Nyugat* published essays by Bartók and Kodály and featured reviews of their music, as well the occasional facsimile of their new scores.[27]

In a review of Bartók's music from May 1, 1908, the music critic Géza Csáth declared that one could hear in the composer's works his entire temperament, which was defined by his "turbulent, sanguine Hungarian spirit . . . equally disposed to taunting, cheerful guffawing, and wrath."[28] Bartók was uniquely able to tap into that "Hungarian spirit," according to Csáth, because of his ethnographic research and encounters with rural subjects. Csáth further echoes Bartók's assessment that rural citizens who had not come into contact with Rom musicians or other outside influences were best able to maintain the authentic traditional music that expressed their "ancestral ethnic souls."[29]

In another review in *Nyugat* two years later, Csáth contrasts works of other Hungarian composers with Bartók's 1907 *Three Hungarian Folksongs from Csík* (*Három Csík megyei népdal*, BB 45b), which was based on folk songs collected during one of his first fieldwork journeys, among the Székely Hungarians of Transylvania:

> Bartók's *Three Hungarian Folksongs from Csík* does not want to be other and to seem other than it is. They are folk song transcriptions, but genuine, elegant, with Bartók's luscious intuition. Bartók feels something entirely different in the folk song than [contemporary Hungarian composer Károly] Agghazy, who stiffly follows the "German" Liszt. Bartók feels the soul of the folk song, its singsong nature, and the milieu from which it arose. If I wanted to define to an Englishman or a Frenchman what a Hungarian folk song is—I would ban Liszt, Székely and Ábrányi-type rhapsodies and I would give him Bartók's simple, easy miniature transcriptions that have no need for runs or warbling.[30]

This description of one of Bartók's earliest arrangements of folk music implies succinctly a number of the principal tenets of his theory of music, including the notion that music can offer an expression of Hungarian national identity; the belief in the importance of innovation and a break from earlier compositional styles; and the assertion that arrangements of folk songs can be created in a mode of authentic realism such that they are more or less equivalent to the artifacts on which they are based.

The composer Géza Vilmos Zágon took a similar approach in a 1911 review of a performance of Bartók's folk music settings: Bartók's pieces, he wrote, "relate the story of Hungarian pleasure and grief, Hungarian pride and pain, but not distorted by the Gypsies' flourishes or the great virtuosi's arrangements; but rather truly, deeply, with almost shocking directness, often with a metaphysical thrill throughout."[31] Like Csáth, Zágon observes in Bartók a unique departure from the familiar virtuosic Rom and Lisztian approaches to Hungarian music. *Nyugat* editors and authors credited Bartók with raising Hungarian musical culture from the peripheral status expected of a nation at the edge between East and West to the quality of its Western counterparts. He was able to do so, they claimed, by studying and assimilating what he called "peasant music" into his compositional idiom. He was thus praised for composing on a par the best European musicians, but creating something essentially Hungarian.

Through the next two decades Bartók continued to promote what he deemed the "pure" musical forms of folk music, and held Rom musicians largely responsible for the hybrid music so popular in Budapest. In his 1921 article "Hungarian Folk Music," for instance, he wrote that when Rom musicians play "dilettante semi-popular melodies" by amateur gentry composers, they alter the tempo, add augmented seconds to the melody, and otherwise employ "strange embellishments which recall certain ornamental passages of Western music."[32] He dubbed these performance tropes "deformations." On the other hand, "Folk music . . . comprises in the broadest sense all the melodies which subsist or have subsisted in the peasant class . . . as a quite spontaneous expression of their musical instincts. . . . It is the entirety of the melodies which, linked this way to peasant life, presents a certain *unity of musical style*."[33]

Similarly, in 1931 Bartók wrote in "Gipsy Music or Hungarian Music" that most listeners associate the music performed by Rom musicians with Hungary and value it over rural folk music: "This official belief . . . is echoed by the multitude, incapable of competent judgment."[34] In rural folk songs, by contrast, "text and music form an indivisible unity."[35] This "unified style" contrasts strongly, in his view, with the music of Rom ensembles, which perform songs without their texts, as instrumental arrangements. Bartók concluded, "This alone suffices to prove the lack of authenticity in gipsy renderings of music."[36] The search for a pure form of folk became one of the primary goals of Bartók's developing ethnographic methodology.

For Bartók, comparative musicology involved the collection of the folk music of neighboring peoples and the analysis of similarities and variances between different musical traditions to establish patterns of influence, as well as to determine the origins of musical traditions by distilling out the main characteristics that, prior to this influence, belonged organically to a particular group. He explained in 1936, "One could and should disclose the ancient cultural connection of peoples who are now far from each other; one could clarify problems of settlement, history; one could point to the form of contact, to the relationship or contrast of the spiritual complexion of neighboring nations."[37] His methodology was founded in part on the fear of the inevitable disappearance of rural cultures. In "Hungarian Folk Music," Bartók laments that "these melodies are about to become extinct; the new musical style prevailing for several decades assails them more and more."[38] Furthermore, he repeats his claim that "we have to look for [folk songs] among the simplest and poorest peasants, far away from the railroads, if we intend to find material untouched by the contaminating influence of the cities."[39] Bartók's project thus combined a preoccupation with the search for musical origins with the restorative aims of salvage ethnography.

Perhaps inspired by his method of comparative musicology, Bartók experimented with the juxtaposition of folk music of different origins in many of his pedagogical works, including his multi-volume piano training system *Mikrokosmos* (1926, 1932–9, BB 105). In his rural miniature collection *Forty-Four Duos for Two Violins*, Bartók provides tools for young musicians and listeners to engage in an amateur version of comparative musicology.[40] Completed in 1931 and published by Universal Edition in 1933, this compendium combines arrangements of folk music artifacts selected from the collections Bartók amassed over many years of fieldwork in and around Hungary. Bartók prefaces the first edition of the work with an explanation of his goals in gathering these diverse arrangements: "They aim at providing the pupils in the first few years of their studies, with performance pieces which possess the unadorned simplicity of old folk-music, with all its melodic and rhythmic particularities."[41] He juxtaposes settings of melodies he heard performed by Ruthenian, Romanian, Arabic, Hungarian, and Slovak musicians.

Bartók writes in his introduction, "Each of the following pieces is based on a peasant melody, with two exceptions. . . . In concert performance it is advisable not to keep to this order but to play the pieces in a group without an interval between the numbers, or in several such groups." He provides five recommended series ranging in length from four to eight movements. One of these suggested sequences, for instance, combines arrangements of one Romanian, one Hungarian, and three Slovak songs (numbers 7, 25, 33, 4, and 34). Another assembles arrangements of two melodies from Slovakia, one from Hungary, and three from different Romanian districts (11, 22, 30, 13, 31, and 32). The musical artifacts represented in *Forty-Four Duos* originated as dances and songs associated with a variety of contexts and functions including lullabies, children's games, weddings, the harvest, and the army. With this work, Bartók permits the performer to produce his own miniature folk music collection and to help listeners draw comparisons between different music cultures.

According to Bartók, the purity of what he called old-style folk song could be heard manifestly in the music's simplicity, succinctness, straightforwardness of expression, and lack of adornment. In a 1921 essay Bartók described folk music as "the classical model of how to express an idea musically in the most concise form, with the greatest simplicity of means, with freshness and life, briefly yet completely and properly proportioned."[42] Eight years later he elaborated on this concept, describing the style of folk music as a manifestation of its authenticity: "Genuine folk music, in its wider sense, contains melodies . . . which are a spontaneous expression of the people's musical instinct. . . . True folk music is always distinguished by absolute purity of style."[43] Bartók returned to this theme in the 1931 essay "What Is Folk Music?": because they are the result of organic processes of change, he writes, folk songs and dances are "the embodiment of an artistic perfection of the highest order; in fact, they are models of the way in which a musical idea can be expressed with utmost perfection in terms of brevity of form and simplicity of means."[44]

The German-language version of Bartók's 1931 essay identifies these musical attributes of brevity and simplicity with the ideal of objectivity, which he denotes with the term "*Objektivität in der Gestaltung*."[45] His complicated conception of objectivity does not preclude musical expression; in fact, combined with brevity and simplicity, it assists in the perfection of expression.[46] In "The Influence of Peasant Music on Modern Music," Bartók explains that folk music, the perfect expression of a musical idea, remains emotionally restrained and straightforward: he writes that folk music's "expressive power is amazing, and at the same time it is devoid of all sentimentality and superfluous ornaments. It is simple, sometimes primitive, but never silly."[47] In his compositions, Bartók employed rural melodies and stylistic effects gleaned from his study of traditional music in an attempt to purify art music. He hoped that by doing so he could use his compositions as a force of purification in urban society.[48] Although these essays came a decade and a half after Bartók's composition of his 1915 folk music arrangements, his early approach to the setting of songs and dances already demonstrated that he associated folk music with the characteristics of brevity, simplicity, objectivity, and expressiveness.

BARTÓK AND REALISM IN COMPOSITION

Early in their collaboration, in 1906, Bartók and Kodály co-authored and published an "Appeal to the Hungarian Public" in which they articulated their motivations for studying folk music, in the hope of garnering financial support for their project. This document expressed their sense of "extreme urgency" to act quickly in their salvage mission to collect Hungarian folk music, because "the traditional stock of folk music dies out at a terrifying rate. . . . Within a few decades Hungarian folk songs will no longer be heard, presumably for ever."[49] Bartók and Kodály hoped to alter this trend by introducing listeners to the music of ethnic Hungarians and other non-Rom groups from rural areas in danger of the hybridizing influence of Rom music: "the influx of light music into the villages, the massive amount of imitation folksongs turned out on a large scale arrested the production of true folksongs and has put the old ones into the shade." In addition to searching out "true folksongs," Bartók and Kodály aimed to replace an old scholarly method that was "not always accurate and authentic" with one characterized by "scholarly exactitude."

This flyer was distributed with an order form that readers could send back to purchase copies of "Hungarian Folksongs," a collection of arrangements compiled by both composers to spread awareness of Hungarian folk culture and solicit interest in funding and following the cause. Although Bartók and Kodály initially planned to publish this booklet of scores in two parts and to follow these with additional serialized collections of folk music arrangements, the number of orders turned out to be meager. As a result, they decided to print all of the twenty songs together in one document and to give up the idea of a subscription series. They adapted six of these from phonograph recordings by their predecessor Vikár and the rest from their own collections. The pamphlet opened with a preface by the two musicians that described two forms of folk song publications they were busy compiling: the "comprehensive dictionary of folksongs," which must contain all songs no matter their aesthetic merit, and the selective song collections, of which the pamphlet was an example, aimed at introducing folk music to the public.[50]

The arrangements in this publication, with their unadorned melodic transcriptions and relatively bare accompaniment, represent a marked departure from Bartók's earlier settings of traditional music, such as the *Four Songs* that he had composed in 1902. Between that earlier compilation of Rom melodies set against complicated piano accompaniments and the new ones in his 1906 pamphlet, Bartók's outlook on the selection and arrangement of folk music had undergone significant change.[51] To describe their new method of setting folk songs to accompaniment, Bartók and Kodály employed a sartorial metaphor whose meaning overlapped with Bartók's analogy between arranging folk music and setting a precious stone:

> If brought in from the fields into the towns, folksongs have to be dressed up. However, attired in their new habit, they might seem shy and out of place. One must take care to cut their new clothes so as not to cramp their fresh country style. Whether arranged for choir or for the piano, the accompaniment should merely try to conjure up the image of fields and villages left behind. As for the authenticity of the melodies, the songs of the popular edition should not be second to those of the complete one.[52]

Bartók and Kodály show no discomfort with the conceptual friction between "dressing up" a folk song and retaining its "authenticity." Thus in this document they outline a theory of musical representation, describing a compositional style that aims to depict folk music research in an apparently authentic manner.

Bartók's aesthetic aims depended on a belief in the close ties between folk song, nationalism, and realism, as his publications with Kodály attest. Bartók developed a number of his related ideals based on his interactions beginning around 1905 with a group of prominent Budapest intellectuals who considered themselves political radicals, in opposition to the conservative principles generally shared by the gentry and noble classes. The group included such figures as the literary critic György Lukács, philosopher Leo Popper, poet Béla Balázs, sociologist Karl Mannheim, and art historian Arnold Hauser. Bartók's relationship with these men frequently involved musical collaboration. He occasionally taught Lukács piano lessons, for instance, and later lived for a time at Lukács's family home. Balázs was the librettist of *Bluebeard's Castle* and scenarist of the ballet *The Wooden Prince*. And in 1918, Bartók delivered a lecture on music at Mannheim's Free School for the Human Sciences.[53] Under the leadership of Lukács, this group formed the Sunday Circle in 1915, meeting weekly to discuss issues they found critical to Hungary's contemporary affairs and to share their work. Bartók performed *The Wooden Prince* in an arrangement for piano at one of these meetings.[54]

For the members of the Sunday Circle, art played a crucial role in modern culture. These figures generally opposed the conception of "art for art's sake," feeling strongly that art had an important social function to rise above mere entertainment and instead reveal society's underlying structures, and even to illuminate the guiding principles of life itself.[55] Using metaphysical terms they described a belief in the presence of an internal essence, an organic soul that was both individual and collectively shared by society. For Mannheim, the responsibility of art was to address the soul; like Bartók, Mannheim suggested that artists incorporate folklore into their work in order to direct modern artistic style in a new, revolutionary direction.[56] The concept of folk music as the authentic expression of the collective Hungarian soul was, of course, developed at length in Bartók's writings. Bartók and his peers held that one of the crucial responsibilities of art was to depict the true, rural Hungarian soul as a way to correct the falsifications that had been imposed on the nation's culture in the city, through the influences of conservatism, modernity, and the lifestyle of the gentry class.

In the essay "What Is Folk Music?" Bartók answers the question posed in the title: "peasant music . . . actually is nothing but the outcome of changes wrought by a natural force whose operation is unconscious in men who are not influenced by urban culture."[57] For Bartók, folk music was natural, organic, and primordial.[58] In the search for the essential elements of life and the drive to create as truthful as possible a depiction of society, Bartók turned to folklore, which he believed to represent the collective soul of the Hungarian nation, by the most technically simple but expressively robust means. Bartók's realist style was founded on the goals of both creating representations of "real" musical artifacts and producing works that were honest to the totality of life. For Bartók, realism meant absolute fealty to the folk music he was recording in the countryside, which he viewed as an antidote for the falsifications of the true Hungarian genius that he could see around him in the city. He attempted to represent an external reality—the folk music artifact—with objective accuracy in his rural miniatures. Through these works, Bartók felt he was making the soul of the Hungarian nation available to listeners in Budapest as well as Western Europe.

BARTÓK'S 1915 RURAL MINIATURES

In 1911, Bartók and Kodály founded the New Hungarian Music Society, which aimed to arrange lectures on music, publish music criticism, and plan concerts featuring abstract musical works and settings of folk songs and dances by Hungarian composers alongside music from other European nations. The Society also proposed the formation of an orchestra devoted to "play[ing] the works of new Hungarian composers, with ambition, conviction, and the fulfillment of the composers' wishes, authentically, and contribut[ing] to the goal of their music taking root in the soul of the audience, and of its not coming before the public distorted or falsified."[59] The goal was no less than to reconfigure the practice of art music in Hungary and to intensify and augment the process by which listeners came to feel that performances by Hungarian musicians and music by Hungarian composers were nationally, authentically theirs. In the manner of the founders of the Society for Jewish Folk Music and the journal *Nyugat*, the New Hungarian Music Society's directors wanted to prove that their music culture was on a par with Western Europe's, but also uniquely local.

The public they hoped to establish as the new audience for Hungarian modernism showed little interest, however, because Bartók and Kodály never managed to accumulate the funding or support to carry out their ambition, and the New Hungarian Music Society was disbanded only one year later. Bartók's disappointment about this failure to attract enthusiasm for his work, in addition to recent criticism of his compositions, drove him to take a hiatus from participating in Hungarian musical life; during this time he rarely performed or composed and lost his business arrangement with his publishers.[60] Instead, Bartók focused his efforts between 1912 and 1915 on another task he found critical to the establishment of authentic Hungarian musical identity: ethnographic fieldwork and analysis.

Bartók developed his techniques for composing rural miniatures in 1915, during which year he devoted his artistic activities almost exclusively to the genre, writing three works for solo piano, *Romanian Christmas Carols*, *Romanian Folk Dances*, and Sonatina (*Szonatina*, BB 69), as well as two unpublished pieces for women's choir and several songs for voice and piano.[61] These works were based on Romanian folk songs and dances selected from the vast collection he amassed during his fieldwork in Transylvania, when it was still within Hungarian borders. The first three incorporate thirty-two folk songs and dances among them. Whereas the Sonatina is structured in a conventional three-movement form, *Romanian Christmas Carols* and *Romanian Folk Dances* are composed of multiple short movements, each devoted to the setting of one song or dance (with the exception of the final movement of *Romanian Folk Dances*, which contains two). In order to enhance the appearance of accuracy in these works, Bartók included background information about the original folk songs and dances in the scores' paratexts. In the 1919 score of Sonatina, Bartók inserted an asterisk at the start of each folk melody, alerting the reader to the bottom of the page, where he supplied the genre name of the song or dance and the village and county in which it was performed; he omitted any descriptive details about the identity of the musicians whose performance he recorded. For instance, Bartók identified the first melody as an *ardeleana* that he initially heard performed in Cserbel, in the county of Hunyad.[62] In the case of the second melody, Bartók additionally provided a cross-reference to the location of his published transcription of the melody in *Cântece populare românești din Comitatul Bihor* (*Ungaria*) (Romanian Folk Songs from the Bihar District [Hungary]), his first compendium of folk music, published in Bucharest in 1913.[63] These details lend credibility to Bartók's folk music settings by demonstrating, in the notational style of objective scholarly footnotes, that the composer has studied the song and published it in a scientific anthology. The footnote makes it possible for the curious performer to refer to Bartók's "comprehensive dictionary of folksongs" in order to locate the original source transcription.

In the 1918 Universal Edition score of *Romanian Folk Dances*, Bartók listed in footnotes the village and county where he recorded the performances on which each movement was based. The 1926 publication of Zoltán Székely's arrangement of the work opens with a page devoted to the ethnographic explication of the genres represented within. For each dance, this preface provides a translation of the title, the regional origin, and a description that refers to its ritual function and steps. "Jocul cu bâtă," for instance, is identified as "*Dance with Sticks*—or a game played with a stick. From Mezőszabad, district of Maros-Torda, in Transylvania. Merry and energetic with a gaily syncopated melody." With such paratextual descriptions Bartók brought his ethnographic research directly into his compositional practice.

Many of the changes Bartók made to the source melodies in his arrangement, such as the editing of ornamentation, appear aimed to create the impression of a simple, pure form of expression among musicians in rural Transylvania. Occasionally, alterations appear to have been unintended, occurring because of gaps in Bartók's ethnographic knowledge at this relatively early stage in his research. Bartók did not form an understanding of complex Bulgarian metric practices, for example, until he read *Grundriss der Metrik und der Rhythmik der bulgarischen Volksmusik* (Outline of the Meter and Rhythm of Bulgarian Folk Music) by Vasil Stoin in the late 1920s or early 1930s, after which time he revisited his Romanian transcriptions and found that 5 percent of these folk melodies and 8 percent of the Christmas carols were based on Bulgarian meters.[64] Thus it appears likely that when he was writing *Romanian Christmas Carols* in 1915, the metric setting of some of the melodies resulted from the attempt to clarify what he heard in his fieldwork, for himself as well as his audience, owing to a limited comprehension of some elements of the region's musical traditions.

By invoking scientific research in Romanian folk music through the addition of ethnographic details in the paratexts of his scores, Bartók invites his performers to participate as amateurs in the field of folk music research. He provides enough information to instruct them about the context and function of each movement and to evoke the world beyond the urban environment in which the performers operated. Performers could thereby introduce these melodies to their listeners, in the role of surrogates of the rural musicians who originally played the musical artifacts. Thus in one concert at which Bartók performed his own works, hosted by the British Music Society in 1922, the program's description of his rural miniatures aimed at persuading them of the performance's accurate, unmediated portrayal of the folk music, with the words, "Roumanian dance tunes are used here in their original form without alteration."[65] For Bartók, art music performance could become an extension of his ethnomusicological work, a means of conveying his discoveries to the urban public.

ROMANIAN FOLK DANCES FROM THE FIELD TO THE PAGE

The primary sources Bartók consulted when arranging folk music for *Romanian Folk Dances*, *Romanian Christmas Carols*, and Sonatina were the initial transcriptions he made rapidly into locational notebooks during his fieldwork in Transylvania, the first time he heard a performance of a song or dance, and before he asked the musician to record it on the phonograph.[66] Transcriptions of field research, for Bartók, were useful early in the process of fieldwork as they helped him determine which melodies he should devote space to on the wax cylinders he brought on his travels. He returned later to the cylinders to produce detailed ethnographic transcriptions and engage in comparative musicological research.[67] Bartók privileged the written record over the aural; he believed that individual performances could be flawed, incorporating mistakes caused by accident or by a performer's lack of ability, and that the transcriber's role was to clean up these mistakes.[68] He began the process of composing all three of these works at once, selecting songs and dances from his notebooks and writing piano arrangements of these directly into a single document.[69] He then separated this large collection of arrangements into three groups, which would become the three works. It is evident from this manuscript that Bartók initially intended to open *Romanian Folk Dances* with an arrangement of an additional dance, an *învârtita* that he collected in 1912; he later decided to omit this dance, crossing out his arrangement in pencil.[70]

The other seven dances that Bartók cordoned off among the arrangements in his manuscript to be included in *Romanian Folk Dances* did make it into the final work. The first movement of *Romanian Folk Dances*, titled "Jocul cu bâtă," is based on a dance Bartók recorded in a performance by a duo of Rom violinists in 1912, in the village of Voiniceni, in Mureş county. The following two movements, "Brâul" and "Pe loc," originated as melodies he transcribed in 1912 in Igriş, Torontal. He collected the remaining four dances in 1910. The source music for the fourth, "Buciumeana," was performed by a Rom violinist in Bistra, Turda-Arieş county; the fifth, "Poargă 'românească,'" was from a melody played by a young violinist in Beiuş, Bihor; and the final two, which together form the sixth movement, "Mărunţel," are derived from a *mărunţel* played for Bartók by another young violinist in Beiuş, Bihor, and a dance of an unidentified genre performed by an adult violinist from Neagra, Turda-Arieş.[71]

A comparison of the manuscript containing the first draft of Bartók's piano arrangements of the folk dances that he separated out to become *Romanian Folk Dances* with the final published edition of the work demonstrates that beyond altering his initial intention to open the piece with an additional movement, Bartók made only a few notable changes between his original conception and final draft. In the first movement, "Jocul cu bâtă," Bartók initially wrote a bass pattern in the first few measures constructed of high chords followed by low bass notes; he then crossed this out on the manuscript, reversing the pattern so that these measures begin instead with a low tone in the bass followed by a chord in a higher range. Heavy downbeats in a low tessitura evoke the uncomplicated authenticity that Bartók described as a trait of rural culture by implying that the dance gestures are simple and repetitive. More specifically, the accentuation patterns and alternating low and high pitches resemble the *esztam* accompaniment pattern. Elsewhere, in measures 17 and 29, the handwritten manuscript shows that in the first beat of the bass, Bartók initially composed a quarter-note chord, before crossing this out and replacing it with a quarter rest, which appears in the final published version. In the third movement, "Pe Loc," Bartók similarly altered his original manuscript setting when editing it for the final published version by crossing out individual chords in the bass voice in measures 20, 28, 32, and 36 and replacing them with rests.

The most significant changes between Bartók's initial handwritten setting in the manuscript and the later published version of the score occur in the final two movements. The entire fifth movement, "Poarga 'românească,'" was originally written in 2/4 time in the manuscript, whereas the final published version appears in alternating measures of 2/4 and 3/4. And in the manuscript draft of movement six, "Mărunţel," Bartók initially experimented with a more syncopated bass rhythm featuring tied notes over every second bar line, before crossing this out and settling on a pattern featuring heavy downbeats, again connoting the simplicity of the dance movements. Other than the metric alteration in movement five, the changes Bartók made between the original handwritten sketch and the final published version demonstrate an interest in paring down his setting, heightening the impression of accuracy in relation to the original sources, and producing a sense of simplicity by creating silences in the bass and straightforward accompaniment patterns with heavy downbeats that emphasize the dance-like qualities of the music's rhythms and imitate *dűvő* and *esztam*. Far more radical alterations occur between Bartók's fieldwork notebook transcriptions of the folk dances and his arrangements of them for piano.[72] The following comparison of the transcriptions and arrangements of folk songs in *Romanian Folk Dances*, with particular attention to the first movement, highlights the kinds of changes Bartók made to his transcriptions in converting them to piano arrangements (measures 1–9 of Bartók's notebook transcription appear in Example 6.1).

The original folk dance was performed by two violinists, one playing the melody and the other close harmonies on three strings at once, on a violin with a flat bridge and scordatura tuning.[73] The dance is formed in two sections and divides conventionally into two-measure units. The first half is eight measures long and repeats with differing first and second endings; the second half is sixteen measures, built of two eight-measure subphrases. The second violin plays a continuous *dűvő* pattern of two notes per bar. Bartók inserts a question mark in the first measure of the accompaniment—presumably the harmony was indiscernible to him during the performance.

The key of this jocul cu bâtă is difficult to determine definitively, although it is clearly centered on the pitch A, which is the final pitch in both halves of the dance. The dance cannot be parsed precisely according to Western diatonic harmonic conventions, of course, because it originates as a Transylvanian folk dance. Although Transylvanian harmonic practices are not entirely different from those in art music,

EXAMPLE 6.1:   "Jocul cu bâtă," measures 1–9, from Béla Bartók's notebooks. Lampert, *Népzene Bartók műveiben*, 96

methods of analysis designed for Western music are generally ill suited to the analysis of Transylvanian music.[74] Because Bartók transcribed this dance using Western notational practices and composed his setting of it according to art music conventions, however, it is revealing to examine this dance through that lens, in order to determine the choices Bartók made in transferring the dance between harmonic languages.

This dance, as Bartók transcribed it, appears to conform in part to the diatonic key of A minor, because of the prevalence of C-natural in the melody, as well as the chord of C major, the relative major key of A minor and thus a key to which A minor tends to modulate. C major chords occur in measure 4 (preceded by a measure in G major, the dominant of C); and the harmony appears to modulate to C major in measures 10–20, during which C major chords alternate with G major and G dominant 7 chords. The A minor triad is never encountered in the accompaniment, however: every triad with a root of A has a raised third degree. Despite the sound of A minor in the melody, therefore, the final effect of the harmony is resoundingly major. Indeed, no minor chords appear in the original transcription of this dance; rather, one finds in the accompaniment only A, C, and G major triads, G dominant 7 chords (absent the third degree), and a double-stopped perfect fourth on A and D (measures 2 and 9).

Bartók makes three significant kinds of alteration to his original transcription in his setting of "Jocul cu bâtă." First, he changes the texture of the music, though mainly retaining the *dűvő* accompaniment. Second, he evokes melancholy by choosing to emphasize the A minor key that is alluded to but never heard in the original transcription, and by including dissonant appoggiaturas in the left hand. Finally, he accentuates the modal quality of the original transcription by elaborating on effects of the original, to hint at the Dorian mode and create weak dominant chords. The following paragraphs address these alterations in order.

Bartók retains the general form of the original dance, while complicating and lengthening it. In lieu of a repeat sign after the first portion of the dance, as appears in the notebook transcription, he writes out the repeated passage (Example 6.2). This allows him to make changes in the accompaniment as the melody recurs. He also notates the repetition of the second half of the melody, lengthening the dance by sixteen measures; here too, he varies the accompaniment for the second airing of the melody. The accompaniment pattern resembles the original *dűvő* accompaniment in the transcription in that it is constructed mostly of quarter notes; Bartók complicates its texture, however, by adding occasional ties over the bar line (measures 5–6, 13–4, 25–6, 27–8, 41–2, and 43–4); silent rests on downbeats (measures 17, 29, 34 and 36); embellishing grace notes (measures 4, 10, 11, and 26); and moving sixteenth and eighth notes (measures 3 and 12). The continuous chordal pattern of the original transcription is altered here in Bartók's setting to accommodate a more varied texture in which he

EXAMPLE 6.2:   Béla Bartók, *Romanian Folk Dances*, movement 1, "Joc cu bâtă," measures 1–17

frequently alternates single-voiced quarter notes with intervals and chords. The overall effect of the left-hand accompaniment is to combine broad leaps between beats one and two with tight voice leading within the chords. Bartók thus emphasizes the downbeats of each measure to denote the dance meter, as he alludes to the voice leading of the scordatura violin.

Although this arrangement is clearly in A minor, Bartók imitates the A major phrase endings in the notebook transcription, writing A major triads at the end of the repeating opening melody (measures 7–8 and 15–16). Bartók also ends the two larger phrases of the second half with A major chords (measures 31–2 and 48). He composes frequent appoggiaturas and descending bass lines in his arrangement. In measure 4, for instance, the B from the previous measure is reiterated, prolonging the descent to A. This appoggiatura, the second degree of the A minor tonic harmony in this measure, produces a dissonance against C in both the right and left hands. The B on the downbeat of measure 19 also acts as an appoggiatura in the midst of a longer descent from D in the middle voice of the chord in the left hand, measure 17, to the F in the bottom voice of the downbeat of measure 21 (Example 6.3a). The bass pattern descends chromatically and again incorporates non-chord tones in measures 32–5, where a line passing from the middle to upper voices falls along the pitch contour C-sharp–C-natural–B–A. Beginning one measure into this pattern and continuing beyond it, passing from middle to bottom voices, is the succession F–E–D–C–B (measures 33–7, Example 6.3b). In the second half of measure 37, this B repeats an octave above and continues to descend chromatically, switching octaves again in measure 39, to the F-natural in measure 41. Bartók continues to compose appoggiaturas in measures 38–41, such as the F in the left hand in measure 39. Finally, the prolonged D in the upper voice of the left hand

EXAMPLE 6.3A: Béla Bartók, *Romanian Folk Dances*, movement 1, "Joc cu bâtă," measures 17–21, left hand

EXAMPLE 6.3B: Béla Bartók, *Romanian Folk Dances*, movement 1, "Joc cu bâtă," measures 32–41, left hand

EXAMPLE 6.3C: Béla Bartók, *Romanian Folk Dances*, movement 1, "Joc cu bâtă," measures 46–8

in the penultimate measure of the movement is an appoggiatura in the midst of a I$^{6/4}$ chord; this resolves to C-sharp in the final measure, in a cadence to A major (Example 6.3c). The frequent appoggiaturas and descending bass lines, both established signifiers of longing and lament, enhance the expressive affect of the minor mode in which they operate.

In Bartók's transcription of the performance he heard in the field, the original dance combines a minor melody with major accompanying chords, and frequent parallel fifths. Bartók alludes once to this parallel-fifth motion, in the bass in measures 34–5 of his arrangement. He also adopts two additional details from this transcription and repeats them in his arrangement. First, the F-sharp in measures 2 and 3 (and in an alternate version of measure 14) of the transcription recurs frequently in both hands in Bartók's piano arrangement. The F-sharp becomes an essential part of the scale on which the piece is based; incorporated into A minor in the place of F-natural, it produces an A Dorian scale. By highlighting the Dorian scale, Bartók illustrates the assertion in many of his essays that the Dorian mode is one of the most common scales in what he calls "old-style" Eastern European folk music and is derived as an expansion of the pentatonic scale, an even more archaic element of the idiom.[75]

Second, Bartók incorporates repeatedly in his arrangement the VII–I progression that appears in the first and second endings of the first half of his notebook transcription. The VII is a weak dominant in this progression because it lacks the leading tone. The VII chord appears repeatedly in Bartók's setting, for example, in measures 3 and 22, where the addition of the seventh above the root G of the chord produces a VII$_7$. Additionally, Bartók employs the harmony of the minor V to resolve to the major tonic in measures 5–7 and 13–14. He even modifies the source melody in order to create this chord, writing in his arrangement a G-natural (measures 6 and 14) where the original transcription features the leading tone G-sharp that resolves to the tonic A on the following downbeat (measures 6–7 and the corresponding measures in the second ending). In order to highlight the difference between traditional music of Transylvania and Western art music composition, Bartók extends and exaggerates the modal techniques beyond what is found in the original transcription.

Within the apparently simple framework of "Jocul cu Bâtă," with its four-measure phrases, repetitions, and clear duple dance meter, Bartók evokes a sense of foreign otherness distinct from Western compositional conventions, through modal mixture, parallel fifths, and weak dominant chords. Bartók illustrates the source melody as different from typical urban fare and as an artifact from another time and place, with an evocative harmony and dancing, two-step simplicity and predictability. Moreover, appoggiaturas and the minor key appear to signify a mood of melancholy nostalgia. This combination of traits recalls Bartók's published descriptions of folk music as simple and uninformed by neighboring musical styles, yet possessed of a metaphysically transcendent expressive power; as pure, serious, and the opposite of what he considered the frivolous urban popular music performed by Rom bands.

The other folk dances that Bartók adapted from his field notebook transcriptions for *Romanian Folk Dances* were originally performed for him as unaccompanied melodies. Bartók makes a number of changes to his transcriptions in adapting them for piano. Movement two, "Brâul," is in D Dorian in Bartók's work, whereas the transcription is notated in B Dorian. The dance on which the following movement, "Pe loc," is based is harmonically ambiguous according to the standard idioms of art music: it could be interpreted to have a tonic of A, although this pitch occurs only rarely, as the lowest note in a melody whose range extends only by a minor sixth, and features augmented seconds between C and D-sharp, which are marked as the key signature (Example 6.4). In Bartók's setting, however, the key signature is shown as B minor, which is entrained at the opening of the movement by three measures of rocking perfect fifths of B and F-sharp in the left hand (Example 6.5). Bartók represents the

EXAMPLE 6.4: "Pă loc," measures 1–2, from Béla Bartók's notebooks. Lampert, *Népzene Bartók műveiben*, 97

EXAMPLE 6.5:   Béla Bartók, *Romanian Folk Dances*, movement 3, "Pe Loc," measures 1–6

scale of the original dance with augmented seconds between D and E-sharp, indicated by accidentals. He also raises the highest note of the scale by a half step, broadening the melodic range to a major sixth. He appends a four-measure coda that resembles an unfinished reiteration of the opening phrase whispered at triple *piano* and concluding with a silent measure-long rest.

In this movement, Bartók provides his melody with a simple bass pattern of slurred pairs of quarter notes, each constructed of an interval followed by a single quarter note. He creates long pedal points by retaining pitches as the melody continues above—in fact, no variation in pitches is registered until measure 13, and then only for two measures before the bass line returns to the original pitches for another two measures. With a dynamic range that does not exceed *più piano* and several measure-long silences in the left hand (measures 20, 28, 32, and 36; the right hand is silent in 37, and both are silent in the last bar), Bartók produces an eerie effect, as swirling arabesques in the right hand contrast with the left hand's lulling insistence.

Bartók retains the original pitches of his notebook transcription in the following movement of *Romanian Folk Dances*, "Buciumeana," and creates a harmonic accompaniment in the tonic key of A major (Example 6.6). The left hand undulates up and down on quarter notes during the first half of the movement; from measures 3–10, pairs of rocking quarter notes create a feeling of duple meter that conflicts with the 3/4 time signature. Bartók also combines twos and threes in the melodic rhythm, by lengthening sixteenth-note patterns from the source melody into triplets (compare measures 4–5 in Example 6.6 with measures 2–3 in Example 6.7). Bartók made a greater alteration to his

EXAMPLE 6.6:   Béla Bartók, *Romanian Folk Dances*, movement 4, "Buciumeana," measures 1–6

EXAMPLE 6.7:   "Buciumeana," measures 1–4, from Béla Bartók's notebooks. Lampert, *Népzene Bartók műveiben*, 97

initial field notebook transcriptions when arranging this dance later for publication in *Romanian Folk Music* than in 1915 for his composition, having in the intervening years become familiar with Bulgarian metrical techniques.[76] In the later transcription, Bartók amended his original 3/4 meter to a complicated alternation of 10/16 and 9/16 in which downbeat pitches remain the same but the rhythms in between are changed. To fit the melody into this new metric construction, Bartók made a number of alterations, including reinterpreting the rhythms he notated as triplets in measures 4 and 5 of his composition as duple rhythms of two sixteenth notes and one eighth note, as they appeared in his initial notebook jottings. The wax cylinder recording that Bartók produced during his fieldwork reveals an exceedingly fast-paced performance. Given Bartók's belief that sound recordings incorporate "mistakes" on the part of the performer that required correction by the ethnographer, it is conceivable that Bartók might have judged irregularities in the meter to be impromptu rhythmic errors in need of correction by fitting them into a stable time signature in his initial transcription and arrangement.

In the melody of "Buciumeana," Bartók accentuates the interval of the augmented second, which he produces by lowering the second scale degree to B-flat and raising the third to C-sharp, and he includes these pitches frequently in the left hand. The prevalence of augmented-second intervals in this and the previous movement might appear surprising in light of the fact that in his 1921 article "Hungarian Folk Music," Bartók would characterize the interval as a trope imported to Hungary from the Balkan regions by itinerant Rom musicians, and thus a "deformation" of pure Hungarian, Slovak, and Romanian music.[77] The effect is, of course, also recognizable as an established exoticizing trope in art music. For the listener, the augmented seconds in *Romanian Folk Dances* might

EXAMPLE 6.8: Béla Bartók, *Romanian Folk Dances*, movement 5, "Poarga 'românească,'" measures 1–8

thus create two seemingly contrasting effects at once, representing both the authenticity of the dance as an artifact of rural Romanian culture, and its exotic distance and difference from the urban setting in which the work is performed.

Movement five, "Poarga 'românească,'" retains the original transcription's alternation of 3/4 and 2/4 meters, and Bartók adds jaunty grace notes that contribute a brisk dance-like quality (Example 6.8). He changes the key from C major to D major, and employs the raised fourth that appears in the first half of the transcribed melody (for example, on the grace note in measure 5), producing the temporary effect of the Lydian scale. Bartók repeats the melody twice, the second time an octave lower and with syncopated, stammered offbeat rhythms in the bass. This movement ends in A major, after which the final movement, "Mărunţel," begins on a D major chord, with A as the first pitch of the melody, transposed from the original C major. Bartók concludes the second part of this movement with a grand finale, a fast-paced rendition of another dance he heard during his research, with a melodic setting that adheres generally to the original field notebook transcription.

Bartók meticulously calculated metronome markings of the tempos of the folk music he collected, both in his field notebook and later in his transcriptions from the wax cylinder recordings. In addition to these descriptive uses of metronome markings, Bartók frequently employed them prescriptively in his compositions, and indeed *Romanian Folk Dances* has metronome markings in each movement. Table 6.1 lists the tempos of the notebook transcriptions beside the metronome markings of each corresponding movement in the Universal Edition 1918 publication of *Romanian Folk Dances*.[78] The variation between the metronome markings in the field notebook and piano solo is not a sign that Bartók was unconcerned with the speed of the original performance when composing his arrangements. To the contrary, his personal markings on a copy

TABLE 6.1:   Tempo comparisons between field notebook transcriptions and their arrangements in *Romanian Folk Dances*

Dance	Field Notebook	Piano Solo
Jocul cu bâtă	♩=96	♩=80
Brâu	♩=92	♩=144*
Pă loc	♩=132	♩=112
Buciumeana	♩=138	♩=100
Poargă românească	♩=120–126	♩=152
Mărunţel	♩=138	♩=152
Unidentified genre	♩=160	♩=160
	From Lampert, *Népzene Bartók műveiben*, 96–9.	From 1918 printed score, Universal Edition

* In the field notebook, the melody of *Brâu* is notated in sixteenth notes, whereas in *Romanian Folk Dances*, Bartók notates it in eighth notes. If one converts the metronome marking of the final version to reflect the sixteenth-note notation of the original, for easy comparison, then ♩=72.

of the Boosey and Hawkes reprint of the Universal Edition score, which he annotated in the 1940s, demonstrate that Bartók always kept in mind the metronome markings of the performances he heard during his fieldwork.[79] Above the metronome marking printed beside the title of the first movement, for instance, he indicates the speed of 100 to the quarter note, conceding, "although the original peasant tempo is 92."[80] At the end of the movement, after the durational marking indicating that the performance should take fifty-seven seconds, Bartók notes, "in the cylinder 1'4"."[81] Bartók writes the "original peasant" tempo over each metronome marking in this document.[82]

As Table 6.1 makes evident, Bartók altered his prescriptive metronome markings considerably from those he originally wrote into his field notebooks. The first four of the seven dances are slower in Bartók's setting than in the original performance he transcribed, with the greatest change occurring in the setting of the buciumeana. The final two create the effect of an energetic, fast-paced setting of three dances that round out the work as a vibrant finale, as Bartók increases the speed of two of his settings, retaining the original metronome marking only in the final dance, already at a rapid 160 to the quarter note.

One effect of these changes is to produce a progression of expressive modes from the solemn, stately first movement to the exhilarating last movement that in its final coda seems to cycle increasingly out of control. This is a typical pattern in some multi-movement forms of art music, from the somber first movement to the spirited finale. This tempo pattern is also common to much traditional music from the area of Transylvania. Somewhat ironically, it also resembles the tempo progression in the traditional *lassú-friss* structure of the *verbunkos*. By slowing down the first four folk dances that he represents in *Romanian Folk Dances*, Bartók also increases the apparent simplicity and straightforwardness of the music clarifying their periodic structures and dance meters. He thus alters his original transcriptions in *Romanian Folk Dances* by manipulating tempos as well as harmonies, melodies, and textures, to represent the authenticity he believes is imbued in the musical artifacts he collected in Transylvania.

A few years after the publication of *Romanian Folk Dances*, Bartók participated in arranging the composition for performance by a variety of ensembles. He reworked the piece for small orchestra in 1917, and in 1925–6 he advised and approved Székely's arrangement for violin and piano duet. Székely studied violin at the Budapest Academy of Music under Jenő Hubay, and during his early career he trained in composition with Kodály. In 1921, when Székely was seventeen, Kodály initiated a meeting between the violinist and Bartók, suggesting that they play together; the two would subsequently begin a partnership, performing duets until 1938.[83] During this first year of their acquaintance, Bartók told Székely the story of his meeting with Lidi Dósa and described his fieldwork with Kodály and the wax cylinders they had accumulated.[84] After Székely's composition of a sonata for solo violin was accepted for the Venice Festival alongside works by Schoenberg and Stravinsky and received positive reviews in the press, the editor of Universal Edition offered Székely a publishing contract for three works, including the edition of Bartók's *Romanian Folk Dances* for violin and piano.[85] This arrangement was first created for a 1925 performance with Bartók in Arnhem, the Netherlands, that juxtaposed the rural miniature with Bartók's "Allegro Barbaro" and the second movement of Ernest Bloch's *Baal Shem*, among other works.[86]

In his edition, Székely takes advantage of the violin's versatility to produce a variety of timbres, some of which evoke the tone qualities of the instruments in Bartók's original recordings. In "Pe loc," for example, Székely sets the melody in artificial harmonics, representing the airy timbre and high tessitura of the *furulya* while also accentuating the eerie quality of Bartók's arrangement. At the opening of movement five and through much of movement six, he writes double stops with rough staccato articulations. Székely occasionally returns to the original timbral indications Bartók included in his field notebook transcriptions of violin performances, for instance, by labeling pizzicato notes in measures 33–4. The timbres of the two-violin instrumentation of the jocul cu bâtă Bartók originally transcribed were perhaps most closely evoked in a lost arrangement Székely made for violin and cello in 1926.[87]

In *Romanian Folk Dances* Bartók employs a variety of techniques for representing the original performances he encountered in Transylvania, by selecting melodies he transcribed in his fieldwork, incorporating sonic tropes that emphasize the simplicity and expressive authenticity he heard in the music, and printing historical and taxonomic details about the source melodies in the scores' paratexts.

For Bartók, unadorned straightforwardness and objectivity were among the attributes of folk music that made it expressively authentic. The compositional techniques in *Romanian Folk Dances* aimed to indicate to listeners and performers that the work accurately depicted an aesthetic and political reality that had been captured by means of his thoroughly contemporary project.

BARTÓK'S ROMANIAN WORKS AFTER THE TREATY OF TRIANON

For his ethnographic research in Transylvania, Bartók received both praise and derision from Hungarian and Romanian critics. While some Romanian writers expressed gratitude to Bartók for studying and spreading the knowledge of Romanian folk music, others were suspicious of whether Bartók was acting in Hungarian national interests. A number of conservative spokespeople in Hungary accused Bartók of paying too close attention to the culture of a neighbor against whom there was a growing sense of antagonism, especially after the destruction caused by World War I and the loss of Transylvania, which was returned to Romania by the Treaty of Trianon. A review of Bartók's 1913 anthology *Romanian Folk Songs from the Bihar District (Hungary)* in the Romanian journal of ethnography *Sezătoarea* (Society) argued that the book was of no value. Bartók defended his work by describing his scholarly method in detail, but he did not address the accusation that his ethnographic fieldwork was conducted in the interest of cultural imperialism.[88]

Bartók faced an onslaught of criticism from the opposite perspective back in Hungary. In 1920 he wrote a letter to the editor of the periodical *Szózat*, responding with vitriol to the accusations that appeared in a column by Hubay, who decried Bartók's decision to republish the article "The Folk Music Dialect of the Hunedoara Romanians" in the Leipzig *Zeitschrift für Musikwissenschaft* during the year of the Trianon losses. Bartók's rebuttal displays none of his previous admiration for the simplicity and purity he hears in Romanian folk music. Instead, Bartók writes that his republication of the article is not "untimely," as Hubay asserted, but to the contrary, "Its publication now is downright desirable, because it makes evident the cultural superiority of the Hungarians." He explains that his article "makes it quite plain that not a single Romanian has appeared who is suitable for the systematic study of the Romanian folk music: a Hungarian had to undertake this scientific research which is extremely important from the Hungarian viewpoint.—Is this not proof of our cultural superiority?"[89] He concludes by casting Hubay's accusations back in his direction: "Is not that man a 'malicious propagandist' who out of ignorance, malevolence or misrepresentation dares to forge the charge of unpatriotic conduct against an article which serves the cause of the Hungarian nation?"[90]

Over a decade later, in 1931, Bartók wrote an extensive and fiery letter to the Romanian author Octavian Beu, who had sent him an early draft of an essay about

Bartók that he intended to read on Romanian Radio, perhaps in honor of the composer's fiftieth birthday.[91] In the outcome of the Treaty of Trianon, Romania had repatriated the city in which Bartók was born, called Nagyszentmiklós in Hungarian and Sânnicolau Mare in Romanian. In spite of the lobby of voices accusing Bartók of working in Hungarian political interests during his research on Romanian music, a countermovement also existed in Romanian culture in which some, honoring Bartók's now-Romanian birthplace and his interest in representing Romania in ethnographic research and composition, in effect claimed Bartók as nationally Romanian after Trianon. In this spirit Beu called Bartók a "Romanian composer," a label at which Bartók took great umbrage. Bartók replied by reasserting his Hungarian identity, in the following terms: "I consider myself a Hungarian composer. The fact that the melodies in some of my own original compositions were inspired by or based on Romanian folk songs is no justification for classing me as a *compositorul roman* [Romanian composer]."[92]

Bartók defends his stance by pointing out that by similar logic one might label him a Slovak composer as well because he also studied Slovak music, or dub Brahms or Schubert Hungarian for evoking Hungary in their music. He momentarily deflects the issue of national identity and its relation to the music he studies, instead evoking loftier ideals: "My own idea . . . is the brotherhood of peoples, brotherhood in spite of all wars and conflicts. I try—to the best of my ability—to serve this idea in my music; therefore I don't reject any influence from another source. . . . The source must only be clean, fresh and healthy!"[93] Following this declaration, Bartók's inconsistent approach to the question of his identity and its effect on his music changes once more. He argues finally, "Whether my style—notwithstanding its various sources—has a Hungarian character or not . . .—is for others to judge, not for me. For my own part, I certainly feel that it has. For character and milieu must somehow harmonize with each other."[94] Here Bartók responds to the Romanian writer's attempt to claim him as Romanian, not only by insisting on his Hungarian character but by implying that his approach to representing the "brotherhood of peoples" in music is to paint the cultural artifacts of his neighbors with a Hungarian brush, in an act that resembles the cultural imperialism of which he had been accused earlier by other Romanian critics.

Bartók's Romanian research and many of the rural miniatures he composed before the conclusion of World War I were thus interpreted in a variety of ways by opposing political and national groups in Hungary and Romania, and Bartók felt threatened by the criticism as well as some of the praise. Nonetheless, his responses to his critics were contradictory: he expressed an egalitarian belief in universal brotherhood while at the same time writing about the cultural superiority of the Hungarian nation. It was partly in the interest of self-protection that Bartók concluded at some point during the first half of the 1920s that he should discontinue his practice of identifying the sources of his folk music appropriations in the paratexts of his new scores.[95] In obscuring the origins of the rural melodies, Bartók could limit the realism of his works, in the hope that listeners would cease to interpret such controversial meanings in the music.

JOSEPH SZIGETI, ZOLTÁN SZÉKELY, AND *ROMANIAN FOLK DANCES*

Sitting at the piano one day in 1915, Bartók used a wax cylinder phonograph to record himself playing *Romanian Folk Dances*. Bartók selected a cylinder he had used in 1913 to capture the sounds of a string player during a trip to North Africa, with the intention of recording over this earlier performance. In the production of the ethnographic recording in Africa, however, the grooves of the stylus had cut deeply into the wax, and as a result, the vibrations caused by Bartók's piano playing were not strong enough to eclipse the other sounds on the cylinder. When the cylinder is played back, the strains of the African musician's instrument emerge partway through Bartók's performance, and gradually overtake the sound of the piano, producing the effect of an inadvertent duet between Bartók at the piano and one of his ethnographic subjects. The aural traces left by these two musicians merge awkwardly, coalescing, despite lacking any unity of musical material, under the rhythmic thud of the extraneous crackling ostinato caused by the corrosion of the cylinder that threatens to overwhelm them both. The sound of this accidental, spectral synthesis of performances from across time and space reminds the listener of Bartók's reference to his fieldwork encounters in his score and performance of *Romanian Folk Dances*, while it also highlights the style that Bartók and a number of his performance collaborators developed in playing *Romanian Folk Dances* and his other folk music arrangements. In particular, Szigeti and Székely, in their 1930s recordings of Székely's edition of *Romanian Folk Dances*, demonstrate the influence of Bartók's descriptions of his fieldwork and of contemporary urban attitudes toward rural cultures, to develop a performance style that evokes rural musicianship as formally untrained but emotionally soulful, spontaneous, and authentic.

Bartók often considered it fruitful to collaborate with performers, and in his work as an editor of piano repertoire, he concerned himself with performance interpretation. He developed a system for notating minutely differentiated articulations as prescriptions for performers in editions of his own piano works and Bach's *Well-Tempered Clavier* and *Notebooks of Anna Magdalena Bach*,[96] and he joined with Székely to create symbols of articulation in some of his compositions for violin.[97] Early in his career he argued against composers' attempts to control all aspects of performance, however, acknowledging that elements such as timbre and intonation cannot be precisely notated but will be decided upon by performers.[98] Bartók wrote of the performance of art and folk music, "[the] interpretation of folk music is very similar to the interpretation of great artists: there is no set uniformity, there is the same diversity in perpetual transformation."[99]

Székely and Szigeti, who was like Székely a violin student of Hubay at the Budapest Academy of Music and began collaborating with Bartók in the 1920s, both developed their styles of performing rural miniatures in a conscious attempt to represent in their playing the sounds of rural violin performances.[100] Bartók played his wax cylinder fieldwork recordings for both musicians. In 1928, he first showed Székely his two Rhapsodies based on his Romanian folk music research—Bartók dedicated the first Rhapsody to Szigeti and the second to Székely—and Székely recalled, "Later that evening after the excitement of seeing the new rhapsodies, Bartók invited me to listen with him to the early recordings of his folk music collection."[101] In his book *With Strings Attached*, Szigeti writes,

> I see Bartók in his villa in the hills of Buda—his tables, couch and piano littered with those hard-earned discs of folk-fiddlers, mostly unaccompanied, which he had recorded during many epic years of folk-lore exploration. He plays them to me while I follow the intricate, almost hieroglyphic signs on the literal transcriptions he has made of these, as he has of thousands of others. Putting me to the test: whether I would recognize the sometimes infinitesimally small rhythmic or melodic shreds that went into the Rhapsody, No. 1, which he dedicated to me in 1928; making the distinction, while discussing these themes, between the unimaginative, premeditated *incorporation* of folk-lore material into a composition, and that degree of *saturation* with the folk-lore of one's country which unconsciously and decisively affects the composer's melodic invention, his palette, his rhythmic imaginings.[102]

A comparison of Bartók's wax cylinder recordings of rural violinists with Szigeti's and Székely's commercial discs shows clearly that the latter musicians did not attempt to sound in their playing exactly like Bartók's ethnographic sources. Szigeti and Székely perform in the style prescribed by their conservatory training: their timbres are generally clear and crisp, and their rhythms steady overall. They play on well-preserved violins. But it is evident that performing with Bartók, discussing his research with him, and listening to the wax cylinder recordings contributed to their development of a style of playing his rural miniatures that involved the use of aural gestures that signified rural performance.

Székely described one of these gestures in a discussion of his rendition of Bartók's second Rhapsody. In a performance of the work in an arrangement for violin and orchestra, with Ernst von Dohnányi as conductor, when Székely reached the violin's entrance in the section marked *friss* (fast), he played a rapid passage of notes with *marcato* (marked) articulation, "on the string in the peasant style."[103] According to Székely, Bartók's rural informants typically played without lifting the bow, and he endeavored to imitate this style. Bartók approved, stating, "You played it very well. You played it like a peasant."[104]

EXAMPLE 6.9:   Fingerings in Béla Bartók, Rhapsody No. 1, reproduced in Szigeti, *Szigeti on the Violin*, 185

Szigeti also explained how he attempted to develop a "folk-like" performance style, in interpreting the first Rhapsody. He devised a complicated scheme of fingerings at the start of the *friss* section of this work: in a passage that can easily be accomplished by using consecutive fingers in the first position on the D string, Szigeti proposed an awkward positioning of the left hand that requires the violinist to perform challenging bow crossing and shifts (Example 6.9). Szigeti writes, "Béla Bartók was in wholehearted agreement" that this passage "should be played mostly on two strings, in order to bring out the 'folk-fiddler' quality of the tune, instead of with the normal, comfortable fingering marked underneath, which makes of it something citified, lacking in precisely the character he was aiming for. . . . [The work] generally breathes this folk-music, outdoor atmosphere."[105]

Szigeti's self-consciously awkward fingering in the first Rhapsody is designed to make "noise": rather than its more simple alternatives, Szigeti's fingering requires the bow to make complicated string crossings, which is likely to produce rough scratching noises, as well as imperfect intonation. Székely's marcato bowing in the second Rhapsody is similarly "noisy," eschewing the clean sound of a bow that is lifted or gently changed in direction at the end of each note, in favor of the crunching that most violinists will produce when sudden starts and stops of the right hand are made when the bow retains contact with the string.

Elsewhere, Szigeti recommends that young violinists take advantage of Bartók's *Forty-Four Duos* as a crucial pedagogical tool possessing "characteristics which will prove to be a key to the Rhapsodies, the Concerto, the two Sonatas of 1921, [and] the Romanian and Hungarian Dances and folk-tunes."[106] In particular, the *Forty-Four Duos* provide schooling "in bow articulation, in the realization of a declamatory or *parlando* line, of accentuating cross rhythms, that at first seem to 'go against the grain' but turn out to be perfectly convincing,"[107] in addition to teaching about different sorts of "*vibrato*, bow articulation, pressure, and bow-speed" that come in handy in the performance of Bartók's compositions based on folk music.[108]

The performance gestures he lists here and recreates in his Rhapsody fingering resemble the fingerings Heifetz published in his editions of Achron's

EXAMPLE 6.10:   Transcription of Joseph Szigeti's 1930 recording of *Romanian Folk Dances*, movement 1, "Joc cu Bâtă." Editorial marks in the printed score appear below the staff; analytical marks appear above

rural miniatures that accentuate the noise caused as the fingers shift along the strings (see Chapter 2): all three of these violinists dictate performance suggestions that are designed to make audible the mechanics of violin performance and the technology of the instrument. As a result of the self-conscious "violinistic" quality of the sound, recordings of rural miniatures by these violinists and others who follow their editorial suggestions evoke the sound of a stereotyped rural violinist, as conjured by the urban imagination. Examples 6.10 and 6.11 are annotated versions of Székely's 1925 arrangement of the first movement of Bartók's *Romanian Folk Dances*, "Joc cu Bâtă," representing what I hear in Szigeti and Székely's recordings. Szigeti's recording was made with Bartók at the piano, for Columbia Records in 1930, and Székely's is accompanied by Géza Frid, for Decca in 1936.[109] Although the sheet music prescribes a tempo of 80 to the quarter note, Szigeti and Bartók take the music considerably faster, at a

EXAMPLE 6.11:   Transcription of Zoltán Székely's 1936 recording of *Romanian Folk Dances*, movement 1, "Joc cu Bâtă." Editorial marks in the printed score appear below the staff; analytical marks appear above

metronome level of approximately 100. Both violinists employ gestures that can be interpreted to evoke rural performance techniques. They play this movement generally in a *marcato* style, with fast-moving bows, initiating the notes with the bow already making firm contact with the string. As their bows change direction on the string without lifting or reducing the tension created by the right hand, Szigeti and Székely produce the "noisy" string changes that Székely advocated as creating sounds representative of the rural violin playing Bartók had heard in his fieldwork.

In Szigeti's recording, he modifies his bowing style at the pickup to measure 21, modulating to a legato technique and playing this quieter phrase (marked *mezzo-forte*, in a sudden reduction of dynamic from the previous accented *forte*) more gently to set it apart from the rough-hewn timbre of the opening melody. When this passage returns at the pickup to measure 37, however, Szigeti plays *marcato*, returning to the forceful timbre in which he opened the piece. Szigeti plays heavily on downbeats; in doing so, he mimics the rhythmic patterns of Hungarian poetry and folk song, in which each line begins with an emphasized syllable, because in the Hungarian language, the first syllable of each word receives stress, and sentences tend to start at a higher pitch and veer downward from the first to last syllables.

In most cases in which measures open with a pair of sixteenth notes followed by a syncopated quarter note (for example, measures 5, 6, and 7), Szigeti plays these sixteenth notes out of phase with the piano, more quickly than the tempo prescribes as though "on top of the beat," and then extends the syncopated quarter to compensate for the extra time remaining in the beat. He also tends to shorten sixteenth-note pickups (for example, in measure 12). Szigeti drags the tempo in some measures and pushes it forward in others. These choices are typical of an expressive rubato style of interpretive playing on the violin. By playing in a less strict time, he also suggests the movements of bodies in dance.

Melodic gestures in Szigeti's playing that do not appear in the score include one grace note, a D in measure 28, and occasional slides between pitches, most notably in measures 6 and 7. In addition, frequently between measures, between phrases, and before long notes, Szigeti breaks the melody by removing the bow from the string, like a brief aspiration. Most of the double- and triple-stopped chords are played in a single violent, crunching bow stroke, hitting all pitches at once; but the quadruple stop in measure 15 is played with an emphatic roll, as the bow hits first the lower two notes and then the upper two after a fraction of a sixteenth beat. While he plays these chords in a grainy timbre, Szigeti extracts a more nuanced expressivity from many of the long notes, like that in measure 45, which he holds as he vibrates with his left hand. Szigeti plays a pair of natural harmonics that do not appear in the score, on the high E's in measures 49 and 50. These predict the higher harmonics on beat two of measure 50.

Despite the rubato that Szigeti employs, speeding up and slowing down individual phrases, Székely exhibits the more radical rhythmic interpretation. He rushes repeatedly through recurring descending melodic patterns, such as appear in measures 8, 16, 25–6, and 42. His grace notes in measures 12, 18, 20, 36, and 44, and an additional unnotated one he adds in measure 23, are short, snappy, and accentuated. At the ends of several measures that lead toward downbeat chords and other accentuated notes, Székely drags the tempo backward (for instance, measures 18, 28, 44, 46, and 48). This stylized gesture allows him to emphasize the following downbeats, which he typically plays with a harsh, "chunky" timbre, taking advantage of the noise produced by a sharp, heavy attack produced by the bottom of the bow against the string. Székely also takes momentary pauses between measures, again to add emphasis to the downbeats—for instance, between measures 10 and 11, 12 and 13, and 28 and 29, and before the pickup sixteenth note at the end of measure 20. Finally, Székely dramatically slows down in the concluding three measures, playing strong accented tenutos on the final two downbeats.

The liberties Székely takes with the tempos and rhythms closely resemble the performance of the solo piano version of *Romanian Folk Dances* that Bartók captured on a 1920 Welte-Mignon piano roll, in which he adopts a faster speed to play the pairs of sixteenth notes that open so many measures, and holds onto syncopated longer notes mid-bar, oscillating between rushing and dragging. He plays chords with a rapid, accented roll and grace notes with a snapped rapidity. This exaggerated, stylized manner of playing rhythms appears in its peculiarity and dance-like nature to be a representation of a performance Bartók heard in the field. When compared with Bartók's wax cylinder recording of the fiddlers playing the *jocul cu bâtă*, however, it becomes apparent that Bartók's rubato style does not directly imitate the performances he captured on his phonograph. The original performance is not steady, to be sure, but the violinists who played into the gramophone trumpet perform the rhythms on the whole more smoothly than Bartók and do not rush sixteenth notes or hold back on longer syncopated notes nearly as much as do Bartók or Székely. The lead violinist plays with a fast bow, which causes him to emphasize each change of direction to produce a forceful pulse, resulting in a timbre that is ebullient and occasionally scratchy, rarely legato or tender.

Szigeti and Székely's interpretations of *Romanian Folk Dances*, in their alterations of the score's rhythmic prescriptions, their *marcato* bowing technique, and the "noisy" chords they play with swift motions of the bow, depict an emphatic, partly improvisational, and aggressively physical performance that comes closer to evoking the conceptions of the authenticity of rural dance described by Aladár Tóth and other critics than the sounds of the ethnographic wax cylinder. In creating a style for the performance of Bartók's folk music arrangements, Szigeti and Székely combine the influence of their discussions with Bartók about his ethnographic discoveries with elements associated, in popular, often nationalist discourse, with the performance techniques of folk musicians.

CONCLUSION

O n the last day of the federal court trial over the copyright status of "Eili, Eili" described in the Introduction to this book, the defense attorney for the publisher charged with copyright infringement, himself a former concert violinist, brought his instrument into the courtroom and performed an arrangement of the melody under dispute. As the reporter for the *New York Times* recounted,

> Abraham I. Menin, counsel for the defendant, obtained the court's permission to play the melody. Mr. Menin, once a professional musician, took his violin and with the score of "Eili, Eili," propped against a pile of law books, played the Jewish lament. The notes reached the corridors and attracted a crowd. An attendant closed and locked the doors of the courtroom and there was a silence until the music ceased. A tendency to applaud was checked by Judge Knox.[1]

This may seem a surprising way for the defense to support the claim of the publisher of "Eili, Eili" that no royalties were owed to composer Jacob Koppel Sandler, who maintained that he wrote the melody.

One might have expected the defense to engage a singer who learned the music through the oral tradition to perform in the courtroom, as proof that the melody had folkloric origins. But Menin's presentation was evidently convincing, and he won the case for his client. That his performance, though apparently virtuosic, was not an improvisation from memory but the rendition of a recent published arrangement of the melody as a rural miniature reveals the complexity of the discourse of authenticity as it was constructed around the genre in the early twentieth century. With no extant recording of the courtroom performance, we cannot know precisely how the lawyer-violinist interpreted the work, but it is likely that his performance engaged expressive tropes like those that can be heard in recordings of rural miniatures by Elman, Jascha Heifetz, and the other violinists discussed in this book, so that the spectators would hear folksy authenticity in the timbres he produced. Thus a composed rural miniature was made to stand in for a folk song and a violin for a voice articulating a religious text in Hebrew; the written tradition, in the form of a score propped against law books, signified the oral; and art music performance became a simulacrum for Eastern European Jewish song.

As shown in the preceding chapters, the rural miniature emerged in the early twentieth century at the intersection of political nationalism, aesthetic modernism, and the development of sound recording technology. Varied conceptions of authenticity and beliefs about the relationship between music and personal and group identities were at the core of the activities of composing, performing, and writing about rural miniatures, from the genre's emergence around the turn of the century through its rapid wane at the conclusion of World War II. A genre that merged elements of the supposedly distinct musical styles of folk, popular, and art musics, the rural miniature reveals the hybridity of musical language during the early twentieth century and the strong and enduring impacts on musical practice of changing perceptions of selfhood and difference in Europe's peripheral nations and borderlands and among non-state ethnic minority groups at this time.

ONE GENRE, THREE CONTEXTS

In spite of the different cultural and political contexts in which the rural miniature emerged in Spain, the Jewish Diaspora, and Hungary, the genre in each of these settings reflected the influence of the nineteenth-century virtuosic violin repertoire in the style hongrois, the style based on the music of Rom ensembles that performed dances, excerpts of operetta, and new compositions by Hungarian gentry composers in cafes and other urban settings throughout Europe. In works by Pablo de Sarasate and Johannes Brahms (as adapted for violin by Joseph Joachim), this genre reached its apex, and indeed Sarasate's "Zigeunerweisen" and Brahms and Joachim's *Hungarian Dances* remained canonic works for violin in the early twentieth century and were regularly recorded and performed alongside the new rural miniatures. Composers of music in the style hongrois were inspired by the performance style in which Rom musicians played, frequently characterized by anthropologists and musicians as spontaneous, improvisational, and emotionally authentic. This exoticizing conception of Rom playing had a lasting impact on classical performance practice, as many violinists developed a performance style in their interpretations of both style hongrois showpieces and rural miniatures that incorporated rough timbres, quasi-improvisational rubato, portamento, ornamentation, and other gestures that operated as signifiers of spontaneity and authenticity.

The juxtaposition of rural miniatures based on Spanish, Jewish, and East Central European melodies demonstrates that despite their shared influences, there is a marked diversity in the genre as well, testifying to the heterogeneity of the ways different communities in Europe's geographic and social peripheries responded to the convergence of modern aesthetic, political, and technological developments, and conceived of race, nation, and their relation to musical practice. An important difference among rural miniatures relates to the distinctive ways music operated within systems of Spanish, Jewish Diaspora, and Hungarian nationalism. The pan-Spanish nature of Manuel de Falla's nationalism, which conflicted with Spanish regionalist movements but corresponded with some race theorists' notions of a Spanish racial fusion of disparate ethnic cultures, prompted him to arrange dance melodies that represented a range of Spanish musical cultures. The rural miniature offered Falla a way of depicting the breadth of idioms and influences that made up the rich folk music of Spain. Diaspora nationalism, on the other hand, offered several unique challenges to composers of rural miniatures based on Jewish themes. It entailed the invention of a sense of community and shared identity and language among a people displaced in exile, in a geographical area that transcended political and linguistic borders. It also involved the attempt at persuading other citizens that a coherent, non-state nation existed within their borders and should be respected as partly autonomous. Composers in the St. Petersburg Society for Jewish Folk Music hoped that the rural miniature was a medium that could assist in achieving both of these political and social goals, perceiving it as able to represent objectively a Jewish cultural identity that was unified throughout the world by a shared folk music tradition. Bartók's brand of Hungarian nationalism, which differed from the mainstream, conservative nationalism more typical in Budapest, involved a different set of challenges. Bartók employed rural miniatures as part of his attempt to define Hungarian borders and promote a Hungarian musical tradition that he believed to be purer than the hybrid musical style of Rom musicians. With his rural miniatures of 1915, he aimed to demonstrate for audiences in Budapest and in other countries that the roots of Hungarian folklore extended beyond the outskirts of the capital, to the borders of greater Hungary. It is because of the political ramifications of Bartók's project that he inspired controversy in both Hungary and Romania after the Treaty of Trianon altered those borders.

The rural miniature developed rapidly in each of these three settings, demonstrating that music was viewed as a powerful force in early twentieth-century nationalist projects across Europe's peripheries. For the composers of rural miniatures, the qualities of authenticity and purity were critical to the understanding of both folk music and its arrangement as art music, though the conception of what these terms meant differed among them. The rural miniature's realism allowed composers to represent the fruits of recent ethnographic discoveries in a seemingly objective manner, though in fact the arrangement of melodies as rural miniatures involved the significant alteration of source melodies. The similar treatment of the genre of the rural miniature across cultures demonstrates how one of the main goals of the music of peripheral nationalisms during the first half of the twentieth century was to show not only the nation's difference from neighboring peoples but also what it shared with them. That is, Spanish, Jewish, and Hungarian artists used the medium of the rural miniature to prove that their nations were comparable in cultural richness to Germany, France, and other groups associated with Europe's cultural "center," because like these others, they too had an authentic folk music that could be seen to represent their national "soul."

Falla looked to *cante jondo* and other Spanish traditional genres, but also reached outside Spanish borders for inspiration in the development of a "Spanish" musical idiom, specifically to Paris and the evocations of Spain in the works of Claude Debussy. Bartók's goals were aligned with *Nyugat*, the journal to which he occasionally contributed articles and compositions. By promoting works that featured Hungarian language and folklore by artists such as Bartók, Kodály, and Béla Balázs, *Nyugat* aimed to show that Budapest's cultural innovation was comparable with that of Western European capitals. Jewish composers and ethnographers had a more difficult task than Falla and Bartók in articulating that Jews of the diaspora possessed an autonomous and unifying folk culture, because they did not have a state of their own, and because they were often subject to repression and to exile to other parts of Europe. Susman Kiselgof, in stating, "Like other peoples, we should be able to say, 'Our folksong unites us,'"[2] made explicit his claim that in searching for what made the dispersed Jewish nation distinct—its own unique body of folk music—his ultimate aim was to demonstrate what made it similar to Europe's other nations. Yet within the community of Jewish musicians and intellectuals, there was significant disagreement over which musical genres should serve as the basis for "Jewish" art music.

The widespread incorporation of rural miniatures into the violin performance canon inevitably led to the gradual assimilation of these works with other emerging musical styles. As historical studies of "Hora Staccato" and "Hebrew Melody" in previous chapters demonstrate, performers and critics over time placed less emphasis on rural miniatures' initially strong ties to ethnography, sound recording technology, and local ethnic musical traditions. During the 1930s and 1940s, many folk music adaptations were arranged in American popular music idioms, for instance, as swing band hits or jazz standards; ethnography gave way to nostalgia as well as to new influences, particularly in the American musical melting pot, while authenticity remained an important value as musical genres and styles were associated with both older (Jewish, Rom, Eastern European) and newer (American, assimilationist, contemporary) aspects of identity in a period of increasing mobility across oceans and diasporas.

DISPLACING AUTHENTICITY: A CONCERT AND A MUSIC VIDEO

As a genre based on folk music, the rural miniature was a product of the trans-formation of music from oral to written traditions through processes of tran-scription, adaptation, and harmonization. But the story of melodic transformation rarely ended there. By conveying folk and religious tunes to international audi-ences, the violinists who performed rural miniatures enabled these melodies to become integrated into new oral traditions. Audiences in New York, for example, could leave a recital by Heifetz with the tune of "Hebrew Melody," Achron's adaptation of what he said was a religious melody from Warsaw, still resonating in their memories. When Seymour Rechtzeit responded to the popularity of the work by adapting it as a Yiddish song, it reentered the oral tradition again among Yiddish radio audiences, this time with text. Old folk tunes thus formed the core of new popular cultural practices, mediated through art music repertoires.

This multi-directional process, the interweaving of oral and written tradi-tions and of folk, popular, and art music styles, was at the heart of the legal dispute over the ownership rights to "Eili, Eili." As noted in the Introduction, Judge Knox determined that whether or not Sandler was the composer of the original song, so much time had elapsed that the melody had passed into the public domain. In effect, as a legal matter, Sandler had acquiesced in the folk-lorization of his own composition. The song had entered the oral tradition, achieving its authenticity as a Jewish folk song through repeated performance both in America and in Russia, as, without Sandler's intervention, record labels, printed scores, and concert reviews began to assert that the music was a "tradi-tional," "religious," "Hebrew," or "Jewish" tune. Thus, with the passing of time, attribution was erased, authenticity was newly minted, and what was originally a composition for a forgotten Yiddish operetta became an internationally rec-ognized signifier of Eastern European Jewish folk song tradition.

Judge Knox's legal imprimatur of folkloric authenticity to the melody he actually believed Sandler created mirrors the aesthetic processes by which the rural miniature ascribed authenticity to folk and popular melodies from around the world. The genre reveals the complexities inherent in the search for origins and the attribution of seemingly simple discourses of authenticity, and in pre-vailing conceptions of music's roles in the construction and performance of cultural and social identities. The following two analyses—the first an anecdote relating a concertgoing experience, the second a description of a recent popular music video—aim to show that authenticity remains an important and complex category in musical practice, as the postmodern conception of identity as a hybrid and mutable construction further complicates the ways music is adapted and recontextualized across media, genres, and borders.[3]

In November 2009, I attended a musicology symposium at Yong Siew Toh Conservatory of Music at the National University of Singapore. I had traveled to the conference to deliver a paper about the performance history of Béla Bartók's *Romanian Folk Dances* in its arrangement for violin and piano by the violinist Zoltán Székely. The presentation, based on material in Chapter 6 of this book, discussed the style in which Székely and Joseph Szigeti interpreted the piece in their early recordings, the influence of Bartók's notion of the purity and authenticity imbuing the folk music he encountered during his research, and the critical reception in Hungary of their performances. That evening, I joined other symposium members at Singapore's waterfront arts center to attend a performance of the Singapore Chinese Orchestra, an ensemble modeled after the European symphony orchestra but containing mostly traditional Chinese instruments.

The concert, billed as an anniversary celebration of Singapore Press Holdings, featured patriotic works dedicated to the history and news media of Singapore, including Kuan Nai-Chung's "Singapore Capriccio" and Iskandar Ismail's "Engaging Moments—25 Years of Photojournalism," which was accompanied by photographs of the country's landscape and citizens. One of the pieces featured on the program, coincidentally, was *Romanian Folk Dances*, in an arrangement for Chinese orchestra by Law Wai Lun. The melodic line, played by the violins in Bartók's version for chamber orchestra and based on Bartók's transcriptions of performances he heard in Transylvania on violin and *furulya* (flute), was taken by a group of musicians on the *erhu*, a bowed two-stringed instrument played upright, the resonating body of the instrument resting in the player's lap. The *erhu* can play sustained notes like the violin, but its timbres differ, and as a result this performance brought a unique sonic character to the work.

Far from Hungary, the audience in Singapore enthusiastically received a performance of Bartok's work as part of a program extolling Singaporean national pride. The formation of a Chinese orchestra in Singapore can be understood to portray a modern Chinese-Singaporean identity by incorporating Chinese traditional instruments into the configuration of the Western symphony. The musical and cultural adaptation involved in the rendition of *Romanian Folk Dances* by the Singapore Chinese Orchestra provides an example of how cultural artifacts perceived to be inextricably linked with the geography and people of one nation can be displaced, transformed, and redefined in representations of the identities of multiple national and ethnic groups. It also demonstrates some of the ways in which the concept of authenticity has remained surprisingly stable over the past century, even in the face of significant social, political, and aesthetic upheaval. While in its early years many listeners associated Bartók's work with the widespread notion of folk music's inherent value as a marker of national identity, the hybrid product that arose out of the Chinese orchestra's performance maintained this association between authenticity and nation while accommodating the fusion of musical forms and artifacts that occurs in the performance of European art music on Chinese instruments.[4] The Singapore Chinese Orchestra's performance relied on the popular conception, entrenched since the nineteenth century, of folklore as a source of spontaneous emotional utterances. At the same time it grafted contemporary values of cross-cultural encounter onto a work famous for its depiction of Bartók's idealization of East Central European rural culture. The performance also appeared to indicate that, like the integration of elements of folk music into compositional practice in the early twentieth century, the aural convergence of Eastern and Western traditions could be considered a site of innovation and virtuosity in music making today.

Another contemporary, postmodern recontextualization of the rural miniature that further challenges our understanding of discourses of musical authenticity can be located in the arena of contemporary popular music. An example is found in the extended opening sequence of photographer Steven Klein's music video for the 2009 song "Alejandro" by the American singer Lady Gaga. The visual track shows a bare, dystopian society, a futuristic landscape populated with half-nude male soldiers in outfits that combine aspects of fascist army uniforms and female stripper garb. Lady Gaga appears wearing deep black lipstick and stylized eyewear, the lenses lined in black lace. She sits by a window among architectural ruins, overlooking army maneuvers like the leader of a post-apocalyptic nation. In a new sequence, she appears in a horned headpiece and black lace, a visual riff on a traditional Spanish mourning veil. She carries a human heart on a pillow before her, reminiscent of an image from a Catholic holy card, and walks slowly at the front of a funeral cortege; stopping before the procession, she announces the end of her relationship with a man named Alejandro.

Throughout this opening passage, the viewer hears a continuous repetition of the first four-bar melodic phrase of the 1904 rural miniature "Csárdás," a work for accompanied violin by the Neapolitan violinist Vittorio Monti, inspired by the Hungarian Rom genre that gives the piece its name. Once the music of "Alejandro" begins, the sample from "Csárdás" repeats as it fades out, overtaken by the electronic introduction to Lady Gaga's song. The landscape remains bare, with videos of flames and warfare projected on screens behind dancing soldiers. The vague sense of a Hispanic geographical location is provided by her repetition of Spanish names, the recurring phrase "Hot like Mexico," Spanish words in the lyrics, and visual references to Catholicism, with crucifix iconography and scenes of the singer in a rubber nun's habit and holding a rosary. Monti's "Csárdás" was a virtuosic showpiece based on the music of Rom bands. But in this video, it is adapted into the context of a fictional local custom, a religious funeral procession in which the participants wear costumes based on traditional mourning attire. Through this simple juxtaposition of aural and visual tracks at the opening of this video, the rural miniature thus becomes the ritual folk music of Lady Gaga's surrealistic vision of a futuristic quasi-Hispanic nation.

As examples of how the rural miniature has continued to develop, then, an arrangement of a Transylvanian folk song can become a medium for the expression of patriotism in the performance of a Singaporean Chinese orchestra, and an early twentieth-century composition in the style of a Rom dance genre can be transformed into the folk music of a fictional postmodern dystopia depicted in a popular music video. The case of "Eili, Eili" also demonstrated how, through the art music genre of the rural miniature—as arranged by Seidel or Elman and performed by the defense attorney—the recently composed melody of an operetta aria was transformed into an "authentic" Russian Jewish folk song. It is evident, then, that the rural miniature exhibited from the very start the contradictions inherent in the project of constructing musical authenticity and the complexities underlying the processes through which music was used in the modernist period to mediate national, social, and ethnic identities.

In the epigraph that opened this book, George Eliot, writing in *Daniel Deronda*, remarks on the human preoccupation with the myth of beginnings. The scholars of folk music and composers of rural miniatures at the turn of the twentieth century were typically concerned with the search for origins—for the sources of traditional music that could be performed as representations or evocations of the identity of the nation.[5] These musicians turned to the objectivity of scientific research, the aesthetic notion of authenticity, and the technology of sound recording to support their projects of finding pure and untouched folk music traditions. But as Eliot avers, origins always remain elusive: "No retrospect will take us to the true beginning."[6] The case studies in this book reveal how the quest for origins can turn in many different directions through folk music research and the quest for authenticity, as music is appropriated, adapted, and recontextualized among musical idioms, genres, and styles across the decades of the twentieth century and among national and ethnic groups. The rural miniature testifies to the complications and contradictions that underlie nationalist projects of folk music collection and the adaptation of traditional melodies in art music, as well as, more generally, the persistent search for authentic musical expressions of identity.

APPENDIX

The following table provides a list of early twentieth-century recordings of rural miniatures, virtuosic violin repertoire in the style hongrois, and other works for accompanied violin based on folk and popular music. It represents a diversity of composers, works, and violinists, but does not seek to be comprehensive. The table is organized alphabetically by composer and composition title; and under each composition, performers are also arranged alphabetically. Recordings are identified by violinist, accompanist, date, location, matrix number, and recording studio number and location, where this information is available. The matrix number is a code attributed uniquely to the master record from which issues are made, and can signify details about the disc including its size, the recording method, and take number.[1] When matrix numbers are unknown, other identifying data is shown, if possible.

Composer/Piece	Performer	Accompanist	Date	Location	Matrix	Other
Joseph Achron						
Hebrew Dance (Op. 35, no. 1)	Jascha Heifetz	Isidor Achron	9/24/1924		C-30931-2	
	Jascha Heifetz	Isidor Achron	9/25/1924		C-30936-1	
Hebrew Lullaby (Op. 35, no. 2)	Jascha Heifetz	Samuel Chotzinoff	10/19/1922		B-27034-1	
Hebrew Melody (Op. 33)	Mischa Elman		1945	Los Angeles		Live
	Mischa Elman	Joseph Seiger	3/26/1956	London	ARL 3081/3082	West Hampstead Studios
	Mischa Elman	Joseph Seiger	10/1961			
	Ida Haendel	Alice Haendel	12/18/1942		AR 7145	
	Josef Hassid	Gerald Moore	11/29/1940	London	2EA 9051	Abbey Road, Studio 3
	Jascha Heifetz	Josef Pasternak (conductor)	12/19/1917	Camden, NJ	C-21268-3	
	Jascha Heifetz	Isidor Achron	12/31/1926	New York	CVE-27034-3	
	Jascha Heifetz	Emanuel Bay	10/19/1946	Hollywood	D6-RC-5637-2A	RCA Studios
	Toscha Seidel	Philip Goodman	1/30/1929	London	98615	
Julián Aguirre						
Huella	Jascha Heifetz	Emanuel Bay	11/29/1945	New York	73183	Decca Studios
	William Primrose	David Stimer	12/17/1947		D7-RC-8252	

Isaac Albéniz

Work	Violinist	Pianist	Date	Location	Matrix	Studio / Cat.
Jota Aragonesa, from 2 morceaux charactéristiques (Op. 164)	Samuel Dushkin	Max Pirani	2/21/1928	Hayes	Bb 12750	
Malaguena, from España (Op. 165, no. 3) (arr. Kreisler)	Ida Haendel	Noel Mewton-Wood	4/2/1941		AR 5537	
	Fritz Kreisler	Carl Lamson	3/25/1927	Camden	BVE-38220-6	Victor Studio 3
	Jacques Thibaud	Tasso Janopoulo	7/1/1933	London	2B 6792-2	Abbey Road, Studio 3
Sevillanas (Op. 47, no. 3)	Ibolyka Zilzer		10/9/1953		CCX 1354	
	Jascha Heifetz	Árpád Sándor	2/21/1934		2B-6056-2	
Tango in D, from España (Op. 165, no. 2) (arr. Dushkin)	Samuel Dushkin	Max Pirani	2/21/1928		Bb 12752-3	
	Fritz Kreisler	Carl Lamson	2/27/1928	Camden	BVE-38221-19	Victor Studio 1
	Manuel Quiroga	Mme. Quiroga	1928-9	Paris	N 300894	
	Jacques Thibaud	Tasso Janopoulo	7/1933	London	OB 6795-1	Abbey Road, Studio 3
Tango in D, from España (Op. 165, no. 2) (arr. Kreisler)	Zino Francescatti	Artur Balsam				Cat. no. Columbia A1533
	Ibolyka Zilzer	F. Eberson				Cat. no. Columbia LDX18

(continued)

Composer/Piece	Performer	Accompanist	Date	Location	Matrix	Other
Anonymous						
Turkey in the Straw	Eddy Brown	Jascha Zayde	1940		US 1563	
Béla Bartók						
Contrasts	Joseph Szigeti	Benny Goodman, Béla Bartók	5/13/1940	New York	WXCO 26819-A	World Broadcasting Studios
Hungarian Folk Tunes (arr. Szigeti)	Joseph Szigeti	Béla Bartók	1/7/1930	London	WAX 5322/3	
Rhapsody no. 1	Joseph Szigeti	Béla Bartók	5/4/1940	New York	WXCO 26790/1	World Broadcasting Studios
	Zoltán Székely	Isobel Moore				
Rhapsody no. 2	Zoltán Székely	Isobel Moore				
Romanian Folk Dances (arr. Székely)	Zoltán Székely	Géza Frid	1936		TA3025-1	
	Joseph Szigeti	Béla Bartók	1/7/1930	London	WA 9908	Petty France Studio
	Ibolyka Zilzer	F. Schröder				Cat. no. Eterna 120043
Georges Bizet						
Carmen Fantasia (arr. Waxman)	Jascha Heifetz	RCA Symphony Orchestra, cond. Donald Voorhees	11/8/1946	New York	D6–RC–6273–2 and 74-3A	
Carmen Fantasy (arr. Hubay)	Harry Solloway	Waldemar Liachowsky			103.5/104bm	
	Franz von Vecsey		7/15/1904	London	5448b-5449b	

	Violinist	Accompanist	Date	Location	Matrix	Venue/Notes
Carmen Fantasy (arr. Sarasate)	Ida Haendel		1939		5978-81	Victor Studios
	Jascha Heifetz	Isidor Achron	12/19/1924	Camden	C 31383-2	
	Jan Kubelik		11/21/1903		4601b	
	Henri Marteau		12/12/1927	Berlin	Cw1425-6	
Ernest Bloch						
Baal Shem:Three Pictures of Chassidic Life	Joseph Szigeti	Andor Földes	6/4/1940	New York	XCO 27411 to 27413	Liederkranz Hall
Nigun (Baal Shem, no. 2)	Mischa Elman	Joseph Seiger	3/26/1956	London	ARL 3081-3082	West Hampstead Studios
	Jascha Heifetz	Brooks Smith	10/23/1972			Live
	Yehudi Menuhin	Louis Persinger	2/12/1929		CV 49849/50	
	Joseph Szigeti	Kurt Ruhrseitz	7/5/1926	London	WAX 3538	Petty France Studio
Johannes Brahms						
Hungarian Dance no. 1 (arr. Joachim)	Leopold Auer	W. Bogutskahein	6/7/1920	New York		Carnegie Hall
	Jeanne Gautier		6/4/1930			
	Jascha Heifetz	Samuel Chotzinoff	9/16/1920		Ki 3358-1	
	Joseph Joachim		8/27/1903	Berlin	B-24468-2	
	Toscha Seidel	Emanuel Bay	10/14/1927		219y	
	Toscha Seidel	Harry Kaufman			98403	
	Toscha Seidel	Eugene Kuzmiak	1940		49690	Cat. no.Victor 4458

(continued)

Composer/Piece	Performer	Accompanist	Date	Location	Matrix	Other
Hungarian Dance no. 2 (arr. Joachim)	Joseph Joachim		8/27/1903	Berlin	217y	
Hungarian Dance no. 3	Alexander Schmuller		1912		3106	
Hungarian Dance no. 4	Cecelia Hansen		1924		C 29623	
Hungarian Dance no. 5 (arr. Joachim)	Fritz Kreisler	George Falkenstein	5/18/1910	New York	B-8969-1	
	Fritz Kreisler	Squire Haddon	11/06/1911		AC 5703	
	Fritz Kreisler	Carl Lamson	2/17/1916	New York	B-8969-2	Victor Studios
	Arnold Rosé		5/1909	Vienna	14681u	
	Joseph Szigeti	Andor Földes	11/24/1941	New York	CO 31950	
Hungarian Dance no. 6	Henri Marteau	Pancho Vladigerov	1929	New York	CLR 4711	
Hungarian Dance no. 7	Mischa Elman	Percy B. Kahn	4/8/1914		B14683-1	
	Jascha Heifetz	Emanuel Bay	12/1/1945		73206	
	Jascha Heifetz	Los Angeles Philharmonic, cond. Alfred Wallenstein	12/9/1953		E3-RC-2551-1	
Hungarian Dance no. 8	Isolde Menges	Hamilton Harty	1915		HO 2127ab	
	Jelly d'Aranyi		1928		145620	

Title	Performer	Accompanist	Date	Location	Matrix	Notes
Hungarian Dance no. 11	Jascha Heifetz	Brooks Smith	4/14/1956		G2-RB-2999	
Hungarian Dance no. 17	Mischa Elman	Arthur Loesser	1/3/1921		B24770	
Hungarian Dance no. 20	Jascha Heifetz	Brooks Smith	4/14/1956		G2-RB-3000	
	Jascha Heifetz	Brooks Smith	4/14/1956		G2-RB-2998	
Julius Chajes						
The Chassid	Mischa Elman	Joseph Seiger				Cat. no.VRS1099
Cécile Chaminade						
Sérénade espagnole (arr. Kreisler)	Michèle Auclair	Otto Schulhof				Cat. no. Remington R199-128
	Fritz Kreisler	Carl Lamson	4/22/1915	New York	B-15938-3	Victor Studios
	Manuel Quiroga	Mme. Quiroga	1928-9	Paris	N 350070	
Grigoraş Dinicu						
Hora Staccato	Grigoraş Dinicu	Orchestra Grigoraş Dinicu	1927-8		WA 7335	
Hora Staccato (arr. Heifetz)	Jascha Heifetz	Emanuel Bay	4/9/1937	London	OEA 4894-1	
Dobrowen						
Hebrew Melody	Carl Flesch	Ignaz Strasfogel	1/2/1929		CLR 4978	

(continued)

Composer/Piece	Performer	Accompanist	Date	Location	Matrix	Other
Ernő Dohnányi						
Gypsy Andante, Ruralia Hungarica (Op. 32c, no. 6)	Jascha Heifetz	Árpád Sándor	3/27/1934		2B-6102-3	
Ruralia Hungarica (Op. 32c)	Fritz Kreisler	Carl Lamson	1/12/1928	New York	BVE 41598-99, 42400-01	
Antonin Dvořák						
Negro Spiritual Melody, from Symphony no. 9, "From the New World," Largo (arr. Kreisler)	Fritz Kreisler	Carl Lamson	8/28/1925		BE-29843-14	
	Yehudi Menuhin	Adolph Baller	10/1951			Cat. no. Victor LS 2004
Slavonic Dance (Op. 46, no. 1) (arr. Kreisler)	Joseph Szigeti	Andor Földes	3/21/1941	New York	CO 30105	Liederkranz Hall
	Jacques Thibaud	Harold Craxton	2/6/1922	London	Bb 978	HMV Studio Hayes Middlesex
Slavonic Dance (Op. 46, no. 2) (arr. Kreisler)	Mischa Elman	Joseph Seiger				Cat. no. Philips A04308L
	Jascha Heifetz	Samuel Chotzinoff	10/14/1919	New York	B-23411-2	
	Fritz Kreisler	Carl Lamson	2/25/1915	New York	B-15738-1	
	Fritz Kreisler	Carl Lamson	12/6/1928	Camden	BVE-15738	Victor Studio 1

Title	Performer	Accompanist	Date	Location	Matrix no.	Catalogue/Studio
Slavonic Dance (Op. 72, no. 2), arr. Kreisler	Yehudi Menuhin	Marcel Gazelle			OLA 925-1	Cat. no. Victor EP3043
	Yehudi Menuhin	A. Baller				Cat. no. Philips A04308L
	Joseph Szigeti	Andor Földes				
	Mischa Elman	Joseph Seiger	3/24/1941	New York	CO 31951	
	Stefi Geyer	Walter Schuldhess	4/11/1927		2-20226	
	Jascha Heifetz	Samuel Chotzinoff	10/20/1922		C-23412-6	
	Fritz Kreisler	Carl Lamson	2/25/1915	New York	C-15742-1	Victor Studios
	Fritz Kreisler	Carl Lamson	3/28/1924	New York	C-15742-3	Victor Studios
	Yehudi Menuhin	Marcel Gazelle			2LA 926-1	
Slavonic Dance (Op. 72, no. 8)	Jascha Heifetz	Samuel Chotzinoff	9/16/1920		C-24467-2	
Slavonic Fantasy (arr. Kreisler)	Fritz Kreisler	Carl Lamson	12/6/1928	Camden	CVE-15737-3	Victor Studio 1
	Mischa Elman	Joseph Seiger	10/16-8 and 22-3/1956	London	ARL 3421/22	West Hampstead Studios
Gypsy Songs (Op. 55, no. 4), "Songs My Mother Taught Me" (arr. Persinger)	Yehudi Menuhin	Marcel Gazelle			OLA 786-2	
Gypsy Songs, (Op. 55, no. 4), "Songs My Mother Taught Me" (arr. Kreisler)	Yehudi Menuhin	Gerald Moore			2EA 17745-1C	

(continued)

Composer/Piece	Performer	Accompanist	Date	Location	Matrix	Other
Mischa Elman						
Eili, Eili (orig. by Jacob Koppel Sandler)	Mischa Elman	Joseph Seiger				
Tango	Mischa Elman	Emanuel Balaban	10/17/1921		C25654	Issued by Victor in set WDM1625
	Mischa Elman	W. Rosé				West Hampstead Studios
	Mischa Elman	Joseph Seiger	10/16–8 and 22–3 10/1956	London	ARL 3421/22	
Tango (orig. by Alben)	Mischa Elman	Joseph Bonime	3/20/1919		B22638	
Cesar Espejo						
Airs tziganes (Op. 11)	Mischa Elman	Marcel van Gool	1948	Los Angeles	2B 1131-3	Live
	Mischa Elman	Joseph Seiger	10/1956	London	ARL 3421/22	West Hampstead Studios
Manuel de Falla						
Canción (arr. Kochański)	Fritz Kreisler	Carl Lamson	3/25/1927	Camden	BVE-37462-2	Victor Studio 3
Suite populaire espagnole (arr. Kochański)	Fritz Kreisler	Carl Lamson	12/23/1929	New York	BVE-57918-5	Victor Studios
	Jeanne Gautier	N. Desouches			PARTX 9261-22/22B, 9262-22/22B, 9263-22/22B	

Title	Violinist	Pianist	Date	Place	No.		
Danse espagnole, from *La vida breve* (arr. Kreisler)	Michèle Auclair	Otto Schulhof					Cat. no. Remington R 199–128
	Jeanne Gautier	John Douglas Todd			CTX 1043		Cat. no. Odeon 171104
	Jeanne Gautier	F. Gaveau					
	Ida Haendel	Adela Kotowska	1940		AR6790		
	Jascha Heifetz	Emanuel Bay	12/11/1935	London	2EA 2581-3		
	Fritz Kreisler	Carl Lamson	2/27/1928	Camden	BVE-40359-7		Victor Studio 1
	Daniel Melsa				L 0442		
	Erica Morini	Louis Kentnor	1926		Bb 12797		
	Jacques Thibaud	Georges de Lausnay	5/29/1929	Paris	CS 3733-1		Salle Chopin
Jota, fom *Suite populaire espagnole* (arr. Kochański)	Carl Flesch	Ignaz Strasfogel	1929		BLR 4980		
	Jascha Heifetz	Isidor Achron	5/8/1928		CVE-43960-2		
	Jascha Heifetz	Emanuel Bay	10/18/1946	Hollywood	D6-RB-3108-2A		
	Jascha Heifetz	Brooks Smith	5/4/1967		UR-A3-1522		
	Fritz Kreisler	Carl Lamson	12/23/1929	New York	BVE-57918-5		RCA Studios
	Manuel Quiroga	Mme. Quiroga	1928–9	Paris	N 300892		
	Jacques Thibaud	Tasso Janopoulo	4/1930	London	Cc 19146-3		Studio A, Hayes, Middlesex

(continued)

Composer/Piece	Performer	Accompanist	Date	Location	Matrix	Other
Miller's Dance, from *El sombrero de tres picos*	Joseph Szigeti	Andor Földes	6/5/1940	New York	XCO 27425	
Nana (Berceuse), from *Suite populaire espagnole*	Jascha Heifetz	Brooks Smith	5/4/1967		UR–A3-1527	
	Jascha Heifetz	Brooks Smith	10/23/1972			Live
Abraham Goldfaden						
Raisins and Almonds (arr. Anthony Collins)	Mischa Elman	Joseph Seiger				Cat. no. Vanguard VRS1099
Enrique Granados						
Andaluza (Op. 37, no. 5) (arr. Kreisler)	Jascha Heifetz	Samuel Chotzinoff	10/19/1922		B-27035-2	
	Fritz Kreisler	Carl Lamson	1/14/1916	New York	B-16986-2	
	Jacques Thibaud	Harold Craxton	2/6/1922	London	Cc 980	HMV Studios, Hayes, Middlesex
	Jacques Thibaud	Harold Craxton	10/21/1927	London	Cc 9912	Queen's Hall, No. 3, Studio C
	Jacques Thibaud	Tasso Janopoulo	4/30/1930	London	Cc 19145-2	HMV Studios, Hayes, Middlesex
	Ibolyka Zilzer	F. Everson	10/9/1953		CCX 1533	

Jenő Hubay

Composition	Violinist	Pianist	Date		
Azt Mondják, *Scènes de la Csárda* no. 8 (Op. 60)	Mary Zentay	Jacques Grunberg		4850	
Geigenmacher von Cremona, Intermezzo (Op. 40)	Jenő Hubay	Otto Herz	12/4/1928	Cw 2046	
	Harry Solloway	Waldemar Liachowsky	c. 1925	102bm	
	Franz von Vecsey		2/17/1911	xPh 4536	
Hejre Kati, *Scènes de la Csárda* no. 4, (Op. 32)	Mischa Elman	Leopold Mittman	4/30/1946		Cat. no. RCA Victor 119433
	Carl Flesch	R. Bauman	3/24/1928	18335	
	Cecilia Hansen	Boris Zakharoff	1925	C 32191	
	Isolde Menges	Eileen Beattie	1925	Cc 9503-3	
	Alexander Mogilevsky		1938	JTW 271/2	
	Maud Powell	George Falkenstein	9/27/1912	C 12427	
	Emil Telemányi	Annette Telemányi	1959		
	Jenő Hubay	Otto Herz	12/4/1928	BW 2048/9	
Hullámzó Balaton, *Scènes de la Csárda* no. 5 (Op. 33)	Joseph Szigeti	Henry Bird	9/30/1908	London	2608f

(continued)

Composer/Piece	Performer	Accompanist	Date	Location	Matrix	Other
	Mischa Weisbord		4/1/1924		CT 2233-2	Cat. no. Polydor 15017
	Ibolyka Zilzer	Michael Raucheisen	c. 1928			Cat. no. Columbia 5076 M
Kis furulyám, *Scènes de la Csárda* no. 2 (Op. 13)	Duci de Kerekjárto	Maurice Eisner				
	Emil Telemányi	Budapest Orchestra, cond. Ferenc Fricsay	1942			Cat. no. Radiola SP 8028
Máros vize, *Scènes de la Csárda* no. 3 (Op. 18)	Joseph Szigeti	Andor Földes	11/24/1941		CO 31947/8	
Mazurka (Op. 45, no. 1)	Ibolyka Gyárfás		c. 1917–8			
Pici tubicám (*Scènes de la Csárda* No. 12, Op. 83)	Jenő Hubay	Budapest Coservatory Orchestra, cond. Nándor Stolz	10/31/1929		CV 696/7	
	Duci de Kerekjárto	Maurice Eisner				Cat. no. Col. 60002-D
Poème Hongroise (Op. 27, no. 6)	Jelly D'Arányi	Ethel Hobday	5/1927			Cat. no. Vocalion X-9981
Ugy-e Jani (Op. 92)	Jenő Hubay	Ottó Herz	11/22/1929		CV 804	

Zoltán Kodály

Composer/Piece	Performer	Accompanist	Date	Location	Matrix	Other
Háry János, Intermezzo (arr. Szigeti)	Joseph Szigeti	Andor Földes	11/24/1941	New York	CO 31949	

Alexander Krein

Work			Date	Location	Matrix	Studio
Dance no. 4 (arr. Heifetz)	Jascha Heifetz	Emanuel Bay	c. 1945		73205	
Fritz Kreisler						
Aloha Oe	Fritz Kreisler	Carl Lamson	8/28/1925		BVE-33189-7	Victor Studio 3
Gypsy Caprice	Fritz Kreisler	Carl Lamson	3/25/1927	Camden	CVE-37461-3	Victor Studios
Song of the Volga Boatmen	Fritz Kreisler	Carl Lamson	8/27/1925	Camden	BVE-33188-3	
Édouard Lalo						
Fantaisie Norvégienne	Jacques Thibaud	Tasso Janopoulo	4/24-5/1930	London	Cc 19151-3/4 and 19270-1/2	Queen's Small Hall, Studio C
Ákos László						
Ungarische Weisen, Op. 5	Joseph Szigeti	Henry Bird	6/8/1909	London	3123f	
Darius Milhaud						
Ipanema	William Primrose	David Stimer	12/17/1947		D7-RC-8249	
Lema	William Primrose	David Stimer	12/17/1947		D7-RC-8249	
Saudades do Brasil no. 7, "Corcovado" (Op. 67)	Joseph Szigeti	Kurt Ruhrseitz	7/9/1926	London	WA 3587	Petty France Studios
Saudades do Brasil no. 10, "Sumaré" (Op. 67) (arr. Levy)	Jascha Heifetz	Árpád Sándor	2/21/1934		0B-6053-3	
	Joseph Szigeti	Andor Földes	6/5/1940	New York	XCO 27425	

(continued)

Composer/Piece	Performer	Accompanist	Date	Location	Matrix	Other
Charles Miller						
Cubanaise	Mischa Elman	Joseph Seiger	10/1956	London	ARL 3421-22	West Hampstead Studios
Joaquín Nin						
20 Cantos populares españolas, nos. 4, 5, 7, and 8	Jeanne Gautier	Joaquín Nin	3/28/1928		Ki 1603-2, 1605-1, 1604-2, 1606-1	
20 Cantos populares españolas, nos. 4, 7, 8, and 16	Jeanne Gautier	M. Orlov			PARTX 9259-1 (nos. 4 and 7), 9260-1 (nos. 8 and 16)	
20 Cantos populares españolas, nos. 1, 15, 16, and 18	Jeanne Gautier	John Douglas Todd				Cat. no. Columbia DOX664
Manuel Ponce						
Estrellita	Jascha Heifetz	Isidor Achron	5/8/1928		BVE-43945-4	
Maude Powell						
Four American Folk Songs	Maud Powell	Joseph Pasternak, cond.	6/1917		C20014	
Manuel Quiroga						
Canto Amoroso	Manuel Quiroga	Mme. Quiroga	5/1928	London	45059	
Danza Española	Manuel Quiroga	Mme. Quiroga	5/1928	London	45057	

Rondalla (Jota)	Manuel Quiroga	Mme. Quiroga	5/1928	London	45058	
Segunda Guajira	Manuel Quiroga	Mme. Quiroga	5/1928	London	45056	
Maurice Ravel						
Pièce en forme de habanera	Jascha Heifetz	Milton Kaye	10/17/1944		72443	Victor Studio 1 RCA 44th St Lab
	Fritz Kreisler	Carl Lamson	11/30/1928	Camden	BVE-49146-3	
	Fritz Kreisler	Carl Lamson	12/16/1929	New York	BVE-49168-3	
Tzigane	Zino Francescatti	Maurice Fauré	1933		WLX 1524/5-1	
	Zino Francescatti	Artur Balsam			XCO 37583/4-1	Cat. no. Doremi DHR 7812
	Zino Francescatti	Orchestre de la Société des Concerts du Conservatoire, cond. André Cluytens	1/1/1951			
	Zino Francescatti	New York Philharmonic, cond. Leonard Bernstein	1/6/1964	New York		Cat. no. CBS BRG72247
	Ida Haendel	Ivor Newton	1940		AR4952-3	
	Jascha Heifetz	Árpád Sándor	2/6/1934		CS-78975-2 and 78976-2	
	Yehudi Menuhin	Arthur Balsam	1932		V7810	

(continued)

Composer/Piece	Performer	Accompanist	Date	Location	Matrix	Other
Camille Saint-Saëns						
Havanaise	Jascha Heifetz	Isidor Achron	12/19/1924	Camden	C-31382-3	Victor Studios
	Jascha Heifetz	London Symphony Orchestra, cond. John Barbirolli	4/9/1937	London	2EA 4744-1A/4745-1A	
	Jascha Heifetz	RCA Victor Symphony Orchestra, cond. William Steinberg	6/1951		E1-RC-2420-3A/2421-1A	
	Jacques Thibaud	Tasso Janopoulo	7/2/1933	London	2B 6796-2/2B 6797-1	Abbey Road, Studio 3
Pablo de Sarasate						
Adios Montaños Mios (Op. 37)	Ossy Renardy	Robert Walter	3/29/1939	New York	WXCO 24284-2	Columbia Studios
Caprice Basque (Op. 24)	Eddy Brown					Cat. no. Columbia A5810
	Mischa Elman	Percy B. Kahn	4/4/1910		C8801	
	Mischa Elman	Joseph Bonime	4/11/1919		C8801	
	Yehudi Menuhin	Marcel Gazelle	12/21/1935	Paris	2LA789	Studio Albert
	Pablo de Sarasate		1904	Paris	4262o	
Danzas Españolas, Malagueña (Op. 21, no. 1)	René Benedetti	Maurice Fauré	10/24/1927		LX 123-1	

Title	Performer	Accompanist	Date	Location	Matrix	Notes
	Carl Flesch	Harry Kaufman	4/1/1924		9254G-1-2-3	
	Jascha Heifetz	André Benoist	12/19/1917		C-21270-3	
	Isolde Menges	Eileen Beattie	9/24/1923		Cc 3491	
	Isolde Menges	Eileen Beattie	12/9/1925		CR 63-2	
	Henri Temianka	Joanna Graudan	7/8/1936	London	CXE 7583	Abbey Road Studios
Danzas Españolas, Habanera (Op. 21, no. 2)	René Benedetti	Maurice Fauré			LX 124-1	
	Guila Bustabo	Heinz Schröter	1941 (?)		CRX 209-1	
	Jascha Heifetz	Isidor Achron	12/18/1924		C-27046-3	
	Miron Polyakin	A. Dyakov	1939		8284/5	
	Ruggiero Ricci	Louis Persinger	10/1/1938		2RA 3333-2	
	Pablo de Sarasate		1904	Paris	4265o	
	Henri Temianka	Joanna Graudan	12/7/1936	London	CXE 7983	Abbey Road Studios
Danzas Españolas (Op. 26, no. 2)	Jan Kubelik	George Falkenstein	5/7/1913 or 9/1914		z7328f	
Danzas Españolas (Op. 26, no. 8)	Arnold Rosé	Alma Rosé	1902	Vienna	(o) 910X–B–2z	
	Maud Powell	Waldemar Liachowsky	10/28/1911		C11089	
Introduction and Caprice-Jota	Pablo de Sarasate		1904	Paris	4259o	

(continued)

Composer/Piece	Performer	Accompanist	Date	Location	Matrix	Other
Jota Aragonesa (Op. 27)	Marie Hall	Harold Craxton (?)	10/3/1918		HO 3476af	
	Joan Manén		1915	Berlin	2-2046	
	Joan Manén	J. Brach	12/21/1921		Cc 813	
	Manuel Quiroga	Mme. Quiroga	1928-9	Paris	N 300918	
Jota Navarra (Op. 22, no. 2)	Manuel Quiroga	Mme. Quiroga	4/18/1912	Paris	17181u	
	Ossy Renardy	Robert Walter	3/29/1939	New York	XCO 23596	Columbia Studios
Miramar–Zortzico (Op. 42)	Manuel Quiroga	Mme. Quiroga	4/18/1912	Paris	17178u	
Navarra (Op. 33)	Pablo de Sarasate		1904	Paris	4261o	
	Eddy Brown	Roman Totenberg, violin	c. 1939		US-121206-1/1207-1	
Playera (Op. 23, no. 1)	Josef Hassid	Gerald Moore	6/28/1940	London	2EA 8801	Abbey Road, Studio 3
Romanza Andaluza (Op. 22, no . 1)	Mischa Elman	Walter Golde	10/6/1915		C16607-3	
	Jascha Heifetz	Emanuel Bay	10/18/1946		D6-RC-5644-2	
	Manuel Quiroga	Mme. Quiroga	1928-9	Paris	N 300901	
	Ossy Renardy	Robert Walter	1/3/1939	New York	XCO 23595	Columbia Studios
	Harry Solloway	Waldemar Liachowsky			105 bm	
	Mischa Weisbord		3/24/1924		CT 2222-3	

Work	Violinist	Accompanist	Date	Location	Matrix no.	Studio
Tarantelle (Op. 43)	Manuel Quiroga	Mme. Quiroga	1928–9	Paris	N 300917	
	Pablo de Sarasate		1904	Paris	4260o	
Zapateado (Op. 23, no. 2)	Guila Bustabo	Heinz Schröter	1941 (?)		CR 790-3	
	John Dunn		5/1/1912		Lxx3680-2	Abbey Road
	Josef Hassid	Gerald Moore	6/12/1940		2EA 8802	Victor Studios
	Jascha Heifetz	André Benoist	10/4/1918	Camden	B-22273-1	Victor Studios
	Jascha Heifetz	Isidor Achron	12/31/1926	Camden	CVE-22273-4	
	Jascha Heifetz	Donald Voorhees, cond.	2/16/1948		J 585 USS 1024	
	Jascha Heifetz	Emanuel Bay	10/19/1946	Hollywood	D6-RB 3114-1	RCA Studios
	Jan Kubelik		1910		XX Ph 4305	
	Jan Kubelik		7/3/1911		5125f/5126f	
	Daniel Melsa				L 0353	
	Manuel Quiroga	Mme. Quiroga	1928–9	Paris	N 350094	
	Ossy Renardy	Walter Robert			xco24286-1	
	Pablo de Sarasate		1904	Paris	4266o	
Zigeunerweisen (Op. 20)	Mischa Elman	Joseph Seiger				Cat. no.VRS1051
	Mischa Elman	Carroll Hollister	1930		A 62242/3	
	Mischa Elman	Marcel van Gool	1930	London	Cc 20366/7	Small Queen's Hall, Studio C

(continued)

Composer/Piece	Performer	Accompanist	Date	Location	Matrix	Other
	Ida Haendel	Ivor Newton	1940		AR 4952-3	
	Jascha Heifetz	Samuel Chotzinoff	10/13–14/1919		C-23410-2/ 23407-2	
	Jascha Heifetz	London Symphony Orchestra, cond. John Barbirolli	4/9/1937	London	2EA 4746-2/4747-2A	
	Jascha Heifetz	Bell Telephone Orchestra, Donald Voorhees, cond.	4/27/1942			
	Jascha Heifetz	RCA Victor Symphony Orchestra, cond. William Steinberg	6/16/1951		El-RC-2418-1/2419-1	
	Jan Kubelik		2/3/1907		xxPh 2405	
	Jan Kubelik		5/30/1911		xPh 4560	
	Jan Kubelik		12/31/1912		Ho 677	
	Daniel Melsa					Broadcast 5130
	Michel Piastro	Maurice Nadelle	c. 1928		10267A/B	
	Miron Polyakin	D. Makarov	1940		10460/1	
	Maud Powell	Waldemar Liachowsky	10/28/1911		B11149	

Work	Performer	Pianist/Conductor	Date	Place	Matrix no.	Catalog/Studio
	Ruggiero Ricci		11/1/1938		2RA3408/9	
	Ruggiero Ricci	Karl Förstner	1939		2RA 3408-2/3409-3	
	Ruggiero Ricci	London Symphony Orchestra, cond. Malcolm Sargent	9/28/1959	London		Cat. no. Decca LXT5571
	Harry Solloway	Waldemar Liachowsky			T 5182	
	Pablo de Sarasate		1904	Paris	4263/4264o	
Albert Spalding						
Old Irish Song and Dance	Mischa Elman	Leopold Mittman	11/16/1943			Cat. no. V-disc 142B
Igor Stravinsky						
Chanson Russe, from *Mavra*	Joseph Szigeti	Igor Stravinsky	5/9/1946	New York	XCO 36310	Columbia Studios
Russian Dance, from *Petrushka* (arr. Dushkin)	Samuel Dushkin	Igor Stravinsky	4/6/1933	Paris	CL 4277	Studio Albert
	Joseph Szigeti	Nikita Magaloff	3/2/1937	London	CA 16270	Abbey Road, Studio 3
Flausino Rodrigues Vale						
Ao Pé Da Figueira (arr. Heifetz)	Jascha Heifetz	Emanuel Bay	11/29/1945	New York	73182	Decca Studios

(*continued*)

Composer/Piece	Performer	Accompanist	Date	Location	Matrix	Other
Ao Pé Da Figueira (for viola)	William Primrose	David Stimer	12/17/1947		D7-RC-8252	
Efrem Zimbalist						
Hebrew Melody and Dance	Efrem Zimbalist		2/24/1912		B-11609	
Polish Dance	Efrem Zimbalist		2/16/1916		B-17172-2	
Sarasateana	William Primrose	David Stimer	12/17/1947	New York	D7-RC-2829/32	RCA Studios

NOTES

Introduction

1. "Programs of the Week," *New York Times*, October 6, 1918, 77.

2. For a description of the various arrangements of "Eili, Eili," see Irene Heskes, *Yiddish American Popular Songs, 1895–1950: A Catalog Based on the Lawrence Marwick Roster of Copyright Entries* (Washington, DC: Library of Congress, 1992), xxxvi.

3. Leo Zeitlin, *Chamber Music*, ed. Paula Eisenstein Baker and Robert S. Nelson (Middleton, WI: A-R Editions, 2009), xxviii. On the history of "Eili, Eili," see Irene Heskes, *Passport to Jewish Music: Its Histories, Traditions, and Culture* (Westport, CT: Greenwood, 1994), 203–5.

4. On cantorial recordings of "Eili, Eili," see Jeffrey Shandler, *Jews, God, and Videotape: Religion and Media in America* (New York: New York University Press, 2009), 23.

5. Anzia Yezierska, "Sorrows into Song," *New York Times*, October 10, 1954, BR26.

6. "Music in the Movies," *New York Times*, September 4, 1921, 51.

7. The story of Sandler's composition of the song and the lawsuit that followed was retold in 1925, in Silas Bent, "Rip Van Winkle Sleep of 'Eili, Eili' Ends," *New York Times*, June 21, 1925, SM12.

8. "'Eili, Eili' Sandler's, Old Actors Testify," *New York Times*, April 30, 1925, 24; and "'Eili, Eili' Played in Court by Lawyer," *New York Times*, May 1, 1925, 7.

9. "'Eili, Eili' Played in Court," 7.

10. John C. Knox, *A Judge Comes of Age* (New York: Charles Scribner's Sons, 1940), 184.

11. "Claimant Loses Suit on 'Eili, Eili,'" *New York Times*, June 10, 1925, 1.

12. Ibid., 11.

13. Knox, *A Judge Comes of Age*, 185.

14. Ibid., 184-5.

15. Ibid., 184.

16. Martin Stokes, introduction to *Ethnicity, Identity and Music: The Musical Construction of Place*, ed. Martin Stokes (Oxford: Berg, 1994), 7.

17. Richard Handler, "Authenticity," *Anthropology Today* 2, no. 1 (February 1986): 2–4.

18. See Ronald Radano and Philip V. Bohlman, "Introduction: Music and Race, Their Past, Their Presence," in *Music and the Racial Imagination*, ed. Ronald Radano and Philip V. Bohlman (Chicago: University of Chicago Press, 2000), 28; Philip

V. Bohlman, *The Study of Folk Music in the Modern World* (Bloomington: Indiana University Press, 1988), 10–11; and Thomas Turino and James Lea, eds., *Identity and the Arts in Diaspora Communities* (Warren, MI: Harmonie Park Press, 2004), 8.

19. Such histories should not be read as teleological: there is no single narrative in any succession of performances and adaptations of a composition. Nevertheless, earlier conceptions of works often furnish essential components of the context that makes such musical rereadings possible. For a discussion of music historiography and the concepts of teleology and context, see Gary Tomlinson, "The Web of Culture: A Context for Musicology," *19th-Century Music* 7, no. 3 (April 1984): 357.

20. Erno Rapée, *Erno Rapée's Encyclopædia of Music for Pictures: As Essential as the Picture* (New York: Belwin, 1925), 13.

21. Philip V. Bohlman, "Erasure: Displacing and Misplacing Race," in *Western Music and Race*, ed. Julie Brown (Cambridge: Cambridge University Press, 2007), 11.

22. Ibid., 12.

23. Quoted in Jann Pasler, "Race and Nation: Musical Acclimatization and the Chansons Populaires in Third Republic France," *Western Music and Race*, ed. Julie Brown (Cambridge: Cambridge University Press, 2007), 148.

24. Quoted in Jann Pasler, *Composing the Citizen: Music as Public Utility in Third Republic France* (Berkeley: University of California Press, 2009), 353; see also 396–7.

25. Quoted in ibid., 355.

26. Franz Liszt, *The Gipsy in Music*, trans. Edwin Evans (London: William Reeves, 1926), 10.

27. Olin Downes published these remarks in a 1923 column in the *Boston Sunday Post*. Quoted in *Ernest Bloch: Biography and Comment* (San Francisco: Mary Morgan, 1925), 16. On Ernest Bloch's conception of race and the role of race in the reception of his music, see Joshua S. Walden, "'An Essential Expression of the People': Interpretations of Hasidic Song in the Composition and Performance History of Ernest Bloch's *Baal Shem*," *Journal of the American Musicological Society* 65, no. 3 (Fall 2012): 777–820.

28. See Harvey E. Goldberg, "Modern Jewish Society and Sociology," in *The Oxford Handbook of Jewish Studies*, ed. Martin Goodman (Oxford: Oxford University Press, 2002), 975–1001; Ivan Hannaford, *Race: The History of an Idea in the West* (Baltimore: Johns Hopkins University Press, 1996); Kenan Malik, *The Meaning of Race: Race, History and Culture in Western Society* (London: Macmillan, 1996); and Radano and Bohlman, "Introduction."

29. Martin Stokes explains the difference between using concepts of race and ethnicity as the basis for research, in his introduction to *Ethnicity, Identity and Music*, 6.

30. Edward W. Said, *Orientalism* (New York: Pantheon, 1978).

31. On Said's orientalist paradigm, see A. L. Macfie, *Orientalism* (London: Longman, 2002), 5–9.

32. John M. Efron, "From Mitteleuropa to the Middle East: Orientalism through a Jewish Lens," *Jewish Quarterly Review* 94, no. 3 (Summer 2004): 490–2.

33. See ibid., 520; and Ivan Davidson Kalmar and Derek J. Penslar, "Orientalism and the Jews: An Introduction," in *Orientalism and the Jews*, ed. Ivan Davidson Kalmar and Derek J. Penslar (Waltham, MA: Brandeis University Press, 2005), xviii

34. Ralph P. Locke, *Musical Exoticism: Images and Reflections* (Cambridge: Cambridge University Press, 2009), 66–8.

35. Mikhail Mikhaïlovich Bakhtin, "Discourse in the Novel," in *The Dialogic Imagination: Four Essays by M.M. Bakhtin*, ed. Michael Holquist and trans. Caryl Emerson and Michael Holquist (Austin: University of Texas Press, 1981), 293–4.

36. Ibid., 358.

37. Ibid., 361, italics in the original.

38. Robert J. C. Young addresses the intertwining histories of the concept of hybridity and racial discourses during the nineteenth and early twentieth centuries, in *Colonial Desire: Hybridity in Theory, Culture and Race* (London: Routledge, 1995).

39. In his study of the music of Górale musicians in Podhale, for example, Timothy J. Cooley argues that "outside interest (ethnographic and touristic) . . . stimulated the very invention of Górale ethnicity and that it now provides, through the tourist industry, an important motivation for maintaining this ethnicity." *Making Music in the Polish Tatras: Tourists, Ethnographers, and Mountain Musicians* (Bloomington: Indiana University Press, 2005), 8.

40. Matthew Gelbart, *The Invention of "Folk Music" and "Art Music": Emerging Categories from Ossian to Wagner* (Cambridge: Cambridge University Press, 2007), 226–7.

41. Ibid., 236. See also Lynn Hooker, "Modernism on the Periphery: Béla Bartók and the New Music Society of 1911–1912," *Musical Quarterly* 88, no. 2 (Summer 2005): 299.

42. Gelbart, *Invention of "Folk Music" and "Art Music,"* 236.

43. Jann Pasler, *Composing the Citizen*, 352.

44. Quoted in Jann Pasler, "The *Chanson Populaire* as a Malleable Symbol in Turn-of-the-Century France," in *Tradition and Its Future in Music: Report of SIMS 1990 Ósaka*, ed. Yoshihiko Tokumaru, Makoto Ohmiya, Masakata Kanazawa, et al. (Tokyo: Mita Press, 1991), 204.

45. Jean-Baptiste Weckerlin, *Échos du temps passé* (Paris: A. Durand et Fils, n.d.), 1:120. "brave cultivateur"; "Nous avons souvent entendu chanter les paysans de Normandie en pleine campagne, ils donnent leur voix à pleins poumons et la soutiennent sur chaque note jusqu'à extinction de respiration. Leurs airs sont presque toujours en mineur, et ressemblent plutôt à des psalmodies qu'à des chansons."

46. Quotations are from the Preface of Edvard Grieg, *Norwegian Peasant Dances (Slåtter)* (New York: C.F. Peters, n.d.). See Daniel M. Grimley, *Grieg: Music, Landscape and Norwegian Identity* (Woodbridge, UK: Boydell, 2006), 147.

47. Grimley, *Grieg*, 152.

48. Quoted in Michael D. Largey, *Vodou Nation: Haitian Art Music and Cultural Nationalism* (Chicago: University of Chicago Press, 2006), 130.

49. Quoted in ibid., 136.

50. Quoted in ibid., 137.

51. Clarence Elkin, *Maori Melodies (with Words) Collected and Arranged for Pianoforte* (Sydney: W. H. Paling, 1923), 1.

52. On Farwell and the *American Indian Melodies*, see Beth Levy, *Frontier Figures: American Music and the Mythology of the American West* (Berkeley: University of California Press, 2012), 26–30. For a study of the goal of authenticity in works based on Native American music at the turn of the twentieth century, see Michael V. Pisani, *Imagining Native America in Music* (New Haven: Yale University Press, 2005), ch. 7.

53. Arthur Farwell, *American Indian Melodies* (New York: G. Schirmer, 1914), 1. Also published by the Wa-Wan Press, the score of Harvey Worthington Loomis's interpretations of Native American music, collected in *Lyrics of the Red Man, Books 1 and 2* (1903 and 1904), similarly featured ethnographic descriptions of each source melody, copied from *A Study of Omaha Indian Music* by Fletcher and Francis La Flesche. Pisani, *Imagining Native America in Music*, 229.

54. Farwell, *American Indian Melodies*, 1–2.

55. Richard Taruskin, "Nationalism," in *Grove Music Online, Oxford Music Online,* http://www.oxfordmusiconline.com/.

56. On the study of borderland musics, see Jolanta T. Pekacz, *Music in the Culture of Polish Galicia, 1772–1914* (Rochester, NY: University of Rochester Press, 2002), 2–9.

57. Ibid., 2–9. On the hybridity of music in peripheral, border, and non-state communities, see Philip V. Bohlman, *The Music of European Nationalism: Cultural Identity and Modern History* (Santa Barbara: ABC Clio, 2004), 219.

58. On Heifetz's musical eclecticism, see Joshua S. Walden, "'The Hora Staccato in Swing!': Jascha Heifetz's Musical Eclecticism and the Adaptation of Violin Miniatures," *Journal of the Society of American Music* 6, no. 4 (November 2012): 405–31.

59. Quoted in Howard Taubman, "Heifetz of Symphony and of Swing," *New York Times*, December 22, 1946, 102.

60. Jean-Jacques Rousseau, *Dictionnaire de Musique* (Paris, 1768), 214. On the violin's universality and broad expressive versatility, see David Schoenbaum, *The Violin: A Social History of the World's Most Versatile Instrument* (New York: W. W. Norton, 2013), xvii–xxvi. Translation of Rousseau's praise for the violin appears on xvii.

Chapter 1

1. Barbara Kirshenblatt-Gimblett examines this form of "eleventh-hour" ethnography in "Folklore's Crisis," *Journal of American Folklore* 111, no. 441 (Summer 1998): 300. See also Roger D. Abrahams, "Phantoms of Romantic Nationalism in Folkloristics," *Journal of American Folklore* 106, no. 419 (Winter 1993): 11.

2. In spite of this tendency in art music, genre persisted as an important factor in popular music in the twentieth century. See the introduction to Fabian Holt, *Genre in Popular Music* (Chicago: University of Chicago Press, 2007), 1–29.

3. Theodor W. Adorno, *Aesthetic Theory*, ed. Gretel Adorno and Rolf Tiedemann and trans. Robert Hullot-Kentor (New York: Continuum, 2004), 262.

4. Carl Dahlhaus, "New Music and the Problem of Musical Genre," in *Schoenberg and the New Music*, trans. Derrick Puffett and Alfred Clayton (Cambridge: Cambridge University Press, 1987), 33. Originally published in 1969 as "Die neue Musik und das Problem der musikalische Gattungen."

5. Fredric Jameson, "Magical Narratives: Romance as Genre," *New Literary History* 7, no. 1 (Autumn 1975): 135. Emphasis in the original. Jameson is responding primarily to literary critics such as Benedetto Croce, who adopts a similar approach to Adorno and Dahlhaus with respect to the field of literature. Croce argues that the classification of literature into constituent genres does injustice to the individuality of particular works, which by their nature constantly break laws of genre. Benedetto Croce, *Aesthetic*, trans. Douglas Ainslie (New York: Noonday, 1968).

6. Northrop Frye, *Anatomy of Criticism: Four Essays* (New York: Atheneum, 1957), 247–8.

7. On art worlds, see Howard Becker, *Art Worlds* (Berkeley: University of California Press, 1982), x. On genre as a social institution or contract, see Tzvetan Todorov, "The Origin of Genres," trans. Richard M. Berrong, *New Literary History* 8, no. 1 (Autumn 1976): 163; and Jameson, "Magical Narratives," 135.

8. Sue Tuohy, "The Social Life of Genre: The Dynamics of Folksong in China," *Asian Music* 30, no. 2 (Spring–Summer 1999): 40.

9. Philip Vilas Bohlman, *The Study of Folk Music in the Modern World* (Bloomington: Indiana University Press, 1988), 35.

10. Ibid., 35.

11. Tuohy, "Social Life of Genre," 41.

12. On the focuses of musical products and processes in ethnomusicological classification systems, see Bohlman, *Study of Folk Music*, 44–6.

13. For a study of the musical category or quality that would seem to contrast most directly with miniaturization, musical monumentality, see Alexander Rehding, *Music and Monumentality: Commemoration and Wonderment in Nineteenth-Century Germany* (New York: Oxford University Press, 2009). Despite the structural differences between musical miniatures and monuments, both become involved in musical commemoration, memorialization, and other such projects. Rehding also addresses arrangements of large-scale works for performance in the home salon as instances of souvenir miniaturization (ch. 3).

14. Tom Phillips, *The Postcard Century: 2000 Cards and Their Messages* (London: Thames and Hudson, 2000), 7.

15. Susan Stewart, *On Longing* (Durham, NC: Duke University Press, 1993), 147.

16. Alan Dundes, *Interpreting Folklore* (Bloomington: Indiana University Press, 1980), 2. See also Raymond Williams, *The Country and the City* (London: Hogarth, 1985), 1.

17. Matthew Gelbart, *Invention of "Folk Music" and "Art Music,"* 15.

18. Ferdinand Tönnies, *Community and Society (Gemeinschaft und Gesellschaft)*, trans. Charles P. Loomis (Newton Abbott, UK: Courier Dover, 2002), 33.

19. Ibid., 35.

20. Ibid., 205–6.

21. C. Hubert H. Parry, *The Art of Music*, 5th ed. (London: Kegan Paul, Trench, Trübner, 1894), 86.

22. Ibid., 86.

23. Robert Redfield, "The Folk Society," *American Journal of Sociology* 52, no. 4 (January 1947): 293.

24. Ibid., 297.

25. Béla Bartók, "The Influence of Peasant Music on Modern Music," in *Béla Bartók Essays*, ed. Benjamin Suchoff (London: Faber and Faber, 1976), 341.

26. Ibid., 341.

27. Judit Frigyesi, "Béla Bartók and the Concept of Nation and *Volk* in Modern Hungary," *Musical Quarterly* 78, no. 2 (Summer 1994): 274.

28. Quoted in ibid., 277.

29. Ibid., 274–5.

30. Ibid., 276–8.

31. Alastair Fowler, *Kinds of Literature: An Introduction to the Theory of Genres and Modes* (Oxford: Clarendon, 1982), 37–8 and 45–6.

32. Roland Barthes, "The Reality Effect," in *The Rustle of Language*, trans. Richard Howard (Berkeley: University of California Press, 1986). Originally published as "L'Effet de réel," *Communications* 11 (1968): 84–9.

33. Barthes, "Reality Effect," 147.

34. Quoted in ibid., 141.

35. Ibid., 142.

36. Ibid., 148.

37. See Hanoch Avenary, "The Concept of Mode in European Synagogue Chant," *Yuval* 2 (1971): 11–21; Hanoch Avenary, "Shtayger," in *Encyclopedia Judaica*, 2nd ed., ed. Michael Berenbaum and Fred Skolnik (Detroit: Macmillan Reference USA, 2007), 18:522–3; Rita Ottens and Joel Rubin, *Klezmer-Musik* (Kassel: Bärenreiter, 1999), 197–200; and Baruch Joseph Cohon, "The Structure of the Synagogue Prayer-Chant," *Journal of the American Musicological Society* 3, no. 1 (Spring 1950): 18–19.

38. Avenary, "Shtayger," 523. Like other synagogue modes, the *Ahavah rabbah* was named for one of the most important prayers in Jewish religious practice that incorporates its particular set of intervals. *Ahavah rabbah* is chanted during the daily morning prayer service.

39. Amnon Shiloah, *Jewish Musical Traditions* (Detroit: Wayne State University Press, 1992), 126.

40. Cohon, "Structure of the Synagogue Prayer Chant," 18; and Mark Slobin, *Tenement Songs: The Popular Music of Jewish Immigrants* (Urbana: University of Illinois Press, 1996), 184 and 187.

41. Slobin, *Tenement Songs*, 187.

42. Mark Slobin, "The Evolution of a Musical Symbol in Yiddish Culture," in *Studies in Jewish Folklore: Proceedings of a Regional Conference of the Association for Jewish Studies Held at the Spertus College of Judaica, Chicago, May 1–3, 1977*, ed. Frank Talmage

(Cambridge, MA: Association for Jewish Studies, 1980), 314. See also Moshe Beregovski, *Jewish Instrumental Folk Music: The Collections and Writings of Moshe Beregovski*, ed. and trans. Mark Slobin, Robert A. Rothstein, and Michael Alpert (Syracuse, NY: Syracuse University Press, 2001); and Abraham Zvi Idelsohn, *Jewish Music in Its Historical Development* (New York: Tudor, 1944), 185.

43. In the original French by C. F. Ramuz, the text is: "On voit que c'est du bon marché/ Il faut tout le temps l'accorder." Translated by Michael Flanders and Kitty Black in *Histoire du soldat* (London: J. and W. Chester, 1955), 5.

44. "Tsen brider" appears in a number of anthologies, including Saul M. Ginzburg and Pesach S. Marek, *Yiddish Folksongs in Russia: Photo Reproduction of the 1901 St. Petersburg Edition*, ed. Dov Noy and trans. Lila Holzman (Ramat Gan: Bar-Ilan University Press, 1991), 142. For historical background on "Tsen Brider," see Joshua R. Jacobson, "'Tsen Brider': A Jewish Requiem," *Musical Quarterly* 84, no. 3 (2000): 452–74; and Joshua S. Walden, "Leaving Kazimierz: Comedy and Realism in the Yiddish Film Musical *Yidl Mitn Fidl*," *Journal of Music, Sound, and the Moving Image* 3, no. 2 (Autumn 2009): 168–9.

45. All Romanization from Yiddish follows YIVO orthography. The names differ in various printed versions of the song; in Ginzburg and Marek's anthology, the refrain opens, "Shmerl mit der fidl/ Yekl mit dem bas,/ Shpilt mir oyf a lidl/ Oyfn mitn gas." Ginzburg and Marek, *Yiddish Folksongs in Russia*, 142.

46. Gérard Genette, *Paratexts: Thresholds of Interpretation*, trans. Jane E. Lewin (Cambridge: Cambridge University Press, 1997), 1.

47. Composers sometimes relied on the persuasive potential of the paratextual space of the score to convince listeners that a composition's sources were other than they actually were. For example, the title could purposefully misidentify the ethnic origins of melodies arranged in a rural miniature and thus deflect the hostility of xenophobic listeners. Heinrich Schenker, for example, wrote a series of dances for four-hand piano in 1899, publishing them under the title *Syrische Tänze* (Syrian Dances). In a letter of 1903, Ferruccio Busoni asked Schenker why he had not given the music the title "Jewish Dance Songs," recognizing that the individual movements were based on the characteristics of Eastern European Jewish dance genres. Nicholas Cook, *The Schenker Project: Culture, Race, and Music Theory in Fin-de-siècle Vienna* (Oxford: Oxford University Press, 2007), 225. A manuscript copy of the work shows that Schenker, a Galician Jew, originally intended to identify his work by the title *Tänze der Chassidim* (Hasidic Dances) but subsequently chose a title that would indicate a more remote, exotic point of origin, apparently in order to evade burgeoning Viennese hostility to representations of Jewish tradition (225). The cover illustration of the printed score further attenuates the connection to Jewish traditional music, and in turn to Schenker's Jewish identity, with an exoticist image of a dancing woman in bangles and flowing fabrics before a landscape of flower blossoms and onion domes (226).

48. Decades earlier, Weckerlin had employed this technique in *Echos du temps passé*, incorporating ethnographic transcriptions of *chansons populaires* in smaller print above his arrangements of the same melodies. Pasler, "Race and Nation," 149.

49. Bartók applied a similar technique in the score of *Improvisations on Hungarian Peasant Songs* (1922), where he provided a preface featuring brief notated transcriptions of the original melodies and the locations (village and county) and dates of collection, as well as the name of the ethnographer when songs did not originate from his own fieldwork.

50. See Pam Morris's definition of realism in the visual arts and literature, in *Realism* (London: Routledge, 2003).

51. Roman Jakobson, "On Realism and Art," trans. Karol Magassy, in *Language in Literature*, ed. Krystyna Pomorska and Stephen Rudy (Cambridge, MA: Belknap, 1987), 20.

52. See Meyer Schapiro, *Modern Art: 19th & 20th Centuries* (New York: G. Braziller, 1982), 195–6; and John Hyman, *The Objective Eye: Color, Form, and Reality in the Theory of Art* (Chicago: University of Chicago Press, 2006), 163–4. On the use of the term "representation," see Peter Kivy, *Sound and Semblance: Reflections on Musical Representation* (Princeton, NJ: Princeton University Press, 1984), 17.

53. My translation, italics in the original. "La reproduction de la nature par l'homme ne sera jamais une *reproduction* ni une *imitation*, ce sera toujours une *interprétation*." Champfleury, *Le réalisme* (Paris: Michel Lévy Frères, 1857), 92.

54. The term "realism" is sometimes used interchangeably with "naturalism," although these words carry differing connotations due to their contrasting uses in nineteenth-century French artistic movements. (For a discussion of naturalism in music, see Walter Frisch, *German Modernism: Music and the Arts* [Berkeley: University of California Press, 2005], ch. 2.) Naturalism was pioneered in the 1860s by the novelist Émile Zola, who attempted in some of his works to represent the daily life of the working classes by depicting collected social types in a manner that would be perceived as scientifically accurate, while avoiding moral judgment. Zola viewed his project in part as a scientific one; in preparing to write *Germinal*, for instance, he undertook research by reading medical and scientific works and visiting mines, in order more accurately to document the life of the working classes. The naturalist movement soon became popular among German, Italian, and French composers and writers and is evident in such musical genres as *verismo* opera. The compositional style of early twentieth-century arrangements of folk music is better described by analogy to the concept of aesthetic realism than to the tenets of the naturalist movement.

55. Parry, *Art of Music*, 320.

56. Norman Cazden also addresses musical realism in "Towards a Theory of Realism in Music," *Journal of Aesthetics and Art Criticism* 10, no. 2 (December 1951): 135–51.

57. Carl Dahlhaus, *Realism in Nineteenth-Century Music*, trans. Mary Whitall (Cambridge: Cambridge University Press, 1985), 26.

58. Ibid., 13–14.

59. Ibid., 26.

60. Ibid., 60.

61. Ibid., 109–10.

62. Ibid., 146.

63. Ibid., 146.

64. Johann Gottfried Herder, *Essay on the Origin of Language*, in *On the Origin of Language*, trans. John H. Moran and Alexander Gode (Chicago: University of Chicago Press, 1986), 85–176. For a discussion of the influence of eighteenth- and nineteenth-century German anthropology on American anthropology of the following century, in particular the intellectual impacts of Herder's concept of *Volksgeist* and Wilhelm von Humboldt's concept of *Nationalcharakter* on the notion of culture as developed by Franz Boas in the first half of the twentieth century, see Matti Bunzl, "Franz Boas and the Humboldtian Tradition: From *Volksgeist* and *Nationalcharakter* to an Anthropological Concept of Culture," in Volksgeist *as Method and Ethic: Essays on Boasian Ethnography and the German Anthropological Tradition*, ed. George W. Stocking Jr., 17–78 (Madison: University of Wisconsin Press, 1996).

65. Philip V. Bohlman, *The Music of European Nationalism: Cultural Identity and Modern History* (Santa Barbara, CA: ABC-Clio, 2004), 43.

66. Translated in Friedrich A. Kittler, *Gramophone, Film, Typewriter*, trans. Geoffrey Winthrop-Young and Michael Wutz (Stanford, CA: Stanford University Press, 1999), 22. "Comme les traits dans les camées/ J'ai voulu que les voix aimées/ Soient un bien qu'on garde à jamais,/ Et puissant répéter le rêve/ Musical de l'heure trop brève;/ Le temps veut fuir, je le soumets."

67. Erika Brady, *A Spiral Way: How the Phonograph Changed Ethnography* (Jackson: University Press of Mississippi, 1999), 60. See also Michael Yates, "Percy Grainger and the Impact of the Phonograph," *Folk Music Journal* 4, no. 3 (1982): 265. On the importance of sound recording in the history of ethnomusicology, see Jaap Kunst, *Ethnomusicology: A Study of Its Nature, Its Problems, Methods, and Representative Personalities to Which Is Added a Bibliography* (The Hague: Martinus Nijhoff, 1959), 12.

68. Quoted in Brady, *Spiral Way*, 63. See also Fewkes's letter to the magazine *Nature*, in which he recounts using the phonograph during fieldwork in New England to collect Passamaquoddy language, folk songs, folk tales, and descriptions of dances. J. Walter Fewkes, "On the Use of the Edison Phonograph in the Preservation of the Languages of the American Indians," *Nature*, April 17, 1890, 560.

69. Brady, *Spiral Way*, 67.

70. Nazir Jairazbhoy, "The 'Objective' and Subjective View in Music Transcription," *Ethnomusicology* 21, no. 2 (May 1977): 263–73.

71. Brady, *Spiral Way*, 65.

72. Béla Bartók, *The Hungarian Folksong*, ed. Benjamin Suchoff, and trans. M. D. Calvocoressi (Albany: State University of New York Press, 1981); and Zoltán Kodály, *Folk Music of Hungary*, enlarged ed. by Lajos Vargyas, trans. Ronald Tempest and Cynthia Jolly, trans. rev. by Laurence Picken (New York: Praeger, 1971). Later in his career, Bartók revised his method of transcription: rather than creating idealized transcriptions of folk music, he produced increasingly detailed annotations of the individual performances he captured on recording. Sándor Kovács, "The Ethnomusicologist," in *The Bartók Companion*, ed. Malcolm Gillies (London: Faber and Faber, 1993), 59.

73. Fritz Mordechai Kaufmann, *Die schönsten Lieder der Ostjuden: siebenundvierzig ausgewählte Volkslieder*, ed. Achim Freudenstein and Karsten Troyke (Edermünde: Achims Verlag, 2001); Yehuda Leib Cahan, *Yidishe folkslider mit melodyes*, ed. Max Weinreich (New York: YIVO, 1957); and Moshe Beregovski, *Old Jewish Folk Music: The Collections and Writings of Moshe Beregovski*, ed. and trans. Mark Slobin (Syracuse, NY: Syracuse University Press, 2000).

74. On the French realist movement, see Linda Nochlin, *Realism* (Baltimore: Penguin, 1971).

75. Quoted in ibid., 35. Lewes's companion, Mary Ann Evans, better known as the realist novelist George Eliot, followed his dictum in depicting rural life in *Scenes from Clerical Life* and in novels including *Mill on the Floss*.

76. Quoted and discussed in Erich Auerbach, *Mimesis: The Representation of Reality in Western Literature*, trans. Willard R. Trask (Princeton, NJ: Princeton University Press, 1953), 475.

77. Nochlin, *Realism*, 43.

78. A copy of this score, personally inscribed by Hubay to the French mezzo-soprano Pauline Viardot, is in the collection of the British Library.

79. István Nemeskürty, László Orosz, Béla G. Németh, and Attila Tamás, *A History of Hungarian Literature*, ed. Tibor Klaniczay, and trans. István Farkas, Enikő Körtvélyessy, Catherine Lőwy, et al. (Budapest: Corvina, 1982), 213.

80. Ibid., 214.

81. S. A. Mansbach, *Two Centuries of Hungarian Painters 1820–1970: A Catalogue of the Nicolas M. Salgó Collection* (Washington, DC: American University Press, 1991), 11.

82. Jenő Hubay, "Petőfi befolyása a magyar zenére," *Petőfi Múzeum* pamphlet (1888): 155–62.

83. Ibid., 160. "A dalzene legprimitivebb foka pedig a népdal."

84. Ibid., 159. "Az egyszerűség, közetlenség [recte: közvetlenség], erősen kifejlett rhythmika s a forma rövidsége."

85. Béla Bartók, "What Is Folk Music?," in *Béla Bartók Essays*, 6.

86. See Gerald Needham, *19th-Century Realist Art* (New York: Harper and Row, 1988), ch. 2. On panoramas and dioramas, see Jonathan Crary, *Suspensions of Perception: Attention, Spectacle, and Modern Culture* (Cambridge, MA: MIT Press, 2001), 134–8.

87. Quoted in Needham, *19th-Century Realist Art*, 19 and 10.

88. Quoted in Miles Orvell, *The Real Thing: Imitation and Authenticity in American Culture, 1880–1940* (Chapel Hill: University of North Carolina Press, 1989), 74.

89. Gerry Farrell, *Indian Music and the West* (Oxford: Oxford University Press, 1997), 32 and 79–80. For more on Bird's and Biggs's publications, see Nicholas Cook, "Encountering the Other, Redefining the Self: Hindostannie Airs, Haydn's Folksong Settings and the 'Common Practice' Style," in *Music and Orientalism in the British Empire, 1780s–1940s*, ed. Martin Clayton and Bennett Zon (Aldershot, UK: Ashgate, 2007).

90. Bohlman, *Music of European Nationalism*, 183; and Ludwig Achim von Arnim and Clemens Brentano, *Des Knaben Wunderhorn* (Munich: Winkler, 1947).

91. Republished in Lisa Feurzeig, ed., *Deutsche Lieder für Jung und Alt* (Middleton, WI: A-R Editions, 2002).

92. Thomas Bewick, *History of British Birds*, Vol. 1, *Containing the History and Description of Land Birds* (Newcastle, 1797), 7; and ibid., 20.

93. Bartók, *Hungarian Folksong*, 4.

94. Béla Bartók, *Rumanian Folk Music*, Vol. 1, *Instrumental Melodies*, ed. Benjamin Suchoff (The Hague: Martinus Nijhoff, 1967), 2 and 4.

95. Orvell, *The Real Thing*, xv.

96. See Roland Gelatt, *The Fabulous Phonograph 1877–1977* (New York: Macmillan, 1977); and George Brock-Nannestad, "The Development of Recording Technologies," in *The Cambridge Companion to Recorded Music*, ed. Nicholas Cook, Eric Clarke, Daniel Leech-Wilkinson, and John Rink (Cambridge: Cambridge University Press, 2009), 149–76.

97. Thomas A. Edison, "The Perfected Phonograph," *North American Review* 146, no. 379 (June 1888): 648–9.

98. Quoted in Susan Sontag, *On Photography* (New York: Dell, 1977), 188.

99. Mark Katz, *Capturing Sound: How Technology Has Changed Music* (Berkeley: University of California Press, 2004), 1.

100. Brady, *Spiral Way*, 34–7. The tendency of advertisers to focus on the realism of recording technology continued throughout the twentieth century and into the twenty-first. In the second half of the twentieth century, for example, posters and television advertisements asked, "Is it real or is it Memorex?"

101. Emily Thompson, "Machines, Music, and the Quest for Fidelity: Marketing the Edison Phonograph in America, 1877–1925," *Musical Quarterly* 79, no. 1 (Spring 1995): 148.

102. Concert program, December 5, 1918, in Jascha Heifetz Collection, Music Division, Library of Congress, Box 218, Folder 2. Further examples of similar advertisements suggesting the fidelity of sound recording to real life appear in Jonathan Sterne, *The Audible Past: Cultural Origins of Sound Reproduction* (Durham, NC: Duke University Press, 2003), 215.

103. Edison, "Perfected Phonograph," 641. Ten years earlier, in Edison's first article about the phonograph, he predicted a rather different range of uses for his new machine. Because of the reduced quality of the sound the phonograph produced early in its development, Edison advertised its employment as a sort of early Dictaphone, useful in the writing of business documents, and as a tool to record and cherish the voice and last words of a dying family member. Regarding music, Edison mentioned only that his invention could be an aid in teaching or provide novel entertainment, as "A friend may in a morning-call sing us a song which shall delight an evening company, etc." Thomas A. Edison, "The Phonograph and Its Future," *North American Review* 126, no. 262 (May–June 1878): 533.

104. Edison, "Perfected Phonograph," 641.

105. Quoted in Thompson, "Machines, Music, and the Quest for Fidelity," 144.

106. Orthophonic Victrola advertisement, *Vanity Fair*, May 1928, 78.

107. Quoted in Pasler, "Race and Nation," 158.

108. Alexander Rehding, "Wax Cylinder Revolutions," *Musical Quarterly* 88, no. 1 (Spring 2005): 139–40.

109. Ibid., 144.

110. Quoted in Vera Lampert, "Nationalism, Exoticism, or Concessions to the Audience? Motivations behind Bartók's Folksong Settings," *Studia Musicologica* 47, nos. 3–4 (September 2006): 339.

111. Béla Bartók and Zoltán Kodály, *Hungarian Folksongs for Voice with Piano*, ed. Denijs Dille, trans. Nancy Bush and Ilona L. Lukács (Budapest: Editio Musica, 1970), 43. For further discussion of this aspect of Bartók and Kodály's project, see Chapter 6.

112. Bohlman, *Music of European Nationalism*, 64–5.

113. Ibid., 65. A more detailed account of the *Landschaftliche Volkslieder* appears in Philip V. Bohlman, "Landscape—Region—Nation—Reich: German Folk Song in the Nexus of National Identity," in *Music and German National Identity*, ed. Celia Applegate and Pamela Potter (Chicago: University of Chicago Press, 2002), 105–27.

114. The recitals of rural miniatures and arrangements of folk songs organized by these groups were anticipated by the concerts of folklore organizations in the nineteenth century such as the French Société des traditions populaires, formed in 1885, whose concerts juxtaposed settings of songs from the French provinces and throughout Europe. Jann Pasler, *Composing the Citizen*, 353–5.

Chapter 2

1. Leopold Auer, *Violin Playing as I Teach It* (New York: Frederick A. Stokes, 1921), 160–1.

2. Michelle Bigenho describes the production of authenticity in the contemporary performance of Bolivian music, a context that shows some points of similarity despite its different era, repertoire, and setting, in *Sounding Indigenous: Authenticity in Bolivian Music Performance* (New York: Palgrave McMillan, 2002), esp. 16–21.

3. Quoted in David E. Schneider, *Bartók, Hungary, and the Renewal of Tradition: Case Studies in the Intersection of Modernity and Nationality* (Berkeley: University of California Press, 2006), 214.

4. Jascha Nemtsov, "Neue jüdische Musik in Polen in den 1920er–30er," in *Jüdische Kunstmusik im 20. Jahrhundert*, ed. Jascha Nemtsov (Wiesbaden: Harrassowitz, 2006), 94.

5. Béla Bartók and Zoltán Kodály, *Hungarian Folksongs for Voice with Piano*, ed. Denijs Dille, trans. Nancy Bush and Ilona L. Lukács (Budapest: Editio Musica, 1970), 40.

6. Lynn Hooker, "Modernism on the Periphery: Béla Bartók and the New Hungarian Music Society of 1911–1912," *Musical Quarterly* 88, no. 2 (Summer 2005): 286.

7. Ibid., 287.

8. Noel Straus, "Ovation to Bartók at Szigeti Recital," *New York Times*, April 22, 1940, 18.

9. Leopold Auer, *Violin Master Works and Their Interpretation* (New York: Carl Fischer, 1925), 179–80.

10. Ibid., 156.

11. Matrix C-30931, with Isidor Achron on piano, September 24, 1924.

12. Matrix 98615, probably with Philip Goodman on piano, January 30, 1927.

13. On the importance of concert programs as historical documents that can reveal important details about cultural tastes and values and the relationships between concert organizers, performers, and audiences, see Jann Pasler, "Concert Programs and their Narratives as Emblems of Ideology," in *Writing through Music: Essays on Music, Culture, and Politics* (New York: Oxford University Press, 2008), ch. 12.

14. Notes by Henry Coates. Jascha Heifetz Collection, Music Division, Library of Congress, Box 218, Folder 8.

15. Notes by F. Gilbert Webb. Quoted here from the concert program for Heifetz's recital performance in Manchester's Free Trade Hall on November 21, 1925, 10. Jascha Heifetz Collection, Music Division, Library of Congress, Box 219, Folder 7.

16. Ibid., 8. Jascha Heifetz Collection, Music Division, Library of Congress, Box 219, Folder 7.

17. Hermann Hoexter, "Biographical Sketch of Jascha Heifetz," in the program of a recital at the Arena Auditorium of Michigan, December 17, 1919, pages 5–7. Jascha Heifetz Collection, Music Division, Library of Congress, Box 218, Folder 1.

18. Ibid., 7.

19. Ibid., 9.

20. *Yehudi Menuhin: The Violin of the Century*, dir. Bruno Monsaingeon (New York: EMI Classics, 1996), DVD.

21. *The Art of Violin*, dir. Bruno Monsaingeon (West Long Branch, NJ: Kultur, 2000), DVD.

22. Quotations from this document appear in Béla Bartók and Zoltán Kodály, *Hungarian Folksongs for Voice with Piano*, 44.

23. Naomi Cumming calls this musical persona the "sonic self," in her discussion of semiotics and musical performance: *The Sonic Self: Musical Subjectivity and Signification* (Bloomington: Indiana University Press, 2000).

24. Rupert Croft-Cooke, "Hungary—Its Gypsies and Their Music," *Gramophone*, November 1927, 223. The recording is identified as Parlo. E. 10248.

25. N.t., *Rimington's Review*, April 1935, 13. The recording is identified as HMV DB2413.

26. C.J., "Instrumental," *Gramophone*, December 1928, 45. Recording data: Col. Masterworks 2073-M, Matrix WA 3587, recorded in Petty France Studios, London, on July 1, 1927, with accompanist Kurt Ruhrseitz.

27. Maiko Kawabata, "Virtuosity, the Violin, the Devil . . . What *Really* Made Paganini 'Demonic'?," *Current Musicology* 83 (Spring 2007): 85–108.

28. "Gramophone Celebrities XIV—Jascha Heifetz," *Gramophone*, November 1925, 278. The claim that Heifetz's playing style was "cold" and "stoic" was not uncommon in critical reviews during his life; Nicholas Slonimsky called Heifetz the "celebrated child prodigy and violin virtuoso of the new school of 'cold tonal beauty.'" Nicholas Slonimsky, *Music since 1900*, 3rd ed. (New York: Coleman-Ross, 1949), 14.

29. "Gramophone Celebrities XIV," 278. Recording data: Matrix C-21268-3. In this recording, Heifetz is accompanied by an orchestra conducted by Josef Pasternak.

30. Szigeti's Jewish identity was also invoked at times as an explanation for his individual virtuosic and expressive performance style, particularly in the Jewish press. The Yiddish newspaper *Afrikaner Idishe Tsaytung* declared, in a 1938 essay titled "My Schmooze with Joseph Szigeti," that his first musical education came from his father, a "simple klezmer" (*pshuter klezmer*) who made a living playing at Jewish weddings; it was in performing wedding dances with his father's band, writes the author, that Szigeti became a wunderkind. "Mayn Shmues mit Yosef Szigeti," *Afrikaner Idishe Tsaytung*, May 13, 1938. In the Joseph Szigeti Collection, Howard Gotlieb Archival Research Center at Boston University, Box 8.

31. Quoted in Claude Kenneson, *Székely and Bartók: The Story of a Friendship* (Portland, OR: Amadeus, 1994), 92.

32. Quoted in ibid., 93.

33. Quoted in ibid., 93.

34. Quoted in ibid., 94.

35. Quoted in ibid., 94.

36. Quoted in ibid., 90.

37. Quoted in ibid., 90.

38. Ayke Agus, *Heifetz as I Knew Him* (Portland, OR: Amadeus, 2001), 56.

39. Jascha Heifetz Collection, Music Division, Library of Congress, Box 1, Folder 20 ("Hebrew Dance"); Folder 214 ("Hebrew Lullaby").

40. The manuscript of this edition with Heifetz's markings is in the Jascha Heifetz Collection, Music Division, Library of Congress, Box 1, Folder 214 ("Hebrew Lullaby").

41. Portamento was a common feature in performances of lullabies during the first half of the twentieth century; see Daniel Leech-Wilkinson, "Portamento and Musical Meaning," *Journal of Musicological Research* 25, nos. 3–4 (December 2006): 233–61.

42. Mark Katz, "Portamento and the Phonograph Effect," *Journal of Musicological Research* 25, nos. 3–4 (December 2006): 214. The history of portamento in nineteenth-century violin playing can be found in David Milsom, *Theory and Practice in Late Nineteenth-Century Violin Performance: An Examination of Style in Performance, 1850–1900* (Aldershot, UK: Ashgate, 2003).

43. A number of these ethnographic recordings have been made available on *Treasure of Jewish Culture in Ukraine* (Kiev: Institute for Information Recording, Vernadsky National Library of Ukraine, 1997), compact disc.

44. Jascha Heifetz Collection, Music Division, Library of Congress, Box 15, Folder 3.

45. Jascha Heifetz Collection, Music Division, Library of Congress, Box 206.

46. I am grateful to Andy Byford for assisting me with the translation from the Russian.

47. The letter of agreement from Dinicu to Heifetz, signed on May 24, 1930, survives in the Jascha Heifetz Collection, Music Division, Library of Congress, Box 5, Folder 7. In 1930, 16,000 lei was equivalent to approximately $100. Dinicu made a recording of his version of "Hora Staccato" around 1930 with the Orchestra Grigoraş Dinicu (Matrix number WA 7335).

48. Jascha Heifetz Collection, Music Division, Library of Congress, Box 5, Folder 8.

49. For discussion of the *esztam* accompaniment pattern, see Schneider, *Bartók, Hungary, and the Renewal of Tradition*, 21–4; Bálint Sárosi, *Cigányzene . . .* (Budapest: Gondolat, 1971), 200–1; and István Pávai, *Az erdélyi és a moldvai magyarság népi tánczenéje* (Budapest: Teleki László Alapítvány, 1993), 87–97.

50. Jascha Heifetz Collection, Music Division, Library of Congress, Box 6, Folder 2.

51. Jascha Heifetz Collection, Music Division, Library of Congress, Box 7, Folder 2. This arrangement was recorded by other trumpeters, including Rafael Méndez.

52. Jascha Heifetz Collection, Music Division, Library of Congress, Box 7, Folder 4.

53. Jascha Heifetz Collection, Music Division, Library of Congress, Box 7, Folder 6. See Agus, *Heifetz as I Knew Him*, 193.

54. Jascha Heifetz Collection, Music Division, Library of Congress, Box 7, Folder 6.

55. Leonard Lyons, "'Jim Hoyl really Jascha Heifetz, Composer of New Bing Crosby Tune," *Miami Daily News*, October 16, 1946, 17-A.

56. "Not According to Hoyl," *Time*, October 21, 1946, 85.

57. "Hora Swing-cato." Lyrics by Marjorie Goetschius, arr. Jim Hoyl. Adapted from "Hora Staccato" by Grigoraş Dinicu and Jascha Heifetz. Copyright © 1945 Carl Fischer, Inc. All rights assigned to Carl Fischer, LLC. International copyrights secured. All rights reserved. Used with permission.

58. For other studies of the ways displaced Eastern European Jewish musicians adapted their techniques to incorporate elements of American popular music as they forged careers in the United States, see, for example, Jeffrey Shandler's essay on changes in cantorial tradition in the early twentieth century, in *Jews, God, and Videotape* (New York: New York University Press, 2009), ch. 1; and Joel E. Rubin's study of klezmer music in the United States during this period, "'They Danced It, We Played It': Adaptation and Revitalization in Post-1920s New York Klezmer Music," in *Studies in Jewish Civilization*, Vol. 19, *"I Will Sing and Make Music": Jewish Music and Musicians throughout the Ages*, ed. Leonard J. Greenspoon, Ronald A. Simkins, and Jean Cahan (Omaha, NE: Creighton University Press, 2008), 181–213.

Chapter 3

1. Jonathan Bellman, *The Style Hongrois in the Music of Western Europe* (Boston: Northeastern University Press, 1993), 65.

2. Bálint Sárosi, "Everyday Hungarian Music in Pest-Buda around 1870," *Studia Musicologica* 40, no. 4 (1999): 339.

3. Nicholas Saul, *Gypsies and Orientalism in German Literature and Anthropology of the Long Nineteenth Century* (London: Legenda, 2007), 2.

4. Ibid., 3.

5. Ibid., 6.

6. Heinrich Moritz Gottlieb Grellmann, *Dissertation on the Gipsies, Being an Historical Enquiry, Concerning the Manner of Life, Œconomy, Customs and Conditions of These People in Europe, and Their Origin*, trans. Matthew Raper (London, 1787), 37.

7. Ibid., 37–8.

8. Ibid., 64–5.

9. Ibid., 166.

10. Saul, *Gypsies and Orientalism*, 7. The tradition of Rom characters in English literature is addressed in David Mayall, *Gypsy Identities, 1500–2000: From Egipcyans and Moon-Men to the Ethnic Romany* (London: Routledge, 2004).

11. Saul, *Gypsies and Orientalism*, 34.

12. Lou Charnon-Deutsch, *The Spanish Gypsy: The History of a European Obsession* (University Park: Pennsylvania State University Press, 2004), 18–19.

13. Louis de Loménie, *Beaumarchais and His Times: Sketches of French Society in the Eighteenth Century from Unpublished Documents*, trans. Henry S. Edwards (London: Addey, 1856), 1:306.

14. Jean-Marie-Jérôme Fleuriot, *Voyage de Figaro en Espagne* (Saint-Malo, 1784), 177. For further discussion, see Charnon-Deutsch, *Spanish Gypsy*, 50.

15. Charnon-Deutsch, *Spanish Gypsy*, 55.

16. Ibid., 64.

17. Kerry Murphy, "*Carmen: Couleur Locale* or the Real Thing?," in *Music, Theater, and Cultural Transfer: Paris, 1830–1914*, ed. Annegret Fauser and Mark Everist (Chicago: University of Chicago Press, 2009), 295.

18. Saul, *Gypsies and Orientalism*, 10.

19. Ibid., 11.

20. Franz Liszt, *The Gipsy in Music*, trans Edwin Evans (London: William Reeves, 1926), 3.

21. Ibid., 3.

22. Ibid., 4.

23. Ibid., 8.

24. Ibid., 8–9.

25. Ibid., 9.

26. Ibid., 10.

27. Ibid., 13.

28. Ibid., 17.

29. Ibid., 333–8.

30. Ibid., 227.

31. Ibid., 266.

32. Ibid., 270.

33. Ibid., 271.

34. Ibid., 297.

35. Ibid., 298.

36. Ibid., 300–301.

37. Ibid., 304–6.

38. Ibid., 306–9.

39. Eliot met Liszt and Sayn-Wittgenstein in 1854. Ruth A. Solie, *Music in Other Words: Victorian Conversations* (Berkeley: University of California Press, 2004), 161–2.

40. On Eliot's depiction of Mirah and Klesmer and the two musical movements they are associated with—the music of the canon and the "music of the future"—see Solie, *Music*, 161–2.

41. George Eliot, *Daniel Deronda* (Edinburgh, 1876), 3:300. For further discussion of this passage, see Shirley Frank Levenson, "The Use of Music in Daniel Deronda," *Nineteenth-Century Fiction* 24, no. 3 (December 1969): 320.

42. Eliot, *Daniel Deronda*, 4:251.

43. On Sarasate's biography, see Julio Altadill, *Memorias de Sarasate* (Pamplona: Imprenta de Aramendía y Onsalo, 1909).

44. Grange Woolley, "Pablo de Sarasate: His Historical Significance," *Music and Letters* 36, no. 3 (July 1955): 244.

45. A. Filare, prologue to Custodia Plantón, *Pablo Sarasate (1844–1908)* (Pamplona: Ediciones Universidad de Navarra, 2000), 13.

46. Carl Flesch, *The Memoirs of Carl Flesch*, ed. and trans. Hans Keller (London: Rockliff, 1957), 36.

47. Ibid., 36.

48. Quoted in ibid., 36. "C'est lui qui nous a appris à jouer juste."

49. Leopold Auer, *My Long Life in Music* (London: Duckworth, 1924), 175.

50. Leopold Auer, *Violin Playing as I Teach It* (New York: Frederick A. Stokes, 1921), 210.

51. Flesch, *Memoirs of Carl Flesch*, 41–2.

52. Auer, *Violin Playing as I Teach It*, 210.

53. Flesch, *Memoirs of Carl Flesch*, 41.

54. Leopold Auer, *Violin Master Works and Their Interpretation* (New York: Carl Fischer, 1925), 157. Emphasis in the original.

55. Ibid., 157–8.

56. "Je tacherais de me montrer en cette occasion un écossais pur sang—moins le costume—et de prouver que la musique nationale de votre pays est l'une des plus belles et poétiques qui existent au monde: vous-savez que j'en suis fanatique." Alexander Mackenzie, "Pablo Sarasate: Some Personal Recollections," *Musical Times*, November 1, 1908, 694.

57. Pablo de Sarasate, "Zigeunerweisen" (New York: Carl Fischer, 1895), 2.

58. László Vikárius, "Bartók and the Ideal of 'Sentimentalitäts-Mangel,'" *International Journal of Musicology* 9 (2000): 217–18.

59. György Kerényi, *Szentirmay Elemér és a magyar népzene* (Budapest: Akadémiai Kiadó, 1966), 416–17.

60. John Weissmann, review of *Szentirmay Elemér és a magyar népzene*, by György Kerényi, *Ethnomusicology* 12, no. 1 (January 1968): 159.

61. Kodály later wrote of his hypothesis that Bartók's frequent thematic use of the interval of the minor third was based on the lasting impression of Szentirmay's song, which Bartók had originally transcribed from a wax cylinder from Béla Vikár's fieldwork. László Vikárius argues that to the contrary, Bartók's interest in Szentirmay's song and its minor third motif is traceable instead to his prior fascination with Richard Strauss's *Salome* and the thematic appearance of the interval in that work. László Vikárius, "Bartók, Kodály and Salome—The Origins of a Bartókian 'Hallmark,'" *Hungarian Quarterly* 48, no. 187 (Autumn 2007): 126–7.

62. J. S. Dale and Francis Korbay, eds. and trans., *Hungarian Melodies*, vol. 1 (London: Pitt and Hatzfeld; and Boston: H.B. Stevens, 1891).

63. Susan Tebbutt, "Disproportional Representation: Romanies and European Art," in *The Role of the Romanies: Images and Counter-Images of the "Gypsies"/Romanies in European Cultures*, ed. Nicholas Saul and Susan Tebbutt (Liverpool: Liverpool University Press, 2005), 164.

64. Quoted in Charnon-Deutsch, *Spanish Gypsy*, 7.

65. Reproduced in Alexandre de la Cerda, *Pablo de Sarasate: le violiniste basque virtuose* (Anglet: Séguier, 2001), 76.

66. "Csak egy szép lány van a világon:/ Az én kedves rózsám, galambom."

67. Sarasate: Matrix number 4263/40; Heifetz: Matrix numbers C-23410-2 and C-23407-2.

68. As in the case of any musical analysis, but perhaps in particular with analyses of aural rather than written texts, the reader is likely to agree with some of my annotations, disagree with others, and hear further interpretive gestures that I have not marked in the examples. The question of transcription and the impossibility of producing a fully precise and objective representation of sound events has been the subject of discussion and debate throughout the history of the study of folk music. Although no man-made transcription of sound can be truly objective, transcription remains a useful scholarly tool in the study of sound recording, even in an age of electronic technologies for performance analysis, because listening is a subjective experience. Bruno Nettl writes that in ethnomusicology, transcription by ear continues to be important: "For better or worse, as we continue significantly to deal with music in its visual form, transcription remains one of the few diagnostic techniques of the ethnomusicologist." Bruno Nettl, *The Study of Ethnomusicology: Thirty-One Issues and Concepts* (Urbana: University of Illinois Press, 2005), 91.

69. The expressiveness of Sarasate's playing in his recording of "Zigeunerweisen" and his ghostly voice at this moment of the disc inspired the surrealistic Japanese movie *Zigeunerweisen* by Seijun Suzuki (1980). In the film's cyclical repetitions, mirrored in the replaying of the record of Sarasate's rendition of the piece at critical structural points

in the narrative, characters are repeatedly unable to discern the sources and meanings of the spectral voices of their deceased relatives. Although the film is too enigmatic to allow any definitive reading, its thematic incorporation of Sarasate's recording can be interpreted as a symbol, like the film's disembodied voices, of the hybridity that emerged from collisions between disparate national cultures and between tradition and modernity in pre–World War II Japan.

Chapter 4

1. Leigh Henry, "The New Direction in Spanish Music," *Musical Times*, August 1, 1919, 401.

2. Ibid., 401.

3. Ibid., 401.

4. Leigh Henry, "The New Direction in Spanish Music (Concluded)," *Musical Times*, September 1, 1919, 465.

5. Ibid., 466.

6. Suzanne Rhodes Draayer, *Art Song Composers of Spain: An Encyclopedia* (Plymouth, UK: Scarecrow Press, 2009), xxiv.

7. Julien Tiersot, *Musiques pittoresques: promenades musicales à l'Exposition de 1889* (Paris: Librairie Fischbacher, 1889), 71–6.

8. Also dedicated to Sarasate are Saint-Saëns's Violin Concertos nos. 2 and 3; Henryk Wieniawksi's Violin Concerto no. 2; Alexander Mackenzie's "*Pibroch*"; Ignacy Paderewski's Sonata for violin and piano; Lalo's *Norwegian Fantasy*; and Leopold Auer's *Hungarian Rhapsody* no. 5. See Custodia Plantón, *Pablo Sarasate (1844–1908)* (Pamplona: Ediciones Universidad de Navarra, 2000), 193.

9. Luis G. Iberni, *Pablo Sarasate* (Madrid: Instituto Complutense de Ciencias Musicales, 1994), 72.

10. Camille Saint-Saëns, *Au courant de la vie* (Paris: Dorbon-aîné, 1914), 37–8.

11. See, for instance, the letter from Camille Saint-Saëns to Pablo de Sarasate of September 17, 1864 (Bibliothèque Nationale VM BOB-23591/LA-Saint Saëns Camille-65), in which Saint-Saëns includes a transcription of the song "On dit, monsieur, que vous êtes" (the song was later included, with an alternate rhythmic pattern, in the 1926 anthology *Chansons populaires des pyrénées Françaises*, by Jean Poueigh); and the August 21, 1889, letter from Sarasate to Saint-Saëns (Bibliothèque Nationale RES VMD MS 11 [FOL 10]), in which Sarasate thanks Saint-Saëns for sending him a recent composition, a "Saraband," and praises it as "a jewel like all that comes from your spirit and from your hands" ("un bijou comme tout ce qui sort de ton esprit et de tes mains").

12. Iberni, *Pablo Sarasate*, 59.

13. Manuel de Falla, *On Music and Musicians*, trans. David Urman and J. M. Thomson (London: Marion Boyars, 1979), 31–2.

14. Ibid., 71.

15. Olin Downes, "Ernest Bloch, the Swiss Composer, on the Influence of Race in Composition," *Musical Observer* 15, no. 3 (1917): 11; quoted in Alexander Knapp, "The Life and Music of Ernest Bloch: Problems and Paradoxes," in *Jüdische Musik und ihre Musiker im 20. Jahrhundert*, ed. Wolfgang Birtel, Joseph Dorfman, and Christoph-Hellmut Mahling (Mainz: Are Musik, 2006), 296.

16. On Bloch's use of quotations of preexisting melodies, see Joshua S. Walden, "'An Essential Expression of the People': Interpretations of Hasidic Song in the Composition and Performance History of Ernest Bloch's *Baal Shem*," *Journal of the American Musicological Society* 65, no. 3 (Fall 2012), esp. 784.

17. See Michael Christoforidis's writings on the subject: "Manuel de Falla's *Siete canciones populares españolas*: The Composer's Personal Library, Folksong Models and the Creative Process," *Anuario Musical* 55 (2000): 213–35; "Folksong Models and Their Sources in Manuel de Falla's *Siete canciones populares españolas*," *Context* 9 (Winter 1995): 12–21; and "From Folksong to Plainchant: Musical Borrowings and the Transformation of Manuel de Falla's Musical Nationalism in the 1920s," in *Manuel de Falla: His Life and Music*, ed. Nancy Lee Harper (Lanham, MD: Scarecrow, 2005).

18. For a history and bibliography of Spanish folk music studies, see Josep Martí, "Folk Music Studies and Ethnomusicology in Spain," *Yearbook for Traditional Music* 29 (1997): 107–40.

19. Michael Christoforidis, "A Composer's Annotations to His Personal Library: An Introduction to the Manuel de Falla Collection," *Context* 17 (Winter 1999): 48–68; and "Manuel de Falla's Personal Library and Insights into the Composer's Annotations," in *Manuel de Falla: His Life and Music*, ed. Nancy Lee Harper (Lanham, MD: Scarecrow, 2005), 308–22.

20. Antonio Gallego, prologue to Manuel de Falla, *Cantares de Nochebuena* (Madrid: Manuel de Falla Ediciones, 1992), 5. Emphasis in the original.

21. Quoted in Walter Aaron Clark, *Isaac Albéniz: Portrait of a Romantic* (Oxford: Oxford University Press, 1999), 55. Emphasis in the original. On the operatic trilogy and Catalan and Spanish nationalism, see Samuel Llano, *Whose Spain? Negotiating Spanish Music in Paris, 1908–1929* (New York: Oxford University Press, 2012), 85–9.

22. Carol A. Hess, *Enrique Granados: A Bio-Bibliography* (Westport, CT: Greenwood, 1991), 22.

23. Walter Aaron Clark, *Enrique Granados: Poet of the Piano* (Oxford: Oxford University Press, 2006), 205, fn. 13.

24. Manuel de Falla, *On Music and Musicians*, trans. David Urman and J. M. Thomson (London: Marion Boyars, 1979), 31.

25. As professor at the Escuela de Estudios Superiores of the Madrid Ateneo, Pedrell delivered lectures between 1896 and 1903 on music history and aesthetics, Spanish popular song and its influence on Spanish composition and modern lyric drama, and Wagner. Francisco Bonastre Bertran, *Felipe Pedrell: Acotaciones a una idea* (Tarragona: Caja de Ahorros Provincial de Tarragona, 1977), 62.

26. Carol A. Hess, *Manuel de Falla and Modernism in Spain, 1898–1936* (Chicago: University of Chicago Press, 2001), 18. Federico Sopeña writes that the attribution of this line to Eximeno is inaccurate, in Falla, *On Music and Musicians*, 49.

27. Falla, *On Music and Musicians*, 54 and 55.

28. Ibid., 60.

29. Joshua Goode, *Impurity of Blood: Defining Race in Spain, 1870–1930* (Baton Rouge: Louisiana State University Press, 2009), 2.

30. Ibid., 13 and 15.

31. Jann Pasler, "Theorizing Race in Nineteenth-Century France: Music as Emblem of Identity," *Musical Quarterly* 89 (2006): 460–3. *La race* was also a term used in France in the sciences in the study of human groups linked by skin color (461).

32. Felipe Pedrell, *Por nuestra música* (Bellaterra: Publicacions de la Universitat Autònoma de Barcelona, 1991), 39. "El canto popular, esa *voz de los pueblos*, la genuina inspiración primitiva del gran cantor anónimo, pasa por el alambique del arte contemporáneo y resulta su quinta esencia: el compositor moderno se nutre con aquella quinta esencia, se la asimila. . . . El canto popular presta el acento, el fondo, y el arte moderno presta también lo que tiene, un simbolismo convencional, la riqueza de formas que son su patrimonio. Perfecta ecuación de un enunciado de encumbradas bellezas dimanada de la relación harmónica que existe entre la forma y su contenido." See discussion in Edgar Istel, "Felipe Pedrell," trans. Theodore Baker, *Musical Quarterly* 11, no. 2 (April 1925): 176.

33. Quoted in Martí, "Folk Music Studies and Ethnomusicology," 110.

34. Felipe Pedrell, "Les artisans du folklore musical espagnol," *La revue musicale*, October 1, 1921, 193–4. "La cellule génératrice de cette musique artificielle, c'est l'autre, la musique naturelle qui n'a exigé de l'individu, pour chanter, qu'une âme en état de grâce ou le stimulant de la passion."

35. Ibid., 193. "douleurs, peines, souffrances, joies, avec une émotion plus ou moins véhémente et d'une manière vague ou précise . . ."

36. Ibid., 194. "le souvenir des âmes et des sentiments qui se sont fondus à travers les âges en d'autres sentiments et en d'autres âmes, transmettant de siècle à siècle le verbe pur de l'émotion d'un individu qui fut et qui créa la musique que d'autres sentirent comme lui."

37. Martí, "Folk Music Studies and Ethnomusicology," 109.

38. Eduardo Ocón, *Cantos Españoles: Colección de aires nacionales y populares* (Málaga: Eigenthum des Herausgebers, 1888), v. "Exactitud y verdad"; "siempre raras y por estremo originales."

39. Hurtado's statements appear in his one-page letter to the Presidente de la Diputación Provincial de Oviedo that introduces the volume. This is dated September 28, 1889, and appears in the reprinted addition, José Hurtado, *100 cantos populares asturianos* (Madrid: Union Musical Española, 1956).

40. Ibid. "La *música Popular*, fuente de bellezas naturales, emanación divina y manifestación expontanea por medio del sonido, del carácter costumbres é inclinaciones de los naturales de una región, presta ancho campo al artista para sus estudios, y es manantial inagotable de inspiración."

41. José Inzenga, *Cantos y bailes de España* (Madrid: A. Romero A., 1888), vii.

42. Ibid., vii. "Con la canción . . . adormece la madre el fruto de su amor en la cuna, el labrador alivia sus penosas tareas del campo, el preso sostiene su abatido espíritu, el marino distrae sus melancolías."

43. Ibid., vii. "El más espontáneo y puro lenguaje del sentimiento representado por la *melodía*, que es el alma, el *sine qua non* del arte de la música."

44. Ibid., xii. "Conservar para siempre, por medio de la notación musica, estas secillas y espontáneas manifestaciones de sentimiento y regocijo de nuestro pueblo."

45. Falla, *On Music and Musicians*, 116.

46. Miguel Manzano Alonso, "Precisiones sobre la Jota en Aragón," *Nassarre: Revista Aragonesa de Musicología* 9, no. 2 (1993): 282–3.

47. Julián Ribera y Tarragó, *La música de la jota aragonesa* (Madrid: Instituto de Valencia de Don Juan, 1928), 6–8.

48. Inzenga, *Cantos y bailes de España*, 8–9.

49. Ibid., 9.

50. Ribera, *La música de la jota aragonesa*, 5. "Tales afirmaciones pueden pasar por hipótesis imaginarias."

51. Carol A. Hess, *Sacred Passions: The Life and Music of Manuel de Falla* (Oxford: Oxford University Press, 2005), 19. See also Leopold Cardona de Bergerac, "The Andalusian Music Idiom," *Music Review* 33, no. 3 (August 1972): 157–66.

52. Hess, *Manuel de Falla and Modernism*, 3.

53. William Washabaugh, *Flamenco: Passion, Politics and Popular Culture* (Oxford: Berg, 1996), 1–2.

54. Timothy Mitchell, *Flamenco Deep Song* (New Haven, CT: Yale University Press, 1994), 67. Mitchell addresses the possible Jewish influence on the development of Andalusian flamenco on page 53.

55. Washabaugh, *Flamenco: Passion*, 10.

56. Ibid., 15.

57. Lou Charnon-Deutsch, *The Spanish Gypsy: The History of a European Obsession* (University Park: Pennsylvania State University Press, 2004), 203.

58. Antonio Machado y Alvarez (Demófilo, pseudo.), *Colección de cantes flamencos, recogidos y anotados por Demófilo* (Madrid: Ediciones Demófilo, 1975). See discussion in William Washabaugh, *Flamenco Music and National Identity in Spain* (Farnham, UK: Ashgate, 2012), 55–6.

59. Washabaugh, *Flamenco Music and National Identity*, 58–60.

60. Ibid., 62–8.

61. Hess, *Manuel de Falla and Modernism*, 55-6.

62. Falla, *On Music and Musicians*, 102.

63. Ibid., 103.

64. Hess, *Sacred Passions*, 128.

65. These recordings are reissued on *I Concurso de cante jondo: Colección Manuel de Falla: Granada, Corpus de 1922. Colección Federico García Lorca: Discografía flamenca utilizada por el poeta* (Madrid: Sonifolk, 1997), compact disc.

66. Washabaugh, *Flamenco: Passion*, 33 and 119.

67. Ibid., 45.

68. Quoted in Christopher Maurer, "'Dramatic Black Moon': Lorca, Deep Song and the Gramophone," CD liner notes, *I Concurso de cante jondo*.

69. Falla, *On Music and Musicians*, 105.

70. Ibid., 105.

71. Christoforidis, "Composer's Annotations, 40–1.

72. Ibid., 39 and 64.

73. F. M. Pabanó, *Historia y costumbres de los gitanos: colección de cuentos viejos y nuevos, dichos y timos graciosos, maldiciones y refranes netamente gitanos: diccionario español-gitano-germanesco, dialecto de los gitanos* (Barcelona: Montaner y Simón, 1915), 75. "Tiernos y sentimentales"; "cada vibración es un beso apasionado, una lágrima, un suspiro."

74. Ibid., 76. "Recuerda la melancolía poética de los pueblos árabes, absorbiendo a los que le escuchan en inexplicable éxtasis."

75. Ibid., 77.

76. Ibid., 78. "Los bailes gitanos no son muy originales ni variados, pero expresan el fuego y la alegría de la vida, provocan eróticas osadías e insolencias ardientes."

77. Mitchell, *Flamenco Deep Song*, 43.

78. Falla, *On Music and Musicians*, 103–4. Federico García Lorca delivered a lecture in 1922 that similarly described *cante jondo* as a natural phenomenon, "close to the trill of the bird, the crowing of the rooster, and the most natural music of forest and fountain . . . a most rare example of primitive song . . . that carries in its notes the naked and spine-chilling emotion of the first oriental races." Quoted in Mitchell, *Flamenco Deep Song*, 167.

79. Chris Collins, "Manuel de Falla, *L'acoustique nouvelle* and Natural Resonance: A Myth Exposed," *Journal of the Royal Musical Association* 128, no. 1 (2003): 75.

80. Ibid., 71.

81. Ibid., 84–6.

82. Manuel de Falla, "Claude Debussy et l'Espagne," translated in Falla, *On Music and Musicians*, 109.

83. Ibid., 108. Samuel Llano shows that Falla elsewhere displayed ambivalence about the ability of composers who were not Spanish to write "Spanish" music: in the same year as "Claude Debussy et l'Espagne" was published, Falla wrote a letter to the editor of *The Chesterian* that appears to imply that only Spanish composers could compose accurately in the style. *Whose Spain?*, 154–6.

84. Clark, *Enrique Granados*, 30.

85. Ibid., 31.

86. Walter Aaron Clark points out that the rhythmic characteristics of this movement resemble the Cuban habanera more closely than the Argentinian tango. *Isaac Albéniz*, 97.

87. Hess, *Sacred Passions*, 42.

88. On the varied history of arrangements and adaptations of "Ritual Fire Dance," see ibid., 293–8.

89. Linton E. Powell, *A History of Spanish Piano Music* (Bloomington: Indiana University Press, 1980), 147.

90. Hess, *Manuel de Falla and Modernism*, 32. On the founding and membership of *les Apaches*, see Jann Pasler, "A Sociology of the Apaches: 'Sacred Battalion' for *Pelléas*," in *Berlioz and Debussy: Sources, Contexts and Legacies: Essays in Honour of François Lesure*, ed. Babara L. Kelly and Kerry Murphy (Aldershot, UK: Ashgate, 2007), esp. 153–6.

91. Quoted in Hess, *Manuel de Falla and Modernism*, 31.

92. Annegret Fauser, *Musical Encounters at the 1889 Paris World's Fair* (Rochester, NY: University of Rochester Press, 2005), 261–8; and Michael Christoforidis, "Manuel de Falla, Flamenco and Spanish Identity," in *Western Music and Race*, ed. Julie Brown (Cambridge: Cambridge University Press, 2007), 231–2.

93. Jann Pasler, "The *Chanson Populaire* as a Malleable Symbol in Turn-of-the-Century France," in *Tradition and Its Future in Music: Report of SIMS 1990 Ōsaka*, ed. Yosihiko Tokumaru, Makoto Ohmiya, Masakata Kanazawa, et al. (Tokyo: Mita Press, 1991), 203.

94. Ibid., 206.

95. Christoforidis, "Manuel de Falla's *Siete canciones populares españolas*," 217.

96. Ronald Crichton, *Falla* (London: British Broadcasting Company, 1982), 28.

97. Jaime Pahissa, *Manuel de Falla: His Life and Works*, trans. Jean Wagstaff (London: Museum Press, 1954), 76–7.

98. Nancy Lee Harper, *Manuel de Falla: His Life and Music* (Lanham, MD: Scarecrow, 2005), 60.

99. Christoforidis, "Manuel de Falla, Flamenco and Spanish Identity," 230.

100. Christoforidis, "Manuel de Falla's *Siete canciones populares españolas*," 219, 224, and 225.

101. Ibid., 225.

102. Alonso, "Precisiones sobre la Jota en Aragón," 283–4.

103. Miguel Manzano Alonso, *La jota como género musical: un estudio musicológico acerca del género más difundido en el repertorio tradicional español de la música popular* (Madrid: Editorial Alpuerto, 1995), 47 and 83.

104. Christoforidis, "Manuel de Falla's *Siete canciones populares españolas*," 223.

105. Hess, *Sacred Passions*, 65.

106. The typical form of the *jota* is described in Elizabeth J. Miles and Loren Chuse, "Spain," in *The Garland Encyclopedia of World Music*, vol. 8, *Europe*, ed. Timothy Rice, James Porter, and Chris Goertzen (New York: Garland, 2000), 594–5.

107. Hess, *Sacred Passions*, 66.

Chapter 5

1. Leonid Sabaneev, "The Jewish National School," trans. S.W. Pring, *Musical Quarterly* 15, no. 3 (July 1929): 448–68.

2. A thorough discussion of Idelsohn's work appears in Eliyahu Schleifer, "Idelsohn's Scholarly and Literary Publications: An Annotated Bibliography," in *Yuval*, Vol. 5,

The Abraham Zvi Idelsohn Memorial Volume, ed. Israel Adler, Bathja Bayer, and Eliyahu Schleifer (Jerusalem: Magnes, 1986), 53–180. The *Thesaurus* was published as *Hebräisch-orientalischer Melodienschatz*, 10 vols. (Leipzig: Breitkopf and Härtel, 1914; Jerusalem, Berlin, and Vienna: Benjamin Harz, 1922–9; and Leipzig: Friedrich Hofmeister, 1932).

3. James Loeffler, "Do Zionists Read Music from Right to Left? Abraham Tsvi Idelsohn and the Invention of Israeli Music," *Jewish Quarterly Review* 100, no. 3 (Summer 2010): 389. On Idelsohn's role in the development of Hebrew song, see also Shai Burstyn, "Inventing Musical Tradition: The Case of the Hebrew (Folk) Song," *Orbis Musicae* 13 (2003): 127–36, esp. 133.

4. Loeffler, "Do Zionists Read Music from Right to Left," 410.

5. On Idelsohn's work in America, see Judah M. Cohen, "Rewriting the Grand Narrative of Jewish Music in the United States," *Jewish Quarterly Review* 100, no. 3 (Summer 2010): 417–53.

6. Ibid., 37–45.

7. Abraham Zvi Idelsohn, *Jewish Music in Its Historical Development* (New York: Tudor, 1944). The following quotations are from page 466.

8. Engel's work was originally published in Moscow in 1916, and by 1923 it appeared in its third edition, with texts and unaccompanied melodies, produced in Berlin by Juwal ferlag-gezelshaft far yudishe muzik, a publishing house run by Engel himself. The sheet music opens with a preface identifying the anthologies from which Engel borrowed the songs he included in the work.

9. Idelsohn, *Jewish Music*, 468.

10. Ibid., 24.

11. Martin Buber, "Address on Jewish Art," in *The First Buber: Youthful Zionist Writings of Martin Buber*, ed. and trans. Gilya G. Schmidt (Syracuse, NY: Syracuse University Press, 1999), 53.

12. Ibid., 60.

13. Judit Frigyesi defines *nusach* as "the traditional way (of singing) according to the given liturgical function and local custom," in "Preliminary Thoughts toward the Study of Music without Clear Beat: The Example of 'Flowing Rhythm' in Jewish 'Nusah,'" *Asian Music* 24, no. 2 (Spring–Summer 1993): 69.

14. On the genres represented in Kiselgof's *Lider-zamelbukh far der yidisher shul un familie* (Collection of Songs for the Jewish School and Family), see Klára Móricz, *Jewish Identities: Nationalism, Racism, and Utopianism in Twentieth-Century Music* (Berkeley: University of California Press, 2008), 23.

15. Eugene M. Avrutin, "Racial Categories and the Politics of (Jewish) Difference in Late Imperial Russia," *Kritika* 8, no. 1 (Winter 2007): 15 and 21.

16. Quoted in ibid., 29.

17. Ibid., 15.

18. Ibid., 32.

19. Quoted in ibid., 30.

20. Ibid., 27 and 38.

21. Ibid., 38.

22. Anthony D. Smith, *Nationalism: Theory, Ideology, History (Key Concepts)* (Cambridge: Polity Press, 2001), 9. Jewish political movements at this time included, among others, Zionist, socialist Bundist, and diaspora nationalist groups. Whereas Zionists sought to create a Jewish homeland where dispersed people could congregate to live in a relatively homogeneous Jewish state, diaspora nationalists aimed to establish ideological connections between Jews throughout Europe, without assimilating or founding a Jewish homeland. The General Jewish Workers' Bund of Russia, Lithuania, and Poland, formed in 1897, was a socialist organization that rejected Zionism and favored the tenets of diaspora nationalism. For discussions of these and other Jewish nationalist groups, see David E. Fishman, *The Rise of Modern Yiddish Culture* (Pittsburgh: University of Pittsburgh Press, 2005).

23. On the concept of diaspora, see James Clifford, "Further Inflections: Toward Ethnographies of the Future," *Cultural Anthropology* 9, no. 3 (August 1994): 307–8.

24. The history of Jewish participation in and reaction to the Revolution can be found in Jonathan Frankel, *Prophecy and Politics: Socialism, Nationalism, and the Russian Jews, 1862–1917* (Cambridge: Cambridge University Press, 1981).

25. Jascha Nemtsov, *Die Neue Jüdische Schule in der Musik* (Wiesbaden: Harrassowitz, 2004), 35–6.

26. Gustaf Herman Dalman, *Jüdischdeutsche Volkslieder aus Galizien und Russland* (Leipzig: Centralbureau der Instituta Judaica [W. Faber], 1888). For discussion, see Philip V. Bohlman and Otto Holzapfel, eds., *The Folk Songs of Ashkenaz* (Middleton, WI: A-R Editions, 2001), viii.

27. Lyudmila Sholokhova, "Jewish Musical Ethnography in Russian Empire: Ideology and Chronology," in *Jüdische Kunstmusik im 20. Jahrhundert: Quellenlage, Entstehungsgeschichte, Stilanalysen*, ed. Jascha Nemtsov (Wiesbaden: Harrassowitz, 2006), 221.

28. Quoted in Nemtsov, *Die Neue Jüdische Schule*, 36. "Schaffen wir es, unsere Kultur lebendig zu machen, werden wir leben, schaffen wir es nicht, werden wir uns quälen bis zum Tode. Einen fremden Kopf und ein fremdes Herz wird uns kein Chirurg annähen können. . . . Ich habe jetzt den Plan . . ., dass die Jüd[ische] ethn[ographische] Ges[ellschaft] mich schickt, . . . jüdische Volklieder, Sprichwörter, Märchen, Sprüche, kurzum die Volkskunst zu sammeln. Wenn es klappt, würde ich mich gern den Rest meines Lebens damit beschäftigen."

29. Sholokhova, "Jewish Musical Ethnography," 222. See also Izaly Zemtsovsky, "The Musical Strands of An-sky's Texts and Contexts," in *The Worlds of S. An-sky: A Russian Jewish Intellectual at the Turn of the Century*, ed. Gabriella Safran and Steven J. Zipperstein (Stanford, CA: Stanford University Press, 2006), 207.

30. Yohanan Petrovsky-Shtern, "'We Are Too Late': An-sky and the Paradigm of No Return," in *The Worlds of S. An-sky: A Russian Jewish Intellectual at the Turn of the Century*, ed. Gabriella Safran and Steven J. Zipperstein (Stanford, CA: Stanford University Press, 2006), 97.

31. Zemtsovsky, "Musical Strands," 207–8. Some of the material gathered during this fieldwork was notated and published in the 1930s by Moshe Beregovski. See his work in, *Old Jewish Folk Music: The Collections and Writings of Moshe Beregovski*, ed. and trans. Mark Slobin (Syracuse, NY: Syracuse University Press, 2000).

32. Quoted in Itzik Nakhmen Gottesman, *Defining the Yiddish Nation: The Jewish Folklorists of Poland* (Detroit: Wayne State University Press, 2003), opening epigraph.

33. Saul M. Ginzburg, and Pesach S. Marek, *Yiddish Folksongs in Russia: Photo Reproduction of the 1901 St. Petersburg Edition*, ed. Dov Noy, trans. Lila Holzman (Ramat Gan: Bar-Ilan University Press, 1991), 25. The original text is in Russian, translated in this edition into Yiddish. ". . . di psikhik fun a folk . . . di meynungen, derinerungen, hofenungen fun dem oder yenem folk, di togteglekhe baderfenishn un di batsiung tsu di arumike dersheynungen."

34. Yehuda Leyb Cahan, *Studies in Yiddish Folklore*, ed. Max Weinreich (New York: YIVO, 1952), 11. "An ekht folkslid . . . iz funem folk gufe geshafn gevorn, un deriber drikt es oykh oys in a natirlekher, nisht-gekinstler forem zayn algemeynem kharakter un shpiglt op di farborgnste vinkelekh fun der kolektiver folks-neshome. An ekht folks-lid ken nisht geleyent, retsitirt oder deklamirt vern; es muz nor gezungen vern, vayl es iz tsuzamengevaksn mit der melodie vi guf un neshome, vos kenen eyns on dos andere nisht eksistirn."

35. Susman Kiselgof, *Lider-zamelbukh far der yidisher shul un familie* (St. Petersburg: Society for Jewish Folk Music; and Berlin: Leo Wintz, 1912). "Dos alts flantst ayn in kinds hartsn a libe tsum folk."

36. Evgeny Khazdan, "Jewish Music in St. Petersburg: A Survey," in *Jüdische Musik und ihre Musiker im 20. Jahrhundert*, ed. Wolfgang Birtel, Joseph Dorfman, and Christoph-Hellmut Mahling (Mainz: Are Edition, 2006), 169.

37. Nemtsov, *Die Neue Jüdische Schule*, 47. On the founding of the Society for Jewish Folk Music, see Móricz, *Jewish Identities*, ch. 1; and James Loeffler, *The Most Musical Nation: Jews and Culture in the Late Russian Empire* (New Haven, CT: Yale University Press, 2010). Analytical studies of compositions by Society members appear in Beate Schröder-Nauenburg, *Der Eintritt des Jüdischen in die Welt der Kunstmusik: Die Anfänge der Neuen Jüdischen Schule: werkanalytische Studien* (Wiesbaden: Harrassowitz, 2007). See also Joshua Walden, "Music of the 'Folks-neshome': 'Hebrew Melody' and Changing Musical Representations of Jewish Culture in the Early Twentieth Century Ashkenazi Diaspora," *Journal of Modern Jewish Studies* 8, no. 2 (July 2009): 151–71.

38. Nemtsov, *Die Neue Jüdische Schule*, 46. Engel's career and influence as an ethnographer and composer are addressed in detail in Loeffler, *Most Musical Nation*.

39. Lazare Saminsky, *Music of the Ghetto and the Bible* (New York: Bloch, 1934), 4.

40. Zemtsovsky, "Musical Strands," 210.

41. Ibid., 210.

42. Joseph Achron, "Notits vegn yidisher muzik," *Bodn* 1, no. 1 (April–June 1934): 55–60.

43. Jewish Music Societies Collection, RG 37, Box 1/Folder 2/128–9, Collection of YIVO, at the Center for Jewish History. "Fun fervaltung fun der gezelshaft

far yudishe folks-muzik. In der tsayt, ven baym yudishen folk dervekt zikh der nat-
sionaler bevustzayn, velkher drikt zikh oys in dem groysen interes tsu alts, vos vert
oyfgeton oyf dem gebit fun der yudisher kultur, ken, fershteyt zikh, nit blayben
on oyfmerkzamkayt di yudishe kunst, un in der ershter reye di yudishe muzik. Di
yudishe folks-lid, velkhe shpigelt in zikh sharf ob di shtimungen un iberlebungen,
di leyden un freyden funem yudishen folk, muz erlernt veren oyfn ergsten oyfn. Di
gezelshaft far yudishe folks-muzik, velkhe shtelt zikh az tsil mitvirken der entviklung
fun der yudisher folks-muzik, hot fun onhoib ir tetigkayt fernumen zikh mit zamlen
folks motiven un kinstlerish bearbayten zey. Yetst hot di gezelshaft aroysgegeben di
ershte serie yudishe folks-lider. Zayendik ibertsaygt, az zi befridigt a noytige lebens-
bederfnish, hot di gezelshaft zikh nit obgeshtelt far keyne shverigkayten un shter-
ungen. Di fervaltung fun gezelshaft far yudishe folks-muzik ruft tsu alemen, vemen
s'zenen tayer di interesen fun yudentum mit ale meglikhkayten mitsuvirken—fersh-
preyten di lider, velkhe di gezelshaft hot aroysgegeben. Oyf di yudishe muzikalishe
ovenden, in der yudisher shul, familie—umedum darf zikh heren di yudishe folks-
lid un farnemen ir pasenden ort. Der erfolg fun der vayterdiger tetigkayt fun der
gezelshaft in derzelber rikhtung, vend zikh yetst nur on dem obklang, velkhen s'vet
gefinen der ershter ferzukh."

44. Alexander Eliasberg, *Ostjüdische Volkslieder: Ausgewählt, übertragen und mit Anmerkungen versehen* (Munich: Georg Müller, 1918).

45. Zemtsovsky, "Musical Strands," 219.

46. Ibid., 220.

47. Ibid., 222.

48. Ibid., 225. This page of the script is reproduced on 227. Idelsohn and Beregovski
would also include transcriptions of the song in their collections.

49. Eliott Kahn, "The Solomon Rosowsky Collection and the Solomon Rosowsky
Addendum at the Library of the Jewish Theological Seminary," in *Jüdische Kunstmusik im
20. Jahrhundert*, ed. Jascha Nemtsov (Wiesbaden: Harrassowitz, 2006), 51.

50. Ibid., 52.

51. A detailed history of Juwal and Jibneh appears in Nemtsov, *Die Neue Jüdische
Schule*, ch. 5.

52. Irene Heskes, "Shapers of American Jewish Music: *Mailamm* and the Jewish
Music Forum, 1931–62," *American Music* 15, no. 3 (Autumn 1997): 305–7. See also Verena
Bopp, *MAILAMM 1932–1941: Die Geschichte einer Vereinigung zur Förderung jüdischer
Musik in den USA* (Wiesbaden: Harrassowitz, 2007).

53. Heskes, "Shapers of American Jewish Music," 307. See also Philip V. Bohlman,
*The World Centre for Jewish Music in Palestine, 1936–1940: Jewish Musical Life on the Eve of
World War II* (Oxford: Clarendon, 1992).

54. Idelsohn, *Jewish Music*, 24.

55. Susman Kiselgof, *Das jüdische Volkslied* (Berlin: Jüdischer Verlag, 1913), 9.

56. Lazare Saminsky, *Music of the Ghetto and the Bible* (New York: Bloch, 1934), 5.
Saminsky refers to Psalm 137: "By the rivers of Babylon, there we sat down, yea, we

wept, when we remembered Zion. We hanged our harps upon the willows in the midst thereof. For there they that carried us away captive required of us a song; and they that wasted us required of us mirth, saying, Sing us one of the songs of Zion. How shall we sing the Lord's song in a strange land?" (King James.)

57. Quoted in Maiko Kawabata, "Violinists 'Singing': Paganini, Operatic Voices, and Virtuosity," *Ad Parnassum* 5, no. 9 (April 2007): 11.

58. Quoted in ibid., 21 and 24. The metaphor of the voice in nineteenth-century descriptions of instrumental playing was not limited to discussions of violin technique: Sigismond Thalberg's piano playing was often characterized as resembling the singing voice—so much so that he would call his treatise on piano playing *L'art du chant appliqué au piano*. See Dana Gooley, *The Virtuoso Liszt* (Cambridge: Cambridge University Press, 2004), 25.

59. Mark Slobin, *Tenement Songs: The Popular Music of Jewish Immigrants* (Urbana: University of Illinois Press, 1996), 16.

60. Robert A. Rothstein, "Klezmer-loshn: The Language of Jewish Folk Musicians," in *American Klezmer: Its Roots and Offshoots*, ed. Mark Slobin (Berkeley: University of California Press, 2002), 28.

61. Quoted in Moshe Beregovski, *Jewish Instrumental Folk Music: The Collections and Writings of Moshe Beregovski*, ed. and trans. Mark Slobin, Robert A. Rothstein, and Michael Alpert (Syracuse, NY: Syracuse University Press, 2001), 36.

62. The theme of the Jewish fiddler continued to be prominent in Jewish art-works after World War II, as part of the revivalist movement, in such works as Lazar Weiner's 1961 lied "Der Yid mitn fidl" (text by A. Lutzky); the 1963 "folk cantata" *The Village Fiddler*, by Arnold M. Rothstein and Alton Meyer Winters, which was based on *Yosl der fidler* and intended to teach children "the worthiness of non-conformity and the values implicit in the standards of life of Eastern-European Jewry" (*The Village Fiddler* [New York: Transcontinental Music, 1963], 3); Vladimir Heifetz's cantata "Oyf'n fidl," based on the Sholem Aleichem story (Heifetz's work was published posthumously in 1992); and, of course, the 1964 Broadway musical and 1971 film *Fiddler on the Roof*.

63. Beregovski, *Jewish Instrumental Folk Music*, 22–3. See also Slobin, *Tenement Songs*, ch. 1; and Hankus Netsky, *Klezmer: Music and Community in 20th-Century Jewish Philadelphia* (Ph.D. Dissertation, Wesleyan University, 2004), 45–8. Kotik's memoir is reprinted in David Assaf, ed., *Journey to a Nineteenth-Century Shtetl: The Memoirs of Yekhezkel Kotik* (Detroit: Wayne State University Press, 2002).

64. Joshua S. Walden, "Leaving Kazimierz: Comedy and Realism in the Yiddish Film Musical *Yidl Mitn Fidl*," *Journal of Music, Sound, and the Moving Image* 3, no. 2 (Autumn 2009): 159–93.

65. "Shpil Klezmer Shpil," by I. Lillian, J. Jacobs and Abraham Ellstein. Performed by Seymour Rechtzeit and Ellstein's orchestra on Columbia Records No. 8235 F, and published by J and J Kammen Music, 1947. Abraham Ellstein Collection, RG 522, Box 1, Collection of YIVO, at the Center for Jewish History. "Shpil mit koykh, zol azh fun

dayn fidl geyn a roykh/ Shpil un mayn neshome gib a glet, oy/ Vey'z mir klezmer ven dayn fidl ret."

66. "Hey du klezmer, nem dem fidl,/ shpil dos naye lidl,/ tantsn vet men dem nayem sher."

67. "Shpil mir, fidele, shpil a doyna. . . . In es shpilen di gefilen/Vi a lidl oyf a fidl."

68. Leib Kvitko, *Dos fidl* (N.p., 1928).

69. See, for example, the postcard depicting a fiddler and young singer in Gerard Silvain, Henri Minczeles, and Donna Wiemann, *Yiddishland* (Corte Madera, CA: Gingko Press, 1999), 442.

70. Benedict Anderson, *Imagined Communities: Reflections on the Origin and Spread of Nationalism* (London: Verso, 1991).

71. On the development of shtetl mythology, see David G. Roskies, *The Jewish Search for a Usable Past* (Bloomington: Indiana University Press, 1999), ch. 4.

72. Mark Zborowski and Elizabeth Herzog, *Life Is with People* (New York: Schocken, 1995), 29.

73. Joseph Cherniavsky, *Moyshe der fidler: a shames un a klezmer, a idishe muzikalishe bild in eyn akt*, United States Library of Congress, American Memory, http://memory.loc.gov/ammem/index.html.

74. Roskies, *Jewish Search*, 64.

75. Rita Ottens and Joel Rubin, *Klezmer-Musik* (Kassel: Bärenreiter, 1999), 175.

76. Quoted in Jed Wyrick, "Yiddish Canon Consciousness and the Dionysiac Spirit of Music," in *Arguing the Modern Jewish Canon: Essays on Literature and Culture in Honor of Ruth R. Wisse*, ed. Justin Cammy, Dara Horn, Alyssa Quint, and Rachel Rubinstein (Cambridge, MA: Harvard University Press, 2008), 480.

77. Ovid, *The Metamorphoses*, trans. Mary M. Innes (Harmondsworth: Penguin, 1955).

78. Quoted in Jim Samson, *Virtuosity and the Musical Work: The* Transcendental Studies *of Liszt* (Cambridge: Cambridge University Press, 2003), 78.

79. Benjamin Harshav, *Marc Chagall and the Lost Jewish World: The Nature of Chagall's Art and Iconography* (New York: Rizzoli, 2006), 189.

80. Benjamin Harshav, "Chagall: Postmodernism and Fictional Worlds in Painting," in *Marc Chagall and the Jewish Theater* (New York: Solomon R. Guggenheim Foundation, 1992), 35. This image became a frequent feature of Chagall's works, appearing in a number of paintings including his 1923–4 *The Green Violinist*. It is based on earlier representations of a fiddler on a roof, in *The Dead Man* (1908) and *The Fiddler* (1912–13). Although Chagall's *Music* was an inspiration for the title of *Fiddler on the Roof*, based on Sholem Aleichem's stories about Tevye and his daughters, it seems that the initial source of Chagall's rooftop musician can be found in Sholem Aleichem's *Stempenyu*. Joshua S. Walden, "The '*Yidishe Paganini*': Sholem Aleichem's *Stempenyu*, the Music of Yiddish Theater, and the Character of the *Shtetl* Fiddler," *Journal of the Royal Musical Association*, 139, no. 1 (Spring 2014, forthcoming).

81. The publication history of the Society is printed in Galina Kopytowa, "Veröffentlichungen der 'Gesellschaft für jüdische Volksmusik' St. Petersburg/Petrograd,"

in *Jüdische Musik in Sowjetrußland: Die 'Jüdische Nationale Schule' der zwanziger Jahre*, ed. Jascha Nemtsov and Ernst Kuhn (Berlin: Ernst Kuhn, 2002), 123–7. The publication history of Jibneh is charted in Nemtsov, *Die Neue Jüdische Schule*, 241–5.

82. Loeffler, *Most Musical Nation*, 179.

83. Móricz, *Jewish Identities*, 38–43. See also Richard Taruskin, "Yevreyi and Zhidy: A Memoir, a Survey, and a Plea," in *On Russian Music* (Berkeley: University of California Press, 2008), 190–201.

84. Jehoash Hirshberg, *Music in the Jewish Community of Palestine 1880–1948: A Social History* (Oxford: Clarendon, 1995), 78–9. In a 1928 article, Rosowsky recalled that Rimsky-Korsakov, "charmed by the special beauty of one of our melodies, in which the soul of the wandering nation is expressed, ... said: 'Hebrew music is yearning for a Glinka of its own.'" Quoted in Hirshberg, *Music in the Jewish Community of Palestine*, 79.

85. Philip V. Bohlman and Ruth F. Davis, "*Mizrakh*, Jewish Music and the Journey to the East," in *Music and Orientalism in the British Empire, 1780s–1940s: Portrayals of the East*, ed. Martin Clayton and Bennett Zon (Aldershot, UK: Ashgate, 2007), 96.

86. Ibid., 97.

87. Idelsohn, *Jewish Music*, 3. See also Philip V. Bohlman, *Jewish Music and Modernity* (Oxford: Oxford University Press, 2008), 44.

88. Ivan Davidson Kalmar and Derek J. Penslar show that one common way in which European Jews responded to anti-Jewish orientalism between the late eighteenth and early twentieth century was "by idealizing and romanticizing the Orient and themselves as its representatives." "Orientalism and the Jews: An Introduction," in *Orientalism and the Jews*, ed. Ivan Davidson Kalmar and Derek J. Penslar (Waltham, MA: Brandeis University Press, 2005), xviii.

89. Jascha Nemtsov, "Joseph Achron (1886–1943)," in *Jüdische Musik in Sowjetrußland: Die 'Jüdische Nationale Schule' der zwanziger Jahre*, ed. Jascha Nemtsov and Ernst Kuhn (Berlin: Ernst Kuhn, 2002), 186. For Achron's biography see Philip Moddel, *Joseph Achron* (Tel Aviv: Israeli Music Publication, 1966).

90. Saminsky, *Music of the Ghetto and the Bible*, 135.

91. Idelsohn, *Jewish Music*, 467.

92. Achron's piano solo "Symphonic Variations and Sonata on the Jewish Theme 'El Jiwneh Hagalil," opus 39, also opens with a small-print transcription of a melody collected by Kiselgof. Achron additionally appropriated melodies from Kiselgof's fieldwork in his incidental music to the plays *The Sorceress* and *Mazl Tov*. Lyudmila Sholokhova, "Zinoviy Kiselgof as a Founder of Jewish Music Folklore Studies in the Russian Empire at the Beginning of the 20th Century," in *Klesmer, Klassik, jiddisches Lied: Jüdische Musikkultur in Osteuropa*, ed. Karl E. Grözinger (Wiesbaden: Harrassowitz, 2004), 65.

93. Heifetz also recorded "Hebrew Dance" and "Hebrew Lullaby" one time each, and "Stimmung" twice, with Isidor Achron and Emmanuel Bay. Heifetz's complete discography can be found in Jean-Michel Molkhou, "Heifetz on Disc and Film," *Strad*,

January 1995, 90–7. On these recordings, see also Joshua S. Walden, "Performing the Rural: Sonic Signifiers in Early Twentieth-Century Violin Playing," in *Before and After Music: Proceedings from the 10th International Congress of the International Project on Musical Signification, Vilnius, 21–25 October 2008*, ed. Lina Navickaitè-Martinelli (Vilnius/Helsinki: Lithuanian Academy of Music and Theatre, Umweb, International Semiotics Institute, 2010), 421–31.

94. Nemtsov, *Die Neue Jüdische Schule*, 91.

95. "Heifetz Plays Benefit," *New York Times*, April 29, 1918, 11.

96. Programs of these concerts are held in the Jascha Heifetz Collection, Music Division, Library of Congress, Boxes 218–20.

97. Horst J. P. Bergmeier, Ejal Jakob Eisler, and Rainer E. Lotz, *Vorbei—Beyond Recall: Dokumentation jüdischen Musiklebens in Berlin, 1933–1938* (Hambergen: Bear Family Records, 2001), 389.

98. Ibid., 387. Like many violinists of his time, Weißgerber played rural miniatures as part of his recital repertoire. During a recording project for Lukraphone in 1935, he performed a "Csárdás" by Hubay, as well as Achron's "Hebrew Melody," and a piece labeled "Spanischer Tanz" by Manuel de Falla; all of these recordings but a fragment of "Csárdás" have been lost (395).

99. Philip V. Bohlman, "Music, Modernity, and the Foreign in the New Germany," *Modernism/Modernity* 1, no. 1 (1994): 128. See also Bohlman, "Musik als Widerstand: jüdische Musik in Deutschland 1933–1940," *Jahrbuch für Volksliedforschung* 40 (1995): 49–74; and Lily E. Hirsch, *A Jewish Orchestra in Nazi Germany: Musical Politics and the Berlin Jewish Culture League* (Michigan: University of Michigan Press, 2010).

100. Bergmeier, et al., *Vorbei*, 137.

101. Review of March 28, 1935, in the *C. V.-Zeitung*, quoted in ibid., 389.

102. The disc was produced by Banner Records, a company Rechtzeit had co-founded in the 1940s with Victor Selzman. Catalogue number B-519, Matrix A-343.

103. Ari Y. Kelman, *Station Identification: A Cultural History of Yiddish Radio in the United States* (Berkeley: University of California Press, 2009), 18–20.

104. For a history of "Yiddish melodies in swing" on Yiddish radio, with multiple audio examples, see the National Public Radio series *Yiddish Radio Project: Stories from the Golden Age of Yiddish Radio*, produced by Dave Isay, Henry Sapoznik, and Yair Reiner (Minneapolis: HighBridge, 2002).

105. David W. Stowe, *Swing Changes: Big-Band Jazz in New Deal America* (Cambridge, MA: Harvard University Press, 1994), 94–5. On "swinging the classics," see also Charles Hiroshi Garrett, "'Shooting the Keys': Musical Horseplay and High Culture," in *The Oxford Handbook of the New Cultural History of Music*, ed. Jane F. Fulcher (New York: Oxford University Press, 2011), 257–59; and John Wriggle, "Jazzing the Classics: Race, Modernism, and the Career of Arranger Chappie Willet," *Journal of the Society for American Music* 6, no. 2 (May 2012): 175–209.

106. "Klangen, es heren zikh/ fun vayten mizrekh dort/ Klangen ayngehilt in a benkshaft/ Mit libe fun a harts vos benkt./ Hert zikh a vider kol,/ Kum tsurik tsu yene mol/ Vi di uves fun amol./ Zeyer oysres hoben uns geshenkt/ . . . Sheyden fun dir/ iz

geven zeyr shver,/ mit dir tsu zayn/ iz geven mayn tsiel, mayn beger/ . . . Lozen vel ikh dikh nit,/ Sheyne kale fun Yisroel." The lyrics are difficult to discern definitively due to the deteriorated quality of the few surviving copies of the record. I am grateful to Judith Schelly for her assistance with this transcription.

107. "Ven ikh derher tsigayner melodi/ A lid fun libe dringt in harts arayn."

108. "Shenk mir libe, khotsh of eyn minit/ Vayl mit dir iz azoy hartsig gut."

109. "Tants far mir, meydl mayn,/ vilder lomir tantsen . . . / Hartsen tsvey, zey klappen on ofher/ Drey zikh meydl, drey zikh shneler mer/ . . . Nu zing tsigayner, shpring tsigayner/ Tants mir mayn gezang."

110. Quoted in Albert Glinsky, *Theremin: Ether Music and Espionage* (Urbana: University of Illinois Press, 2000).

111. Barbara Kirshenblatt-Gimblett, introduction to Mark Zborowski and Elizabeth Herzog, *Life Is with People* (New York: Schocken, 1995), xi.

112. Quoted in ibid., xi.

Chapter 6

1. Vera Lampert, *Népzene Bartók műveiben: A feldolgozott dallamok forrásjegyzéke: Magyar, szlovák, román, rutén, szerb és arab népdalok és táncok* (Budapest: Hagyományok Háza, Helikon Kiadó, Néprajzi Múzeum, Zenetudományi Intézet, 2005), 96. This book has been published in English translation: Vera Lampert, *Folk Music in Bartók's Compositions: A Source Catalog: Arab, Hungarian, Romanian, Ruthenian, Serbian, and Slovak Melodies* (Budapest: Hungarian Heritage House; and Germany: G. Henle, 2008).

2. Béla Bartók, *Rumanian Folk Music*, ed. Benjamin Suchoff, Vol. 1, *Instrumental Melodies* (The Hague: Martinus Nijhoff, 1967), 136.

3. Bartók's concert performances of *Romanian Folk Dances* from the 1920s to mid-1930s include recitals in Hungary, Russia, Germany, and elsewhere. These are listed in the card catalogue of Bartók's performances in the Bartók Archívum at the Institute for Musicology of the Hungarian Academy of Sciences.

4. The original text of this essay was published as "A parasztzene hatása az újabb műzenére," *Új Idők* 37, no. 23 (May 31, 1931): 718–19. It is reprinted in *Bartók Béla Írásai*, Vol. 1, *Bartók Béla önmagáról, műveiről, az új magyar zenéről, műzene és népzene viszonyáról*, ed. Tibor Tallián (Budapest: Zeneműkiadó, 1989), 141–4.

5. Béla Bartók, "The Influence of Peasant Music on Modern Music," in *Béla Bartók Essays*, ed. Benjamin Suchoff (London: Faber and Faber, 1976), 341.

6. Ibid., 344.

7. Ibid., 341.

8. David E. Schneider, *Bartók, Hungary, and the Renewal of Tradition: Case Studies in the Intersection of Modernity and Nationality* (Berkeley: University of California Press, 2006), 21–4.

9. See, for instance, Béla Bartók, "Hungarian Folk Music [1921]," in *Béla Bartók Essays*, ed. Benjamin Suchoff (London: Faber and Faber, 1976).

10. Tamás Hofer, "Construction of the 'Folk Cultural Heritage' in Hungary, and Rival Versions of National Identity," *Ethnologia Europaea* 21, no. 2 (1991): 157.

11. Quoted in ibid., 155.

12. Ibid., 156.

13. Ibid., 155.

14. Judit Frigyesi, *Béla Bartók and Turn-of-the-Century Budapest* (Berkeley: University of California Press, 1998), 55–60.

15. Katie Trumpener, "Béla Bartók and the Rise of Comparative Ethnomusicology: Nationalism, Race Purity, and the Legacy of the Austro-Hungarian Empire," in *Music and the Racial Imagination*, ed. Ronald Radano and Philip V. Bohlman (Chicago: University of Chicago Press, 2000), 404.

16. Sándor Kovács, "The Ethnomusicologist," in *The Bartók Companion*, ed. Malcolm Gillies (London: Faber and Faber, 1993), 52.

17. Ibid., 54.

18. Quoted in Linda Dégh, "Bartók as Folklorist: His Place in the History of Research," in *Bartók and Kodály Revisited*, ed. György Ránki (Budapest: Akadémiai Kiadó, 1987), 109.

19. Béla Bartók, "Why and How Do We Collect Folk Music?," in Bartók, *Béla Bartók Essays*, 14.

20. Julie Brown, "Bartók, the Gypsies, and Hybridity in Music," in *Western Music and Its Others: Difference, Representation, and Appropriation in Music*, ed. Georgina Born and David Hesmondhalgh (Berkeley: University of California Press, 2000). See also Julie Brown, *Bartók and the Grotesque: Studies in Modernity, the Body, and Contradiction in Music* (Aldershot, UK: Ashgate, 2007), 41–2.

21. Brown, "Bartók, the Gypsies, and Hybridity," 123.

22. Béla Bartók, *Béla Bartók Letters*, ed. János Demény, trans. Péter Balabán, István Farkas, et al. (London: Faber and Faber, 1971), 29.

23. Ibid., 29.

24. Ibid., 30. Emphasis in the original.

25. Ibid., 50. Emphasis in the original.

26. Hofer, "Construction of the 'Folk Cultural Heritage,'" 158–9. On the role of music in the discourse regarding Hungarian identity between East and West, see Lynn Hooker, "Solving the Problem of Hungarian Music: Contexts for Bartók's Early Career," *International Journal of Musicology* 9 (2001): 11–42.

27. For further discussion of Bartók and Kodály's work with *Nyugat*, see Marianne D. Birnbaum, "Bartók, Kodály and the 'Nyugat'," in *Bartók and Kodály Revisited*, ed. György Ránki (Budapest: Akadémiai Kiadó, 1987), 55–64.

28. Géza Csáth, "Bartók Béla," *Nyugat*, May 1, 1908, http://epa.oszk.hu/00000/00022/00009/. "Szilaj, szangvinikus magyar kedély, gúnyolódásra, vidám hahotázásokra és haragra egyaránt hajlamos."

29. Ibid. The entire passage appears as follows: "Bartók, aki mint etnográfus kutató is jelentős szolgálatokat tett a magyar muzsika ügyének, azt látta, hogy Magyarországon az eredeti fajiságot a cigány befolyás elrontotta és ez különösen az Alföldön végre egészen el is vesztette eredeti jellemét. A székelyek, csángók, dunántúliak népdalaiban ellenben megmaradtak a kontrapunktos felhasználásra sokkal inkább alkalmas ősi faji elemek."

30. Géza Csáth, "Musique moderne hongroise," *Nyugat*, October 16, 1910, http:// epa.oszk.hu/00000/00022/00066/. "Bartók 'Három csikmegyei népdala' nem akar más lenni és másnak látszani, mint ami. Népdal-átiratok, de eredetiek, finomak, a Bartók zamatos megérzéseivel. Bartók egészen mást érez a népdalban, mint Aggházy, aki mereven követi a 'német' Lisztet. Bartók érzi a népdal lelkét, a monotóniáját, a miliőt, amelyből keletkezett. Ha egy angolnak vagy egy franciának meg akarnám magyarázni, mi a magyar népdal -, eltiltanám a Liszt, Székely és Ábrányi-féle rapszódiáktól és odaadnám neki a Bartók egyszerű, könnyű, futamok és tremolók nélkül szűkölködő apró átiratait."

31. Quoted in Lynn Hooker, "Modernism on the Periphery: Béla Bartók and the New Hungarian Music Society of 1911–1912," *Musical Quarterly* 88, no. 2 (Summer 2005), 296.

32. Béla Bartók, "Hungarian Folk Music [1921]," 59 and 70.

33. Ibid., 59. Emphasis in the original.

34. Béla Bartók, "Gipsy Music or Hungarian Music," in Bartók, *Béla Bartók Essays*, 219.

35. Ibid., 221.

36. Ibid., 222.

37. Béla Bartók, "Why and How Do We Collect Folk Music?" in Bartók, *Béla Bartók Essays*, 12.

38. Bartók, "Hungarian Folk Music [1921]," 63.

39. Ibid., 60.

40. For a study of the pedagogical function of *Forty-Four Duos for Two Violins*, see Christiano Pesavento, *Musik von Béla Bartók als pädagogisches Programm* (Frankfurt am Main: P. Lang, 1994), 131–235.

41. Quoted in Joseph Szigeti, *Szigeti on the Violin* (London: Cassell, 1969), 216.

42. Béla Bartók, "The Relation of Folk Music to the Development of the Art Music of Our Time," in Bartók, *Béla Bartók Essays*, 321.

43. Bartók, "Hungarian Folk Music [1929]," in Bartók, *Béla Bartók Essays*, 3-4.

44. Bartók, "What Is Folk Music?" in Bartók, *Béla Bartók Essays*, 6.

45. László Vikárius, "Bartók and the Ideal of 'Sentimentalitäts-Mangel,'" *International Journal of Musicology* 9 (2000), 211–12. Vikárius shows that Bartók settled in the 1930s on the term "*Sentimentalitäts-Mangel*," or "lack of sentimentality," to describe the expressive manner of folk music, as well as his preferred style of art music composition and performance.

46. Ibid., 211–12.

47. Bartók, "Influence of Peasant Music," 341.

48. Klára Móricz, "'From Pure Sources Only': Bartók and the Modernist Quest for Purity," *International Journal of Musicology* 9 (2000): 252.

49. Quotations in this paragraph are from Béla Bartók and Zoltán Kodály, *Hungarian Folksongs for Voice with Piano*, ed. Denijs Dille, trans. Nancy Bush and Ilona L. Lukács (Budapest: Editio Musica, 1970), 50.

50. Ibid., 43.

51. Vera Lampert, "Nationalism, Exoticism, or Concessions to the Audience? Motivations behind Bartók's Folksong Settings," *Studia Musicologica* 47, nos. 3–4 (September 2006), 340.

52. Bartók and Kodály, *Hungarian Folksongs for Voice with Piano*, 43.

53. Leon Botstein, "Out of Hungary: Bartók, Modernism, and the Cultural Politics of Twentieth-Century Music," in *Bartók and His World*, ed. Peter Laki (Princeton, NJ: Princeton University Press, 1995), 46.

54. Ibid., 46.

55. Ibid., 47.

56. Ibid., 48.

57. Bartók, "What Is Folk Music?," 6.

58. Frigyesi, *Béla Bartók and Turn-of-the-Century Budapest*, 104.

59. Quoted in Lynn Hooker, "Modernism on the Periphery," 273.

60. László Somfai, "Written and Performed Form in Bartók's Piano Works of 1915–1920," in *Musik als Text: Bericht über den Internationalen Kongress der Gesellschaft für Musikforschung, Freiburg im Breisgau 1993*, Vol. 1, ed. Hermann Danuser and Tobias Plebuch (Kassel: Bärenreiter, 1998), 104. Bartók did not acquire another formal publishing contract until he signed with Universal Edition in 1918.

61. János Kárpáti, "Piano Works of the War Years," in *The Bartók Companion*, ed. Malcolm Gillies (London: Faber and Faber, 1993), 147. Bartók accumulated a sheet music library containing an extensive collection of arrangements of traditional songs and dances from around the world. Among these, the folk culture of Hungary was represented by works including Ernő Balogh's "Peasant Dance"; Palestine's folk culture by a copy of Israel Brandmann's "Variations on a Palestinian Folk Dance," signed by the composer "in admiration" (*in Verehrung*) of Bartók; the Eastern European Jewish folk tradition, by *Deux danses Hassides*, by Max Eisikovits; and Croatian folk culture, by folk song settings by Anton Dobronič. Other works represented folk cultures of Egypt, Kyrgyzstan, Spain, Turkey, and elsewhere. The most comprehensive itemization of Bartók's library can be found in Vera Lampert, "Zeitgenössische Musik in Bartóks Notensammlung," in *Documenta Bartókiana*, Vol. 5, ed. Denijs Dille (Mainz: B. Schott und Sohne; and Budapest: Akadémiai Kiadó, 1977), 142–68.

62. "'Ardeleana;' előadták Cserbelen, Hunyad m[egye]."

63. The footnote to the second folk song arrangement reads, "táncdallam; előadták Veskohmezőn (Câmp), Bihar m. (Bartók: *Chansons populaires roumaines du département Bihar*; Bucureşti, 1913; 337. lap, 350. szám.)" (Dance melody; performed in Veskohmező [Câmp], Bihar County [Bartók: *Chansons populaires roumaines du département Bihar*; Bucharest, 1913; page 337; number 350]).

64. Timothy Rice, "Béla Bartók and Bulgarian Rhythm," in *Bartók Perspectives: Man, Composer, Ethnomusicologist*, ed. Elliott Antokoletz, Victoria Fischer, and Benjamin Suchoff (Oxford: Oxford University Press, 2000), 196–7.

65. Béla Bartók, *Bartók Béla Írásai*, 263.

66. Lampert, *Népzene Bartók műveiben*, 16. For studies of these works in relation to the original musical artifacts on which they are based, see Ingrid Arauco, "Bartók's

Romanian Christmas Carols: Changes from the Folk Sources and Their Significance," *Journal of Musicology* 5, no. 2 (Spring 1987): 191–225; David Yeomans, "Background and Analysis of Bartók's *Romanian Christmas Carols for Piano* (1915)," in *Bartók Perspectives: Man, Composer, and Ethnomusicologist*, ed. Elliott Antokoletz, Victoria Fischer, and Benjamin Suchoff (Oxford: Oxford University Press, 2000), 185–95; and László Vikárius "Erinnern an die 'Stimmung' der Sache. Das Konkrete und das Schwebende im Komponieren Bartóks," in *Resonanzen: Vom Erinnern in der Musik*, ed. Andreas Dorschel (Vienna: Institut für Wertungsforschung, 2007), 165.

67. Bartók published transcriptions of the phonograph recordings gradually: some appeared in the 1913 collection from Bucharest, others were included in 1923 in *Volksmusik der Rumänen von Maramureş*, and still more in 1935 in *Melodien der rumänischen Colinde*. Many of his Romanian music transcriptions were not published until after his death, when Benjamin Suchoff compiled and edited the five-volume *Rumanian Folk Music* in 1967.

68. Vikárius, "Erinnern an die 'Stimmung' der Sache," 162–3.

69. Bartók Archívum, Institute for Musicology of the Hungarian Academy of Sciences, manuscript number PB 36–37–38PS1.

70. The published transcription of the wax cylinder recording of this dance, which had been played for him by two violinists in harmony, can be found as number 240 in Bartók, *Rumanian Folk Music*, 1:224.

71. Lampert, *Népzene Bartók műveiben*, 96–9.

72. These notebook transcriptions can be found as numbers 128–34 in ibid.

73. Bartók describes the customary tuning of the accompanying violinist in *Rumanian Folk Music*, 1:16.

74. For a study of harmonic practices in traditional instrumental music from Transylvania, see István Pávai, "Sajátos szempontok az erdélyi hangszeres népi harmónia vizsgálatában," in *A Magyar népi tánczene: Tanulmányok*, ed. Márta Virágvölgyi and István Pávai (Budapest: Planétás Kiadó, 2000), 161–85.

75. For example, see Bartók, "Hungarian Folk Music," 61.

76. Rice, "Béla Bartók and Bulgarian Rhythm," 201.

77. Bartók, "Hungarian Folk Music," 70.

78. A detailed table of tempo markings in all extant manuscript versions of *Romanian Folk Dances* as well as Bartók's wax cylinder recordings and transcriptions of the original dances and his performances of the work appears in László Somfai, *Béla Bartók: Composition, Concepts, and Autograph Sources* (Berkeley: University of California Press, 1996), 248–51.

79. Bartók Archívum, Institute for Musicology of the Hungarian Academy of Sciences, manuscript number PB 37PFC1.

80. "de az eredeti paraszt tempo 92."

81. "a hengerben 1'4"."

82. In movement two, he indicates, "original peasant is 184" to the quarter (paraszt eredeti 184); in movement three, "original peasant goes from 130 to 138!" (paraszt eredeti 130-tól 138ig megy!); in movement four, he marks that the original sixteenth

note was 570; in movement five, the original tempo was 145 to the quarter note; and in the final movement he writes that the "peasant" tempos of each dance were 138 and 160 to the quarter note. Bartók Archívum, manuscript PB 37PFC1.

83. Claude Kenneson, *Székely and Bartók: The Story of a Friendship* (Portland, OR: Amadeus, 1994), 33.

84. Ibid., 42.

85. Ibid., 88–9.

86. Ibid., 90.

87. János Breuer, "*Román népi táncok*: Egy Bartók-mű két lappangó atirata," *Zenetudományi dolgozatok* (1982): 155–8.

88. Schneider, *Bartók, Hungary, and the Renewal of Tradition*, 193.

89. Béla Bartók, "Reply to Jenő Hubay," in Bartók, *Béla Bartók Essays*, 201.

90. Ibid., 203.

91. Schneider, *Bartók, Hungary, and the Renewal of Tradition*, 185.

92. Demény, *Béla Bartók Letters*, 201.

93. Ibid., 201. See Malcolm Gillies, "Bartók and His Music in the 1990s," in *The Bartók Companion*, ed. Malcolm Gillies (London: Faber and Faber, 1993), 12.

94. Demény, *Béla Bartók Letters*, 201.

95. Schneider, *Bartók, Hungary, and the Renewal of Tradition*, 196.

96. See László Somfai, "Nineteenth-Century Ideas Developed in Bartók's Piano Notation in the Years 1907–14" *19th-Century Music* 11, no. 1 (Summer 1987): 73–91; and Victoria Fischer, "Articulation Notation in the Piano Music of Béla Bartók: Evolution and Interpretation," *Studia Musicologica* 36, nos. 3–4 (1995): 285–301.

97. László Somfai, "Idea, Notation, Interpretation: Written and Oral Transmission in Bartók's Works for Strings" *Studia Musicologica* 37, no. 1 (1996): 41.

98. Fischer, "Articulation Notation," 300–301.

99. Ibid., 301.

100. On this subject, see also Joshua S. Walden, "'On the String in the Peasant Style': Performance Style in Early Recordings of Béla Bartók's *Romanian Folk Dances*," in *Performers' Voices across Centuries, Cultures, and Disciplines*, ed. Ann Marshman (London: Imperial College Press), 151–63.

101. Quoted in Kenneson, *Székely and Bartók*, 113.

102. Szigeti, *Szigeti on the Violin*, 127.

103. Kenneson, *Székely and Bartók*, 114.

104. Ibid., 114.

105. Szigeti, *Szigeti on the Violin*, 185.

106. Ibid., 216–17.

107. Ibid., 217.

108. Ibid., 223.

109. Szigeti and Bartók's recording: Matrix numbers LB 6 and WA 9908-WA 9909; re-released on Hungaroton CD series "Bartók at the Piano," CD 3, HCD 12328. Székely and Frid's recording: original catalogue number Decca K 872; Matrix number TA 3025-1.

Conclusion

1. "'Eili, Eili' Played in Court by Lawyer," *New York Times*, May 1, 1925, 7.

2. Susman Kiselgof, "Das jüdische Volkslied," in *Jüdische Musik in Sowjetrußland: Die "Jüdische Nationale Schule" der zwanziger Jahre*, ed. Jascha Nemtsov and Ernst Kuhn (Berlin: Ernst Kuhn, 2002), 45. "Gleich anderen Völkern sollen wir sagen können: 'Unser Volkslied vereint uns.'"

3. On postmodern theories of identity, see Madan Sarup, *Identity, Culture and the Postmodern World* (Edinburgh: Edinburgh University Press, 1996), 45.

4. John O'Flynn describes the concepts of old and new authenticities in relation to music, in "National Identity and Music in Transition: Issues of Authenticity in a Global Setting," in *Music, National Identity and the Politics of Location: Between the Global and the Local*, ed. Ian Biddle and Vanessa Knights (Aldershot, UK: Ashgate, 2007), 34.

5. This book focuses on the music of European peripheries, but it is helpful to note that the search for musical beginnings was also a preoccupation of German scholars in the field of *Musikwissenschaft* during the early years of the twentieth century, as they sought evidence that musical art possessed Germanic origins. On this historical and intellectual project and its relation to conceptions of authenticity, purity, and identity, see Alexander Rehding, "The Quest for the Origins of Music in Germany Circa 1900," *Journal of the American Musicological Society* 53, no. 2 (Summer 2000): 345–85.

6. George Eliot, *Daniel Deronda*, 4 vols. (Edinburgh, 1876), 1:3.

Appendix

1. For a useful explanation of discography and the matrix number, see Simon Trezise, "The Recorded Document: Interpretation and Discography," in *The Cambridge Companion to Recorded Music*, ed. Nicholas Cook, Eric Clarke, Daniel Leech-Wilkinson, and John Rink (Cambridge: Cambridge University Press, 2009), 186–209.

BIBLIOGRAPHY

Abrahams, Roger D. "Phantoms of Romantic Nationalism in Folkloristics." *Journal of American Folklore* 106, no. 419 (Winter 1993): 3–37.

Achron, Joseph. "Notits vegn yidisher muzik." *Bodn* 1, no. 1 (April–June 1934): 55–60.

Adorno, Theodor W. *Aesthetic Theory*. Edited by Gretel Adorno and Rolf Tiedemann. Translated by Robert Hullot-Kentor. New York: Continuum, 2004.

Agus, Ayke. *Heifetz as I Knew Him*. Portland, OR: Amadeus, 2001.

Alonso, Miguel Manzano. *La jota como género musical: un estudio musicológico acerca del género más difundido en el repertorio tradicional español de la música popular*. Madrid: Editorial Alpuerto, 1995.

———. "Precisiones sobre la Jota en Aragón." *Nassarre: Revista aragonesa de musicología* 9, no. 2 (1993): 281–5.

Altadill, Julio. *Memorias de Sarasate*. Pamplona: Imprenta de Aramendía y Onsalo, 1909.

Anderson, Benedict. *Imagined Communities: Reflections on the Origin and Spread of Nationalism*. London: Verso, 1991.

Arauco, Ingrid. "Bartók's Romanian Christmas Carols: Changes from the Folk Sources and Their Significance." *Journal of Musicology* 5, no. 2 (Spring 1987): 191–225.

Arnim, Ludwig Achim von, and Clemens Brentano. *Des Knaben Wunderhorn*. Munich: Winkler, 1947.

The Art of Violin. Directed by Bruno Monsaingeon. West Long Branch, NJ: Kultur, 2000. DVD.

Assaf, David. *Journey to a Nineteenth-Century Shtetl: The Memoirs of Yekhezkel Kotik*. Detroit: Wayne State University Press, 2002.

Auer, Leopold. *Violin Master Works and Their Interpretation*. New York: Carl Fischer, 1925.

———. *My Long Life in Music*. London: Duckworth, 1924.

———. *Violin Playing as I Teach It*. New York: Frederick A. Stokes, 1921.

Auerbach, Erich. *Mimesis: The Representation of Reality in Western Literature*. Translated by Willard R. Trask. Princeton, NJ: Princeton University Press, 1953.

Avenary, Hanoch. "Shtayger." In *Encyclopaedia Judaica*, 2nd ed., edited by Michael Berenbaum and Fred Skolnik, 18:522–3. Detroit: Macmillan Reference USA, 2007.

———. "The Concept of Mode in European Synagogue Chant." *Yuval* 2 (1971): 11–21

Avrutin, Eugene M. "Racial Categories and the Politics of (Jewish) Difference in Late Imperial Russia." *Kritika* 8, no. 1 (Winter 2007): 13–40.

Bakhtin, Mikhail Mikhaïlovich. "Discourse in the Novel." In *The Dialogic Imagination: Four Essays by M.M. Bakhtin,* edited by Michael Holquist, and translated by Caryl Emerson and Michael Holquist, 259–422. Austin: University of Texas Press, 1981.

Barthes, Roland. "The Reality Effect." In *The Rustle of Language,* translated by Richard Howard, 141–8. Berkeley: University of California Press, 1986.

———. "L'Effet de réel." *Communications* 11 (1968): 84–9.

Bartók, Béla. *Bartók Béla Írásai.* Vol. 1, *Bartók Béla önmagáról, műveiről, az új magyar zenéről, műzene és népzene viszonyáról.* Edited by Tibor Tallián. Budapest: Zeneműkiadó, 1989.

———. *The Hungarian Folksong.* Edited by Benjamin Suchoff. Translated by M.D. Calvocoressi. Albany, NY: State University of New York Press, 1981.

———. *Béla Bartók Essays.* Edited by Benjamin Suchoff. London: Faber and Faber, 1976.

———. *Béla Bartók Letters.* Edited by János Demény. Translated by Péter Balabán, István Farkas. Translation revised by Elisabeth West and Colin Mason. London: Faber and Faber, 1971.

———, and Zoltán Kodály. *Hungarian Folksongs for Voice with Piano.* Edited by Denijs Dille. Translated by Nancy Bush and Ilona L. Lukács. Budapest: Editio Musica, 1970.

———. *Rumanian Folk Music.* Edited by Benjamin Suchoff. Vol. 1, *Instrumental Melodies.* The Hague: Martinus Nijhoff, 1967.

———. "A parasztzene hatása az újabb műzenére." *Új Idők,* May 31, 1931, 718–19.

Becker, Howard. *Art Worlds.* Berkeley: University of California Press, 1982.

Bellman, Jonathan. *The Style Hongrois in the Music of Western Europe.* Boston: Northeastern University Press, 1993.

Benjamin, Walter. *Illuminations.* Translated by Harry Zohn. New York: Schocken, 1968.

Bent, Silas. "Rip Van Winkle Sleep of 'Eili, Eili' Ends." *New York Times,* June 21, 1925.

Beregovski, Moshe. *Jewish Instrumental Folk Music: The Collections and Writings of Moshe Beregovski.* Edited and translated by Mark Slobin, Robert A. Rothstein, and Michael Alpert. Syracuse, NY: Syracuse University Press, 2001.

———. *Old Jewish Folk Music: The Collections and Writings of Moshe Beregovski.* Edited and translated by Mark Slobin. Syracuse, NY: Syracuse University Press, 2000.

Bergerac, Leopold Cardona de. "The Andalusian Music Idiom." *Music Review* 33, no. 3 (August 1972): 157–66.

Bergmeier, Horst J.P., Ejal Jakob Eisler, and Rainer E. Lotz. *Vorbei . . . Beyond Recall: Dokumentation jüdischen Musiklebens in Berlin, 1933–1938.* Hambergen: Bear Family Records, 2001.

Bertran, Francisco Bonastre. *Felipe Pedrell: Acotaciones a una idea.* Tarragona: Caja de Ahorros Provincial de Taragona, 1977.

Bewick, Thomas. *History of British Birds.* Vol. 1, *Containing the History and Description of Land Birds.* Newcastle, 1797.

Bigenho, Michelle. *Sounding Indigenous: Authenticity in Bolivian Music Performance.* New York: Palgrave Macmillan, 2002.

Birnbaum, Marianne D. "Bartók, Kodály and the 'Nyugat.'" In *Bartók and Kodály Revisited*, edited by György Ránki, 55–67. Budapest: Akadémiai Kiadó, 1987.

Bohlman, Philip Vilas. *Jewish Music and Modernity*. New York: Oxford University Press, 2008.

———. "Erasure: Displacing and Misplacing Race." In *Western Music and Race*, edited by Julie Brown, 3–23. Cambridge: Cambridge University Press, 2007.

———, and Ruth F. Davis. "*Mizrakh*, Jewish Music and the Journey to the East." In *Music and Orientalism in the British Empire, 1780s–1940s: Portrayals of the East*, edited by Martin Clayton and Bennett Zon, 95–127. Aldershot, UK: Ashgate, 2007.

———. *The Music of European Nationalism: Cultural Identity and Modern History*. Santa Barbara: ABC-Clio, 2004.

———. "Landscape—Region—Nation—Reich: German Folk Song in the Nexus of National Identity." In *Music and German National Identity*, edited by Celia Applegate and Pamela Potter, 105–27. Chicago: University of Chicago Press, 2002.

———, and Otto Holzapfel, editors. *The Folk Songs of Ashkenaz*. Middleton, WI: A-R Editions, 2001.

———. "Musik als Widerstand: jüdische Musik in Deutschland 1933–1940." *Jahrbuch für Volksliedforschung* 40 (1995): 49–74.

———. "Music, Modernity, and the Foreign in the New Germany." *Modernism/Modernity* 1, no. 1 (1994): 121–52.

———. *The World Centre for Jewish Music in Palestine, 1936–1940: Jewish Musical Life on the Eve of World War II*. Oxford: Clarendon, 1992.

———. *The Study of Folk Music in the Modern World*. Bloomington: Indiana University Press, 1988.

Bopp, Verena. *MAILAMM 1932–1941: Die Geschichte einer Vereinigung zur Förderung jüdischer Musik in den USA*. Wiesbaden: Harrassowitz, 2007.

Botstein, Leon. "Out of Hungary: Bartók, Modernism, and the Cultural Politics of Twentieth-Century Music." In *Bartók and His World*, edited by Peter Laki, 3–63. Princeton: Princeton University Press, 1995.

Brady, Erika. *A Spiral Way: How the Phonograph Changed Ethnography*. Jackson: University Press of Mississippi, 1999.

Breuer, János. "*Román népi táncok*: Egy Bartók-mű két lappangó átirata." *Zenetudományi dolgozatok* (1982): 155–8.

Brock-Nannestad, George. "The Development of Recording Technologies." In *The Cambridge Companion to Recorded Music*, edited by Nicholas Cook, Eric Clarke, Daniel Leech-Wilkinson, and John Rink, 149–76. Cambridge: Cambridge University Press, 2009.

Brown, Julie. *Bartók and the Grotesque: Studies in Modernity, the Body, and Contradiction in Music*. Aldershot, UK: Ashgate, 2007.

———. "Bartók, the Gypsies, and Hybridity in Music." In *Western Music and Its Others: Difference, Representation, and Appropriation in Music*, edited by Georgina Born and David Hesmondhalgh, 119–42. Berkeley: University of California Press, 2000.

Buber, Martin. "Address on Jewish Art." In *The First Buber: Youthful Zionist Writings of Martin Buber*, edited and translated by Gilya G. Schmidt, 46–64. Syracuse, NY: Syracuse University Press, 1999.

Bunzl, Matti. "Franz Boas and the Humboldtian Tradition: From *Volksgeist* and *Nationalcharakter* to an Anthropological Concept of Culture." In Volksgeist *as Method and Ethic: Essays on Boasian Ethnography and the German Anthropological Tradition*, edited by George W. Stocking Jr., 17–78. Madison: University of Wisconson Press, 1996.

Burstyn, Shai. "Inventing Musical Tradition: The Case of the Hebrew (Folk)Song." *Orbis Musicae* 13 (2003): 127–36.

Cahan, Yehuda Leib. *Yidishe folkslider mit melodyes*. Edited by Max Weinreich. New York: YIVO, 1957.

———. *Studies in Yiddish Folklore*. Edited by Max Weinreich. New York: YIVO, 1952.

Cazden, Norman. "Towards a Theory of Realism in Music." *Journal of Aesthetics and Art Criticism* 10, no. 2 (December 1951): 135–51.

Cerda, Alexandre de la. *Pablo de Sarasate: le violoniste basque virtuose*. Anglet: Séguier, 2001.

Champfleury. *Le réalisme*. Paris: Michel Lévy Frères, 1857.

Charnon-Deutsch, Lou. *The Spanish Gypsy: The History of a European Obsession*. University Park: Pennsylvania State University Press, 2004.

Cherniavsky, Joseph. *Moyshe der fidler: a shames un a klezmer, a idishe muzikalishe bild in eyn akt*. United States Library of Congress, American Memory. http://memory.loc.gov/ammem/index.html.

Christoforidis, Michael. "Manuel de Falla, Flamenco and Spanish Identity." In *Western Music and Race*, edited by Julie Brown, 230–43. Cambridge: Cambridge University Press, 2007.

———. "From Folksong to Plainchant: Musical Borrowings and the Transformation of Manuel de Falla's Musical Nationalism in the 1920s." In *Manuel de Falla: His Life and Music*, edited by Nancy Lee Harper, 209–46. Lanham, MD: Scarecrow, 2005.

———. "Manuel de Falla's Personal Library and Insights into the Composer's Annotations." In *Manuel de Falla: His Life and Music*, edited by Nancy Lee Harper, 297–325. Lanham, MD: Scarecrow, 2005.

———. "Manuel de Falla's *Siete canciones populares españolas*: The Composer's Personal Library, Folksong Models and the Creative Process." *Anuario Musical* 55 (2000): 213–35.

———. "A Composer's Annotations to His Personal Library: An Introduction to the Manuel de Falla Collection." *Context* 17 (Winter 1999): 48–68.

———. "Folksong Models and Their Sources in Manuel de Falla's *Siete canciones populares españolas*." *Context* 9 (Winter 1995): 12–21.

C. J. "Instrumental." *Gramophone*, December 1928, 44–5.

"Claimant Loses Suit on 'Eili, Eili.'" *New York Times*, June 10, 1925.

Clark, Walter Aaron. *Enrique Granados: Poet of the Piano*. Oxford: Oxford University Press, 2006.

———. *Isaac Albéniz: Portrait of a Romantic*. Oxford: Oxford University Press, 1999.

Clifford, James. "Further Inflections: Toward Ethnographies of the Future." *Cultural Anthropology* 9, no. 3 (August 1994): 302–38.

Cohen, Judah M. "Rewriting the Grand Narrative of Jewish Music in the United States." *Jewish Quarterly Review* 100, no. 3 (Summer 2010): 417–53.

Cohon, Baruch Joseph. "The Structure of the Synagogue Prayer-Chant." *Journal of the American Musicological Society* 3, no. 1 (Spring 1950): 17–32.

Collins, Chris. "Manuel de Falla, *L'acoustique nouvelle* and Natural Resonance: A Myth Exposed." *Journal of the Royal Musical Association* 128, no. 1 (2003): 71–97.

Cook, Nicholas. "Encountering the Other, Redefining the Self: Hindostannie Airs, Haydn's Folksong Settings and the 'Common Practice' Style." In *Music and Orientalism in the British Empire, 1780s–1940s: Portrayal of the East*, edited by Martin Clayton and Bennett Zon, 13–37. Aldershot, UK: Ashgate, 2007.

———. *The Schenker Project: Culture, Race, and Music Theory in Fin-de-siècle Vienna*. Oxford: Oxford University Press, 2007.

Cooley, Timothy J. *Making Music in the Polish Tatras: Tourists, Ethnographers, and Mountain Musicians*. Bloomington: Indiana University Press, 2005.

Crary, Jonathan. *Suspensions of Perception: Attention, Spectacle, and Modern Culture*. Cambridge, MA: MIT Press, 2001.

Crichton, Ronald. *Falla*. London: British Broadcasting Company, 1982.

Croce, Benedetto. *Aesthetic*. Translated by Douglas Ainslie. New York: Noonday, 1968.

Croft-Cooke, Rupert. "Hungary – Its Gypsies and Their Music." *Gramophone*, November 1927, 222–3.

Csáth, Géza. "Musique moderne hongroise." *Nyugat*, October 16, 1910. http://epa.oszk.hu/00000/00022/00066/.

———. "Bartók Béla." *Nyugat*, May 1, 1908. http://epa.oszk.hu/00000/00022/00009/.

Cumming, Naomi. *The Sonic Self: Musical Subjectivity and Signification*. Bloomington: Indiana University Press, 2000.

Dahlhaus, Carl. "New Music and the Problem of Musical Genre." In *Schoenberg and the New Music*, translated by Derrick Puffett and Alfred Clayton, 32–44. Cambridge: Cambridge University Press, 1987.

———. *Realism in Nineteenth-Century Music*. Translated by Mary Whitall. Cambridge: Cambridge University Press, 1985.

Dale, J. S., and Francis Korbay, editors and translators. *Hungarian Melodies*. Vol. 1. London: Pitt and Hatzfeld; and Boston: H.B. Stevens, 1891.

Dalman, Gustaf Herman. *Jüdischdeutsche Volkslieder aus Galizien und Russland*. Leipzig: Centralbureau der Instituta Judaica (W. Faber), 1888.

Dégh, Linda. "Bartók as Folklorist: His Place in the History of Research." In *Bartók and Kodály Revisited*, edited by György Ránki, 107–21. Budapest: Akadémiai Kiadó, 1987.

Downes, Olin. "Ernest Bloch, the Swiss Composer, on the Influence of Race in Composition." *Musical Observer* 15, no. 3 (1917): 11–12.

Draayer, Suzanne Rhodes. *Art Song Composers of Spain: An Encyclopedia*. Plymouth, UK: Scarecrow Press, 2009.

Dundes, Alan. *Interpreting Folklore*. Bloomington: Indiana University Press, 1980.

Edison, Thomas A. "The Perfected Phonograph." *North American Review* 146, no. 379 (June 1888): 641–50.

———. "The Phonograph and Its Future." *North American Review* 126, no. 262 (May–June 1878): 527–36.

Efron, John M. "From Mitteleuropa to the Middle East: Orientalism through a Jewish Lens." *Jewish Quarterly Review* 94, no. 3 (Summer 2004): 490–520.

"'Eili, Eili' Played in Court by Lawyer." *New York Times*, May 1, 1925.

"'Eili, Eili' Sandler's, Old Actors Testify." *New York Times*, April 30, 1925.

Eisenberg, Evan. *The Recording Angel: Music, Records and Culture from Aristotle to Zappa*. New Haven, CT: Yale University Press, 2005.

Eliasberg, Alexander. *Ostjüdische Volkslieder: Ausgewählt, übertragen und mit Anmerkungen versehen*. Munich: Georg Müller, 1918.

Eliot, George. *Daniel Deronda*. 4 vols. Edinburgh, 1876.

Elkin, Clarence. *Maori Melodies (with Words) Collected and Arranged for Pianoforte*. Sydney: W.H. Paling, 1923.

Ernest Bloch: Biography and Comment. San Francisco: Mary Morgan, 1925.

Falla, Manuel de. *On Music and Musicians*. Translated by David Urman and J.M. Thomson. London: Marion Boyars, 1979.

Farrell, Gerry. *Indian Music and the West*. Oxford: Oxford University Press, 1997.

Farwell, Arthur. *American Indian Melodies*. New York: G. Schirmer, 1914.

Fauser, Annegret. *Musical Encounters at the 1889 Paris World's Fair*. Rochester, NY: University of Rochester Press, 2005.

Feurzeig, Lisa, editor. *Deutsche Lieder für Jung und Alt*. Middleton, WI: A-R Editions, 2002.

Fewkes, J. Walter. "On the Use of the Edison Phonograph in the Preservation of the Languages of the American Indians." *Nature*, April 17, 1890, 560.

Filare, A. Prologue to Custodia Plantón, *Pablo Sarasate (1844–1908)*, 7–14. Pamplona: Ediciones Universidad de Navarra, 2000.

Fischer, Victoria. "Articulation Notation in the Piano Music of Béla Bartók: Evolution and Interpretation." *Studia Musicologica* 36, nos. 3–4 (1995): 285–301.

Fishman, David E. *The Rise of Modern Yiddish Culture*. Pittsburgh: University of Pittsburgh Press, 2005.

Flesch, Carl. *The Memoirs of Carl Flesch*. Edited and translated by Hans Keller. London: Rockliff, 1957.

Fleuriot, Jean-Marie-Jérôme. *Voyage de Figaro en Espagne*. Saint-Malo, 1784.

Fowler, Alastair. *Kinds of Literature: An Introduction to the Theory of Genres and Modes*. Oxford: Clarendon, 1982.

Frankel, Jonathan. *Prophecy and Politics: Socialism, Nationalism, and the Russian Jews, 1862–1917*. Cambridge: Cambridge University Press, 1981.

Frigyesi, Judit. *Béla Bartók and Turn-of-the-Century Budapest*. Berkeley: University of California Press, 1998.

———. "Béla Bartók and the Concept of Nation and *Volk* in Modern Hungary." *Musical Quarterly* 78, no. 2 (Summer 1994): 255–87.

———. "Preliminary Thoughts toward the Study of Music without Clear Beat: The Example of 'Flowing Rhythm' in Jewish 'Nusah,'" *Asian Music* 24, no. 2 (Spring–Summer 1993): 59–88.

Frisch, Walter. *German Modernism: Music and the Arts.* Berkeley: University of California Press, 2005.

Frye, Northrop. *Anatomy of Criticism: Four Essays.* New York: Atheneum, 1957.

Gallego, Antonio. Prologue to Manuel de Falla, *Cantares de Nochebuena*, 5–9. Madrid: Manuel de Falla Ediciones, 1992.

Garrett, Charles Hiroshi. "'Shooting the Keys': Musical Horseplay and High Culture." In *The Oxford Handbook of the New Cultural History of Music*, edited by Jane F. Fulcher, 245–63. New York: Oxford University Press, 2011.

Gelatt, Roland. *The Fabulous Phonograph, 1877–1977.* New York: Macmillan, 1977.

Gelbart, Matthew. *The Invention of "Folk Music" and "Art Music": Emerging Categories from Ossian to Wagner.* Cambridge: Cambridge University Press, 2007.

Genette, Gérard. *Paratexts: Thresholds of Interpretation.* Translated by Jane E. Lewin. Cambridge: Cambridge University Press, 1997.

Gershwin, Ira. *Lyrics on Several Occasions.* Winona, MN: Hal Leonard, 1997.

Gillies, Malcolm. "Bartók and His Music in the 1990s." In *The Bartók Companion*, edited by Malcolm Gillies, 3–17. London: Faber and Faber, 1993.

Ginzburg, Saul M., and Pesach S. Marek. *Yiddish Folksongs in Russia: Photo Reproduction of the 1901 St. Petersburg Edition.* Edited by Dov Noy. Translated by Lila Holzman. Ramat Gan: Bar-Ilan University Press, 1991.

Glinsky, Albert. *Theremin: Ether Music and Espionage.* Urbana: University of Illinois Press, 2000.

Goldberg, Harvey E. "Modern Jewish Society and Sociology." In *The Oxford Handbook of Jewish Studies*, edited by Martin Goodman, 975–1001. Oxford: Oxford University Press, 2002.

Goode, Joshua. *Impurity of Blood: Defining Race in Spain, 1870–1930.* Baton Rouge: Louisiana State University Press, 2009.

Gooley, Dana. *The Virtuoso Liszt.* Cambridge: Cambridge University Press, 2004.

Gottesman, Itzik Nakhmen. *Defining the Yiddish Nation: The Jewish Folklorists of Poland.* Detroit: Wayne State University Press, 2003.

"Gramophone Celebrities XIV—Jascha Heifetz." *Gramophone*, November 1925, 278–9.

Grellmann, Heinrich Moritz Gottlieb. *Dissertation on the Gipsies: Being an Historical Enquiry, Concerning the Manner of Life, Œconomy, Customs and Conditions of These People in Europe, and Their Origin.* Translated by Matthew Raper. London, 1787.

Grieg, Edvard. *Norwegian Peasant Dances (Slåtter).* New York: C.F. Peters, n.d.

Grimley, Daniel M. *Grieg: Music, Landscape and Norwegian Identity.* Woodbridge, UK: Boydell, 2006.

Handler, Richard. "Authenticity." *Anthropology Today* 2, no. 1 (February 1986): 2–4.

Hannaford, Ivan. *Race: The History of an Idea in the West*. Baltimore, MD: Johns Hopkins University Press, 1996.

Harper, Nancy Lee. *Manuel de Falla: His Life and Music*. Lanham, MD: Scarecrow, 2005.

Harshav, Benjamin. *Marc Chagall and the Lost Jewish World: The Nature of Chagall's Art and Iconography*. New York: Rizzoli, 2006.

———. "Chagall: Postmodernism and Fictional Worlds in Painting." In *Marc Chagall and the Jewish Theater*, 15–64. New York: Solomon R. Guggenheim Foundation, 1992.

"Heifetz Plays Benefit." *New York Times*, April 29, 1918.

Henry, Leigh. "The New Direction in Spanish Music." *Musical Times*, August 1, 1919, 401–2.

———. "The New Direction in Spanish Music (Concluded)." *Musical Times*, September 1, 1919, 465–8.

Herder, Johann Gottfried. *Essay on the Origin of Language*. In *On the Origin of Language*, translated by John H. Moran and Alexander Gode, 85–176. Chicago: University of Chicago Press, 1986.

Heskes, Irene. "Shapers of American Jewish Music: *Mailamm* and the Jewish Music Forum, 1931–62." *American Music* 15, no. 3 (Autumn 1997): 305–20.

———. *Passport to Jewish Music: Its Histories, Traditions, and Culture*. Westport, CT: Greenwood, 1994.

———. *Yiddish American Popular Songs, 1895–1950: A Catalog Based on the Lawrence Marwick Roster of Copyright Entries*. Washington, DC: Library of Congress, 1992.

Hess, Carol A. *Sacred Passions: The Life and Music of Manuel de Falla*. Oxford: Oxford University Press, 2005.

———. *Manuel de Falla and Modernism in Spain, 1898–1936*. Chicago: University of Chicago Press, 2001.

———. *Enrique Granados: A Bio-Bibliography*. Westport, CT: Greenwood, 1991.

Hirsch, Lily E. *A Jewish Orchestra in Nazi Germany: Musical Politics and the Berlin Jewish Culture League*. Ann Arbor: University of Michigan Press, 2010.

Hirshberg, Jehoash. *Music in the Jewish Community of Palestine 1880–1948: A Social History*. Oxford: Clarendon, 1995.

Hofer, Tamás. "Construction of the 'Folk Cultural Heritage' in Hungary, and Rival Versions of National Identity." *Ethnologia Europaea* 21, no. 2 (1991): 145–70.

Holt, Fabian. *Genre in Popular Music*. Chicago: University of Chicago Press, 2007.

Hooker, Lynn. "Modernism on the Periphery: Béla Bartók and the New Hungarian Music Society of 1911–1912." *Musical Quarterly* 88, no. 2 (Summer 2005): 274–319.

———. "Solving the Problem of Hungarian Music: Contexts for Bartók's Early Career." *International Journal of Musicology* 9 (2001): 11–42.

Hubay, Jenő. "Petőfi befolyása a magyar zenére." *Petőfi Múzeum* pamphlet (1888): 155–62.

Hurtado, José. *100 cantos populares asturianos*. Madrid: Unión Musical Española, 1956.

Hyman, John. *The Objective Eye: Color, Form, and Reality in the Theory of Art*. Chicago: University of Chicago Press, 2006.

Iberni, Luis G. *Pablo Sarasate*. Madrid: Instituto Complutense de Ciencias Musicales, 1994.

Idelsohn, Abraham Zvi. *Jewish Music in Its Historical Development*. New York: Tudor, 1944.

———. *Hebräisch-orientalischer Melodienschatz*. 10 vols. Leipzig: Breitkopf and Härtel, 1914; Jerusalem, Berlin, and Vienna: Benjamin Harz, 1922–9; and Leipzig: Friedrich Hofmeister, 1932.

Inzenga, José. *Cantos y bailes de España*. Madrid: A. Romero A., 1888.

Isay, Dave, Henry Sapoznik, and Yair Reiner. *Yiddish Radio Project: Stories from the Golden Age of Yiddish Radio*. Minneapolis: HighBridge, 2002, compact disc.

Istel, Edgar. "Felipe Pedrell." Translated by Theodore Baker. *Musical Quarterly* 11, no. 2 (April 1925): 164–91.

Jacobson, Joshua R. "'Tsen Brider': A Jewish Requiem." *Musical Quarterly* 84, no. 3 (2000): 452–74.

Jairazbhoy, Nazir. "The 'Objective' and Subjective View in Music Transcription." *Ethnomusicology* 21, no. 2 (May 1977): 263–73.

Jakobson, Roman. "On Realism and Art." Translated by Karol Magassy. In *Language in Literature*, edited by Krystyna Pomorska and Stephen Rudy, 19–27. Cambridge, MA: Belknap, 1987.

Jameson, Fredric. "Magical Narratives: Romance as Genre." *New Literary History* 7, no. 1 (Autumn 1975): 135–63.

Kahn, Eliott. "The Solomon Rosowsky Collection and the Solomon Rosowsky Addendum at the Library of the Jewish Theological Seminary." In *Jüdische Kunstmusik im 20. Jahrhundert*, edited by Jascha Nemtsov, 47–58. Wiesbaden: Harrassowitz, 2006.

Kalmar, Ivan Davidson, and Derek J. Penslar. "Orientalism and the Jews: An Introduction." In *Orientalism and the Jews*, edited by Ivan Davidson Kalmar and Derek J. Penslar, xiii–xl. Waltham, MA: Brandeis University Press, 2005.

Kárpáti, János. "Piano Works of the War Years." In *The Bartók Companion*, edited by Malcolm Gillies, 146–61. London: Faber and Faber, 1993.

Katz, Mark. "Portamento and the Phonograph Effect." *Journal of Musicological Research* 25, nos. 3–4 (December 2006): 211–32.

———. *Capturing Sound: How Technology Has Changed Music*. Berkeley: University of California Press, 2004.

Kaufmann, Fritz Mordechai. *Die schönsten Lieder der Ostjuden: siebenundvierzig ausgewählte Volkslieder*. Edited by Achim Freudenstein and Karsten Troyke. Edermünde: Achims Verlag, 2001.

Kawabata, Maiko. "Violinists 'Singing': Paganini, Operatic Voices, and Virtuosity." *Ad Parnassum* 5, no. 9 (April 2007): 7–39.

———. "Virtuosity, the Violin, the Devil . . . What *Really* Made Paganini 'Demonic'?" *Current Musicology* 83 (Spring 2007): 85–108.

Kelman, Ari Y. *Station Identification: A Cultural History of Yiddish Radio in the United States*. Berkeley: University of California Press, 2009.

Kenneson, Claude. *Székely and Bartók: The Story of a Friendship*. Portland, OR: Amadeus, 1994.

Kerényi, György. *Szentirmay Elemér és a magyar népzene.* Budapest: Akadémiai Kiadó, 1966.

Khazdan, Evgeny. "Jewish Music in St. Petersburg: A Survey." In *Jüdische Musik und ihre Musiker im 20. Jahrhundert,* edited by Wolfgang Birtel, Joseph Dorfman, and Christoph-Hellmut Mahling, 169–81. Mainz: Are Edition, 2006.

Kirshenblatt-Gimblett, Barbara. "Folklore's Crisis." *Journal of American Folklore* 111, no. 441 (Summer 1998): 281–327.

———. Introduction to Mark Zborowski and Elizabeth Herzog, *Life Is with People,* ix–xlviii. New York: Schocken, 1995.

Kiselgof, Susman. "Das Jüdische Volkslied." In *Jüdische Musik in Sowjetrußland: Die "Jüdische Nationale Schule" der zwanziger Jahre,* edited by Jascha Nemtsov and Ernst Kuhn, 25–45. Berlin: Ernst Kuhn, 2002.

———. *Das Jüdische Volkslied.* Berlin: Jüdischer Verlag, 1913.

———. *Lider-zamelbukh far der yidisher shul un familie.* St. Petersburg: Society for Jewish Folk Music; and Berlin: Leo Wintz, 1912.

Kittler, Friedrich A. *Gramophone, Film, Typewriter.* Translated by Geoffrey Winthrop-Young and Michael Wutz. Stanford: Stanford University Press, 1999.

Kivy, Peter. *Sound and Semblance: Reflections on Musical Representation.* Princeton, NJ: Princeton University Press, 1984.

Knapp, Alexander. "The Life and Music of Ernest Bloch: Problems and Paradoxes." In *Jüdische Musik und ihre Musiker im 20. Jahrhundert,* edited by Wolfgang Birtel, Joseph Dorfman, and Christoph-Hellmut Mahling, 287–301. Mainz: Are Edition, 2006.

Knox, John C. *A Judge Comes of Age.* New York: Charles Scribner's Sons, 1940.

Kodály, Zoltán. *Folk Music of Hungary.* Enlarged edition by Lajos Vargyas. Translated by Ronald Tempest and Cynthia Jolly. Translation rev. by Laurence Picken. New York: Praeger, 1971.

Kopytowa, Galina. "Veröffentlichungen der 'Gesellschaft für jüdische Volksmusik' in St. Petersburg/Petrograd." In *Jüdische Musik in Sowjetrußland: Die 'Jüdische Nationale Schule' der zwanziger Jahre,* edited by Jascha Nemtsov and Ernst Kuhn, 123–7. Berlin: Ernst Kuhn, 2002.

Kovács, Sándor. "The Ethnomusicologist." In *The Bartók Companion,* edited by Malcolm Gillies, 51–63. London: Faber and Faber, 1993.

Kunst, Jaap. *Ethnomusicology: A Study of Its Nature, Its Problems, Methods, and Representative Personalities to Which Is Added a Bibliography.* The Hague: Martinus Nijhoff, 1959.

Kvitko, Leib. *Dos fidl.* N.p., 1928.

Lacombe, P., and J. Puig Y Absubide. *Echos d'Espagne: chansons & danses populaires.* Paris: Durand, Schoenewerk, 1872.

Lampert, Vera. *Folk Music in Bartók's Compositions: A Source Catalog: Arab, Hungarian, Romanian, Ruthenian, Serbian, and Slovak Melodies.* Budapest: Hungarian Heritage House; and Germany: G. Henle, 2008.

————. "Nationalism, Exoticism, or Concessions to the Audience? Motivations behind Bartók's Folksong Settings." *Studia Musicologica* 47, nos. 3–4 (September 2006): 337–43.

————. *Népzene Bartók műveiben: A feldolgozott dallamok forrásjegyzéke: Magyar, szlovák, román, rutén, szerb és arab népdalok és táncok.* Budapest: Hagyományok Háza, Helikon Kiadó, Néprajzi Múzeum, Zenetudományi Intézet, 2005.

————. "Zeitgenössische Musik in Bartóks Notensammlung." In *Documenta Bartókiana*, vol. 5, edited by Denijs Dille, 142–68. Mainz: B. Schott und Sohne; and Budapest: Akadémiai Kiadó, 1977.

Largey, Michael D. *Vodou Nation: Haitian Art Music and Cultural Nationalism.* Chicago: University of Chicago Press, 2006.

Leech-Wilkinson, Daniel. "Portamento and Musical Meaning." *Journal of Musicological Research* 25, nos. 3–4 (December 2006): 233–61.

Levenson, Shirley Frank. "The Use of Music in Daniel Deronda." *Nineteenth-Century Fiction* 24, no. 3 (December 1969): 317–34.

Levy, Beth. *Frontier Figures: American Music and the Mythology of the American West.* Berkeley: University of California Press, 2012.

Liszt, Franz. *The Gipsy in Music.* Translated by Edwin Evans. London: William Reeves, 1926.

Llano, Samuel. *Whose Spain? Negotiating Spanish Music in Paris, 1908–1929.* New York: Oxford University Press, 2012.

Locke, Ralph P. *Musical Exoticism: Images and Reflections.* Cambridge: Cambridge University Press, 2009.

Loeffler, James. "Do Zionists Read Music from Right to Left? Abraham Tsvi Idelsohn and the Invention of Israeli Music." *Jewish Quarterly Review* 100, no. 3 (Summer 2010): 385–416.

————. *The Most Musical Nation: Jews and Culture in the Late Russian Empire.* New Haven: Yale University Press, 2010.

Loménie, Louis de. *Beaumarchais and His Times: Sketches of French Society in the Eighteenth Century from Unpublished Documents.* Vol. 1. Translated by Henry S. Edwards. London: Addey, 1856.

Lyons, Leonard. "'Jim Hoyl Really Jascha Heifetz, Composer of New Bing Crosby Tune." *Miami Daily News*, October 16, 1946, 17–A.

Macfie, A. L. *Orientalism.* London: Longman, 2002.

Machado y Álvarez, Antonio (Demófilo, pseud.). *Colección de cantes flamencos recogidos, y anotados por Demófilo.* Madrid: Ediciones Demófilo, 1975.

Mackenzie, Alexander. "Pablo Sarasate: Some Personal Recollections." *Musical Times*, November 1, 1908, 693–5.

Malik, Kenan. *The Meaning of Race: Race, History and Culture in Western Society.* London: MacMillan, 1996.

Mansbach, S. A. *Two Centuries of Hungarian Painters 1820–1970: A Catalogue of the Nicolas M. Salgó Collection.* Washington, DC: American University Press, 1991.

Martí, Josep. "Folk Music Studies and Ethnomusicology in Spain." *Yearbook for Traditional Music* 29 (1997): 107–40.

Maurer, Christopher. "'Dramatic Black Moon': Lorca, Deep Song and the Gramophone." In *I Concurso de cante jondo: Colección Manuel de Falla: Granada, Corpus de 1922. Colección Federico García Lorca: Discografía flamenca utilizada por el poeta*. Madrid: Sonifolk, 1997, compact disc.

Mayall, David. *Gypsy Identities, 1500–2000: From Egipcyans and Moon-Men to the Ethnic Romany*. London: Routledge, 2004.

Miles, Elizabeth J., and Loren Chuse. "Spain." In *The Garland Encyclopedia of World Music*, Volume 8, *Europe*, edited by Timothy Rice, James Porter, and Chris Goertzen, 588–603. New York: Garland, 2000.

Milsom, David. *Theory and Practice in Late Nineteenth-Century Violin Performance: An Examination of Style in Performance, 1850–1900*. Aldershot, UK: Ashgate, 2003.

Mitchell, Timothy. *Flamenco Deep Song*. New Haven, CT: Yale University Press, 1994.

Moddel, Philip. *Joseph Achron*. Tel Aviv: Israeli Music Publication, 1966.

Molkhou, Jean-Michel. "Heifetz on Disc and Film." *Strad*, January 1995, 90–7.

Móricz, Klára. *Jewish Identities: Nationalism, Racism, and Utopianism in Twentieth-Century Music*. Berkeley: University of California Press, 2008.

———. "'From Pure Sources Only': Bartók and the Modernist Quest for Purity." *International Journal of Musicology* 9 (2000): 243–61.

Morris, Pam. *Realism*. London: Routledge, 2003.

Murphy, Kerry. "*Carmen: Couleur Locale* or the Real Thing?" In *Music, Theater, and Cultural Transfer: Paris, 1830–1914*, edited by Annegret Fauser and Mark Everist, 293–315. Chicago: University of Chicago Press, 2009.

"Music in the Movies." *New York Times*, September 4, 1921.

Needham, Gerald. *19th-Century Realist Art*. New York: Harper and Row, 1988.

Nemeskürty, István, László Orosz, Béla G. Németh, and Attila Tamás. *A History of Hungarian Literature*. Edited by Tibor Klaniczay. Translated by István Farkas, Enikő Körtvélyessy, Catherine Lőwy, et al. Budapest: Corvina, 1982.

Nemtsov, Jascha. "Neue jüdische Musik in Polen in den 1920er–30er." In *Jüdische Kunstmusik im 20. Jahrhundert*, edited by Jascha Nemtsov, 91–106. Wiesbaden: Harrassowitz, 2006.

———. *Die Neue Jüdische Schule in der Musik*. Wiesbaden: Harrassowitz, 2004.

———. "Joseph Achron (1886–1943)." In *Jüdische Musik in Sowjetrußland: Die 'Jüdische Nationale Schule' der zwanziger Jahre*, edited by Jascha Nemtsov and Ernst Kuhn, 185–98. Berlin: Ernst Kuhn, 2002.

Netsky, Hankus. *Klezmer: Music and Community in 20th-Century Jewish Philadelphia*. Ph.D. diss., Wesleyan University, 2004.

Nettl, Bruno. *The Study of Ethnomusicology: Thirty-One Issues and Concepts*. Urbana: University of Illinois Press, 2005.

Nochlin, Linda. *Realism*. Baltimore: Penguin, 1971.

"Not According to Hoyl." *Time*, October 21, 1946, 85.

N.t. *Rimington's Review*, April 1935, 13.

Ocón, Eduardo. *Cantos Españoles: Colección de aires nacionales y populares*. Málaga: Eigenthum des Herausgebers, 1888.

O'Flynn, John. "National Identity and Music in Transition: Issues of Authenticity in a Global Setting." In *Music, National Identity and the Politics of Location: Between the Global and the Local*, edited by Ian Biddle and Vanessa Knights, 19–38. Aldershot, UK: Ashgate, 2007.

Orvell, Miles. *The Real Thing: Imitation and Authenticity in American Culture, 1880–1940*. Chapel Hill: University of North Carolina Press, 1989.

Ottens, Rita, and Joel Rubin. *Klezmer-Musik*. Kassel: Bärenreiter, 1999.

Ovid. *The Metamorphoses*. Translated by Mary M. Innes. Harmondsworth: Penguin, 1955.

Pabanó, F. M. *Historia y costumbres de los gitanos: colección de cuentos viejos y nuevos, dichos y timos graciosos, maldiciones y refranes netamente gitanos: diccionario español-gitano-germanesco, dialecto de los gitanos*. Barcelona: Montaner y Simón, 1915.

Pahissa, Jaime. *Manuel de Falla: His Life and Works*. Translated by Jean Wagstaff. London: Museum Press, 1954.

Parry, C. Hubert H. *The Art of Music*. 5th ed. London: Kegan Paul, Trench, Trübner, 1894.

Pasler, Jann. *Composing the Citizen: Music as Public Utility in Third Republic France*. Berkeley: University of California Press, 2009.

———. *Writing through Music: Essays on Music, Culture, and Politics*. New York: Oxford University Press, 2008.

———. "Race and Nation: Musical Acclimatisation and the *Chansons Populaires* in Third Republic France." In *Western Music and Race*, edited by Julie Brown, 147–67. Cambridge: Cambridge University Press, 2007.

———. "A Sociology of the Apaches: 'Sacred Battalion' for *Pelléas*." In *Berlioz and Debussy: Sources, Contexts and Legacies: Essays in Honour of François Lesure*, eds. Babara L. Kelly and Kerry Murphy, 149–66. Aldershot, UK: Ashgate, 2007.

———. "Theorizing Race in Nineteenth-Century France: Music as Emblem of Identity." *Musical Quarterly* 89, no. 4 (2006): 459–504.

———. "The *Chanson Populaire* as a Malleable Symbol in Turn-of-the-Century France." In *Tradition and Its Future in Music: Report of SIMS 1990 Ôsaka*, edited by Yosihiko Tokumaru, Makoto Ohmiya, Masakata Kanazawa, et al., 203–9. Tokyo: Mita Press, 1991.

Pávai, István. "Sajátos szempontok az erdélyi hangszeres népi harmónia vizsgálatában." In *A Magyar népi tánczene: Tanulmányok*, edited by Márta Virágvölgyi and István Pávai, 161–85. Budapest: Planétás Kiadó, 2000.

———. *Az erdélyi és a moldvai magyarság népi tánczenéje*. Budapest: Teleki László Alapítvány, 1993.

Pedrell, Felipe. *Por nuestra música*. Bellaterra: Publicacions de la Universitat Autònoma de Barcelona, 1991.

———. "Les artisans du folklore musical espagnol." *La revue musicale*, October 1, 1921, 193–204.

Pekacz, Jolanta T. *Music in the Culture of Polish Galicia, 1772–1914.* Rochester, NY: University of Rochester Press, 2002.

Pesavento, Christiano. *Musik von Béla Bartók als pädagogisches Programm.* Frankfurt am Main: P. Lang, 1994.

Petrovsky-Shtern, Yohanan. "'We Are Too Late': An-sky and the Paradigm of No Return." In *The Worlds of S. An-sky: A Russian Jewish Intellectual at the Turn of the Century,* edited by Gabriella Safran and Steven J. Zipperstein, 83–102. Stanford: Stanford University Press, 2006.

Phillips, Tom. *The Postcard Century: 2000 Cards and Their Messages.* London: Thames and Hudson, 2000.

Pisani, Michael V. *Imagining Native America in Music.* New Haven, CT: Yale University Press, 2005.

Plantón, Custodia. *Pablo Sarasate (1844–1908).* Pamplona: Ediciones Universidad de Navarra, 2000.

Powell, Linton E. *A History of Spanish Piano Music.* Bloomington: Indiana University Press, 1980.

"Programs of the Week." *New York Times,* October 6, 1918.

Radano, Ronald, and Philip V. Bohlman. "Introduction: Music and Race, Their Past, Their Presence." In *Music and the Racial Imagination,* edited by Ronald Radano and Philip V. Bohlman, 1–53. Chicago: University of Chicago Press, 2000.

Ramuz, C. F. *Histoire du soldat.* Translated by Michael Flanders and Kitty Black. London: J. and W. Chester, 1955.

Rapée, Erno. *Erno Rapée's Encyclopædia of Music for Pictures: As Essential as the Picture.* New York: Belwin, 1925.

Redfield, Robert. "The Folk Society." *American Journal of Sociology* 52, no. 4 (January 1947): 293–308.

Rehding, Alexander. *Music and Monumentality: Commemoration and Wonderment in Nineteenth-Century Germany.* New York: Oxford University Press, 2009.

———. "Wax Cylinder Revolutions." *Musical Quarterly* 88, no. 1 (Spring 2005): 123–60.

———. "The Quest for the Origins of Music in Germany Circa 1900." *Journal of the American Musicological Society* 53, no. 2 (Summer 2000): 345–85.

Ribera y Tarragó, Julián. *La música de la jota aragonesa.* Madrid: Instituto de Valencia de Don Juan, 1928.

Rice, Timothy. "Béla Bartók and Bulgarian Rhythm." In *Bartók Perspectives: Man, Composer, Ethnomusicologist,* edited by Elliott Antokoletz, Victoria Fischer, and Benjamin Suchoff, 196–210. Oxford: Oxford University Press, 2000.

Roskies, David G. *The Jewish Search for a Usable Past.* Bloomington: Indiana University Press, 1999.

Rothstein, Arnold M., and Alton Meyer Winters. Introduction to *The Village Fiddler.* New York: Transcontinental Music, 1963.

Rothstein, Robert A. "Klezmer-loshn: The Language of Jewish Folk Musicians." In *American Klezmer: Its Roots and Offshoots*, edited by Mark Slobin, 24–34. Berkeley: University of California Press, 2002.

Rousseau, Jean-Jacques. *Dictionnaire de Musique*. Paris, 1768.

Rubin, Joel E. "'They Danced It, We Played It': Adaptation and Revitalization in Post-1920s New York Klezmer Music." In *Studies in Jewish Civilization*. Vol. 19, *"I Will Sing and Make Music": Jewish Music and Musicians throughout the Ages*, edited by Leonard J. Greenspoon, Ronald A. Simkins, and Jean Cahan, 181–213. Omaha, NE: Creighton University Press, 2008.

Sabaneev, Leonid. "The Jewish National School." Translated by S. W. Pring. *Musical Quarterly* 15, no. 3 (July 1929): 448–68.

Said, Edward W. *Orientalism*. New York: Pantheon, 1978.

Saint-Saëns, Camille. *Au courant de la vie*. Paris: Dorbon-aîné, 1914.

Saminsky, Lazare. *Music of the Ghetto and the Bible*. New York: Bloch, 1934.

Samson, Jim. *Virtuosity and the Musical Work: The* Transcendental Studies *of Liszt*. Cambridge: Cambridge University Press, 2003.

Sarasate, Pablo de. "Zigeunerweisen." New York: Carl Fischer, 1895.

Sárosi, Bálint. "Everyday Hungarian Music in Pest-Buda around 1870," *Studia Musicologica* 40, no. 4 (1999): 325–52.

———. *Cigányzene . . .* Budapest: Gondolat, 1971.

Sarup, Madan. *Identity, Culture and the Postmodern World*. Edinburgh: Edinburgh University Press, 1996.

Saul, Nicholas. *Gypsies and Orientalism in German Literature and Anthropology of the Long Nineteenth Century*. London: Legenda, 2007.

Schapiro, Meyer. *Modern Art: 19th & 20th Centuries*. New York: G. Braziller, 1982

Schleifer, Eliyahu. "Idelsohn's Scholarly and Literary Publications: An Annotated Bibliography." In *Yuval*. Vol. 5, *The Abraham Zvi Idelsohn Memorial Volume*, edited by Israel Adler, Bathja Bayer, and Eliyahu Schleifer, 53–180. Jerusalem: Magnes Press, 1986.

Schneider, David E. *Bartók, Hungary, and the Renewal of Tradition: Case Studies in the Intersection of Modernity and Nationality*. Berkeley: University of California Press, 2006.

Schoenbaum, David. *The Violin: A Social History of the World's Most Versatile Instrument*. New York: W. W. Norton, 2013.

Schröder-Nauenburg, Beate. *Der Eintritt des Jüdischen in die Welt der Kunstmusik: Die Anfänge der Neuen Jüdischen Schule: werkanalytische Studien*. Wiesbaden: Harrassowitz, 2007.

Shandler, Jeffrey. *Jews, God, and Videotape: Religion and Media in America*. New York: New York University Press, 2009.

Shiloah, Amnon. *Jewish Musical Traditions*. Detroit: Wayne State University Press, 1992.

Sholokhova, Lyudmila. "Jewish Musical Ethnography in Russian Empire: Ideology and Chronology." In *Jüdische Kunstmusik im 20. Jahrhundert: Quellenlage, Entstehungsgeschichte, Stilanalysen*, edited by Jascha Nemtsov, 217–26. Wiesbaden: Harrassowitz, 2006.

————. "Zinoviy Kiselgof as a Founder of Jewish Music Folklore Studies in the Russian Empire at the Beginning of the 20th Century." In *Klesmer, Klassik, jiddisches Lied: Jüdische Musikkultur in Osteuropa*, edited by Karl E. Grözinger, 63–72. Wiesbaden: Harrassowitz, 2004.

Silvain, Gerard, Henri Minczeles, and Donna Wiemann. *Yiddishland*. Corte Madera, CA: Gingko Press, 1999.

Slobin, Mark. *Tenement Songs: The Popular Music of Jewish Immigrants*. Urbana: University of Illinois Press, 1996.

————. "The Evolution of a Musical Symbol in Yiddish Culture." In *Studies in Jewish Folklore: Proceedings of a Regional Conference of the Association for Jewish Studies Held at the Spertus College of Judaica, Chicago, May 1–3, 1977*, edited by Frank Talmage, 313–30. Cambridge, MA: Association for Jewish Studies, 1980.

Slonimsky, Nicholas. *Music since 1900*, 3rd ed. New York: Coleman-Ross, 1949.

Smith, Anthony D. *Nationalism: Theory, Ideology, History (Key Concepts)*. Cambridge: Polity Press, 2001.

Solie, Ruth A. *Music in Other Words: Victorian Conversations*. Berkeley: University of California Press, 2004.

Somfai, László. "Written and Performed Form in Bartók's Piano Works of 1915–1920." In *Musik als Text: Bericht über den Internationalen Kongress der Gesellschaft für Musikforschung, Freiburg im Breisgau 1993*, edited by Hermann Danuser and Tobias Plebuch, 1:103–7. Kassel: Bärenreiter, 1998.

————. *Béla Bartók: Composition, Concepts, and Autograph Sources*. Berkeley: University of California Press, 1996.

————. "Idea, Notation, Interpretation: Written and Oral Transmission in Bartók's Works for Strings." *Studia Musicologica* 37, no. 1 (1996): 37–49.

————. "Nineteenth-Century Ideas Developed in Bartók's Piano Notation in the Years 1907–14." *19th-Century Music* 11, no. 1 (Summer 1987): 73–91.

Sontag, Susan. *On Photography*. New York: Dell, 1977.

Sterne, Jonathan. *The Audible Past: Cultural Origins of Sound Reproduction*. Durham, NC: Duke University Press, 2003.

Stewart, Susan. *On Longing*. Durham, NC: Duke University Press, 1993.

Stokes, Martin. Introduction to *Ethnicity, Identity and Music: The Musical Construction of Place*, edited by Martin Stokes, 1–27. Oxford: Berg, 1994.

Stowe, David. *Swing Changes: Big-Band Jazz in New Deal America*. Cambridge, MA: Harvard University Press, 1994.

Straus, Noel. "Ovation to Bartók at Szigeti Recital." *New York Times*, April 22, 1940.

Szigeti, Joseph. *Szigeti on the Violin*. London: Cassell, 1969.

Taubman, Howard. "Heifetz of Symphony and of Swing." *New York Times*, December 22, 1946.

Taruskin, Richard. "Yevreyi and Zhidy: A Memoir, a Survey, and a Plea." In Richard Taruskin, *On Russian Music*, 190–201. Berkeley: University of California Press, 2008.

————. "Nationalism." In *Grove Music Online. Oxford Music Online.* http://www.oxford musiconline.com/.

Tebbutt, Susan. "Disproportional Representation: Romanies and European Art." In *The Role of the Romanies: Images and Counter-Images of the "Gypsies"/Romanies in European Cultures*, edited by Nicholas Saul and Susan Tebbutt, 159–77. Liverpool: Liverpool University Press, 2005.

Thompson, Emily. "Machines, Music, and the Quest for Fidelity: Marketing the Edison Phonograph in America, 1877–1925." *Musical Quarterly* 79, no. 1 (Spring 1995): 131–71.

Tiersot, Julien. *Musiques pittoresques: promenades musicales à l'Exposition de 1889.* Paris: Librairie Fischbacher, 1889.

Todorov, Tzvetan. "The Origin of Genres." Translated by Richard M. Berrong. *New Literary History* 8, no. 1 (Autumn 1976): 159–70.

Tomlinson, Gary. "The Web of Culture: A Context for Musicology." *19th-Century Music* 7, no. 3 (April 1984): 350–62.

Tönnies, Ferdinand. *Community and Society (Gemeinschaft und Gesellschaft).* Translated by Charles P. Loomis. Newton Abbott, UK: Courier Dover, 2002.

Treasure of Jewish Culture in Ukraine. Kiev: Institute for Information Recording, Vernadsky National Library of Ukraine, 1997, compact disc.

Trezise, Simon. "The Recorded Document: Interpretation and Discography." In *The Cambridge Companion to Recorded Music*, edited by Nicholas Cook, Eric Clarke, Daniel Leech-Wilkinson, and John Rink, 186–209. Cambridge: Cambridge University Press, 2009.

Trumpener, Katie. "Béla Bartók and the Rise of Comparative Ethnomusicology: Nationalism, Race Purity, and the Legacy of the Austro-Hungarian Empire." In *Music and the Racial Imagination*, edited by Ronald Radano and Philip V. Bohlman, 403–34. Chicago: University of Chicago Press, 2000.

Tuohy, Sue. "The Social Life of Genre: The Dynamics of Folksong in China." *Asian Music* 30, no. 2 (Spring–Summer 1999): 39–86.

Turino, Thomas, and James Lea, editors. *Identity and the Arts in Diaspora Communities.* Warren, MI: Harmonie Park Press, 2004.

Vikárius, László. "Bartók, Kodály and Salome—The Origins of a Bartókian 'Hallmark.'" *Hungarian Quarterly* 48, no. 187 (Autumn 2007): 124–37.

————. "Erinnern an die 'Stimmung' der Sache. Das Konkrete und das Schwebende im Komponieren Bartóks." In *Resonanzen: Vom Erinnern in der Musik*, edited by Andreas Dorschel, 162–84. Vienna: Institut für Wertungsforschung, 2007.

————. "Bartók and the Ideal of 'Sentimentalitäts-Mangel.'" *International Journal of Musicology* 9 (2000): 197–242.

Walden, Joshua S. "The '*Yidishe Paganini*': Sholem Aleichem's *Stempenyu*, the Music of Yiddish Theater, and the Character of the *Shtetl* Fiddler." *Journal of the Royal Musical Association* 139, no. 1 (Spring 2014, forthcoming).

————. "'An Essential Expression of the People': Interpretations of Hasidic Song in the Composition and Performance History of Ernest Bloch's *Baal Shem*." *Journal of the American Musicological Society* 65, no. 3 (Fall 2012): 777–820.

————. "'The Hora Staccato in Swing!': Jascha Heifetz's Musical Eclecticism and the Adaptation of Violin Miniatures." *Journal of the Society of American Music* 6, no. 4 (November 2012): 405–31.

————. "'On the String in the Peasant Style': Performance Style in Early Recordings of Béla Bartók's *Romanian Folk Dances*." In *Performers' Voices across Centuries, Cultures, and Disciplines*, edited by Ann Marshman, 151–63. London: Imperial College Press, 2011.

————. "Performing the Rural: Sonic Signifiers in Early Twentieth-Century Violin Playing." In *Before and After Music: Proceedings from the 10th International Congress of the International Project on Musical Signification, Vilnius, 21–25 October 2008*, edited by Lina Navickaitė-Martinelli, 421–31. Vilnius/Helsinki: Lithuanian Academy of Music and Theatre, Umweb, International Semiotics Institute, 2010.

————. "Leaving Kazimierz: Comedy and Realism in the Yiddish Film Musical *Yidl Mitn Fidl*." *Journal of Music, Sound, and the Moving Image* 3, no. 2 (Autumn 2009): 159–93.

————. "Music of the '*Folks-neshome*': 'Hebrew Melody' and Changing Musical Representations of Jewish Culture in the Early Twentieth Century Ashkenazi Diaspora." *Journal of Modern Jewish Studies* 8, no. 2 (July 2009): 151–71.

Washabaugh, William. *Flamenco Music and National Identity in Spain*. Farnham, UK: Ashgate, 2012.

————. *Flamenco: Passion, Politics and Popular Culture*. Oxford: Berg, 1996.

Weckerlin, Jean-Baptiste. *Échos du temps passé*. Paris: A. Durand et Fils, n.d.

Weissmann, John. Review of *Szentirmay Elemér és a magyar népzene*, by György Kerényi. *Ethnomusicology* 12, no. 1 (January 1968): 156–60.

Williams, Raymond. *The Country and the City*. London: Hogarth, 1985.

Woolley, Grange. "Pablo de Sarasate: His Historical Significance." *Music and Letters* 36, no. 3 (July 1955): 237–52.

Wriggle, John. "Jazzing the Classics: Race, Modernism, and the Career of Arranger Chappie Willet." *Journal of the Society for American Music* 6, no. 2 (May 2012): 175–209.

Wyrick, Jed. "Yiddish Canon Consciousness and the Dionysiac Spirit of Music." In *Arguing the Modern Jewish Canon: Essays on Literature and Culture in Honor of Ruth R. Wisse*, edited by Justin Cammy, Dara Horn, Alyssa Quint, and Rachel Rubinstein, 467–85. Cambridge, MA: Harvard University Press, 2008.

Yates, Michael. "Percy Grainger and the Impact of the Phonograph." *Folk Music Journal* 4, no. 3 (1982): 265–75.

Yehudi Menuhin: The Violin of the Century. Directed by Bruno Monsaingeon. New York: EMI Classics, 1996. DVD.

Yeomans, David. "Background and Analysis of Bartók's *Romanian Christmas Carols for Piano* (1915)." In *Bartók Perspectives: Man, Composer, and Ethnomusicologist*, edited by Elliott Antokoletz, Victoria Fischer, and Benjamin Suchoff, 185–95. Oxford: Oxford University Press, 2000.

Yezierska, Anzia. "Sorrows into Song." *New York Times*, October 10, 1954.

Young, Robert J. C. *Colonial Desire: Hybridity in Theory, Culture and Race*. London: Routledge, 1995.

Zborowski, Mark, and Elizabeth Herzog. *Life Is with People*. New York: Schocken, 1995.

Zeitlin, Leo. *Chamber Music*. Edited by Paula Eisenstein Baker and Robert S. Nelson. Middleton, WI: A-R Editions, 2009.

Zemtsovsky, Izaly. "The Musical Strands of An-sky's Texts and Contexts." In *The Worlds of S. An-sky: A Russian Jewish Intellectual at the Turn of the Century*, edited by Gabriella Safran and Steven J. Zipperstein, 203–31. Stanford, CA: Stanford University Press, 2006.

Archives Consulted

Abraham Ellstein Collection, RG 522, Box 1, Collection of YIVO, at the Center for Jewish History.

Bartók Archívum. Institute for Musicology of the Hungarian Academy of Sciences, Budapest.

British Library Sound Archive, London.

Département de Musique. Bibliothèque Nationale de France, Paris.

Jascha Heifetz Collection. Music Division, Library of Congress, Washington, DC.

Jewish Music Societies Collection, RG 37. Collection of YIVO, at the Center for Jewish History, New York.

Joseph Szigeti Collection, Howard Gotlieb Archival Research Center at Boston University, Boston.

Mischa Elman Collection, Howard Gotlieb Archival Research Center at Boston University, Boston.

INDEX